PC Technician's Troubleshooting Pocket Reference

2nd Edition

P9-EMG-547

PC Technician's Troubleshooting Pocket Reference

2nd Edition

Stephen J. Bigelow

McGraw-Hill

New York   San Francisco   Washington, D.C.   Auckland   Bogotá
Caracas   Lisbon   London   Madrid   Mexico City   Milan
Montreal   New Delhi   San Juan   Singapore
Sydney   Tokyo   Toronto

McGraw-Hill

A Division of The McGraw·Hill Companies

Copyright © 2000 by The McGraw-Hill Companies, Inc. All rights reserved. Printed in the United States of America. Except as permitted under the United States Copyright Act of 1976, no part of this publication may be reproduced or distributed in any form or by any means, or stored in a data base or retrieval system, without the prior written permission of the publisher.

6 7 8 9 0   DOC/DOC   0 5 4 3 2

ISBN 0-07-212945-X

The sponsoring editor for this book was Michael Sprague and the production manager was Clare Stanley. It was set in Century Schoolbook by D&G Limited, LLC.

Printed and bound by R. R. Donnelley & Sons.

Disclaimer and Cautions

It is important that you read and understand the following information. Please read it carefully!

Personal Risk and Limits of Liability

The repair of personal computers and their peripherals involves some amount of personal risk. Use extreme caution when working with AC and high-voltage power sources. Every reasonable effort has been made to identify and reduce areas of personal risk. You are instructed to read this book carefully *before* attempting the procedures discussed. If you are uncomfortable following any of the procedures that are outlined in this book, do not attempt them. Refer your service to qualified service personnel.

NEITHER THE AUTHOR, THE PUBLISHER, NOR ANYONE DIRECTLY OR INDIRECTLY CONNECTED WITH THE PUBLICATION OF THIS BOOK SHALL MAKE ANY WARRANTY EITHER EXPRESSED OR IMPLIED, WITH REGARD TO THIS MATERIAL, INCLUDING, BUT NOT LIMITED TO, THE IMPLIED WARRANTIES OF QUALITY, MERCHANTABILITY, AND FITNESS FOR ANY PARTICULAR PURPOSE.

Further, neither the author, publisher, nor anyone directly or indirectly connected with the publication of this book shall be liable for errors or omissions contained herein, or for incidental or consequential damages, injuries, or financial or material losses (including the loss of data) resulting from the use, or inability to use, the material contained herein. This material is provided *as is*, and the reader bears all responsibilities and risks connected with its use.

Contents

1

Preparing for Service

Troubleshooting is a lot like taking a test. A problem needs to be solved, and you are "graded" on the speed and success by which that problem is solved. Like any test, a certain amount of preparation is required, and you often have to make some basic assumptions about the problem in order to solve it. Unfortunately, many less experienced technicians are quick to jump at a solution without performing essential checks and observations. Too often this results in lost time and wasted materials. This chapter presents you with the set of checklists and guidelines that can help to speed your diagnosis of a problem and keep your troubleshooting on track.

Rules of the Troubleshooting Business

Troubleshooting is a strange pursuit, not an art, not a science, but somewhere in between. Calling yourself a technician is easy, but being a *successful* technician is *not* so easy. The PC industry changes and grows almost daily, profit margins for repair shops are razor-thin, and products become obsolete (and unavailable) seemingly overnight. With so much pressure, PC troubleshooting can be a demanding and unforgiving

career. Still, rewards are awaiting those with the dedi-
cation and motivation to persevere. Whether you're
already a professional technician trying to get ahead or
a computer enthusiast hoping to go professional, the
following sections offer some rules to work by.

Rule 1: Time Is Money

PCs are an integral (sometimes vital) part of today's
society. Even entry-level jobs require *some* amount of
computer literacy. As a consequence, every computer
that fails means that someone somewhere is sitting
idle. They can't do their jobs; they can't make money;
they can't even play Solitaire until that PC is back in
operation. Your job is to return that broken PC to operation as quickly, efficiently, and cost-effectively as possible while providing the maximum profit for your
employer and the minimum cost for your customer.
This brings us to Rule 2.

Rule 2: Focus on Sub-Assembly Replacement

Current schematics are virtually impossible to come
by. Unless you're a depot technician or an authorized
repair center, chances are that you will never actually
see the circuitry you're repairing. That's a hard fact to
face (especially if you're an electronics purist like me),
but it's a fact of life. As a result, you'll need to focus on
sub-assembly repairs (if a video board fails, you replace
it). The advantage of sub-assembly replacement is that
it can be performed quickly and easily, two factors that
lend themselves well to profitability, and leads us to
Rule 3.

Rule 3: Cultivate Suppliers

The phrase "quickly and easily" assumes that you
have a readily available source of spare parts (video
boards, hard drive controllers, motherboards, and so
on). However, resist the urge to become a warehouse;

nothing eats up profit faster than *inventory*, so stock as *little* as possible. To accomplish this delicate balance, cultivate relationships with as many *quality* suppliers as you can, starting with suppliers in your region. If you have one or two computer stores in your area, establish credit accounts there ASAP, and keep their current catalogs on hand at all times. Finally, remember that there is *nothing* more terrifying than an irate delivery person, so be nice to them *all*.

Rule 4: Turn-Around Wins Customers

Customers don't want to wait two weeks or a month before getting their system back; they want it *now*. If your suppliers are any good, you should shoot for a turn-around time of less than a week. Fast turn-around is a competitive advantage and is a sure way to win customers.

Rule 5: Stand Behind Your Work

Fast turn-around doesn't mean much if the PC still doesn't work right. Always be sure to double-check the system's configuration and applications after a repair, and offer a warranty on the service. Warranties not only protect the customer, but they demonstrate professionalism and confidence in the work (two things a customer will remember later on). Even short warranties (15 or 30 days) serve as a tweaking period to ensure that all the applications still work.

Rule 6: Limit Your Liability

Unfortunately, we live in a litigious society where seemingly innocent mistakes or oversights can have enormous consequences (especially for small businesses). Consider having your customers sign a work order each time they drop off a system. As a minimum, a work order should cover the following points (a local lawyer can help you with specific verbiage):

1. You're not responsible for any data on the hard drive(s) or any data lost on the hard drive(s). The customer should have a complete system backup on hand before delivering a system for service.

2. Check the system for viruses, but you're not responsible for any computer virus(es) that might be transmitted during the service or viruses that escape detection.

3. Try to make exact replacements where possible, but you have permission to replace assemblies or components with devices of similar (or better) design and capability.

4. The customer must understand that some applications may no longer work properly after a repair due to the installation of different hardware or drivers. It is the customer's responsibility to reconfigure or reinstall any such applications.

Rule 7: Invest in Education

Another fact of life is that as companies struggle to remain profitable, people often lose their jobs. If you work for someone else, *education* is the key to your long-term employability. Even if you get laid off anyway, you'll stand a better chance of being hired somewhere else. Consider pursuing a certificate such as CST, A+, or cross-train in a related discipline such as *Certified Network Engineer* (CNE).

Troubleshooting Guidelines

Guidelines serve an important purpose in the troubleshooting industry. They provide technicians with a foundation of principles and practices that ensure safety for both the technician, and the customer's equipment. This book provides you with guidelines for static control, electricity control, guards and shielding, boot disks, and virus disks.

Static Control

Modern PCs depend on extremely complex integrated circuits, and those chips are very sensitive to *Electrostatic Discharge* (ESD). Unfortunately, static electricity is commonplace and is generated constantly by such innocent means as passing a comb through our hair or putting on a sweater. When ESD is allowed to discharge through a chip, the chip is destroyed. No outward signs of ESD damage occur: no smoke, no fire, and rarely any shock or other physical sensation. Still, the damage is quite real. ESD is controlled by a combination of grounding, protective materials, and environmental management. Here are some tips to prevent ESD:

- *Use wrist straps.* Grounding wrist straps are the first line of defense against ESD. They attach to your wrist and connect to a grounded surface or outlet through a wire. When properly connected, a wrist strap "bleeds off" any charge on your body and clothing, making it safer to handle delicate electronics.

- *Use anti-static containers.* You have probably noticed that all delicate electronics come packaged in blue or pink bags. These act as "Faraday cages" that dissipate charges before they can reach the device contained inside. Always keep devices inside anti-static containers until you are ready to actually install them, and then place any removed device into an anti-static container immediately.

- *Use an anti-static mat.* A mat works like a wrist strap by connecting to ground and bleeding off any accumulated charges. You can place boards, chips, or *single inline memory modules* (SIMMs) safely on a properly connected anti-static mat without having to place them in containers. Anti-static mats are very popular on PC repair workbenches where sensitive items are regularly installed and removed.

■ *Use anti-static chemicals.*   Monitor screens, most synthetic surfaces, and virtually all plastic enclosures are major sources of ESD. When properly and regularly applied, anti-static chemicals can go a long way toward preventing ESD damage from accidental or casual contact with sensitive electronics.

■ *Manage temperature and humidity.*   Static builds up discharges easily in cool, dry environments. Work in a warm area with adequate *relative humidity* (RH). Use a humidifier if necessary to maintain adequate RH.

Electricity Control

PCs and their peripherals use a raw *alternating current* (AC) as a power source. Although the myriad of plugs, outlets, and line cords used today are generally regarded as quite safe for end-users, technicians must often work in close proximity to exposed circuitry. In reality, the odds of electrocution are actually quite slim, but electricity *can* injure or kill when handled carelessly. Follow these guidelines to prevent any electrical mishaps:

■ *Keep the PC unplugged when working inside it.*   As a rule, unplug the PC (don't just turn it off) during upgrades or repairs.

■ *Use one hand only for "hot" measurements.*   If you must make measurements or probe around inside a powered system (especially inside the power supply), keep one hand behind your back. If you should contact a live wire, there is no pathway through your heart.

■ *Use properly rated test probes.*   If you attempt to measure high voltages through commercial test probes, you can be electrocuted right through the probe's insulation. Make sure the probe you're using is rated for the expected voltage levels.

Guards and Shielding

Modern PCs and peripherals often employ an assortment of metal and plastic shields or guards within the device. Shields and guards serve a variety of purposes, but all should be replaced when service is complete:

- *Replacing EMI shields.* PCs operate at very high frequencies, and the signals generated by that operation can sometimes be transmitted to nearby receivers such as radios and televisions. Ideally, the PC's design should prevent such *electromagnetic interference* (EMI), but it may also be necessary to add metal shields to attenuate excessive interference. Whenever you remove metal housings or shields from a PC, be sure to replace them before returning the system to service.

- *Replacing X-ray shields.* Monitors use extremely high voltages at the *Cathode Ray Tube* (CRT), which in turn can liberate X-rays through the CRT glass. The lead contained in the CRT glass itself is usually a sufficient shield, but larger CRTs often employ supplemental X-ray shields around the CRT funnel. When you remove X-ray shields from a monitor, be sure to replace them before running the monitor or returning it to service.

- *Replace all guards and other mechanical assemblies.* Printers typically employ a large assortment of guards and covers (both plastic and metal) to protect delicate mechanical assemblies from dust and accidental contact. You can typically operate a printer for short periods without guards in place, but you should always make it a point to replace any protective assemblies before returning the device to service.

Boot Disks

PCs rely heavily on the use of hard drives as the boot drive that holds the boot sector and the *operating system* (OS) needed to complete the computer's initialization. Unfortunately, hard drives are also one of the most delicate devices used in a computer. When a boot drive fails, the drive (and its vast contents) becomes inaccessible. Still, in order to begin troubleshooting the computer, it must be successfully booted to an OS. As a result, one of the most valuable tools at your disposal is a boot disk. Generally speaking, a boot disk is little more than a floppy disk that has been formatted as a system disk and is loaded with files and utilities needed to complete the PC's initialization if the boot hard drive cannot. You can follow the procedure below to make a full-featured boot disk:

> **NOTE**:   The procedure below assumes that your floppy disk is A:, your main hard drive is C:, and your CD-ROM (if installed) is D:. If your particular system is configured differently, please substitute the correct drive letters.

1. *Start at the DOS command line.* You should exit Windows or Windows 95/98 before proceeding.

2. *Format the floppy disk as a bootable (system) disk.* If your diskette is totally blank, use the FORMAT command such as

   ```
   C:\DOS\> format a:<Enter>
   ```

   Next, make the diskette bootable by transferring system files. Use the SYS command to make the diskette bootable such as

   ```
   C:\DOS\> sys a:   <Enter>
   ```

   If you purchase your diskettes preformatted, simply use the SYS command.

3. *Test the diskette.* Reboot your computer and see that the system will boot successfully to the A:

DOS prompt. If so, you have created a simple boot disk, but other steps are required to complete a full-featured boot disk.

4. Copy your startup files. Copy the AUTOEXEC. BAT and CONFIG.SYS files from your hard drive to the boot diskette:

```
C:\> copy config.sys a:          <Enter>
C:\> copy autoexec.bat a:        <Enter>
```

5. Copy your CONFIG.SYS-related files. You should also copy all the files referenced in your startup files. For example, a CONFIG.SYS file typically has memory managers, low-level plug-and-play drivers, and low-level CD-ROM drivers, such as the CONFIG.SYS file below:

```
REM memory managers first
device=c:\windows\himem.sys
device=c:\windows\emm386.exe   ram   i=b000-b7ff
i=e000-e7ff i=ee00-efff
dos=umb,high
files=60
buffers=40
REM low-level CD-ROM driver
devicehigh=c:\cdd\wcd.sys   /d:wp_cdrom
REM low-level PnP driver
devicehigh=c:\plugplay\drivers\dos\dwcfgmg.syd
```

If this was your CONFIG.SYS file, you would copy the HIMEM.SYS, EMM386.EXE, WCD.SYS, and DWCFGMG.SYS files to your floppy diskette. Your particular system may be a bit different.

6. *Copy your AUTOEXEC.BAT-related files.* As with CONFIG.SYS, you should copy over all of the files referenced in AUTOEXEC.BAT. The AUTOEXEC. BAT file usually sets paths, configures the sound

card and environment, loads the CD-ROM DOS extension (MSCDEX.EXE), and starts your mouse driver. For the following AUTOEXEC.BAT file,

```
PATH=C:\NETMANAG;C:\WINDOWS;C:\WINDOWS\COMMAND

LH C:\CDD\MSCDEX.EXE /D:WP_CDROM /M:20

SET BLASTER=A220 IXX DX T1

SET SNDSCAPE=C:\SNDSCAPE

LH C:\SNDSCAPE\SSINIT /I

LOADHIGH C:\MOUSE.EXE
```

you would need to copy the MSCDEX.EXE, SSINIT.EXE, and MOUSE.EXE files to the floppy disk.

7. Redirect the CONFIG.SYS and AUTOEXEC.BAT files. Use the startup programs from your floppy disk rather than from the hard drive. This helps because it enables the boot disk to start your PC just as if the hard drive were still working and will enable such necessary functions as sound, CD-ROM access, and mouse operation. Using any text editor like the DOS EDIT utility, you can rewrite the diskette's CONFIG.SYS file, such as

```
device=a:\himem.sys

device=a:\emm386.exe ram i=b000-b7ff i=e000-e7ff
i=ee00-efff

dos=umb,high

files=60

buffers=40

devicehigh=a:\wcd.sys   /d:wp_cdrom

devicehigh=a:\dwcfgmg.syd
```

Save the edited file to your floppy disk (not to your hard drive) as CONFIG.SYS. The original CONFIG.SYS file will be renamed CONFIG.BAK. Next, load AUTOEXEC.BAT into EDIT and alter it, such as

```
LH A:\MSCDEX.EXE /D:WP_CDROM /M:20

SET BLASTER=A220 IXX DX T1

SET SNDSCAPE=A:\SNDSCAPE

LH A:\SSINIT /I

LH A:\MOUSE.EXE
```

Save the edited file to your floppy disk (not your hard drive) as AUTOEXEC.BAT. The original AUTOEXEC.BAT file will be renamed AUTOEXEC. BAK. Now the PC will start *entirely* from the floppy diskette instead of from the hard drive.

8. *Test the diskette again.*   Reboot the PC and make sure that the boot diskette is capable of starting the entire PC without errors. You should still be able to access things like your CD-ROM drive or play .WAV files through the sound board and so on. If any errors occur, you probably forgot to change a line in CONFIG.SYS or AUTOEXEC. BAT. Restart EDIT and check both startup files again. Retest your boot disk until the PC can initialize to the A: prompt without errors. At this point, your boot disk is just about complete.

9. *Add some DOS utilities.*   Although you should now be able to boot the system normally from your floppy disk, you will still need tools to deal with hard drive problems. Chances are that you still have plenty of space left on the floppy disk, so go to your DOS directory and copy the following utilities to your boot disk: CHKDSK.*, SCANDISK.*, FDISK.*, FORMAT.*, MEM.*, SYS.*, EDIT.*, MSAV.*, and DEFRAG.*. Of course, if your hard drive is using compression such as DoubleSpace or Stacker, you'll need to copy those operating files as well.

10. *Store the new boot disk in a safe place.*   Mark the new boot disk clearly and put it away with your other diskettes.

Problems with Boot Disks

Boot disks are handy tools for any troubleshooter, but you should also be aware that they have three major drawbacks:

- *Boot disks become obsolete fast.* Every time you make a change to your system (that is, replace a CD-ROM drive or add a new mouse), your startup files also change, so you will need to update your boot disk(s) to reflect the changes. Too often, end-users and technicians alike forget to do this, and the boot disk winds up useless when it if finally needed.

- *Boot disks are very "system-specific."* Exchanging boot disks was a simple matter in the early days of PCs since there were few (if any) drivers or *Terminate and Stay Residents* (TSRs) to worry about. As computers have become more sophisticated, each CD-ROM, sound board, mouse, and so on requires its own drivers. PCs are now quite unique, and a full-featured boot disk created for one system will not necessarily work on any other system.

- *Boot disks are ideal virus carriers.* If you *do* make a habit of trying your boot disk in multiple systems, use extra caution to prevent the spread of computer viruses. First, write-protect your boot disk to help prevent contracting a virus from other systems. Also check your disk regularly to see that it remains virus-free.

Viruses and Computer Service

Few developments in the PC field have caused more concern and alarm than the computer virus. Although viruses do not physically *damage* computer hardware, they can irrevocably destroy vital data, disable your PC (or shutdown a network), and propagate to other systems through networks, disk swapping, and online services. Even though virus infiltration is generally regarded as rare, a good PC technician will always protect themselves (and their customers) by checking the system for viruses *before* and *after* using their diagnostic disks on the PC. A careful process of virus isolation can detect viruses on the customer's system before any hardware-level work is done. Virus isolation tactics also prevent your diagnostic disks from becoming infected and prevent you from subsequently transferring the virus to other systems (for which you might be legally liable). This section of the chapter outlines a virus-screening procedure for PCs.

Many attempts have been made to define a computer virus, and most definitions have a great deal of technical merit. For the purposes of this book, however, we can consider a *virus* to be some length of computer code (a program or a program fragment) that performs one or more, often destructive, functions and replicates itself wherever possible to other disks and systems. Since viruses generally want to escape detection, they may often hide by copying themselves as hidden, system, or read-only files. However, this only prevents casual detection. More elaborate viruses affect the boot sector code on floppy and hard disks or attach themselves to other executable programs. Each time the infected program is executed, the virus has a chance to wreck havoc. Still other viruses infect the partition table. Most viruses exhibit a code sequence that can be detected. Many virus scanners work by checking the contents of memory and disk files for such virus "signatures." As viruses become more complex, however, viruses are using encryption techniques to escape detection. Encryption changes the virus signature each time the virus replicates itself. For a well-designed virus, this can make detection extremely difficult.

Just as a biological virus is an unwanted (and sometimes deadly) organism in a body, "viral" code in software can lead to a slow, agonizing death for your customer's data. In actual practice, few viruses *immediately* crash a system (with notable exceptions such as the much-publicized Michealangelo virus). Most viruses make only small changes each time they are executed and create a pattern of chronic problems. This slow manifestation gives viruses a chance to replicate, infecting backups and floppy disks that are frequently swapped to infect other systems.

> **NOTE**:   Frequent system backups are an effective protection against computer viruses because you can restore files damaged by viruses. Even if the backup is infected, the infected files can often be cleaned once they are restored from the backup.

The Tell-Tale Signs.   Viruses are especially dangerous since you are rarely made aware of their presence until it is too late and the damage is already done. However, a number of characteristics could suggest the presence of a virus in your system. Once again, remember that one of the best protections against viruses (or other drive failures) is to maintain regular backups of your data. None of these symptoms *alone* guarantee the presence of a virus (there *are* other reasons why such symptoms can occur), but when symptoms *do* surface, it is always worth running an anti-virus checker just to be safe. The following symptoms are typical of virus activity:

- *The hard drive is running out of disk space for no apparent reason.*   Some viruses multiply by attaching copies of themselves to executable (.EXE) and .COM files, often multiple times. This increases the file size of infected files (sometimes dramatically) and consumes more disk space. If left unchecked, files can grow until the disk runs short of space. However, disk space can also be gobbled up by many CAD, graphics, and multimedia applications such as video capture systems. Be aware of what kind of applications are on the disk.

- *You notice that various .EXE and .COM programs have increased in size for no reason.*   This is a classic indicator of a virus at work. In actual practice, few rational people make it a habit to keep track of file sizes, but dates can be a giveaway. For example, if most of the files in a subdirectory are dated six months ago when the package was installed, but the main .EXE file is dated yesterday, it's time to run that virus checker.

■ *You notice substantial hard drive activity but were not expecting it.* It is hardly unusual to see the drive indicator's *light-emitting diode* (LED) register activity when programs are loaded and run. In disk-intensive systems such as Windows 98 or NT, you should expect to see extensive drive activity due to swap file operations. However, you should not expect to see regular or substantial disk activity when the system is idle. If the drive runs for no apparent reason, especially under MS-DOS, run the virus checker.

■ *System performance has slowed down noticeably.* This symptom is usually coupled with low drive space and may very well be the result of a filled and fragmented disk such as those found in systems that deal with CAD and multimedia applications. Run the virus checker first. If no virus is detected, try eliminating any unneeded files and defragment the drive completely.

■ *Files have been lost or corrupted for no apparent reason, or an unusual number of access problems are occurring.* Under ordinary circumstances, files should not be lost or corrupted on a hard drive. Even though bad sectors will crop up on extremely rare occasions, you should expect the drive to run properly. Virus infiltration can interrupt the flow of data to and from the drives and result in file errors. Such errors may occur randomly, or they may be quite consistent. You may see error messages such as *"Error in .EXE file"*. Regular errors may even simulate a drive failure. Try running a virus checker before running a diagnostic like ScanDisk.

Inadequate power problems can also have an effect on drive reliability.

■ *The system locks up frequently or without explanation.* Faulty applications and corrupted files can freeze a system. Memory and motherboard problems can also result in system lockups. Although viruses rarely manifest themselves in this fashion, it is possible that random or consistent system lockups may suggest a virus (or virus damage to key files).

■ *Unexplained problems occur in system memory or memory allocation.* Although one or more memory defects may occur, it is quite common for viruses to exist in memory where other files can be infected. In some cases, this can effect the amount of free memory available to other applications. You may see error messages such as *"Program too big to fit in memory."* If you are having trouble with free memory or memory allocation, run a virus checker that performs a thorough memory check. If the system checks clear of viruses, you can run diagnostics to check the memory.

Anti-Virus Software. In the race between "good and evil", it is "evil" that usually has the head start. As a result, anti-virus detection and elimination packages are constantly trying to keep up with new viruses and their variations (in addition to dealing with more than 45,000 viruses that have already been identified). This leads to an important conclusion about anti-virus software: they all quickly become *obsolete*. Even though first-class shareware and commercial packages can be quite comprehensive, they must all be updated frequently. Some of the most notable anti-virus products are found in Symantec's *Norton Anti-Virus* (NAV) and VirusScan from Network Associates. If you use MS-DOS 6.0 or later, you already own *Microsoft Anti-Virus* (MSAV).

Another important factor in anti-virus programs is their incapability to successfully remove all viruses from .EXE files. Files with a .COM extension are simply reflections of memory, but .EXE files contain header information that is easily damaged by a virus (and are subsequently unrecoverable). It is always worth *trying* to eliminate the virus. If the .EXE header is damaged, you've lost nothing in the attempt, and you can reload the damaged .EXE file from a backup or its original distribution disks if necessary. Remember that there is no better protection against viruses and other hardware faults than keeping regular backups. It is better to restore an infected backup and clean it than to forego backups entirely.

Virus Disks. In order to check a system for viruses, you'll need to create an anti-virus boot diskette. The following procedure explains how to create a batch of virus work disks.

> **NOTE:** This procedure assumes that your floppy disk is A:, your main hard drive is C:, and your CD-ROM (if installed) is D:. If your particular system is configured differently, please substitute the correct drive letters.

1. *Start at the DOS command line.* You should exit Windows or Windows 95/98 before proceeding.

2. *Ensure your system is virus-free.* Run a current virus checker that checks for the most important types of viruses, including memory-resident viruses. Once the system is clean, you can proceed.

3. *Format 10 floppy disks as bootable (system) disks.* If your diskettes are totally blank, use the command FORMAT, such as

```
C:\DOS\> format a:        <Enter>
```

   Next, make the diskettes bootable by transferring system files. Use the SYS command to make the diskettes bootable, such as

```
C:\DOS\> sys a:                <Enter>
```

If you purchase your diskettes preformatted, simply use the SYS command.

4. *Test a diskette.*   Reboot your computer and see that the system will boot successfully to the A: DOS prompt. If so, you have created simple boot disks (you need only test one disk), but other steps are required to complete a virus-checking disk.

5. *Copy the virus checker to your first bootable floppy disk.*   Virus checkers are typically self-contained, single-file tools such as Norton's NAV.EXE, Microsoft's MSAV.EXE, or the shareware tool FPROT.EXE. Copy the necessary executable file to your diskette.

6. *Create an AUTOEXEC.BAT file that will start the virus checker* Ideally, you want the virus checker to start automatically, so create a simple AUTOEXEC.BAT file that will start the virus checker. For example, MSAV.EXE could use a command line such as

```
a:\msav.exe
```

You might also add command-line arguments to streamline the virus checker even further. Save the AUTOEXEC.BAT file to your floppy disk.

7. *Test the diskette again.* Reboot the system with your anti-virus floppy disk. The system should boot "clean" with no drivers or TSRs loaded that might confuse the virus checker and the anti-virus program should load. Depending on exactly which virus checker and command-line options you choose, the checker may run through a complete scan automatically, or you may have to manually start testing from the program's menu.

8. *Duplicate the original disk to the other work disks.* Use the DOS DISKCOPY command to duplicate

your original virus-checking diskette to the other nine diskettes you have prepared. You may have to swap back and forth between the source (original) and target (new) diskettes several times. When the new diskette is done, DISKCOPY will ask if you want to repeat the procedure.

9. *Mark the diskettes carefully.* You have just created a batch of anti-virus work disks. They should be immediately write-protected and kept together as a set.

   NOTE: Step 7 asks you to create 10 copies of the virus-checking software. Even though the disks are exclusively for your use, and you will only use one disk at a time, this kind of multiple duplication may violate the license agreement for your anti-virus software. Be sure your license allows multiple copies of the software before proceeding.

Using Virus Work Disks.   Whenever a PC comes in for service, use one of your anti-virus work disks to boot and check the system first before trying a boot disk or diagnostic disk. Professionals always create anti-virus diskettes in batches because the diskettes are *disposable*. That is, if a virus is detected and cleaned, the diskette that detected the infection should be *destroyed*, and you should boot the system with a new work disk to locate any other instances of the same virus or any different viruses. This may seem radical, but it is cheap insurance against cross-contamination of the diskette. Once a system is booted with a work disk and checks clean, you can put that work disk away and boot the system again with a diagnostic or boot disk as required. It is also advisable to check the PC for viruses again once the repair is complete.

Problems with Anti-Virus Tools.   The protocol outlined earlier should help to protect you (and your customer) from virus attacks. Still, other troubles can occur:

- *Virus checkers get obsolete fast.*   Viruses are prolif-
erating with the aid of powerful new programming
languages and vast avenues of distribution such as
the Internet. You will need to update your virus
work disks regularly with the latest anti-virus software. Too often, technicians buy an anti-virus package and continue to use it for years. The software
certainly remains adept at detecting the viruses it
was designed for but does not take into account the
many new strains that crop up regularly. As a
result, older virus checkers may enable newer
viruses to pass undetected.

- *Technicians get cheap with their floppy disks.*   If a
work disk detects and eliminates a virus, it should be
considered contaminated and you should *throw it
away*. Start again with a fresh work diskette. Continue
checking and eradicating viruses until the system
checks clean. The 30 cents or so that the diskette is
worth is not worth the risk of contracting the virus.

Quick-Start Bench Testing

Many problems can plague the PC, but perhaps the
most troubling problems occur during startup when the
computer fails to start at all or does not start completely.
Startup problems make it almost impossible to use
diagnostics or other utilities that we depend on to help
isolate problems. With the advent of graphics-oriented
operating systems such as Windows 95/98, even more
difficulties can develop. This part of the chapter offers
you a series of possible "quick-start" explanations for
full and partial system failures.

The System Doesn't Start at All

**Symptom 1.1. The power light does not come on, and you
cannot hear any cooling fan.**   Chances are that there is
insufficient power reaching the computer. Thus, check
the following areas:

- *Check the AC voltage.*   Use a voltmeter and confirm that there is adequate AC voltage at the wall outlet.

- *Check the AC cord.*   The AC cord may be loose or disconnected.

- *Check the power supply fuse(s).*   The main fuse may have opened. Replace any failed fuse.

> **NOTE**:   If you replace a main fuse and the fuse continues to fail, you may have a serious fault in the power supply. Try replacing the power supply.

Symptom 1.2. There is no power light, but you hear the cooling fan running.   Chances are that AC power is reaching the PC, but the supply is not providing adequate energy to the motherboard, drives, and other system components. Thus, perform the following checks:

- *Check the AC voltage.*   Use a voltmeter and confirm that there is adequate AC voltage at the wall outlet. Unusually low AC voltages (such as during "brownout" conditions) can cause the power supply to malfunction.

- *Check the power supply cables.*   Verify that the power supply cables are attached properly and securely to the motherboard and drives.

- *Check the power supply voltages.*   Use a voltmeter to verify that each output from the power supply is correct. Table 1.1 illustrates the proper voltage for each wire color, while Tables 1.2 and 1.3 outline the wiring layouts for AT and ATX motherboards respectively. If any output is very low or absent (especially the +5 volt output), replace the power supply.

- *Check the "Power Good" signal.* Use a voltmeter and verify that the Power Good signal is +5 volts. If this signal is below 1.0 volts, it may inhibit the CPU

TABLE 1.1   Index of Power Supply Outputs

Wire Color	Voltage or Designation
Black	Ground
Blue	−12Vdc
Brown	+3.3V Sense (ATX and NLX supplies)
Gray	Power OK (~ +5Vdc in ATX and NLX supplies)
Green	Power Supply on ("Soft control signal" for ATX and NLX supplies)
Orange	+3.3Vdc (ATX and NLX supplies)
Orange	Power Good (~ +5Vdc in AT-style supplies)
Purple	+5Vdc Standby (ATX and NLX supplies)
Red	+5Vdc
White	−5Vdc
Yellow	+12Vdc

TABLE 1.2   AT-style Motherboard Power Connections

Pin	P8 Assignment	Color	Pin	P9 Assignment	Color
1	Power Good	Orange	1	GND	Black
2	+5v (or NC)	Red	2	GND	Black
3	+12v	Yellow	3	−5v	White
4	−12v	Blue	4	+5v	Red
5	GND	Black	5	+5v	Red
6	GND	Black	6	+5v	Red

TABLE 1.3   ATX-style Motherboard Power Connections

Pin 1	-	+3.3Vdc	Pin 11	-	+3.3Vdc
Pin 2	-	+3.3Vdc	Pin 12	-	−12Vdc
Pin 3	-	Ground	Pin 13	-	Ground
Pin 4	-	+5Vdc	Pin 14	-	PS-ON ("soft" power control signal)
Pin 5	-	Ground	Pin 15	-	Ground
Pin 6	-	+5Vdc	Pin 16	-	Ground
Pin 7	-	Ground	Pin 17	-	Ground
Pin 8	-	Power Good	Pin 18	-	−5Vdc
Pin 9	-	+5Vdc (standby)			
			Pin 19	-	+5dc
Pin 10	-	+12Vdc	Pin 20	-	+5dc

from running by forcing a continuous reset condition. Since the Power Good signal is generated by the power supply, replace the power supply.

Symptom 1.3. The power light is on, but there is no apparent system activity.   Many possible problems can cause this kind of behavior, but a systematic approach should help you isolate the trouble quickly:

■ *Check the power supply voltages.*   Use a voltmeter to verify that each output from the power supply is correct. Refer to Table 1.1 for the proper voltage for each wire color. If any output is very low or absent (especially the +5 volt output), replace the power supply.

■ *Check the "Power Good" signal.*   Use a voltmeter and verify that the Power Good signal is +5 volts. If this signal is below 1.0 volts, it may inhibit the CPU from running by forcing a continuous reset condition. Since the Power Good signal is generated by the power supply, replace the power supply.

■ *Check the CPU.*   Check to see that the CPU is cool, that the heat-sink/fan assembly is fitted on correctly, and that the CPU itself is inserted properly and completely into its socket/slot.

■ *Check the CPU socket / slot.*   If the CPU is seated in a *Zero Insertion Force* (ZIF) socket, make sure that the socket's tension lever is closed and locked into place. If the CPU is seated in a slot (Slot 1 or Slot A), see that the retention mechanism is securely in place.

■ *Check the MCP.*   If there is a separate math co-processor on the motherboard (i286 and i386 systems), make sure that the MCP is inserted properly and completely into its socket.

■ *Check the expansion boards.*   Make sure that all expansion boards are seated properly. Any boards that are not secured properly or that are inserted unevenly can short bus signals and prevent the PC from starting.

- *Check the motherboard for shorts.* Inspect the motherboard at every metal standoff and see that no metal traces are being shorted against a standoff or screw. You may want to free the motherboard and see if the system starts. If it does, use non-conductive spacers (such as a small piece of manila folder) to insulate the motherboard from each metal standoff. If the system still fails to start (and all voltages from the power supply are correct), replace the motherboard.

The System Starts but Won't Initialize

Symptom 1.4. The power light is on, but you hear two or more beeps. There is also no video. In most cases, the trouble is with the video system or the motherboard. Thus, make the following checks:

- *Check the video board.* Video problems can easily halt the initialization process. Turn off and unplug the PC. Then make sure that your video board is inserted completely into its expansion slot.

- *Determine the beep code.* A catastrophic fault has been detected in the *Power On Self-Test* (POST) before the video system could be initialized. BIOS makers use different numbers and patterns of beeps to indicate failures. You can determine the exact failure by finding the BIOS maker (usually marked on the motherboard BIOS IC) and then finding the error message in Section 5. In the vast majority of cases, the fault will be traced to the *Central Processing Unit* (CPU), RAM, motherboard circuitry, video controller, or drive controller.

Symptom 1.5. The power light is on, but the system hangs during initialization. Video may be active, but there may be no text in the display. The POST has detected a fault and is unable to continue with the initialization process.

The main task here is to determine the POST code. BIOS makers mark the completion of each POST step by writing hexadecimal completion codes to port 80h. Turn off and unplug the PC, and then insert a POST board to read the completion codes. Reboot the computer and find the last code to be written before the initialization stops; that is the likely point of failure. You can determine the meaning of that POST code by finding the BIOS maker (usually displayed in the initial moments of powerup) and then locating the corresponding error message in Section 5. Note that without a POST board available, it will be extremely difficult to identify the problem.

Symptom 1.6. You see a message indicating a (CMOS) Setup problem. The system parameters entered into CMOS RAM do not match the hardware configuration found during the POST.

To find a solution, try the following steps:

- *Start the CMOS Setup.* Most systems use one of the key combinations listed in Table 1.4. If you are working on an older system (early i386 and i286 systems), you will probably need to boot the PC from a setup disk. If no setup disk is available, you may be able to find a suitable routine at *oak.oakland.edu* or *ftp.uu.net:/systems/msdos/simtel/at.*

- *Check the CMOS Setup.* Review each entry in the CMOS setup, especially things like drive parameters and installed memory, and make sure that the CMOS entries accurately reflect the actual hardware installed on your system. If not, correct the error(s),

TABLE 1.4   Setup Key Combinations for Typical BIOS Makers

AMI BIOS	\<Del\> key during the POST
Award BIOS	\<Ctrl\> + \<Alt\> + \<Esc\>
DTK BIOS	\<Esc\> key during the POST
IBM PS/2 BIOS	\<Ctrl\>+\<Alt\>+\<Ins\> after \<Ctrl\>+\<Alt\>+\<Del\>
Phoenix BIOS	\<Ctrl\>+\<Alt\>+\<Esc\> or \<Ctrl\>+\<Alt\>+\<S\>

save your changes, and reboot the system. If your CMOS setup offers a set of BIOS Defaults, try selecting the defaults.

■ *Test the CMOS battery.* See if CMOS RAM will hold its contents by turning off the PC, waiting several minutes, and then rebooting the PC. If setup problems persist and you find that the values you entered have been lost, change the CMOS backup battery.

Symptom 1.7. You see no drive light activity and the boot drive cannot be located.   In most cases, there is a problem with the drive's power, signal connections, or system configuration, but the following steps should help to isolate the trouble:

■ *Check the drive's power cable.* The most frequent cause of drive problems is power connections. Inspect the four-pin power cable and see that it is attached properly and completely to the drive.

■ *Check the power supply voltages.* Use a voltmeter and verify that the +5 and +12 voltage levels (especially +12 volts) are correct at the four-pin connector. Table 1.5 shows the values of each pin. If either voltage is low or absent, replace the power supply.

■ *Check the drive's signal cable.* Locate the wide ribbon cable that connects to the drive and make sure it is attached correctly and completely at the drive *and* controller ends. Look for any scrapes or nicks

TABLE 1.5   **Pin Assignments* of a Four-Pin Power Connector**

Pin	Level
1	+12 volts
2	+12 GND*
3	+5 GND*
4	+5 volts

*In actual practice, the +12 and +5 GND lines are combined
together at the power supply.

along the cable that might cause problems. You
might try a reliable signal cable.

- *Start the CMOS Setup.* Most systems use one of the
  key combinations listed in Table 1.2. If you are
  working on an older system (early i386 and i286 systems), you will probably need to boot the PC from a
  setup disk. If no setup disk is available, you may be
  able to find a suitable routine at *oak.oakland.edu* or
  ftp.uu.net:/systems/msdos/simtel/at.

- *Check the CMOS setup.* Review the drive parameters entered in the CMOS setup, and make sure that
  the CMOS entries accurately reflect the actual boot
  drive installed on your system. If not, correct the
  error(s), save your changes, and reboot the system.
  You may want to try letting the BIOS auto-detect
  and/or auto-configure your hard drive(s).

- *Check the drive's controller.* Make sure that the
  drive controller board is installed properly and completely in its expansion slot, and see that any
  jumpers are set correctly.

- *Try the boot diskette.* Try booting the system from
  your boot floppy. If the system successfully boots to
  the A: prompt, your problem is limited to the hard
  drive system. Try switching to the C: drive. If the
  drive responds (and you can access its information),
  there may be a problem with the boot sector. Try a
  package like PC Tools or Norton Utilities to try and

fix the boot sector. If you can't access the hard drive, try a diagnostic to check the drive controller and drive.

- *Check for boot sector viruses.* A boot sector virus can render the hard drive unbootable. If you haven't checked for viruses yet, use your anti-virus work disk now and focus on boot sector problems.

- *Replace the drive.* If you cannot determine the problem at this point, try replacing the drive with a reliable working drive. Remember that you will have to change the CMOS setup parameters to accommodate the new drive.

- *Replace the drive controller.* If all else fails, try a new drive controller board.

Symptom 1.8. The drive light remains on continuously and the boot drive cannot be located. This typically happens if the signal cable is inserted backwards at one end. In most cases, this type of problem happens after replacing a drive or upgrading a controller. To fix the situation, try the following checks:

- *Check the drive's signal cable.* Make sure the cable is inserted in the correct orientation at both ends.

- *Replace the drive.* If you cannot determine the problem at this point, try replacing the drive with a reliable working drive. Remember that you will have to change the CMOS Setup parameters to accommodate the new drive.

- *Replace the drive controller.* If all else fails, try a new drive controller board.

Symptom 1.9. You see normal system activity but no video. In virtually every case, the system is working, but the video system is not installed or connected properly. The following checks can help remedy the problem:

- *Check monitor power.* Make sure the monitor is plugged in and turned on. This type of oversight is really more common than you might think.

- *Check the monitor itself.* Check to make sure that the monitor works (you may want to try the monitor on a known, reliable system). If the monitor fails, replace it.

- *Check the monitor cable.* Trace the monitor cable to its connection at the video board and verify that the connector is inserted securely.

- *Check the video board.* It is possible that the video board has failed. Try a reliable monitor. If the problem persists, replace the video board.

The System Starts but Crashes/Reboots Intermittently

Symptom 1.10. The system randomly crashes/reboots for no apparent reason. This type of trouble can occur from a wide range of problems, both hardware and software related. The following protocol will help you identify hardware-related problems in a systematic fashion:

- *Check for viruses.* Some viruses (especially memory-resident viruses) can cause the PC to crash or reboot unexpectedly. If you haven't run your virus checker yet, do so now.

- *Check the power supply cables.* Verify that the power supply cables are attached properly and securely to the motherboard.

- *Check the power supply voltages.* Use a voltmeter to verify that each output from the power supply is correct. Refer to Table 1.1 for the proper voltage for each wire color. If any output is low (especially the +5 volt output), replace the power supply.

- *Check the CPU.* With all power off, check to see that the CPU is cool, that the heat-sink/fan assembly is fitted on correctly, and that the CPU itself is inserted properly and completely into its socket/slot. If the CPU overheats, it will stall, taking the entire system with it.

■ *Check the CPU socket/slot.*   If the CPU is seated in a ZIF socket, make sure that the socket's tension lever is closed and locked into place. If the CPU is seated in a slot (a Slot 1 or Slot A connection), see that the retention mechanism is securely attached.

■ *Check all SIMMs and Dual In-Line Memory Modules (DIMMs).*   With all power off, make sure that all SIMMs/DIMMs are seated properly in their holders and locked into place. You may try removing each SIMM/DIMM, cleaning the contacts, and gently reinstalling the SIMMs/DIMMs.

■ *Check the expansion boards.*   Make sure that all expansion boards are seated properly. Any boards that are not secured properly or that are inserted unevenly can short bus signals and cause spurious reboots. If you've recently installed new expansion hardware, make sure that no hardware conflicts exist between the interrupts, DMA channels, or I/O addresses. You can find an index of these resources in Section 5, "Motherboard Troubleshooting."

■ *Check the motherboard for shorts.*   Inspect the motherboard at every metal standoff and see that no metal traces are being shorted against a standoff or screw. You may want to free the motherboard and see if the crashes or reboots go away. If so, use nonconductive spacers (such as a small piece of manila folder) to insulate the motherboard from each metal standoff. If the system continues to crash or reboot (and all voltages from the power supply are correct), replace the motherboard.

Conflict Troubleshooting

The PC only provides a limited number of interrupts (IRQs), *Direct Memory Access* (DMA) channels, and I/O addresses for devices to use. No two devices can use the same resources. If that happens, the two devices will compete for control. Conflicts can result in problems ranging from erratic device behavior to system lockups and crashes. The following procedure offers a reliable method for locating and eliminating device conflicts:

1. Power the computer down and remove the new expansion device.

2. Start the machine to the DOS mode and run the MSD.EXE program that is in your \WINDOWS directory (you can also try any number of shareware or commercial diagnostics that detect resource assignments).

3. The MSD program will let you look at which interrupts, DMA channels, and I/O addresses are currently in use on your system. Record those on a sheet of paper (or print the report to a printer) and exit the program.

4. Examine the new device and check its resource assignments against the resources already in use. Chances are that the new device will be using an IRQ, DMA, or I/O assignment already shown in your MSD report.

5. Change the conflicting resource. For example, if you find an IRQ conflict, change the IRQ on your new device to an IRQ that is not in use. If the device's resources are set through software, simply proceed to the next step.

6. Turn the system off again and place the device back in your computer.

7. Run any setup software for the new device. It should be recognized properly.

8. If you cannot find any available resources, you will have to disable at least one other device in order to free up the resources for your new device.

9. If the new device works under Windows, be sure to run any Windows installation software. If the device is running under Windows 95, run the Add New Hardware wizard.

After an Upgrade

Symptom 1.11. The system fails to boot, freezes during boot, or freezes during operation for no apparent reason. This is the classic sign of a hardware conflict. A PC is designed with a limited number of resources (memory, I/O addresses, interrupt (IRQ) lines, DMA channels, and so on). For the PC to function properly, each device added to the system must use its *own* unique resources. For example, no two devices can use the same IRQ, DMA, or I/O resources. When such an overlap of resources occurs, the PC can easily malfunction and freeze. Unfortunately, it is virtually impossible to predict when the malfunction will occur, so a conflict can manifest itself early (any time during the boot process) or later on (after DOS is loaded) while an application is running.

Resolving a conflict is not difficult, but it requires patience and attention to detail. Examine the upgrade and its adapter board and check the IRQ, DMA, and I/O address settings of other boards in the system. Make sure that the upgrade hardware is set to use resources that are *not* in use by other devices already in the system. For example, some motherboards offer built-in video controller circuits. Before another video adapter can be added to the system, the motherboard video adapter must be disabled, usually with a single motherboard jumper. Some sophisticated adapter boards (especially high-end video adapters and video capture boards) require the use of extra memory space. If memory exclusions are needed, be sure that the appropriate entries are made in CONFIG.SYS and AUTOEXEC.BAT files. If memory exclusions are not followed, multiple devices may attempt to use the same memory space and result in a conflict.

Symptom 1.12. The system fails to recognize its upgrade device. Even if the hardware is installed in a system correctly, the PC may not recognize the upgrade device(s) without the proper software loaded. A great example of this is the CD-ROM drive. It is a simple matter to install the drive (and a controller card if necessary), but the PC will not even recognize the drive unless the low-level CD-ROM device driver is added to CONFIG.SYS and the MS-DOS CD-ROM driver (MSCDEX.EXE) is included in AUTOEXEC.BAT. If the PC is running in a stable fashion, but it does not recognize the expansion hardware, make sure that you have loaded all required software correctly.

If you are mixing and matching existing subassemblies from new and old systems, make sure that each device is fully compatible with the PC. Incompatibilities between vintages and manufacturers can lead to operational problems. For example, adding a 3.5-inch floppy drive to an i286 AT system can result in problems since the older BIOS could not format 3.5-inch, high-density (1.44 MB) floppy disks. A DOS utility (such as DRIVER.SYS) is needed to correct this deficiency.

It is also possible that the upgrade device may simply be defective or installed incorrectly. Open the system and double-check your installation. Pay particular attention to any cables, connectors, or drive jumpers. When you confirm that the hardware and software installation is correct, suspect a hardware defect. Try the upgrade in another system if possible. If the problem *persists* when you attempt the upgrade on another PC, one or more elements of the upgrade hardware are probably defective. Return it to the vendor for a prompt refund or replacement. If the upgrade *works* on another system, the original system may be incompatible with the upgrade, or you may have missed a jumper or DIP switch setting on the motherboard.

Symptom 1.13. One or more applications fail to function as expected after an upgrade. This is not uncommon among video adapter and sound board upgrades. Often, applications are configured to work with various sets of hardware. When that hardware is altered, the particular application(s) may no longer run properly (this is especially true under Windows). The best way to address this problem is to check and change the hardware configuration for each affected application. Most DOS applications come with a setup utility. Under Windows 95/98, you can access system configuration settings through the System icon under the Control Panel (a.k.a. the Device Manager).

Windows 95/98 Boot Symptoms

Symptom 1.14. The Windows 95/98 boot drive is no longer bootable after restoring data with the DOS Backup utility. This happens frequently when a replacement drive is installed, and you attempt to restore the Windows 95/98 backup data. Unfortunately, the DOS version of Backup is not configured to restore system files. Start Backup and restore your root directory with System Files, Hidden Files, and Read-Only Files checked. Next, boot the system from MS-DOS 6.x Upgrade Setup Disk 1 or a Windows 95/98 startup disk. Then use the SYS command to make the hard drive bootable, such as

```
A:\> sys c:                    <Enter>
```

You should then be able to restore the remainder of your files. When backing up a Windows 95/98 system, your best approach is to use the Windows Backup program. Once the new drive is installed, partitioned, and formatted, install a new copy of Windows 95/98, start Windows Backup, and *then* restore the remaining files to the drive.

Symptom 1.15. Windows 95/98 will not boot, and ScanDisk reports bad clusters that it cannot repair. This is a problem encountered with *Western Digital* (WD) hard drives. If your WD drive fails in this way, you can recover the drive, but you will lose all information on it. Backup as much information from the drive as possible before proceeding and peform these steps:

1. Download the Western Digital service files WDATIDE.EXE and WD_CLEAR.EXE from WD at *www.wdc.com*. You can also get these files from AOL by typing keyword WDC.

2. Copy these files to a clean boot floppy diskette.

3. Boot to DOS from a clean diskette (no CONFIG. SYS or AUTOEXEC.BAT files) and run WD_ CLEAR.EXE. This utility clears all data on the media (and destroys all data).

4. Next, run the WDATIDE.EXE utility to perform a comprehensive surface scan.

5. Repartition and reformat the drive. Then restore your data.

Symptom 1.16. You see a Bad or missing <filename> error on startup. A file used by Windows 95/98 during startup has probably become corrupt. Locate the file mentioned in the error message. If you can find the file, erase it and try reinstalling it from the original Windows 95/98 installation CD.

Symptom 1.17. Windows 95/98 reports damaged or missing files, or a VxD error. During startup, Windows 95/98 depends on several key files being available. If a key file is damaged or missing, Windows will not function properly (if it loads at all). Run Windows Setup again and select the *Verify* option in *Safe Recovery* to replace the missing or damaged file(s). Otherwise, you may need to reinstall Windows from scratch.

Symptom 1.18. After installing Windows 95/98, you can't boot from a different drive. The Windows Setup program checks all hard disks to find just one that contains the drive type (80h) designator in the DriveNumber field of a boot sector. Windows 95/98 will typically force the first drive to be bootable and prevent other drives from booting. However, the problem can be corrected in two ways after Windows 95/98 is installed:

- Use the version of FDISK included with Windows 95/98 to set the primary active partition.

- Use a disk editor utility to change a disk's Drive-Number field so that you can boot from that hard disk.

Symptom 1.19. Windows 95/98 Registry files are missing. Two registry files exist: USER.DAT and SYSTEM. DAT. They are backed up automatically as USER.DA0 and SYSTEM.DA0. If a .DAT file is missing, Windows 95/98 will automatically load the corresponding .DA0 file. If both the .DAT and .DA0 Registry files are missing or corrupt, Windows 95/98 will start in the Safe Mode offering to restore the Registry. However, this cannot be accomplished without a backup. Either restore the Registry files from a tape or diskette backup, or run Windows Setup to create a new Registry. Unfortunately, restoring an old registry or creating a new registry from scratch will reload programs and re-add hardware to restore the system to its original state, a long and difficult procedure. Use the following DOS procedure to backup the Registry files to a floppy disk:

```
attrib -r -s -h system.da?
attrib -r -s -h user.da?
copy system.da? A:\
```

```
copy user.da? A:\

attrib +r +s +h system.da?

attrib +r +s +h user.da?
```

Symptom 1.20. During the Windows 95/98 boot, I get an Invalid System Disk error. This often happens during the first reboot during Windows Setup or when you boot from the startup disk. When you a see a message such as *Invalid system disk. Replace the disk and then press any key,* there may be several possible problems. First, your disk may be infected with a boot-sector virus. Run your anti-virus work disk and check closely for boot sector viruses. Windows Setup may also fail if anti-virus software is running as a TSR, or your BIOS has enabled boot sector protection. Make sure that any boot sector protection is turned off before installing Windows 95/98. Check for disk overlay software. Windows 95/98 may not detect overlay software such as Disk Manager, EZ-Drive, or DrivePro and will over-write the *master boot record* (MBR). See the documentation that accompanies your particular management software for recovering the MBR. To reinstall the Windows 95/98 system files, follow these steps:

1. Boot the system using the Windows 95/98 Emergency Boot Disk.

2. At the DOS command prompt, type the following lines:

```
c:

cd\windows\command

attrib c:\msdos.sys -h -s -r

ren c:\msdos.sys c:\msdos.xxx

a:

sys c:

del c:\msdos.sys
```

```
ren c:\msdos.xxx c:\msdos.sys
attrib c:\msdos.sys +r +s +h
```

3. Remove the Emergency Boot Disk and reboot the system.

Symptom 1.21. Windows 95/98 will not install on a compressed drive. You are probably using an old version of the compression software that Windows 95/98 does not recognize. Although Windows 95/98 should be compatible with all versions of SuperStor, it does require version 2.0 or later of Stacker. Make sure your compression software is recent, and see that there is enough free space on the host drive to support Windows 95/98 installation. If you have the PlusPack for Windows 95/98, you should be able to install DriveSpace 3 for best Windows support.

Symptom 1.22. The drive indicates that it is in MS-DOS compatibility mode. For some reason, Windows 95/98 is using a real-mode (DOS) driver instead of a protected-mode (32-bit) driver. Make sure that any software related to the hard drive (especially hard disk drivers) are using the protected-mode versions. Windows 95/98 should install equivalent protected-mode software, but you may need to contact the drive manufacturer and obtain the latest Windows 95/98 drivers. If you are using Disk Manager, make sure that you're using version 6.0 or later. You can get the latest patch (DMPATCH.EXE) from the Ontrack web site at *www.ontrack.com.* Finally, check your motherboard BIOS. Windows 95/98 may use DOS compatibility mode on large EIDE hard disks (hard disks with more than 1,024 cylinders) in some computers. This may occur because of an invalid drive geometry translation in the system ROM BIOS that prevents the protected-mode IDE device driver from being loaded. Contact your system manufacturer for information about obtaining an updated BIOS.

Symptom 1.23. Disabling protected-mode disk driver(s) hides the partition table when FDISK is used. As with Symptom 1.22, some problem is preventing 32-bit operation of your hard drive(s). Do not use the Disable all 32-bit protected-mode disk drivers option. Instead, upgrade your motherboard BIOS to a later version.

Symptom 1.24. You cannot achieve 32-bit disk access under Windows 95/98. If the Windows 95/98 system refuses to enable 32-bit disk access, there may be a conflict between the motherboard CMOS Setup entries and the BIOS on your EIDE controller. For example, if both BIOS have settings for *Logical Block Addressing* (LBA), make sure only one entry is in use.

Symptom 1.25. Windows 95/98 does not recognize a new device. In some cases, Windows 95/98 is unable to recognize a new device. When this happens, check to see if there is a hardware conflict between the device and other devices in the system (you can see conflicts represented in the Device Manager with small yellow exclamation marks). Also make sure that any necessary drivers have been installed properly. If problems continue, remove the new device through your Device Manager and reinstall it through the Add New Hardware wizard (or perform a full reboot and allow Windows to redetect the device at start time).

Symptom 1.26. Windows 95/98 malfunctions when installed over Disk Manager. Disk Manager should typically be compatible with Windows 95/98, but certain points must be kept in mind. Check your Disk Manager version first. If you are using Disk Manager, make sure that you're using version 6.0 or later. You can get the latest patch (DMPATCH.EXE) from the Ontrack web site at *www.ontrack.com*. Check the slave drive with Disk Manager. Although the Windows 95/98 file system is supposed to work properly with a slave drive only using Disk Manager, problems can occur in some circumstances:

- When a Windows 3.1x virtual driver replaces the Windows 95 protected-mode driver (WDCDRV.386)

- When the cylinder count in CMOS for the slave drive is greater than 1,024 cylinders

- When the motherboard CMOS settings for the slave drive are set to auto-detect

Symptom 1.27. You have problems using a manufacturer-specific hard disk driver (such as Western Digital's FastTrack driver WDCDRV.386) for 32-bit access under Windows 95/98. Generally speaking, Windows 95/98 has 32-bit, protected-mode drivers for a wide variety of EIDE devices. In actual practice, you should not need a manufacturer-specific driver. If Windows 95/98 has not removed all references to the driver from the file SYSTEM.INI, you should edit it, remove those references manually, and then reboot the system. Be sure to make a backup copy of SYSTEM.INI before editing it.

Tips for Slow Windows Startups

Windows 95/98 is a complex OS, and it takes time to load the many components and drivers that are required to make it run. However, certain circumstances can make Windows really drag. If it seems that your Windows 98 system is taking an unusually long time to start, follow these tips to help streamline your setup:

Shut Down Unneeded Programs. The first thing to do is examine which programs you're launching at startup and decide whether you really need them. Remember that programs can be launched from the Startup folder (under the Start menu), the RUN= and LOAD= lines of your WIN.INI file, or from entries in the Registry. Under Windows 95 you'd have to check each of these locations manually, but Windows 98 has a convenient one-stop location to tweak them all (see Figure 1.1). Just click Start, select Run, then type MSCONFIG.

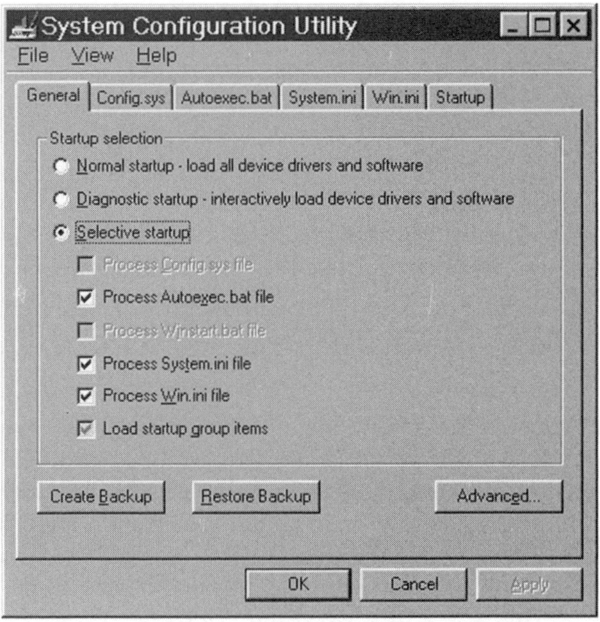

Figure 1.1 The MSCONFIG dialog under Windows 98

Under the Startup tab, you'll see all the programs you are launching. By clearing the check box next to any item, you'll prevent it from running at startup.

Disable Real-Time Virus Scanning. Many of today's antivirus utilities offer real-time scanning for viruses. Unfortunately, since the scanner loads at startup, it can seriously impact performance because it must scan every program file as they are being loaded into memory. If you're willing to accept a bit less virus protection, you can accelerate your boot times by turning off real-time scanning. Instead, schedule a task to run a standard virus scan at least once a day. Not only will this shorten boot times, but it will make your system faster during any disk access.

Don't Check the Floppy Drive.   Among its many other startup checks, Windows 98 checks to see if you've added or changed floppy drives each time the system starts up. Chances are that you'll *never* reconfigure your floppy, so tell Windows to stop checking it. Click Start, highlight Settings, select Control Panel, and then double-click the System icon. Click the Performance tab, click the File System button, and then select the Floppy Disk tab. Clear the checkbox marked "Search for new floppy disk drives each time your computer starts." Apply your changes and try rebooting the computer.

Check Your Network Settings.   Network settings are often a cause of slow boot times. One common problem occurs when a network card has the TCP/IP protocol loaded and is set to obtain an IP address from a DHCP server, but no server is available. The PC will wait up to a minute for an answer from the server before it continues booting. Click Start, highlight Settings, select the Control Panel, and double-click the Network icon (don't make changes if you're on a company network that is supported by a network administrator; check with them first).

  If you're *not* using TCP/IP on your local network (only for ISP dialup), then just remove the binding between the network card and the TCP/IP protocol. You'll see this in the Network dialog as a line that reads `TCP/IP -> (network card name)`. Select that item and click Remove. If you *are* using TCP/IP on your local network, you either need to have a DHCP server running on the network or use manually assigned IP addresses. For most small networks of Windows 98 systems, manually assigned addresses work fine. For each PC on the network, assign a unique IP number in a sequence such as 10.0.0.1, 10.0.0.2, 10.0.0.3, and so on. You set this number in the Network dialog. Select the entry `TCP/IP -> (network card name)` and click Properties. On the IP Address tab, choose `Specify an IP address` and enter the unique IP number that you've chosen for this system. For the subnet mask, try using 255.0.0.0 for all systems.

Tweak Your CMOS Setup. Check your CMOS Setup routine for options that can speed your system's boot time. Enabling options such as Quick Boot or Quick POST, and shortening drive initialization delays can shave a few seconds off the system's POST process. You'll also get a faster boot sequence if the system can boot directly from the C: drive rather than first checking for a floppy (this also prevents viruses from infecting your system via a boot floppy).

Examine the Boot Log. You may be faced with a problematic hardware component or software driver. These can be a bit difficult to diagnose, but the BOOTLOG. TXT feature can help. This enables you to generate a boot log that indicates each step in the boot process. You'll need to access the Windows Startup menu, which will give you the option to generate a boot log. After the BIOS has completed its POST, hold down the Ctrl key. The boot menu should appear (if the Windows 98 logo appears instead, you probably didn't press the Ctrl key soon enough).

From the boot menu, select a "logged startup." Once Windows has finished booting up, the BOOTLOG.TXT file will be in the root of your C: drive, and you can view this file with Notepad. On a normal system, it's unusual to have any step in the boot process take more than a second or two. Large delays (10 or 20 seconds) usually indicate some sort of problem with a driver or its associated hardware.

Tips for Windows Startup Problems

It's bad enough when Windows takes a long time to load, but when Windows fails to start at all, it may be difficult (or impossible) to use diagnostics and

Windows tools to correct the problem. This part of the chapter outlines a suite of tips that can help you track down and correct serious startup faults.

Try the Safe Mode.   One of your first options is to try starting Windows 98 in the Safe Mode. Hold down the Ctrl key right after the BIOS finishes its POST (but before Windows starts to load). You should get a Startup Menu of options to select from. Choose Safe Mode from the menu and allow Windows to boot. If the boot is successful, right-click My Computer and select Properties. Then click the Device Manager tab. If any hardware is malfunctioning, it will be shown there with a yellow exclamation point (you can also use Device Manager to disable hardware manually and see if that lets you boot normally). If you cannot boot Windows to the Safe Mode, chances are that there's a serious hardware problem in the system.

Check for Disk Errors.   If you cannot start Windows due to a disk error, it may be that the drive's power or signal cable has become loose. Check the cables and see that the drive is receiving adequate power. Try booting from a floppy diskette. If you can reach a DOS prompt from a boot diskette, the system hard drive may be defective. If you *can* access your hard drive(s), try running ScanDisk and Disk Defragmenter (Defrag) to weed out any potential file system trouble.

Use the Automatic Skip Driver Agent.   If your system crashes or hangs during the startup process, Windows 98 tries to avoid crashing again by skipping the operation that it "thinks" caused the problem; this is the *Automatic Skip Driver agent* (ASD). However, the ASD may cause other problems (such as disabling some of your hardware) when a driver is skipped. To see if Windows is skipping any bootup operations on your system, select Start, choose Run, and type ASD. If everything is okay, you'll receive a dialog that says `There are no current ASD critical operation failures on this machine.` If your system has had boot problems, they will be listed in this dialog. You can put a check next to any or all of the skipped drivers to have Windows 98 retry them the next time you boot. After you boot the system again, run ASD and see if the function is disabled again. If so, you may have a problem with that hardware (or your BIOS).

Check for Missing Files.   If you see the message `A file needed by Windows is missing` during a boot cycle, it's often due to a poor uninstallation of an application. This can sometimes occur when you uninstall and then immediately reinstall an application without rebooting first. Take a look at the name of the missing file and see if it yields any clue to the application that might be causing the problem. Then try to uninstall, reboot, and reinstall that application. If the offending file relates to an application that you no longer need, you can use RegEdit to find and delete the Registry keys that refer to the file (be sure that you have good backups before trying this). As a last resort, you may need to reinstall Windows to fix this problem cleanly.

Windows Protection Errors.   In some cases, Windows may refuse to boot, returning the message `Windows Protection Error. You need to restart your computer.` At this point, you're stuck unless you boot from a floppy disk. One cause in Windows 95/98 could be a problem between SmartDrive and a large number of installed device drivers. If you see something about initializing IOS in the error message, try booting from a floppy, find the file SMARTDRV.EXE (usually in the Windows directory), and rename it to SMARTDRV. BAD. Now try booting the system from the hard drive again.

There is also a known problem in Windows 95 that affects AMD K6 processors that run at 350 MHz or higher speeds. This will sometimes give a Windows protection error message (you can refer to Microsoft's document Q192841 for more detailed information and a patch file). Other solutions to Windows protection errors can be identified in Microsoft's document Q149962.

2

Drive Troubleshooting

Computers serve little purpose without some means of reliable long-term storage, and over the years, a large number of versatile drives have developed to provide access to vast amounts of information. This chapter highlights the troubleshooting procedures for floppy drives, hard drives, and CD-ROMs, CD recorders (CD-Rs), and CD-rewritable disk (CD-RW) drives.

Floppy Drives

In spite of their age, the venerable floppy disk drive remains a standard removable-media, mass-storage device. Although they're remarkably slow and offer puny storage capacities when compared to hard drives and other mass-storage devices, their high reliability, inexpensive media, and universal compatibility will keep floppy drives around for years to come.

Floppy Drive Interface

Floppy drives use a 34-pin signal interface and a 4 pin "mate-and-lock" power connector. Both connections are illustrated in Figure 2.1.

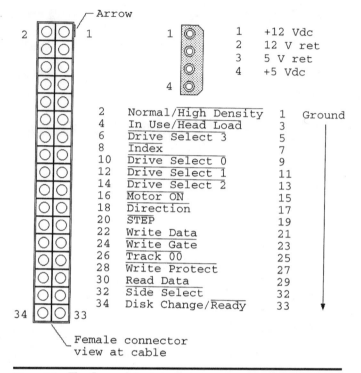

Figure 2.1   The floppy drive interface

Windows 95/98 Guidelines

A great deal of everyday work takes place under Windows 95/98. As a result, floppy drive problems are often first noticed under Windows. When Windows reports trouble reading a floppy drive, try the following steps to identify and resolve the issue through Windows.

Check the Floppy Controller Using the Safe Mode. Start Windows in Safe mode and try to access the floppy drive. To start Windows 95 in Safe mode, restart the computer and then press the F8 key when you see the message Starting Windows 95. Then choose Safe Mode from the Startup menu. To start Windows 98 in Safe mode, restart your computer, press and hold down the Ctrl key after your computer completes the *Power-On Self-Test* (POST), and then choose Safe Mode from the Startup menu. If you can access the floppy drive in Safe mode, follow these steps:

1. Right-click the My Computer icon from your desktop and then click Properties on the menu that appears.

2. Click the Device Manager tab and then double-click the Floppy Disk Controllers entry.

3. Highlight the floppy disk controller for the drive you are having problems with, and then click Properties.

4. In Windows 95, click the Original Configuration (Current) check box to clear it. In Windows 98, click the Disable In This Hardware Profile check box to select it. This disables the Windows protected-mode driver for the floppy disk drive controller.

5. Click OK and restart Windows normally.

If you can now access the floppy disk drive successfully after following the procedure above, you may be faced with one or more of the following conditions:

■ The floppy disk drive controller may not be supported in protected mode.

■ Drivers are loading in the file CONFIG.SYS or AUTOEXEC.BAT that may be necessary for protected mode access.

■ Drivers are loading in the file CONFIG.SYS or AUTOEXEC.BAT that may be causing conflicts in Windows and need to be disabled.

If you still cannot access the floppy disk drive, follow these steps to redetect the floppy drive controller:

1. Right-click the My Computer icon from your desktop and then click Properties on the menu that appears.

2. Click the Device Manager tab and then double-click the Floppy Disk Controllers entry.

3. Highlight the floppy disk controller, click Remove to remove the controller, and then click OK.

4. Open your Control Panel, then double-click the Add New Hardware icon.

5. Click Next and then click Yes to enable Windows to detect the hardware in your computer.

6. When the Add New Hardware wizard is finished, restart the computer and try the floppy drive again.

Redetecting the floppy disk controller should correct addressing problems with the controller by detecting the correct address range. If the floppy disk controller is *not* detected correctly, there may be a problem with the floppy disk controller. If the floppy disk controller *is* redetected, but you still cannot access the floppy drive, there may be a problem with the diskette itself.

Suspect Your Diskette(s).   One or more of your diskettes may be damaged. Use a disk utility (such as ScanDisk) to test the diskette for damage or try a reliable high-quality diskette.

> **NOTE**:   Never use a disk utility that is *not* compliant with Windows 95 or Windows 98. Non-compliant disk utilities can damage DMF (compressed) disks. The Windows ScanDisk tool recognizes DMF disks and does not damage them.

You may also try the following command from a DOS command prompt:

```
C:\> copy a:\*.* nul        <Enter>
```

For example, if you are having problems with drive A:, insert a disk you are having problems with in drive A: and type the command. This command copies the files on the disk to a null device. If there is a problem copying the files, error messages will appear on the screen notifying you that diskette is probably defective.

Suspect Your Tape Backup. Floppy problems are known to occur under Windows when using an Irwin tape backup unit under Windows 95/98. Windows 95/98 Setup should remove the following statement from the [386Enh] section of the SYSTEM.INI file:

```
device=<path>\VIRWT.386
```

If you reinstall the Irwin Tape Backup software *after* you install Windows 95/98 , this statement is placed in the SYSTEM.INI file again and can cause conflicts with floppy disk access in Windows. When this occurs, you must comment-out that line in SYSTEM.INI.

Check the CMOS Setup. Reboot your computer and verify that the floppy drive entries in your CMOS Setup are correct. If not, Windows will not be able to recognize your floppy drive hardware. If you must make changes to your CMOS Setup, remember to save your changes as you exit.

Check for Device Conflicts. Device conflicts (reported by the Device Manager) can cause problems reading from and writing to floppy disks. You can generally resolve device conflict problems by changing or removing the resources from the Device Manager that are causing the conflict. Typical conflicts occur with hard drive controller cards, video cards, or COM ports.

Floppy Disk Troubleshooting

Symptom 2.1. The floppy drive is completely dead. The system boots, but the disk does not even initialize when inserted. This behavior can be caused by a number of important problems, so consider each possibility carefully before acting:

- *Check the diskette.* Make sure that the disk is properly inserted into the floppy drive assembly. If the diskette does not enter and seat just right within the drive, disk access will be impossible. If you cannot get the diskettes to insert properly, replace the floppy drive.

- *Check the drive power.* Loose connectors or faulty cable wiring can easily disable a floppy drive. Use your multimeter to measure DC voltages at the power connector. Place your meter's ground lead on pin 2 and measure +12 Vdc at pin 1. Ground your meter on pin 3 and measure +5 Vdc at pin 4. If either of both of these voltages is low or missing, troubleshoot your computer power supply or replace the supply outright.

- *Check the signal cable.* Verify that the drive's 34-pin ribbon cable is attached securely at the drive(s) and at the drive controller. Re-attach the signal cable if it's loose and try another signal cable if necessary.

- *Replace the floppy drive.* If the problem persists, chances are that the floppy drive is defective (perhaps the "disk-in-place" sensor has failed). Try replacing the floppy drive with a reliable drive from another system.

- *Replace the floppy drive controller.* If a new floppy drive still does not resolve the problem, you may have a defective floppy drive controller circuit. If so, you may also receive a floppy drive or controller error from the system *Basic Input/Output System*

(BIOS) at boot time. Try disabling the existing floppy controller and install an expansion card controller (with only the floppy controller portion enabled).

Symptom 2.2. The floppy drive rotates a disk but will not seek to the desired track.   This type of symptom generally suggests that the head positioning stepping motor is inhibited or defective, but all other floppy drive functions are working properly. Thus, check the following areas:

- *Check the drive for obstructions.*   Carefully inspect the head positioning assembly to be certain that no broken parts or obstructions could jam the read/write heads. Gently remove any obstructions that you may find. Be careful not to accidentally misalign any linkages or mechanical components in the process of clearing an obstruction.

- *Check the drive power.*   Remove any diskette from the drive and reconnect the drive's signal and power cables. Apply power to the computer and measure drive voltages with your multimeter. Ground your multimeter on pin 2 of the power connector and measure +12 Vdc at pin 1. Move the meter ground to pin 3 and measure +5 Vdc on pin 4. If either voltage is low or absent, troubleshoot your computer power supply or replace the supply outright.

- *Check the signal cable.*   Verify that the drive's 34-pin ribbon cable is attached securely at the drive(s) and at the drive controller. Re-attach the signal cable is it's loose and try another signal cable if necessary.

- *Replace the floppy drive.*   If the problem persists, chances are that the floppy drive is defective (perhaps the head positioning system has failed). Try replacing the floppy drive with a reliable drive from another system.

- *Replace the floppy drive controller.* If a new floppy drive still does not resolve the problem, you may have a defective floppy drive controller circuit. If so, you may also receive a floppy drive or controller error from the system BIOS at boot time. Try disabling the existing floppy controller and install an expansion card controller (with only the floppy controller portion enabled).

Symptom 2.3. The floppy drive heads seek properly, but the spindle does not turn. This symptom suggests that the spindle motor is inhibited or defective, but all other floppy drive functions are working properly. Thus, make the following checks:

- *Check the drive for obstructions.* Power down the computer and remove the floppy drive. Carefully inspect the spindle motor, drive belt (if used), and spindle assembly. Make certain that no broken parts or obstructions could jam the spindle. If there is a belt between the motor and spindle, make sure the belt is reasonably tight; it should not slip. You should also examine the floppy drive with a diskette inserted to be certain that the disk's insertion or alignment is not causing the problem. Double-check your observations using several different diskettes. Gently remove any obstruction(s) that you may find. Be careful not to cause any accidental damage in the process of clearing an obstruction. Do *not* add any lubricating agents to the assembly, but gently vacuum or wipe away any significant accumulations of dust or dirt.

- *Check the drive power.* Remove any diskette from the drive and reconnect the drive's signal and power cables. Apply power to the computer and measure drive voltages with your multimeter. Ground your multimeter on pin 2 of the power connector and measure +12 Vdc at pin 1. Move the meter ground to pin 3 and measure +5 Vdc on pin 4. If either voltage is low or absent, troubleshoot your computer power supply or replace the supply outright.

- *Check the signal cable.* Verify that the drive's 34-pin ribbon cable is attached securely at the drive(s) and at the drive controller. Re-attach the signal cable is it's loose and try another signal cable if necessary.

- *Replace the floppy drive.* If the problem persists, chances are that the floppy drive is defective (perhaps the spindle motor control system has failed). Try replacing the floppy drive with a reliable drive from another system.

- *Replace the floppy drive controller.* If a new floppy drive still does not resolve the problem, you may have a defective floppy drive controller circuit. If so, you may also receive a floppy drive or controller error from the system BIOS at boot time. Try disabling the existing floppy controller and install an expansion card controller (with only the floppy controller portion enabled).

Symptom 2.4. The floppy drive will not read from/write to the diskette. All other operations appear normal. This type of problem can manifest itself in several ways, but your computer's *operating system* (OS) will usually inform you when a disk read or write error has occurred. The following checks can help you spot the problem:

- *Check the diskette.* Begin by trying a properly formatted diskette in your suspect drive. A faulty diskette can generate some very perplexing read/write problems.

- *Clean the floppy drive.* If a reliable diskette does not resolve the problem, try cleaning the read/write heads thoroughly. Do *not* run the drive with a head-cleaning disk inserted for more than 30 seconds at a time or you risk damaging the heads with excessive friction.

- *Check the signal cable.* Verify that the drive's 34-pin ribbon cable is attached securely at the drive(s) and at the drive controller. Re-attach the signal cable is it's loose and try another signal cable if necessary.

- *Replace the floppy drive.* If the problem persists, chances are that the floppy drive is defective (perhaps the head read/write system has failed). Try replacing the floppy drive with a drive from another system.

- *Replace the floppy drive controller.* If a new floppy drive still does not resolve the problem, you may have a defective floppy drive controller circuit. If so, you may also receive a floppy drive or controller error from the system BIOS at boot time. Try disabling the existing floppy controller and install an expansion card controller (with only the floppy controller portion enabled).

Symptom 2.5. The drive is able to write to a write-protected disk. When this kind of problem occurs, it is almost always the drive itself that is defective. The following checks are recommended:

- *Check the diskette.* Remove and examine the diskette itself to verify that it is actually write-protected. If the disk is *not* write-protected, write-protect it appropriately and try the diskette again. You might also like to try a different diskette.

- *Clean the floppy drive.* Try cleaning the drive by blowing clean compressed air into the drive (pay particular attention to cleaning off the write-protect sensor).

- *Replace the floppy drive.* If the problem persists, chances are that the floppy drive is defective. Perhaps the write-protect sensor or on-board drive electronics have failed. Try replacing the floppy drive with a reliable drive from another system.

Symptom 2.6. The drive can only recognize either high or double-density media, but not both. This type of problem usually appears in 3.5-inch drives during the disk format process when the drive must check the media type. The following checks can help spot the cause of the problem:

- *Check the diskette.*   Verify that you're using the correct disk type (this is actually a common oversight since many generic diskettes are unmarked).

- *Clean the floppy drive.*   Try cleaning the drive by blowing clean compressed air into the drive (pay particular attention to cleaning off the Media-type sensor).

- *Check the signal cable.*   Verify that the drive's 34-pin ribbon cable is attached securely at the drive(s) and at the drive controller. Re-attach the signal cable is it's loose and try another signal cable if necessary.

- *Replace the floppy drive.*   If the problem persists, chances are that the floppy drive is defective. Perhaps the Media-type sensor or on-board drive electronics has failed. Try replacing the floppy drive with a reliable drive from another system.

Symptom 2.7. When a new diskette is inserted in the drive, a directory from a previous diskette appears. You may have to reset the system in order to get the new diskette to be recognized. This is the classic "phantom directory" problem and is usually due to a drive or cable fault. The following checks will tell you for sure:

- *Check the signal cable.*   Verify that the drive's 34-pin ribbon cable is attached securely at the drive(s) and at the drive controller. Re-attach the signal cable is it's loose and try another signal cable if necessary.

- *Check the drive's jumpers.*   If this is a new drive installation, check the floppy drive's jumpers. Some floppy drives enable the DISK CHANGE signal to

be enabled or disabled. Make sure that the DISK
CHANGE signal is enabled.

- *Replace the floppy drive.*   If the problem persists,
chances are that the floppy drive is defective.
Perhaps the disk change logic has failed in the
drive's electronics. Try replacing the floppy drive
with a drive from another system.

> **NOTE**:   If you suspect a phantom directory, *do not* ini-
> tiate any writing to the diskette. Its *file allocation table*
> (FAT) table and directories could be overwritten ren-
> dering the disk's contents inaccessible without careful
> data-recovery procedures.

**Symptom 2.8. No jumpers are available on the floppy disk,
so it is impossible to change settings.**   This is not a
problem as much as it is an inconvenience. Typically,
you can expect unjumpered floppy disks to be set to the
following specifications:

- Drive Select 1 (B: drive)
- Disk Change (pin 34) enabled
- Frame Ground enabled

This configuration supports traditional single and dual
(1.44-MB) floppy drive systems using twisted floppy
cables.

**Symptom 2.9. DOS reports an error such as "Cannot read
from drive A:."**   A diskette is fully inserted in the drive,
and the drive *light-emitting diode* (LED) indicates that
access is being attempted. Thus, make the following
checks:

- *Check the diskette.*   Begin by trying a reliable, properly formatted diskette in your suspect drive. A
faulty diskette can generate some very perplexing
read/write problems.

- *Check the drive for obstructions.* Carefully inspect the spindle motor, drive belt (if used), and read/write head assembly. Make certain that no broken parts or obstructions can jam the heads. You should also examine the floppy drive with a diskette inserted to be certain that the disk's insertion or alignment is not causing the problem. Double-check your observations using several different diskettes. Gently remove any obstruction(s) that you may find. Be careful not to cause any accidental damage in the process of clearing an obstruction.

- *Clean the floppy drive.* If a reliable diskette does not resolve the problem, try cleaning the read/write heads thoroughly. Do *not* run the drive with a head-cleaning disk inserted for more than 30 seconds at a time or you risk damaging the heads with excessive friction.

- *Check the signal cable.* Verify that the drive's 34-pin ribbon cable is attached securely at the drive(s) and at the drive controller. Re-attach the signal cable is it's loose and try another signal cable if necessary.

- *Replace the floppy drive.* If the problem persists, chances are that the floppy drive is defective (perhaps the head read/write system has failed). Try replacing the floppy drive with a drive from another system.

- *Replace the floppy drive controller.* If a new floppy drive still does not resolve the problem, you may have a defective floppy drive controller circuit. If so, you may also receive a floppy drive or controller error from the system BIOS at boot time. Try disabling the existing floppy controller and install an expansion card controller (with only the floppy controller portion enabled).

Symptom 2.10. The floppy drive activity LED stays on as soon as the computer is powered up. This is a classic signaling problem that occurs after changing or upgrading a drive system. In virtually all cases, one end of the drive cable has been inserted backwards. Make sure that pin 1 on the 34-pin cable is aligned properly with the connector on both the drive and controller. If problems remain, the drive controller may have failed. This is rare, but try a new drive controller.

Symptom 2.11. The new drive does not work or the system does not recognize the new drive.   This is a classic problem where the system does not recognize the newly installed drive and is typically the result of incorrect or overlooked CMOS settings. Perform the following checks:

- *Check the CMOS settings.*   Reboot the system and start the CMOS Setup routine. Verify the floppy drive parameters against the actual physical drives in the system and then make sure that the correct data is entered in CMOS. You may have forgotten to save the data initially. Save the new data correctly and try the system again.

- *Check the signal cables.*   Inspect the power and signal cables at the drive. Loose or incorrectly attached cables can effectively disable the drive. Install each cable carefully and try the system again.

- *Replace the floppy drive.*   If the problem persists, chances are that the new floppy drive is defective. Try replacing the floppy drive with a drive from another system.

Symptom 2.12. You cannot boot the system from the new floppy drive.   If the drive is recognized properly and operates as expected, the failure to boot actually may not be a failure. Rather, the boot order established in your CMOS Setup may not include the new drive. Often, the boot order is A: then C:, or C: then A:. If you installed a new floppy as B:, the system will not attempt to boot because it is not included in the boot order. Restart the CMOS Setup routine and adjust the boot order to address your new floppy drive first (that is, B:/C: or A:/B:/C: or so on).

Symptom 2.13. After the second floppy is installed, many signal problems occur, such as read or write errors. Chances are that you left the terminating resistors in place on the second (middle) floppy drive, resulting in signal errors. You should have a terminating resistor pack on the drive at the *end* of the daisy chain cable. Check that the terminating resistors are in place on drive A: and remove the terminating resistors from the middle drive (B:). Also check that the signal cables are installed securely on both drives. Loose or damaged cables can cause signal problems.

Symptom 2.14. You cannot create a Windows 95/98 startup disk. Many possible causes may prevent Windows from properly creating a startup disk, but the points below outline many of the most common issues:

- *Check the diskette.*   The diskette itself may have 10 or more bad sectors, or the first sector may be damaged. Try a reliable diskette (preferably a high-quality or premium-grade diskette). Also, Windows 95/98 generally requires a high-density (1.44-MB) floppy disk in order to create a startup disk.

- *Check your anti-virus software.*   Many anti-virus tools can interfere with floppy disk operations. Disable or uninstall your anti-virus software according to the manufacturer's instructions.

- *Check the CMOS settings.*   Reboot the system and start the CMOS setup routine. Verify the floppy drive parameters against the actual physical drives in the system. Then make sure that the correct data is entered in CMOS. You may have forgotten to save the data initially. Save the new data correctly and try the system again.

- *Disable/remove floppy tape devices.* Some older tape backup devices utilizing the floppy controller may prevent you from gaining access to the floppy drive. To work around this behavior, disconnect the tape backup device from the floppy controller *before* you attempt to create a Windows 95/98 startup disk or disable the tape backup driver.

- *Replace the floppy drive.* If the problem persists, chances are that the new floppy drive is defective. Try replacing the floppy drive with a drive from another system.

Hard Drives

Hard drives have quickly become one of the most powerful and progressive parts of the PC. Tremendous storage capacities and outstanding speed enable an unmatched data transfer performance, including virtual memory usage. However, PCs also *depend* on proper hard drive operation. Drive problems can prevent a system from booting, and data loss can render weeks (or months) of work inaccessible.

Hard Drive Interfaces

Two major interfaces are used with modern hard drives: IDE/EIDE and *Small Computer System Interface* (SCSI). The IDE/EIDE interface is shown in Figure 2.2. IDE/EIDE drives (including the more recent UDMA/33 and UDMA/66 drives) are extremely popular and most end-user systems made since 1989 carry some vintage of the IDE drive. *Small Computer System Interface* (SCSI) drives are outstanding in server or multitasking systems. Figure 2.3 shows a standard 50-pin SCSI connection and Figure 2.4 shows a 68-pin SCSI connection.

Pin	Name	Pin	Name
1	Reset	2	Ground
3	DD7	4	DD8
5	DD6	6	DD9
7	DD5	8	DD10
9	DD4	10	DD11
11	DD3	12	DD12
13	DD2	14	DD13
15	DD1	16	DD14
17	DD0	18	DD15
19	Ground	20	Key (slot only)
21	DMARQ	22	Ground
23	−I/O write data (−DIOW)	24	Ground
25	−I/O read data (−DIOR)	26	Ground
27	−I/O channel ready (−IORDY)	28	unused
29	−DMA acknowledge (−DMACK)	30	Ground
31	Interrupt request (INTRQ)	32	−Host 16-bit I/O (−IOCS16)
33	DA1	34	−Passed diagnostics (−PDIAG)
35	DA0	36	DA2
37	−Host chip sel 0 (−CS1FX)	38	−Host chip sel 1 (−CS3FX)
39	−Drive active (−DASP)	40	Ground

Figure 2.2　The standard IDE cable pinout

Understanding Drive Capacity Limits

Capacity limitations are encountered whenever a computer system BIOS (and an OS) is unable to identify (or address) physical locations on a hard drive. This is *not* a problem with the design or structure of the hard drive itself, but rather a limitation of the system's BIOS or OS. For the BIOS, it is not capable of translating the addresses of the sectors beyond a certain number of cylinders, thus limiting the capacity of the

Signal	Pin	Pin	Signal	
Ground	1	2	Data 0	
Ground	3	4	Data 1	
Ground	5	6	Data 2	
Ground	7	8	Data 3	
Ground	9	10	Data 4	
Ground	11	12	Data 5	
Ground	13	14	Data 6	
Ground	15	16	Data 7	
Ground	17	18	Data parity	
Ground	19	20	Ground	
Ground	21	22	Ground	
Reserved	23	24	Reserved	
Open	25	26	TERMPWR	
Reserved	27	28	Reserved	
Ground	29	30	Ground	
Ground	31	32	−ATN	(−Attention)
Ground	33	34	Ground	
Ground	35	36	−BSY	(−Busy)
Ground	37	38	−ACK	(−Acknowledge)
Ground	39	40	−RST	(−Reset)
Ground	41	42	−MSG	(−Message)
Ground	43	44	−SEL	(−Select)
Ground	45	46	−C/D	(−Control/Data)
Ground	47	48	−REQ	(−Request)
Ground	49	50	−I/O	(−Input/Output)

Figure 2.3 The standard 50-pin SCSI cable pinout

hard drive to less than its full amount. For the OS, the file structure, that is, the *File Allocation Table* (FAT), is limited in the number of physical locations (or addresses) that can be entered in the FAT. Drive manufacturers first encountered BIOS limitations in 1994 with the release of 540-MB (ATA-2/EIDE) hard drives. OS limitations were discovered with the release of hard drives larger than 2.1 GB. Your exact limitations will vary depending on your BIOS version and the OS. Today you'll probably encounter BIOS with limitations at 2.1-GB, 4.2-GB, and 8.4-GB levels. OSs like DOS and Windows 95 have a 2.1-GB partition size limita-

Signal	Pin	Pin	Signal	
Ground	1	35	Data 12	
Ground	2	36	Data 13	
Ground	3	37	Data 14	
Ground	4	38	Data 15	
Ground	5	39	Data parity 1	
Ground	6	40	Data 0	
Ground	7	41	Data 1	
Ground	8	42	Data 2	
Ground	9	43	Data 3	
Ground	10	44	Data 4	
Ground	11	45	Data 5	
Ground	12	46	Data 6	
Ground	13	47	Data 7	
Ground	14	48	Data parity 0	
Ground	15	49	Ground	
Ground	16	50	Ground	
TERMPWR	17	51	TERMPWR	
TERMPWR	18	52	TERMPWR	
Reserved	19	53	Reserved	
Ground	20	54	Ground	
Ground	21	55	−ATN	(−Attention)
Ground	22	56	Ground	
Ground	23	57	−BSY	(−Busy)
Ground	24	58	−ACK	(−Acknowledge)
Ground	25	59	−RST	(−Reset)
Ground	26	60	−MSG	(−Message)
Ground	27	61	−SEL	(−Select)
Ground	28	62	−C/D	(−Control/data)
Ground	29	63	−REQ	(−Request)
Ground	30	64	−I/O	(−Input/output)
Ground	31	65	Data 8	
Ground	32	66	Data 9	
Ground	33	67	Data 10	
Ground	34	68	Data 11	

Figure 2.4   The standard 68-pin SCSI cable pinout

tion, and Windows NT has a 4.2-GB partition size limit, but Windows 95 OSR2 and Windows 98 can access much larger drives using the FAT32 file system. This part of the chapter is intended to help you understand and correct these drive size limitations.

Cylinder Limits in BIOS

BIOS is the key to hard drive addressing through the use of BIOS-based (INT 13) services. Today you'll find three major BIOS limitations:

- BIOS versions dated *prior* to July of 1994 will typically experience a 528-MB drive size limit. BIOS cannot support more than 1,024 cylinders. The *Logical Block Addressing* (LBA) mode capability did not become widely accepted until after this point.

- BIOS versions dated *after* July 1994 will typically experience a 2.1-GB drive size limit. BIOS cannot support more than 4,093 to 4,096 cylinders. Even though LBA is being used correctly, the BIOS makers simply imposed an artificial limit on the number of addressable cylinders.

- BIOS versions dated *after* 1996 can support drives over 528 MB and support drives over 2.1 GB, but they may experience a 4.2-GB or 8.4-GB drive size limit. Once again, the BIOS cannot support the number of cylinders (around 8,190) needed to handle these larger drives even though LBA is being used correctly.

Here are some more specifics:

- Phoenix Technologies' (*www.ptltd.com*) BIOS version 4 revision 6 or greater can support capacities greater than 8.4 GB. If the BIOS is revision 5.12, it does not support extended INT 13. All Phoenix BIOS are version 4, so 5.12 is an older release than 6. Phoenix recommends MicroFirmware (*http://max. firmware.com*) for BIOS upgrades.

- Award's (*www.award.com*) BIOS dated after November 1997 will support drives greater than 8.4 GB. Award recommends Unicore (*www.unicore.com*) for BIOS upgrades.

- American Megatrends' (AMI) (*www.megatrends.com*) BIOS versions with a date of January 1, 1998 or greater support drives greater than 8.4 GB.

Partition Limits in the OS

File systems used by various OSs are also subject to drive size limits. FAT16-type operating systems (DOS, the commercial release of Windows 95, Windows NT with FAT16, and OS/2 with FAT16) are typically limited to 2.1-GB drive sizes. Windows NT using *NT File System* (NTFS) suffers a 4-GB drive size limit. When using a physical hard drive that is larger than these limits, you'll need to create multiple partitions on the drive in order to access all the available space. With the introduction of FAT32 with Windows 95 OSR2 and Windows 98, drives up to two *terabytes* (TB) can be accessed as a single partition.

Overcoming Capacity Limits

Since 1994, the PC industry has been working hard to overcome the drive size limits imposed by BIOS and OSs. Unfortunately, drive size limits still plague older systems. This is particularly prevalent because many systems a few years old are now being upgraded with the huge hard drives that are on the market. As a result, drive size support problems are the most frequent issues encountered during drive upgrades. Still, several tactics have become available for technicians.

The 528-MB Limit. Supporting large (EIDE) hard drives over 528 MB will clearly require a system upgrade. Three possible solutions exist to fix the problem: upgrade the motherboard BIOS to support LBA, upgrade the drive controller using an on-board BIOS that supports LBA, or partition the drive with a drive overlay utility like Disk Manager or EZ-Drive. If the system is older than 1994, a new drive controller and an on-board BIOS will probably yield a noticeable drive system performance improvement. If price is the primary concern, drive overlay software is free (included with most new hard drives) and requires no invasive hardware upgrade.

2.1-GB, 4.2-GB, 8.4-GB, and 32-GB Limits. The difficulty with these limits is that several possible symptoms can crop up:

- *Truncation of cylinders.* Cylinder truncation is when the BIOS limits the number of cylinders reported to the operating system to 4,095. The BIOS may display the drive as having more than this many cylinders, but it still only reports a total of 4,095.

- *System hang-up at POST.* A system hang-up occurs when the BIOS has a problem truncating the cylinders and locks the system up during the *power-on self-test* (POST). This is most frequently caused by the auto-detect feature some BIOS versions have implemented.

- *Cylinder wrap.* Cylinder wrapping is when the BIOS takes the remaining number of cylinders from the maximum allowed (4,095) and reports it to the OS. For example, if the drive listed 4,096 cylinders, the BIOS would report only one cylinder to the OS.

- *System hangs at boot time.* This usually occurs for drives larger than 4.2 GB (8-GB or 32-GB drives). A system hang is when the operating system hangs up during the initial loading (either from the floppy diskette or the existing hard drives). This can be caused by the BIOS reporting the number of heads to the OS as 256 (100h). The register size DOS and Windows 95/98 uses for the head count has a capacity of two hex digits (equivalent to decimal values 255).

In virtually all cases, these symptoms represent a BIOS compatibility problem and can be corrected by a BIOS upgrade. You should contact the system or motherboard maker to inquire if a BIOS update is available. If you cannot upgrade the motherboard BIOS directly, you can install a new drive controller with an LBA-compatible BIOS that will support additional cylinders.

You may also be able to adjust the drive's translation to overcome BIOS cylinder limits. You may find that these huge hard drives seem to auto-detect correctly in BIOS, and the problem crops up when trying to partition the drive. The partition may seem to be created properly through FDISK, but the system hangs when rebooting. Although this is an OS limitation, it appears that the appropriate way to deal with this problem is to account for it in the system BIOS. Fortunately, there is a temporary workaround to the problem (until you get the BIOS upgraded).

> **NOTE**:   You should first verify that you have a recent-enough BIOS to handle drives over 2 GB, 4 GB, 8.1 GB, or 32 GB correctly.

To set up a drive over 4 GB (under an older BIOS), perform the following steps:

1. Auto-detect the drive in CMOS Setup.

2. Manually adjust the number of heads from 16 to 15.

3. Multiply the number of cylinders by 16/15 (rounded down to whole number). Since 16/15 is 1.06667, the simplest way to multiply by 16/15 would be to multiply by 1.06667 (and then round down to a whole number).

4. Adjust the number of cylinders to this larger amount.

5. Write down these adjusted values for cylinders, heads, and sectors.

6. Save changes to CMOS and then partition and format the drive.

NOTE: The important thing to keep in mind when using the previous workaround is that you must keep a record of the translation values used so that they can be re-entered if the contents of CMOS RAM are lost or if the drive is moved to another system. Write the values on masking tape and stick the tape on the drive itself.

OS Limits.   You basically have two solutions for overcoming drive size limits through an OS. If you continue to use FAT16, you'll need to create partitions equal to or smaller than two GB. If the drive is larger than 2 GB, you can make multiple partitions on the drive. This makes more than one logical drive for the system to deal with, but it will enable you to use the entire drive capacity. As an alternative, you can upgrade to a FAT32 system such as the OSR2 version of Windows 95 (or Windows 98) that should easily handle partitions over 32 GB.

But some other issues must be considered. For example, hard disks and other media larger than 32 GB in size are not supported in any version of Windows 95. Media at this capacity were not available at the time Windows 95 and OSR versions were developed. If you want to use media larger than 32 GB in size, you should upgrade to Windows 98 or Microsoft Windows NT. Note that you must use Windows NT 4.0, Service Pack 4 (or newer) to address this capacity limitation.

Also, the protected-mode (Windows) version of ScanDisk may misreport cluster sizes on IDE hard drives whose capacity exceeds 32 GB. The resulting symptoms may also include an inability to access areas of the hard drive beyond the first 32 GB. You can correct this problem by downloading the file 243450US8.EXE (release date 12/10/99) from the Microsoft Web site (see Microsoft Knowledge Base article Q243450 for more information). Note this problem does not occur if the BIOS uses true LBA Assist translation instead of BitShift translation.

Hard Drive Troubleshooting Guide

Fortunately, not all hard drive problems are necessarily fatal. True, you may loose some programs and data (so back up your hard drive frequently), but many drive problems are recoverable without resorting to drive replacement. Instead of focusing on repairing a hard drive's electronics or mechanics, today's repair tactics focus on repairing a drive's *data*. By reconstructing or relocating faulty drive information, it is often possible to recover from a wide variety of drive problems. If that fails, the drive (and/or its controller) must be replaced. Before you begin any sort of drive troubleshooting, you should perform the following tasks:

1. Gather a DOS boot disk or a Windows 95/98 startup disk. If you don't have a boot disk on hand, you should make one now *before* continuing.

2. Gather your DOS installation disk(s) or Windows 95/98 Installation CD-ROM. If you need to reinstall the OS or any of its components at some point, these will be invaluable.

3. Gather any hard drive/controller diagnostics that you'll need.

4. Back up as much as you can from your hard drive(s) before attempting any sort of drive service.

   NOTE: Drive troubleshooting has the potential of destroying any data on the drive(s). Before attempting to troubleshoot hard disk drive problems, be sure to back up as much of the drive as possible. If no backup is available, do not repartition or reformat the drive unless absolutely necessary, and all other possible alternatives have been exhausted.

General Troubleshooting Guidelines. Although most drive installations and replacements will proceed flawlessly, problems will often crop up. If you've installed a hard drive and it does not function properly, perform the following basic checks before examining specific symptoms:

- *Watch for power and static problems.*   Always turn off the computer before changing jumpers or unplugging cables and cards. Wear an anti-static wrist strap (or use other anti-static precautions) while working on your computer or handling a drive.

- *Verify compatibility.*   Verify that the drive controller and drive are appropriately matched to each other (and to your computer). For example, an Ultra-DMA/66 drive will not run at top speed on an Ultra-DMA/33 controller.

- *Check all cards.*   Verify that all expansion cards (including the drive controller card) are seated in their slots on the motherboard and are secured with mounting screws. Often one or more cards may be displaced when a PC is opened for service.

- *Check all connectors and cables.*   Make sure that all ribbon and power cables are securely connected. Ribbon cables are easily damaged (especially at the connectors). Try a new cable that you know is good. Make sure no connector pins are bent. Verify that pin 1 on the interface cable is aligned with pin 1 on the drive and the controller.

- *Verify drive jumper settings.*   Review the instructions in your drive's manual (and in your host adapter installation guide), and see that all appropriate jumpers are installed or removed as necessary. Incorrect or duplicated jumper settings (two master drives on the same channel) can easily interfere with drive operation.

- *Check your power supply capacity.*   Each time you add a new device to your computer, make sure your computer's power supply can support the total power demand. Install a larger (higher wattage) power supply if necessary.

- *Verify the drive settings in your CMOS Setup.* The drive settings in the CMOS Setup must not exceed the physical specifications of your drive. Also, the settings must not exceed the limitations set by the OS and BIOS. Try the CMOS Setup's auto-detect feature to identify the drive or consider upgrading the BIOS and/or drive controller.

- *Check for viruses.* Before you use an unknown diskette in your system for the first time, scan the diskette for viruses. Also scan the system for viruses periodically.

Potential Problems with Y-Splitters.   In rare instances, you may find that a drive will not function or is damaged outright when using a Y power adapter (or a Y-splitter). This can happen because a number of Y-splitters on the market are incorrectly wired. Y-splitters consist of a clear plastic plug with four metal prongs on one end (which attaches to an existing power connector from the power supply) and two sets of wires leading to two plugs with female connections on the other ends (which are attached to internal devices such as hard drives, CD-ROM drives, and so on). The problem with some of these newer connectors is that the wires are attached incorrectly on one of the female connectors.

Examine both female connectors. Make certain that both the female connectors are lined up with the two rounded corners facing up and both of the squared corners facing down. The four wires attached to the female connectors should now be in the following order (from left to right):

Yellow (112Vdc), Black (ground), Black (ground), and Red (15Vdc)

If this order is reversed on one of the connectors, then your Y-splitter is faulty and should not be used. As a rule, you should never split power from the hard drive under any circumstances.

Potential Problems with Bus Speeds Above 66 MHz. Many Pentium and later motherboards offer an adjustable system bus clock that may be set by either the system BIOS or with jumpers. This bus speed setting enables you to increase the system bus clock above 66 MHz, usually to 75 MHz or 83 MHz. Most drives have no problem with the higher bus clock speeds, but some problems may result because of the way that some motherboards handle the interaction between the higher bus speeds (above 66 MHz) and the IDE-type interface.

On some motherboards, when the system clock is increased above 66 MHz, the PCI bus (ideally 33 MHz) is also increased. This higher speed reduces the PCI bus I/O cycle time. This change in the I/O cycle time violates the IDE specification and may cause disruptions in the communications between the hard drive and the PCI bus. This is not a faulty hard drive or drive design. When the PCI bus speed is forced over 33 MHz because of higher bus speed settings, you may see problems such as data loss, data corruption, and failure of the system to recognize the hard drive on bootup. Higher bus speeds will not cause any kind of permanent hard drive failure and returning the system bus speed to 66 MHz can usually eliminate the problem(s). The best solution to this problem is to either return the motherboard to a 66-MHz bus speed or upgrade the motherboard with a model where the PCI bus speed is asynchronous of the bus speed. This allows you to increase the bus speed, but the PCI clock will remain fixed at 33 MHz.

> **NOTE**:   Due to the differences between drive designs, it is possible that some drives may not have any problems responding at higher bus speeds, while other drive models may produce serious problems. It's virtually impossible to determine which drives will or won't be affected.

Current Pentium II and Pentium III motherboards designed to operate up to 100 MHz or higher are almost all asynchronous and should not pose a problem. This issue, however, may crop up when working with slightly older motherboards or systems.

Troubleshooting DOS Compatibility-Mode Problems. One of the great advantages enjoyed by Windows 95/98 is that it operates in protected mode. Drivers and software can be executed beyond the traditional real-mode RAM limit of one MB. By comparison, DOS is a real-mode environment. DOS programs and drivers can only be executed within the first 640 KB of RAM (the conventional memory area). If Windows 95/98 cannot establish protected-mode operation for a drive, it will fall back to real-mode driver support. This is known as *DOS compatibility mode*. Unfortunately, real-mode support often impairs system performance. If you notice that one or more of the hard drives in a system is using DOS compatibility mode (there may be an error message such as `Compatibility mode paging reduces overall system performance`), you'll need to track down and correct the cause. In general, Windows 95/98 may invoke the DOS compatibility mode for any of the following reasons:

- A questionable device driver, *Terminate and Stay Resident* (TSR), or computer virus has hooked the INT 21h or INT 13h chain before Windows 95/98 loaded.

- The hard disk controller in your computer is not detected by Windows 95/98.

- The hard disk controller is removed from the current configuration in Device Manager.

- A resource conflict is taking place between the hard disk controller and another hardware device.

- The Windows 95/98 protected-mode driver is missing or damaged.

- The Windows 95/98 protected-mode driver detects incompatible or unsupportable hardware.

You can use the following procedure to isolate and correct the cause of DOS compatibility mode problems:

1. Open the Control Panel, double-click the System icon, and then choose the Performance tab in the System Properties dialog. You can identify which drive is using DOS compatibility mode and why.

2. If the driver name listed as causing the DOS compatibility mode is MBRINT13.SYS, your computer may be infected with a boot-sector virus or you are running real-mode disk overlay software (for an IDE hard disk with more than 1024 cylinders) that is *not* compatible with Windows 95/98 protected-mode disk drivers.

   - Run a current anti-virus program to detect and remove boot sector viruses such as *Norton Anti-Virus* (NAV). You may need to rewrite your boot sector using a DOS command, for example FDISK/MBR.

   - If you cannot detect any virus activity, check any drive overlay software. For example, if you're using Disk Manager, make sure that you're using Disk Manager 7.0 or later (use Disk Manager 7.04 if you're running DriveSpace 3 included with the Microsoft Plus! pack). You may need to make similar updates if you're running other drive overlay software.

3. If the driver name that is listed in Step #2 is also in the CONFIG.SYS file, contact the driver's manufacturer to determine whether a more recent version of the driver will enable protected-mode operations in Windows 95/98. You may be able to download and install the latest driver version from the driver manufacturer's Web site.

4. If no driver is listed on the Performance tab, check to make sure that the hard disk controller is listed in the Device Manager. If not, install it through

the Add New Hardware wizard. If the wizard cannot detect the controller automatically, run the wizard again but do not let it attempt to detect the hardware in your computer. Instead select the controller specifically from the hardware list. If your particular controller is not listed, contact the manufacturer of the disk controller to obtain a Windows 95/98 protected-mode disk driver (or a Windows 3.1x 32-bit disk access FastDisk driver if available).

NOTE: If the hard disk controller is listed in Device Manager but has a red X over it, it has been removed from the current hardware profile. Click Properties for the controller in Device Manager and then click the check box corresponding to the current hardware profile under Device Usage.

5. If the hard disk controller is listed in the Device Manager but has a yellow exclamation mark over it, there is a resource conflict (IRQ, I/O, DMA, or BIOS address range) with another device, the protected-mode driver is missing or damaged, or the `Disable all 32-bit protected-mode disk drivers` check box has been selected in File System properties. Thus, one of the following steps will help solve the problem:

   ▪ Double-click the System icon in the Control Panel, click the Performance tab, and then click File System. Select the Troubleshooting tab and be sure that the `Disable all 32-bit protected-mode disk drivers` check box has not been selected.

   ▪ Resolve any resource conflicts with other devices in the system.

   ▪ Check to make sure that the protected-mode driver is in the \Windows\SYSTEM\IOSUBSYS directory and is loading properly. To find which driver is providing 32-bit disk access, click Properties for the disk controller in Device Manager and click the Driver tab to see which driver files are associated with the controller. For most IDE, EIDE, and ESDI disk controllers, 32-bit disk access is provided by the ESDI_ 506.PDR driver. For SCSI controllers, Windows 95 often uses SCSIPORT.PDR and a mini-port (or .MPD) driver. Restart Windows 95/98, press F8 when the Starting Windows 95/98 message appears, and then select a Logged (BOOTLOG. TXT) start. If the 32-bit driver is listed as loading properly, you're all set. Otherwise, the driver may be missing or damaged, so try reinstalling the respective 32-bit drivers.

6. Load SYSTEM.INI into a text editor and see if the MH32BIT.386 driver is being loaded (check for a line that reads: `device=mh32bit.386`). This driver is installed by MicroHouse EZ-Drive software and is not compatible with the Windows 95/98 protected-mode disk drivers. Unfortunately, this driver is not removed by Windows 95/98 Setup, so you'll need to disable the line manually, save your changes, and reboot the PC.

7. If all else fails, you may be able to achieve protected-mode support from the disk controller by disabling any of the controller's advanced features (caching and fast or turbo modes) or reducing data transfer rates. You may also try systematically disabling advanced IDE controller features in the CMOS Setup.

8. If problems persist, you may have to replace the drive controller with a model that better supports protected-mode operations.

Detecting a Dynamic Drive Overlay.   A *Dynamic Drive Overlay* (DDO) is used to support access to a large hard drive when the system BIOS or drive controller is unable to. Since the DDO can sometimes cause problems with drive access and system performance, it must be detected before removal. You can use the following tell-tale signs to identify the presence of a DDO on a Windows 95/98 system:

- *DDO startup message.* When you boot your computer, a message may be displayed on the screen that shows the DDO manufacturer's name (or prompts you to press a key to boot to a floppy disk). Current versions of drive overlay software may not display this message by default.

- *BIOS revision date.* Computers made before 1994 generally do not support LBA. If your BIOS shows an early revision date, it will probably need a DDO in order to support hard drives over 528 MB.

- *FDISK/status switch.* Boot your computer with a Windows 95/98 Startup Disk and type `fdisk/status` from the command prompt. Verify that the sum of the existing partitions is larger than the total hard disk space. If so, a DDO is at work.

- *Windows 95/98 Startup Disk.* Reboot your computer with the Windows 95/98 Startup Disk (this will prevent the DDO program from loading) and then boot to a command prompt. Check to see if files on the C: drive are accessible. If not, the drive is inaccessible because a DDO has not been loaded for the hard drive.

- *Verify file names.* Some drive overlay files use an .OVL or a .BIN extension. At the command prompt, type `dir /a *.bin` or `dir /a *.ovl` to check for the existence of files other than DRVSPACE.BIN and DBLSPACE.BIN. If other such files exist, a DDO is probably installed.

- *Check CONFIG.SYS.* Drive overlay software may be loaded from the CONFIG.SYS file in order to access drives *other* than the active boot partition of the master drive on the primary IDE controller. If

DDO software is called in CONFIG.SYS, you'd disable it there if necessary.

Removing a DDO.   When you install a drive overlay utility like EZ-Drive or MaxBlast (or other similar software), there may be a point where it's necessary to remove it. You may need to do this when upgrading the BIOS and/or drive controller, and the DDO software is no longer required. In most cases, you can remove your DDO without losing any data as long as you have an alternative means of accessing the drive (such as an updated BIOS or drive controller). The following example illustrates the use of Disk Manager, but other utilities will follow a similar process:

> **NOTE**:   Before you remove a DDO from a drive, make a complete backup copy of all the data on your hard drive. Also run CHKDSK or ScanDisk (or a third-party equivalent) to detect and repair any damaged files. If the DDO removal program encounters a serious file problem (or is interrupted by a power loss or hardware failure), the removal will fail and your data can be lost.

1. Boot the computer to drive C: and then insert your DiscWizard diskette (or CD).

2. Type DM to start Disk Manager and choose the Select Installation Options Menu.

3. Select the Maintenance Menu.

4. Select Migrate Dynamic Drive. This option moves the data on your drive so that it can be accessed without the DDO. Remember that this conversion may take up to an hour to complete (depending on the size of your drive).

5. When the conversion has finished, exit Disk Manager, remove the diskette, and reboot the computer.

6. Enter your CMOS Setup program and configure the hard drive with the appropriate number of

cylinders, heads, and sectors as specified for your drive model.

7. Save your changes in the CMOS Setup and reboot again.

8. When your computer has rebooted, insert the DiscWizard diskette into drive A:.

9. Type A:\DM to start Disk manager and choose the Maintenance Menu.

10. Select Uninstall Disk Manager.

11. Select the correct drive to uninstall from and allow the process to complete.

12. When the uninstall is complete, exit Disk Manager and reboot the system.

> **NOTE**:   Disk Manager can also remove a drive overlay placed by the EZ-Drive program. Simply select Convert Drive Format from the Maintenance Menu.

Drive Not Recognized by the OS.   Occasionally, a hard drive is recognized correctly by the BIOS (the drive is properly auto-detected), but it is not properly identified by the OS. In virtually all cases, the problem can be traced to installation issues or drive software (code-related) issues. Check the essential installation points first:

1. Check the parameters in the CMOS Setup and verify that the drive parameters *and* translation mode are set correctly.

2. Contact the system or motherboard manufacturer to verify potential BIOS capacity limitations. For example, you may need a BIOS upgrade to accommodate the drive sizes that you're using.

3. Ensure that newly installed EIDE or UDMA controller cards do not conflict with the existing system BIOS. You may need to disable the motherboard's

existing drive controller channel(s) through the CMOS Setup before the new controller card will be recognized by the OS.

4. Systematically step down the enhanced features of your BIOS (block mode, multi-sector transfers, 32-bit transfers, PIO mode settings, and so on) to their minimum values or disable the features entirely. You may also try the BIOS Default settings in your CMOS Setup.

5. If your motherboard uses ISA bus slots, check the AT BUS Clock speed in your CMOS Setup and verify that it's set between 8 and 10 MHz (ideally 8.33 MHz).

6. Increase the boot process time in your CMOS Setup. You can enable Floppy Seek at Boot, Test Memory Above 1 MB, and/or set the Boot Sequence to A: then C:.

7. Set Boot Speed to its lowest value in the CMOS Setup and set the Boot Pre-delay entry (if present) to its highest value.

8. Double-check your partitions using FDISK. If the drive was not previously partitioned, create a Primary DOS partition on the drive. Use option 2 to set the partition active. Exit FDISK and reboot. Now format the new partition and install the system files. If the drive was previously partitioned, make sure the first partition is PRI DOS and its status is A. Compare the sum of all partition sizes to the Total Disk Space; this should be same within about one MB. If the total is different, correct the drive parameters or translation mode in CMOS Setup and repartition the drive.

NOTE: If the drive was previously partitioned, but no partitions are currently seen in FDISK, do not attempt to create new partitions if data on the drive is to be saved.

9. Double-check the master/slave jumpers on all drives using the primary controller.

10. Install (set) the jumper for I/O Channel Ready on the drive (if that option is present).

11. If you're using a SCSI drive, verify that the Parity jumper is installed.

12. Check all of your cable connections and try a shorter replacement cable (or connect the drive to the middle cable connector).

13. Replace the drive controller card.

14. Remove the slave drive (if present) to determine the presence of any compatibility issues.

You may also need to check for data corruption or errors on the drive:

1. Clean boot the system to a boot diskette and execute FDISK /MBR and SYS C:. Make sure the DOS version on the floppy diskette is the same version as on the hard drive before using the SYS command.

2. Bypass the CONFIG.SYS and AUTOEXEC.BAT files to check for problems in your startup files. If this works, use the step-by-step boot mode in the Windows Startup menu to walk through each step of these files until the problem is found. Then edit both the CONFIG.SYS and AUTOEXEC.BAT files and comment-out the statement(s) causing the problem.

3. Check for drive compression and try removing the compression drivers if no important data is on the drive.

4. Delete the partition using FDISK; then repartition and reformat the drive.

5. Replace the hard drive.

Checking for FAT16 and FAT32.   It may be necessary for you to identify the presence of a FAT16 or FAT32 partition before using disk utilities, backup software, or other applications. This will prevent accidental data loss from using an incompatible software version (using a FAT16 version of ScanDisk on a FAT32 partition):

1. Under Windows 98, double-click the My Computer icon on your desktop and then right-click the drive you're interested in. Click Properties from the drop-down menu. Look at the General tab on the line marked File system. A FAT16 partition will simply say FAT, while a FAT32 partition will specify FAT32.

2. Try the `version` command from a DOS prompt:

```
Windows 95A. [Version 4.00.950]
Windows 95B. [Version 4.00.1111]
Windows 98. [Version 4.10.1998]
```

If you need a FAT32 version of FDISK, check to see that FDISK asks, `Do you wish to enable large disk support? (Y/N)`. If it does not ask this question, it's probably a FAT16 version.

You can also check the partition type using a FAT32 version of FDISK. Select option 4 to display the partition information. The System field will read FAT32 if the partition is FAT32 or FAT16 if the partition is FAT16. If the partition has not been formatted, the System field will read `Unknown`.

Dealing with Drive Noise.   All hard drives make a certain amount of noise during normal operation, and the noise level will vary depending on whether the drive is spinning or accessing. However, when the drive makes substantial or abnormal noises, this may indicate an impending failure. The trick here is to tell the normal noises from the abnormal noises. A drive makes three basic sounds:

- A whining noise during the drive spin-up (and a mild whir while the system is on)

- Regular clicking or tapping sounds during drive access (the R/W heads stepping across the platters)

- Hard clicks when the drive heads park before power off

You should develop a keen ear for abnormal drive sounds:

- A high-pitched whining sound (such as a screech or squeal) can be an indication of problems.

- Noises (vibrations) caused by mounting issues due to either a high frequency vibration in the mounting hardware or a potential drive failure

- Repeated, regular tapping, grinding, or beeping. When the hard drive is suspect, it is always important to make an immediate backup of your data.

> **NOTE**:   To isolate the drive further, try disconnecting the drive's signal cable and power the system up. If the noise persists, the drive should be backed up and replaced at your earliest convenience. If the noise stops, there may be an issue with the cable or controller that you should investigate further.

Dealing with Spin Problems.   All hard drives must spin their platters at a constant rate of speed, so any spin problems can render the drive inaccessible. Spin problems can usually be broken down into three types:

- *Drive does not spin at all.*   When a system is turned on, the characteristic hard drive wind up sounds are not present. This can also occur if the hard drive spins down (without cause) after working for a period of time.

- *Drive spins up and spins down again.*   This normally occurs during the initial power up. The hard drive will start spinning and then slow down again (or it cycles up to a point and ceases to spin).

- *Drive spins down following a period of inactivity.*
  The hard drive fails to spin up when access is
  attempted.

The first thing to check for are installation errors:

1. Check the jumper settings on all hard drives
   attached to the same interface cable. For example,
   check the master/slave jumpers on each drive and
   then check for energy management or deferred
   spinup jumpers. Most SCSI (and a few IDE) hard
   drives contain one or both jumper options.

2. Check all of the power supply cable connections.

3. Check the interface (ribbon) cable connections.

4. Check for any system software for power management and disable or uninstall that software if necessary.

Next check for "green" or "power management" features that might be set improperly:

1. Disable your drive-related power management
   features in the CMOS Setup.

2. Disable the power management jumper on your
   hard drive (if present).

3. Some overlay software has the capability to set
   power management features. For example, you can
   disable power management under Maxtor's Max-
   Blast software (versions 7.04 – 7.12) by removing
   the /E switch. Clean boot the system if other power
   management software is the suspected culprit.

4. Windows 95 and Windows 98 can enable power
   management. This feature will need to be disabled
   through the OS's Power Management icon in the
   Control Panel.

Finally, check for hardware failures with the drive
and/or its controller:

1. Try installing the drive in another system. This will verify the problem is with the drive, not the system.

2. Use a different power supply plug.

3. Use a different interface (ribbon) cable.

4. Use a different drive controller (try a PCI drive controller card).

5. Disconnect the ribbon cable from the drive.

6. Replace the drive outright.

Hardware Symptoms

Now it's time to review some problems and solutions. The important concept here is that a hard drive *problem* does not necessarily mean a hard drive *failure*. The failure of a sector or track does not automatically indicate physical head or platter damage. That is why software tools have been so successful at restoring operations (and even recovering data).

> **NOTE**: Drive troubleshooting has the potential to destroy any data on the drive(s). Before attempting to troubleshoot hard disk drive problems, be sure to back up as much of the drive as possible. If no backup is available, do not repartition or reformat the drive unless absolutely necessary, and all other possible alternatives have been exhausted.
>
> The term *IDE-type drive* is taken to mean any drive using a 40-pin IDE-style interface such as IDE, EIDE, ATAPI IDE, Ultra-DMA/33, and Ultra-DMA/66 (using the 40-pin/80-conductor cable). Specific drive types or exceptions will be denoted.

Symptom 2.15. The hard drive is completely dead. The drive does not spin up, the drive light doesn't illuminate during power-up, or you see an error message indicating that the drive is not found or ready. The following checks will help you find a solution:

- *Check the drive power.* Make sure the four-pin power connector is inserted properly and completely. If the drive is being powered by a Y-connector, make sure any interim connections are secure. Use a voltmeter and measure the +5 volt (pin 4) and +12 volt (pin 1) levels. If either voltage (especially the +12 volt supply) is unusually low or absent, replace the power supply.

- *Check the signal cable.* Also check your signal cable. See that the drive's signal interface cable is connected securely at both the drive and controller ends. For IDE-type drives, this is the 40-pin ribbon cable. If the cable is visibly worn or damaged, try a new cable.

- *Check the CMOS Setup.* The PC cannot use a hard drive that it can't recognize, so enter the CMOS Setup routine and see that all the parameters entered for the drive are correct. Heads, cylinders, sectors per track, landing zone, and write precompensation must all be correct. Otherwise, POST will not recognize the drive. If you have an auto-detect option available, try that also. Remember to save your changes in CMOS and reboot the system.

- *Replace the drive or controller.* If problems continue, the hard drive itself may be defective. Try a reliable hard drive. If it works as expected, your original drive is probably defective and should be replaced. If it fails to operate, replace the drive controller board.

Symptom 2.16. You see drive activity, but the computer will not boot from the hard drive.   In most cases, there is a drive failure, boot sector failure, or DOS/Windows file corruption. The following checks are recommended:

- *Check the signal cable.* Make sure that the drive's signal cable is connected securely at both the drive and controller. If the cable is visibly worn or damaged, try a new one.

- *Check the CMOS Setup.*   Verify that all the parameters entered for the drive are correct. Heads, cylinders, sectors per track, landing zone, and write precompensation must all be correct. Otherwise, POST will not recognize the drive. If the BIOS provides an option to auto-detect the drive, try that as well.

- *Check the boot sector.*   Boot from a floppy disk and try accessing the hard drive. If the hard drive is accessible, chances are that the boot files are missing or corrupt. Try a utility such as DrivePro's Drive Boot Fixer. You might also try running FDISK /MBR, which will rebuild the drive's master boot record, but be *careful*. The FDISK /MBR command may render the files on your drive inaccessible.

- *Check the drive and controller.*   You may have a problem with your drive system hardware. If you cannot access the hard drive, run a diagnostic such as Windsor Technologies' PC Technician. Test the drive and drive controller. If the controller responds but the drive does not, try repartitioning and reformatting the hard drive. If the drive still doesn't respond, replace the hard drive outright. If the controller doesn't respond, replace the hard drive controller.

Symptom 2.17. Errors occur during drive reads or writes. Magnetic information does not last forever and sector ID information can gradually degrade to a point where you encounter file errors. A solution can be found by performing one of the following checks:

- *Check for file problems.*   Start by checking for any file structure problems on the drive. Use a utility such as ScanDisk to examine the drive and search for bad sectors. If a failed sector involves part of an .EXE or .COM file, that file is now corrupt and should be restored from a backup.

- *Try a low-level format.*   If you cannot isolate file problems, you may need to consider a *low-level* (LL) format. LL formatting rewrites sector ID information, but the sophistication of today's drives makes LL formatting almost impossible. If the drive manufacturer provides a drive preparation utility, you should back up the drive; run the utility, FDISK, and FORMAT; and restore the drive from its backup.

Symptom 2.18. Hard drive performance appears to be slowing down over time.   In virtually all cases, diminishing drive performance can be caused by file fragmentation. To a far lesser extent, you may be faced with a computer virus. Thus, perform the following tasks:

■ *Boot the system clean.*   Start the PC with a clean boot disk and make sure no TSRs or drivers are being loaded.

■ *Check for viruses.*   After a clean boot, run your anti-virus checker and make sure that no memory-resident or file-based viruses are in the system.

■ *Check for file fragmentation.*   If the system checks clean for computer viruses, you should check for file fragmentation next. Start Disk Defragmenter (Defrag) and check the percentage of file fragmentation. If there is more than 10 percent fragmentation, you should consider running the defragmentation utility after preparing Windows.

Symptom 2.19. You can access the hard drive correctly, but the drive light stays on continuously.   A continuous LED indication is not necessarily a problem as long as the drive seems to be operating properly. Check the drive and the drive controller for drive "light jumpers." Examine the drive itself for any jumper that might select latched mode versus activity mode. If no such jumpers are on the drive, check the drive controller or motherboard. Set the jumper to activity mode to see the drive light during access only. Next, consider the possibility of drive light error messages. Some drive types (especially SCSI drives) use the drive activity light to signal drive and controller errors. Check the drive and controller documents to determine if any error is indicated by the light remaining on.

Symptom 2.20. You cannot access the hard drive, and the drive light stays on continuously. This usually indicates a reversed signal cable and is most common when upgrading or replacing a drive system. Thus, make the following checks:

■ *Check the signal cable.* In virtually all cases, one end of the signal cable is reversed. Make sure that both ends of the cable are installed properly (remember that the red or blue stripe on one side of the cable represents pin 1).

■ *Replace the drive controller.* If problems persist, replace the drive controller. It is rare for a fault in the drive controller to cause this type of problem, but if trouble persists, try a reliable drive controller board.

Symptom 2.21. You see a "No Fixed Disk Present" error message on the monitor. This kind of problem can occur during installation or at any point in the PC's working life. The following checks are recommended:

■ *Check the power connector.* Make sure the four-pin power connector is inserted properly and completely. If the drive is being powered by a Y-connector, make sure any interim connections are secure. Use a voltmeter and measure the +5 volt (pin 4) and +12 volt (pin 1) levels. If either voltage (especially the +12 volt supply) is unusually low or absent, replace the power supply.

■ *Check the signal connector.* Make sure the drive's signal cable is connected securely at both the drive and controller. If the cable is visibly worn or damaged, try a new one.

- *Check the CMOS Setup.* Enter the CMOS Setup routine and see that all the parameters entered for the drive are correct. Heads, cylinders, sectors per track, landing zones, and write precompensation must all be correct. Otherwise, POST will not recognize the drive. You might also try auto-detecting the drive.

- *Check for hardware conflicts.* Make sure that no other expansion devices in the system are using the same IRQs or I/O addresses used by your drive controller. If so, change the resources used by the conflicting device. If your drive system uses a SCSI interface, make sure that the SCSI cable is terminated properly.

- *Replace the hard drive or controller.* If problems continue, try a reliable hard drive. If it works as expected, your original drive is probably defective. If problems persist with the drive, replace the drive controller board.

Symptom 2.22. Your drive spins up, but the system fails to recognize the drive. Your computer may flag this as a hard-disk error or a hard-disk controller failure during system initialization. The following checks will help you find a solution:

- *Check the signal connector.* Make sure that the interface signal cable is inserted properly and completely at the drive and controller. Try a new signal cable.

- *Check the drive jumpers.* See that a primary (master) drive is configured as primary, and a secondary (slave) drive is configured as secondary. For SCSI drives, see that each drive has a unique ID setting and check that the SCSI bus is terminated properly.

- *Check the CMOS Setup.* Enter the CMOS Setup routine and see that all the parameters entered for the drive are correct. Heads, cylinders, sectors per track, landing zones, and write precompensation must all be correct. Otherwise, POST will not recognize the drive. Try using the auto-detect feature if it is available.

- *Check the partition.* If the CMOS is configured properly, you should suspect a problem with the partition. Boot from a floppy disk and run FDISK to check the partitions on your hard drive. Make sure that at least one DOS partition exists. If the drive is to be your boot drive, the primary partition must be active and bootable. Repartition and reformat the drive if necessary.

- *Try another hard drive or controller.* If a reliable drive works as expected, your original drive is probably defective. If the hard drive fails to work as expected, replace the drive controller. If problems persist with a reliable floppy drive, replace the drive controller board.

Symptom 2.23. Your IDE drive spins up when power is applied and then rapidly spins down again. The drive is defective or it is not communicating properly with its host system. The following checks can help spot the cause of the problem:

- *Check the power connector.* Make sure the four-pin power connector is inserted properly and completely into the drive.

- *Check the signal connector next.* See that the interface signal cable is inserted properly and completely at the drive and controller. Try a new signal cable.

- *Check the drive jumpers.* The primary (master) drive should be configured as primary, and a secondary (slave) drive should be configured as secondary. For SCSI drives, see that each drive has a unique ID setting, and check that the SCSI bus is terminated properly.

- *Replace the drive.*   If problems persist, try a reliable hard drive. If it works as expected, your original drive is probably defective.

Symptom 2.24. You see a "Sector not found" error message.   This problem usually occurs after the drive has been in operation for quite some time and is typically the result of a media failure. Fortunately, a bad sector will only effect one file. Thus, make the following checks:

- *Try recovering the file.*   Use a utility such as SpinRite from Gibson Research (or another data recovery utility) and attempt to recover the damaged file. Note that you may be unsuccessful and have to restore the file from a backup later.

- *Check the disk media.*   Use a disk utility (such as ScanDisk) to evaluate the drive. Then locate and map out any bad sectors that are located on the drive.

- *Try a low-level format.*   If problems persist, perform a low-level format (if possible). Lost sectors often occur as drives age and sector ID information degrades. LL formatting restores the sector IDs, but LL formatting is performed at the factory for IDE/EIDE and SCSI drives. If there is an LL formatting utility for your particular drive (available right from the drive manufacturer), and ScanDisk reveals a large number of bad sectors, you may consider backing up the drive completely, running the LL utility, repartitioning, reformatting, and then restoring the drive. If ScanDisk maps out bad sectors, you may need to restore those files from a backup.

Symptom 2.25. You see a 1780 or 1781 ERROR on the system.   The classical 1780 error code indicates a Hard Disk 0 Failure, while the 1781 error code marks a Hard Disk 1 Failure. The following steps will help you solve the problem:

- *Boot the system clean.* Start the PC with a clean boot disk and make sure no TSRs or drivers are being loaded.

- *Check for viruses.* If you haven't done so already, run your anti-virus checker and make sure that no memory-resident or file-based viruses are on the system.

- *Check the boot files.* If you can access the hard drive once your system is booted, chances are that the boot files are missing or corrupt. Try a utility such as DrivePro's Drive Boot Fixer to recover the boot files or recopy the boot files with SYS and recreate the master boot record with FDISK /MBR. Otherwise, you will need to repartition and reformat the disk, and then restore disk files from a backup.

- *Replace the hard drive or controller.* If you cannot access the hard drive, run a diagnostic such as Windsor Technologies' PC Technician. Test the drive and drive controller. If the controller responds but the drive does not, try repartitioning and reformatting the hard drive. If the drive still doesn't respond, replace the hard drive outright. If the controller doesn't respond, replace the hard drive controller.

Symptom 2.26. You see a 1790 or 1791 ERROR on the system. The classical 1790 error code indicates a Hard Disk 0 Error, while the 1791 error code marks a Hard Disk 1 Error. Thus, make the following checks:

- *Check the signal connector.* Make sure that the interface signal cable is inserted properly and completely at the drive and controller. Try a new signal cable.

- *Check the partition.* Boot from a floppy disk and run FDISK to check the partitions on your hard drive. Make sure that there is at least one DOS partition. If the drive is to be your boot drive, the primary partition must be active and bootable. Repartition and reformat the drive if necessary.

- *Replace the hard drive or controller.* If a reliable drive works as expected, your original drive is probably defective. If problems persist with a reliable floppy drive, replace the drive controller board.

Symptom 2.27. You see a 1701 ERROR on the system. The 1701 error code indicates a hard drive POST error and the drive did not pass its POST test. The following checks will help you narrow down the problem:

- *Check the power connector.* Make sure the four-pin power connector is inserted properly and completely. If the drive is being powered by a Y-connector, make sure any interim connections are secure. Use a voltmeter and measure the +5 volt (pin 4) and +12 volt (pin 1) levels. If either voltage (especially the +12 volt supply) is unusually low or absent, replace the power supply.

- *Check the CMOS Setup.* Enter the CMOS Setup routine and see that all the parameters entered for the drive are correct. Heads, cylinders, sectors per track, landing zones, and write precompensation must all be correct. Otherwise, POST will not recognize the drive. Also try auto-detecting the drive.

- *Try a low-level format.* If problems persist, perform a LL format (if possible). If there is an LL formatting utility for your particular drive (available right from the drive manufacturer), you may consider backing up the drive completely, running the LL utility, repartitioning, reformatting, and then restoring the drive.

Symptom 2.28. The system reports random data, seek, or format errors. Random errors rarely indicate a permanent problem, but identifying the problem source can be a time-consuming task. The following checks can help you start to do so:

- *Check the power connector.* Make sure the four-pin power connector is inserted properly and completely. If the drive is being powered by a Y-connector, make sure any interim connections are secure. Use a volt-meter and measure the +5 volt (pin 4) and +12 volt (pin 1) levels. If either voltage (especially the +12 volt supply) is unusually low, replace the power supply.

- *Check the signal connector.* Make sure that the interface signal cable is inserted properly and com-pletely at the drive and controller. Try a new signal cable. Also try rerouting the signal cable away from the power supply or noisy expansion devices.

- *Check the drive orientation.* If problems occur after remounting the drive in a different orientation, you may need to repartition and reformat the drive or return it to its original orientation. Try relocating the drive controller away from cables and noisy expansion devices.

- *Check the turbo mode.* If your system has a turbo mode, your ISA drive controller may have trouble operating while the system is in this mode. Take the system out of turbo mode.

- *Replace the drive controller.* If the problem disap-pears, try a new drive controller.

- *Check the media.* The disk media may also be defective. Use a utility such as ScanDisk to check for and map out any bad sectors. Once bad sectors are mapped out, you may need to restore some files from your backup.

- *Try the hard drive and controller in another system.* If the drive and controller work in another system, there is probably excessive noise or grounding prob-lems in the original system. Reinstall the drive and controller in the original system and remove all extra expansion boards. If the problem goes away, replace one board at a time and retest the system until the problem returns. The last board you inserted when the problem returned is probably the culprit. If the problem persists, there may be a ground problem on the motherboard. Try replacing the motherboard as an absolute last effort.

Symptom 2.29. You see an "Error reading drive C:" error message. Read errors in a hard drive typically indicate problems with the disk media but may also indicate viruses or signaling problems. Thus, make the following checks:

- *Check the signal connector.* Make sure that the interface signal cable is inserted properly and completely at the drive and controller. Try a new signal cable.

- *Boot the PC clean.* Start the PC with a clean boot disk and make sure no TSRs or drivers are being loaded.

- *Check for viruses.* If you haven't done so already, run your anti-virus checker and make sure that no memory-resident or file-based viruses are on the system.

- *Consider the drive's orientation.* If problems occur after remounting the drive in a different orientation, you may need to repartition and reformat the drive or return it to its original orientation.

- *Check the disk media.* Use a utility such as ScanDisk to check for and map out any bad sectors. Once bad sectors are mapped out, you may need to restore some files from your backup.

- *Try another hard drive.* If a reliable drive works as expected, your original drive is probably defective and should be replaced.

Symptom 2.30. You see a "Track 0 not found" error message. A fault on track 00 can disable the entire drive since track 00 contains the drive's FAT. This can be a serious error that may require you to replace the drive. The following checks can tell you for sure:

- *Check the signal connector.* Examine the drive signal connector and verify that the interface signal cable is inserted properly and completely at the drive and controller. Try a new signal cable.

- *Check your partitions.* Boot from a floppy disk and run FDISK to check the partitions on your hard drive. Make sure there is at least one DOS partition. If the drive is to be your boot drive, the primary partition must be active and bootable. Repartition and reformat the drive if necessary.

- *Replace the hard drive.* Try a reliable hard drive. If it works as expected, your original drive is probably defective.

Symptom 2.31. You see a Hard Disk Controller Failure or a large number of defects in last logical partition. This is typically a CMOS Setup or drive controller problem. Enter the CMOS Setup routine and see that all of the parameters entered for the drive are correct. If the geometry specifies a larger drive, the system will attempt to format areas of the drive that don't exist, resulting in a large number of errors. If CMOS is configured correctly, there may be a problem with the hard drive controller, so try a new one. If a new drive controller does not correct the problem, the drive itself is probably defective and should be replaced.

Symptom 2.32. The IDE drive (greater than 528 MB) does not partition or format to full capacity. When relatively small hard drives do not realize their full capacity, the CMOS Setup is usually at fault. The drive parameters entered into CMOS must specify the full capacity of the drive using a geometry setup that is acceptable. If you use parameters that specify a smaller drive, any extra capacity will be ignored. If there are over 1024 cylinders, you must use an alternate translation geometry to realize the drive's full potential. The drive maker can provide you with the right translation geometry. Also check your DOS version. Older versions of DOS use a partition limit of 32 MB. Upgrade your older version of DOS to 6.22 (or MS-DOS 7.0 with Windows 95).

Symptom 2.33. The EIDE drive (less than 528 MB) does not partition or format to full capacity. This type of problem may be due to a CMOS Setup error but is almost always due to poor system configuration. Thus, make the following checks:

- *Check the CMOS Setup.* The drive parameters entered into CMOS must specify the full capacity of the drive. If you use parameters that specify a smaller drive, any extra capacity will be ignored. If there are over 1024 cylinders, you must use an alternate translation geometry to realize the drive's full potential. The drive maker can provide you with the right translation geometry. Also check the CMOS Setup for LBA. EIDE drives need LBA to access over 528 MB. Make sure that there is an entry such as LBA Mode in CMOS. Otherwise, you may need to upgrade your motherboard BIOS to have full drive capacity.

- *Check the drive controller.* If you cannot upgrade an older motherboard BIOS, install an EIDE drive controller with its own controller BIOS. This will supplement the motherboard BIOS.

- *Check the drive overlay software.* If neither your motherboard nor controller BIOS will support LBA mode, you will need to install drive overlay software (such as EZ-Drive or Drive Manager).

Symptom 2.34. You see "Disk Boot Failure," "non-system disk," or "No ROM Basic—SYSTEM HALTED" error messages. Several possible reasons for these errors exist and the following steps will help narrow down the problem:

- *Check the signal connector.* Make sure that the interface signal cables are inserted properly and completely at the drive and controller. Try some new signal cables.

- *Boot the PC clean.* Start the PC with a clean boot disk and make sure no TSRs or drivers are being loaded that might interfere with drive operations. If you haven't done so already, run your anti-virus checker and make sure no memory-resident or file-based viruses are on the system.

- *Check the CMOS Setup.* Enter the CMOS Setup routine and see that all the parameters entered for the drive are correct. Heads, cylinders, sectors per track, landing zones, and write precompensation must all be entered accurately.

- *Check your partitions.* Boot from a floppy disk and run FDISK to check the partitions on your hard drive. Make sure that there is at least one DOS partition. If the drive is to be your boot drive, the primary partition must be active and bootable.

- *Replace the drive or controller.* It is also possible that the hard drive itself is defective. Try a reliable hard drive. If it works as expected, your original drive is probably defective. If problems persist with a reliable floppy drive, replace the drive controller.

Symptom 2.35. The hard drive in a PC is suffering frequent breakdowns (between 6 to 12 months). When drives tend to fail within a few months, some factors should be considered:

- *Check the PC power.* If the AC power supplying your PC is dirty (with lots of spikes and surges), power anomalies can often make it through the power supply and damage other components. Remove any high-load devices such as air conditioners, motors, or coffee makers from the same AC circuit used by the PC, or try the PC on a reliable AC circuit. You might also consider a good-quality *uninterruptable power supply* (UPS) to power your PC.

- *Consider drive utilization.* Excessive drive use may be another factor. If the drive is being worked hard by applications and swap files, consider upgrading RAM, adding cache, or disabling virtual memory to reduce dependency on the drive.

- *Defragment the drive.* Periodically run a utility like DEFRAG to reorganize the files. This reduces the amount of drive thrashing that occurs when loading and saving files.

- *Consider the environment.* Constant, low-level vibrations, such as those in an industrial environment, can kill a hard drive. Smoke (even cigarette smoke), high humidity, very low humidity, and caustic vapors can ruin drives. Make sure the system is used in a stable office-type environment.

Symptom 2.36. A hard drive controller is replaced, but during initialization the system displays error messages such as "Hard Disk Failure" or "Not a recognized drive type." The PC may also lock-up. Some drive controllers may be incompatible in some systems. Check with the controller manufacturer and see if there have been any reports of incompatibilities with your PC. If so, try a different drive controller board.

Symptom 2.37. A new hard drive is installed, but it will not boot or a message appears such as "HDD controller failure." The new drive has probably not been installed or prepared properly. The following checks will help you spot the problem:

- *Check the power connector.* Make sure the four-pin power connector is inserted properly and completely. If the drive is being powered by a Y-connector, make sure any interim connections are secure. Use a voltmeter and measure the +5 volt (pin 4) and +12 volt (pin 1) levels. If either voltage (especially the +12 volt supply) is unusually low or absent, replace the power supply.

- *Check the signal cable.* Make sure the drive's signal interface cable is connected securely at both the drive and controller. If the cable is visibly worn or damaged, try a new one.

- *Check the CMOS Setup.* Enter the CMOS Setup routine and see that all the parameters entered for the drive are correct. Heads, cylinders, sectors per track, landing zones, and write precompensation must all correct. Otherwise, POST will not recognize the drive.

- *Check the drive's preparation.* The drive may not be prepared properly. Run FDISK from a bootable diskette to partition the drive, and run FORMAT to initialize the drive. Then run SYS C: to make the drive bootable.

Symptom 2.38. The drive will work as a primary drive, but not as a secondary (or vice versa). In most cases, the drive is simply jumpered incorrectly, but there may also be timing problems. Perform the following checks:

- *Check the drive jumpers.* Make sure that the drive is jumpered properly as a primary (single drive), primary (dual drive), or secondary drive.

- *Check the drive relationship.* The drive signal timing may also be off. Some IDE/EIDE drives do not work as primary or secondary drives with certain other drives in the system. Reverse the primary/secondary relationship. If the problem persists, try the drives separately. If the drives work individually, there is probably a timing problem, so try a different drive as the primary or secondary.

Symptom 2.39. You install a Y-adapter that fails to work. Some Y-adapters are incorrectly wired and can cause severe damage to any device attached to it. Examine the power connector first. Make certain that both the female connectors are lined up with the two chamfered (rounded) corners facing up and both of the squared corners facing down. The four wires attached to the female connectors should now be in the following order from left to right: Yellow (112Vdc), Black (ground), Black (ground), and Red (15Vdc). If this order is reversed on one of the connectors, then your Y power adapter is faulty and should not be used.

Symptom 2.40. During the POST, you hear a drive begin to spin up and produce a sharp noise. This problem can be encountered with some combinations of drives, motherboards, and motherboard BIOS. This type of problem can easily result in data loss (and media damage). Check the motherboard BIOS version first, then contact the PC system manufacturer, and see if a BIOS upgrade is necessary. Try a BIOS upgrade. Otherwise, replace the drive controller. Often a new drive controller may resolve the problem if the motherboard BIOS cannot be replaced.

Symptom 2.41. You're using an Ultra-DMA hard drive, but no DMA check box is available in the drive's Properties dialog. If the DMA checkbox is unavailable, this may suggest that Windows does not view the drive as Ultra-

DMA-capable. This could be a driver issue or your hard drive (or motherboard drive controller) does not support Ultra-DMA. Assuming the drive and motherboard both support Ultra-DMA operation, make sure that you are running the latest bus-mastering drivers (these are installed by default if your motherboard supports them). You may need to download the latest bus-master drivers from the drive controller maker or the motherboard manufacturer. Once the proper drivers are installed, Windows 98 will automatically handle all transfer rates that the drive and motherboard support.

Symptom 2.42. After installing a large HDD (unpartitioned), you cannot access the floppy drive.   This will effectively hang the system and prevent you from completing the hard drive's installation. In most cases, this is due to an issue with the drive size. Some BIOS versions cannot perform the proper translation on an 8.4-GB (or larger) drive and will hang the system as a result. Try setting the drive up using the following parameters:

- Cylinders: 1023
- Heads: 16
- Sectors: 63

Of course, this represents a small IDE drive and the system will tell you that this is a 504-MB or 528-MB drive. If you can then boot to a floppy disk, then you can either upgrade the BIOS or drive controller to support the large hard drive natively or install drive overlay software such as Disk Manager or MaxBlast.

Symptom 2.43. After configuring a drive with the correct parameters (16383 $\times$ 16 $\times$ 63), the system still indicates that the drive is only 504 MB or 528 MB.   Keep in mind that 528 MB (or 504 MB) is the limitation of the original cylinder/head/sector translation method used on

IDE drives. This problem was resolved with the LBA translation technique. Make sure that the CMOS Setup is configured to use LBA if it is available. If not, you may need to upgrade the BIOS (or drive controller) or install drive overlay software such as Disk Manager or MaxBlast.

Symptom 2.44. You detect hard drive errors caused by damaged data or physical damage.   You may receive one of the following error messages when you are starting or using your computer:

- `Serious Disk Error Writing Drive <X>`
- `Data Error Reading Drive <X>`
- `Error Reading Drive <X>`
- `I/O Error`
- `Seek Error–Sector not found`

These error messages indicate either damaged data or physical damage on the hard disk. Run ScanDisk to examine the hard drive. Running ScanDisk with the Thorough option selected examines the drive for physical damage. If damaged data is detected, ScanDisk enables you to save the damaged data to a file (or discard the data). Keep in mind that ScanDisk's surface scan may take a considerable amount of time on large hard disks. If ScanDisk is unable to repair damaged data (or indicates that the drive suffers from physical damage), you'll need to replace the drive.

Symptom 2.45. You find that a PC using an Ultra-DMA controller/drive may lock up when running Windows 95 (OSR2).   The lockup occurs when the drive is being accessed. This problem occurs when there's a hardware error while data is being read from the hard drive. When the error happens during an Ultra-DMA data transfer, the Windows device driver does not successfully recover from the error and does not retry the operation, so the system halts. This is a known issue with Windows 95 OSR2, and an update file (REMIDEUP.EXE) is available for download from the Microsoft Web site. The updated file ESDI_506.PDR version 4.00.1116 (dated 8/25/97 or later) should fix the problem under Windows 95 OSR2.

Symptom 2.46. You encounter errors accessing a hard drive with its spin-down feature enabled. This frequently occurs under Windows 95 (and OSR2), and you may find that incorrect data is read or written to the drive or you may encounter *General Protection Faults* (GPFs). This type of problem is known to occur under Windows 95 (and OSR2) if the drive requires more than 7.5 seconds to spin up. An error is then generated in the Windows 95 driver, resulting in incorrect data being read from the drive (which can result in GPFs).

You can work around this problem by disabling the hard disk spin-down on the Disk Drives tab using the Power tool in the Control Panel. An update file (REMIDEUP.EXE) is available for download from the Microsoft Web site. The updated file ESDI_506.PDR version 4.00.1113 (dated 12/6/96 or later) should fix the problem under Windows 95 (and OSR2). For Windows 95, the VOLTRACK.VXD version 4.00.954 (dated 3/6/96 or later) file is also installed.

File System Symptoms

This section will focus on problems with your file system and we'll examine some solutions for fixing it.

Symptom 2.47. The hard drive's root directory is damaged. A faulty root directory can cripple the entire disk, rendering *all* subdirectories inaccessible. You may be able to recover the root directory structure. Use a utility like DISKFIX (with PC Tools) to reconstruct the damaged

FATs and directories. If you have been running MIR-ROR, DISKFIX should be able to perform a reliable recovery. You may also try other recovery/corrective utilities such as DrivePro or ScanDisk. However, if you cannot recover the root directory reliably, you'll need to reformat the drive and then restore its contents from a backup.

Symptom 2.48. The hard drive is infected by a bootblock virus. You may detect the presence of a bootblock virus (a virus that infects the MBR) by running an anti-virus utility or receiving an warning from the BIOS bootblock protection feature. In every case, you should attempt to use the anti-virus utility to eradicate the virus. You may also remove a bootblock virus by using FDISK /MBR (though that could render the contents of your disk inaccessible). If you're using drive overlay software such as Disk Manager, you can usually rewrite the code through the Maintenance Menu within the Disk Manager utility itself.

Symptom 2.49. You see a "File Allocation Table Bad" error. The OS has encountered a problem with the FAT. Normally, two copies of the FAT are on a drive. Chances are that one of the copies has become damaged. It may also be possible that there is no partition on the drive to begin with. Run ScanDisk, which may be able to correct the problem by allowing you to select which copy of the FAT you want to use. If the problem continues, you'll need to backup as many files as possible and reformat the drive.

Symptom 2.50. DOS requires you to enter the volume label, but the label is corrupt.   Some versions of DOS (such as DOS 3.x) require you to enter the volume label when formatting a hard drive or deleting a logical drive partition using the FDISK command. However, if the volume label is corrupted (or was changed by a third-party utility to contain lowercase letters), this is impossible. To correct this problem, use the LABEL command to delete the volume label and then use FORMAT or FDISK. When you are prompted for the volume label, press Enter (which indicates no volume label). If LABEL doesn't successfully delete the volume label, you can use the following debug script to erase the first sector of the drive and make it appear unformatted. Then repartition and reformat the drive. Start DEBUG and then type the following:

```
-   F 100 L 200 0    ;Create a sector of zeros at
address 100

-   W 100 2 0 1                ;Write information at
address 100 to sector 0 of drive 2

-   Q                          ;Quit DEBUG
```

For DOS versions 5.x and later, you can use the following command to handle the problem:

```
format /q /v:VOLUME x:
```

where VOLUME is the new volume name you want to assign to the hard disk drive, and x: is the drive letter you want to format.

Software-Oriented Symptoms

Symptom 2.51. Software diagnostics indicate an average access time that is longer than specified for the drive. The average access time is the average amount of time needed for a drive to reach the track and sector where a needed file begins. The following checks are recommended:

- *Check your timing.* Review your drive specifications and verify the timing specifications for your particular drive. Its timing may be correct.

- *Defragment the drive.* Start your defragmentation utility (such as DEFRAG) and check to see the percentage of file fragmentation. If there is more than 10 percent fragmentation, you should consider running the defragmentation utility.

- *Check your software.* Also keep in mind that different software packages measure access time differently. Make sure that the diagnostic subtracts system overhead processing from the access time calculation. Try one or two other diagnostics to confirm the measurement.

- *Check similar drives.* Before you panic and replace a drive, try testing several similar drives for comparison. If only the suspect drive measures incorrectly, you may not need to replace the drive itself just yet, but you should at least maintain frequent backups in case the drive is near failure.

Symptom 2.52. Software diagnostics indicate a slower data transfer rate than specified. This is often due to less than ideal data transfer rates, rather than an actual hardware failure. Thus, make the following checks:

- *Check your timing.* Review your drive specifications and verify the timing specifications for your particular drive. Its timing may be correct.

- *Check your data transfer modes.* Enter the CMOS Setup routine and verify that any enhanced data transfer modes are enabled (such as PIO Mode 4). This can increase the data transfer rate substantially.

- *Defragment the drive.* Start your defragmentation utility (such as DEFRAG), and check to see the percentage of file fragmentation. If there is more than 10 percent fragmentation, you should consider running the defragmentation utility.

- *Check your software.* Also keep in mind that different software packages measure access time differently. Make sure that the diagnostic subtracts system overhead processing from the access time calculation. Try one or two other diagnostics to confirm the measurement.

- *Check for low-level formatting.* If the drive is an IDE/EIDE type, make sure that no one performed a low-level format. This may remove head and cylinder skewing optimization and result in a degradation of data transfers. This error generally cannot be corrected by end-user software.

- *Check termination.* If the drive is a SCSI type, make sure the SCSI bus is terminated properly. Poor termination can cause data errors and result in retransmissions that degrade overall data transfer rates.

Symptom 2.53. The FDISK procedure hangs up or fails to create or save a partition record for the drive(s). You may also see an error message such as a Runtime error. This type of problem often indicates a problem with track 00 on the drive. The following checks will help you narrow down the problem:

- *Check the signal connector.* Make sure that the interface signal cables are inserted properly and completely at the drive and controller. Try some new signal cables.

- *Check the drive setup.* Enter the CMOS Setup routine and see that all the parameters entered for the drive are correct. Heads, cylinders, sectors per track, landing zones, and write precompensation must all be appropriate. Check with the drive maker and see if there is an alternate translation geometry that you can enter instead. If the BIOS supports auto-detection, try auto-detecting the drive.

- *Check your version of FDISK.* The version of FDISK you are using must be the same as the DOS version on your boot diskette. Older versions may not work.

- *Check your partition(s).*   Run FDISK and see if any partitions are already on the drive. If so, you may need to erase any existing partitions and then create your new partition from scratch. Remember that erasing a partition will destroy any data already on the drive.

- *Check for media defects.*   Use a utility such as ScanDisk to check the media for physical defects, especially at track 00. If there is physical damage in the boot sector, you should replace the drive.

- *Check for emergency drive utilities.*   Some drive makers provide low-level preparation utilities that can rewrite track 00. For example, Western Digital provides the WD_CLEAR.EXE utility.

- *Replace the hard drive.*   If problems still persist, replace the hard defective hard drive.

Symptom 2.54. After using FDISK to partition a large hard drive, the system hangs when booting from a floppy disk. This is almost always an issue with the system BIOS (or drive controller) that cannot properly support a large (8.4-GB1) drive. Some BIOS versions are confused when they encounter an 8.4-GB or larger hard drive, and they assign it zero heads by mistake. Under these conditions, you'll be able to partition the drive with FDISK, but the partition table that it creates will contain invalid information. When you boot to a floppy disk, the OS on that floppy disk attempts to access the partition table on the hard drive. The invalid information created by FDISK causes the OS to hang. The solution is to upgrade the system BIOS (or the drive controller) to support the large drive natively or install drive overlay software such as Disk Manager or MaxBlast.

Symptom 2.55. FDISK reports an error such as "no space to create partition" or "disk is write-protected." Several possible issues may cause this type of behavior, and the following checks will help you solve the problem:

- *Check the CMOS Setup.* Chances are that your BIOS has enabled virus protection for the master boot record (also referred to as Boot Sector Write Protect). You must go into the system's CMOS Setup and disable that feature before partitioning a drive (or installing/upgrading an OS).

- *Check the drive jumpers.* Some hard drives require the use of two jumpers rather than just one. Verify that your drive is jumpered properly for its place in your particular drive configuration (such as single master, master with slave, or slave).

- *Upgrade the BIOS or drive controller.* If the problem persists, the BIOS may not be able to support your drive properly. Check for a BIOS upgrade (or upgrade the drive controller) or install drive overlay software such as Disk Manager or MaxBlast.

Symptom 2.56. FDISK refuses to partition the drive and hangs the system or returns a runtime error. In many cases, track 00 on the drive has been corrupted. If you can perform a low-level format of the drive, try using the disk manufacturer's LL formatting (or drive preparation) utility to reconstruct track 00. For example, Western Digital's Data Lifeguard Tools utility (*www.wdc.com / service / ftp / drives.htmladlgtools*) can be used to perform a pseudo-LL format on Western Digital drives. From the main menu, choose Diagnostics, select the correct drive, and choose Write Zeros. After the operation completes, run FDISK again. Your particular drive manufacturer may offer other similar utilities. If this does not resolve the problem, the drive itself may need to be replaced.

Symptom 2.57. You install Disk Manager to a hard drive and then install DOS, but DOS formats the drive back to 528 MB.   After Disk Manager is installed, you must create a rescue disk to use in conjunction with your DOS installation.

1. Create a clean DOS bootable disk.

2. Copy two files from the original Disk Manager disk to your bootable disk, XBIOS.OVL and DMDRVR.BIN.

3. Create a CONFIG.SYS file on this bootable disk with these three lines:

```
DEVICE=DMDRVR.BIN

FILES=35

BUFFERS=35
```

4. Remove the bootable diskette and reboot the system.

5. When you see `Press space bar to boot from diskette`, do so and the system will halt

6. Insert the rescue disk in drive A:, and press any key to resume the boot process.

7. At the A: prompt, remove your rescue disk, insert the DOS installation disk, and then type `SETUP`.

8. You will now install DOS files without overwriting the Disk Manager files.

Symptom 2.58. ScanDisk reports some bad sectors but cannot map them out during a surface analysis.   You may need a surface analysis utility for your particular drive that is provided by the drive maker. For example, Western Digital provides the WDATIDE.EXE utility for its Caviar series of drives. It will mark all grown defects and compensate for lost capacity by utilizing spare tracks.

NOTE: These types of surface analysis utilities are typically destructive. Make sure to have a complete backup of the drive before proceeding. Also, the utility may take a long time to run depending on your drive's capacity.

Symptom 2.59. ScanDisk reports an Out of Memory error after copying data from a smaller drive to a larger one. The data seems to copy successfully, but when you run ScanDisk, you get an Out of Memory error (or you have a problem using Defrag). Chances are that you've copied data from a smaller drive to a larger drive that uses FAT32 (you're running Windows 95 OSR2 or Windows 98) using some utility that can copy the contents of one hard drive to another. The utility may have created an image of the drive that was copied to the other or it copied data sector by sector from one drive to the other.

If you used an older utility (or version of EZ-Drive) to copy the data, the clusters were probably not correctly resized for the new FAT32 partition. When a partition becomes formatted, it is divided into clusters or small blocks. These clusters are used to store data and the size of a cluster is determined by the size of the partition. Older copy utilities often do not support FAT32 properly and will incorrectly size the cluster on the new FAT32 partition when they transfer data from the old drive to the new one. You can verify if this has occurred by running CHKDSK from a DOS prompt. The correct cluster sizes for FAT32 partitions are listed here:

- 512 MB to 8.2 GB = 4-KB cluster size
- 8.2 GB to 16.4 GB = 8-KB cluster size
- 16.4 GB to 32.8 GB = 16-KB cluster size
- 32.8 GB and higher = 32-KB cluster size

If CHKDSK reports an incorrect cluster size for your partition, you need to erase the data and copy it using an updated utility.

Symptom 2.60. Drive diagnostics reveal a great deal of wasted space on the drive.   You probably have a large drive partitioned as one or more FAT16 logical volumes. If you deal with large numbers of small files, it may be more efficient to create multiple smaller partitions utilizing smaller clusters. As an alternative, you may choose to repartition the drive using FAT32 that supports much larger partitions (while allowing for smaller clusters).

Symptom 2.61. After installing a new hard drive, Windows 98 only detects the drive if it's noted as removable in the Device Manager.   Chances are that you missed one or two steps and neglected to partition and format the drive. All hard disk drives must be partitioned before they can be formatted, even if the drive is only going to have a single partition. Windows 98 incorrectly enables you to format an unpartitioned drive if you designate the drive as removable. Using a drive this way will almost certainly result in a data loss. The solution is to backup any data on the drive and then remove the checkmark from the removable box in the Windows 98 Device Manager. Next, use FDISK to create at least one primary and active partition. Reboot the system and then format the partition(s) with FORMAT. This process will destroy any data on the drive but should correct the recognition issue.

Symptom 2.62. ScanDisk incorrectly reports hard drive problems under Windows 98.   When you upgrade from Windows 3.x to Windows 98, Setup may quit and recommend you run ScanDisk to repair your hard disk, but no errors are found after you run ScanDisk. This is a known problem with Windows 98 and occurs when your Windows 3.x-based computer is configured to use a network server for virtual memory. To work around this issue, run Windows 98 Setup with the /is parameter (Setup runs normally, but skips ScanDisk) such as

```
setup /is
```

Symptom 2.63. Defrag causes a GPF in USER.EXE under Windows 95/98.   When you try to run Defrag from System Agent or Task Scheduler, you may receive a GPF in USER.EXE. This may occur if the task information for Defrag has become damaged. Delete the Defrag task from System Agent or Task Scheduler and then create a new task.

FAT32 Symptoms

Symptom 2.64. You cannot place a FAT32 partition on a drive.   The trick to establishing a FAT32 partition on a drive is to partition the drive correctly. Try the following steps to partition a drive:

1. In the Windows 95/98 Device Manager, select the drive, and then click on Properties.

2. Click Settings and then click the INT 13 Unit check box to select it.

3. Quit the Device Manager and restart Windows 95/98.

4. Once Windows 95/98 is restarted, open an MS-DOS session and use the FDISK command to partition the drive (careful not to partition an existing drive accidentally).

5. Restart Windows 95/98 again. You should be able to format the drive and use the FAT32 file system.

Symptom 2.65. After moving a FAT32 SCSI hard drive from one controller to another, you cannot read or write reliably to the SCSI drive.   This is because SCSI drives are highly controller-dependent to begin with, and you should be prepared to repartition and reformat SCSI drives whenever changing the SCSI host controller. This behavior is particularly evident when you partition and format a hard disk using a SCSI controller that fully supports INT 13 extensions, and you then move the hard disk to a controller that does not fully support INT 13 extensions. To move a drive using the FAT32 file system to a different controller, you must verify that both controllers fully support INT 13 extensions in the same manner. If they do not, data loss will most likely occur.

Symptom 2.66. When you try to compress a drive with DriveSpace or DriveSpace 3, you receive the error message, "Drive C cannot be compressed because it is a FAT32 drive." This is because DriveSpace was designed to work with the FAT12 and FAT16 file systems and cannot be used on drives with the FAT32 file system. Unfortunately, this problem has no correction, and Microsoft is considering an update for a future release. In the mean time, your only options are to avoid using drive compression or use a third-party drive compression tool that is FAT32-compatible. Check out the Stacker site (*www.stac.com*).

Symptom 2.67. When booting from a diskette, you cannot access your FAT32 hard drive partition(s). The system boots fine from the hard drive. This is an issue with the boot diskette. Boot diskettes made with older versions of DOS or Windows are not FAT32-aware and cannot support access to your FAT32 hard drive partition(s). For example, you cannot access your Windows 98 FAT32 drive when booting from a Windows 95a startup disk. Create a Windows 98 startup disk in order to boot your FAT32 system.

Symptom 2.68. The system may hang up when certain drive software is used under FAT32. After installing the drive software (PC Tools Pro 9.0), the computer will probably hang up during startup after you see the following message:

```
Analyzing drive C:

Reading system areas
```

In virtually all cases, this occurs because your drive software is not compatible with the FAT32 file system in Windows 95 OSR2 (or Windows 98). You can contact the software maker (such as Symantec for PC Tools Pro 9.0 at *www.symantec.com*) for a FAT32-aware version of the software. As a workaround, you can use a text editor (EDIT or Notepad) to edit the AUTOEXEC.BAT file and disable the command line that starts the software. For PC Tools Pro 9.0, you'd REM-out its line such as

```
REM call pctools.bat
```

Symptom 2.69. When using Defrag on a FAT32 system, you encounter an error message such as "DEFRAG0026, Make sure disk is formatted." You may also see an error such as

```
Windows cannot defragment this drive. Make sure the
disk is formatted and free of errors. Then try
defragmenting the drive again.
```

This error can be caused when running an earlier version of DEFRAG.EXE than the version included with Windows 95 OSR2 (or Windows 98). To resolve this problem, extract a new copy of the DEFRAG.EXE file from your original Windows 95 OSR2 (or Windows 98) CD.

Symptom 2.70. You see an "Invalid Media" error message when formatting a FAT32 partition. When you try to format a FAT32 file system partition larger than 8025 MB (8 GB) from within Windows 95/98, you may receive the following error message:

```
Verifying <xxx.xx>M

Invalid media or track 0 bad-disk unusable

Format terminated
```

where `<xxx.xx>` is the size of the partition. This error occurs if a non-DOS partition is preceding the extended DOS partition and the primary DOS partition has been formatted using the real-mode FORMAT.EXE command. To correct this problem, you'll need to reformat the volume using the following steps:

1. Click the Start button, click Shut Down, click Restart the Computer in MS-DOS Mode, and then click Yes.

2. Type the following command and then press Enter:

   ```
   format <drive>:
   ```

   where `<drive>` is the drive letter for the partition you want to format.

3. When the partition is formatted, type `exit` to restart Windows 95/98.

Symptom 2.71. After you install Windows 98 (or convert a partition to FAT32), Windows 98 reports DOS Compatibility mode.   This can occur when the drive controller has not been detected properly under Windows 98. Try rebooting the PC and see if Windows 98 will redetect the drive controller (you may need to remove the drive controller entry from the Device Manager before rebooting the system). For specific details about resolving Compatibility mode problems, refer to the DOS Compatibility mode troubleshooting guide at the beginning of this section.

Symptom 2.72. After converting a drive to FAT32, you notice that tools like ScanDisk and Defrag take much longer to run.   This is an undesired side effect of the FAT32 file system. It takes Defrag and ScanDisk the same amount of time to examine a single cluster, regardless of that cluster's size. Since FAT32 uses smaller clusters, many times more clusters exist, and such utilities take considerably longer than they used to. Microsoft compensates for this by including the Tune-Up Wizard, which enables you to schedule such tasks to take place when you're away from the computer.

Symptom 2.73. The FAT32 conversion utility crashed after reporting that it found bad sectors. This is a side effect of ScanDisk. If ScanDisk has marked any sectors as bad, the FAT32 converter will refuse to run, even if they are fixed by third-party disk utilities (such as Data Lifeguard Tools). ScanDisk uses the FAT table to keep track of bad sectors. But even if third-party utilities remap bad sectors at the hardware level, ScanDisk is not aware of those changes. One solution is to wipe the hard drive clean and start over (in which case you'd just partition the drive using FAT32 to begin with).

Symptom 2.74. The FAT32 converter under Windows 98 cannot locate the drive partition to be converted. When using the Windows 98 Drive Converter tool to convert a drive from FAT16 to FAT32, you may receive an error message such as `Drive converter unable to find the drive partition`. This problem can occur if you try to convert a FAT16 logical drive that begins above the 8.0-GB mark. For example, if you have a 10-GB hard disk with five 2.0-GB FAT16 partitions, you may have trouble converting the fifth drive (drive G:) to FAT32. To work around this problem, delete all of your partitions above the 8.0-GB mark, and then recreate your partitions.

Upgrade/Installation Symptoms

This section will cover problems concerning upgrades and installations.

Symptom 2.75. Your drive fails to spin up properly after power is applied. This problem usually occurs when a new drive or controller board is installed or upgraded. A signal cable between the drive and controller board is probably flipped on one side. Check the signal cable alignments and ensure that both ends of the cable(s) are inserted properly. Also verify that the drive is properly identified in the CMOS Setup.

Symptom 2.76. You see a "Drive not ready" error or similar message displayed on the monitor. This problem is typically encountered during installations and upgrades. The system is not recognizing your drive, so the following checks are necessary:

- *Check the signal cable.* Begin your inspection by checking the signal cable between the controller and drive. One end of the cable may be reversed.

- *Check the power cable.* Power is typically through a four-pin mate-and-lock connector. The middle two pins are ground. One end provides +5 Vdc and the other end provides +12 Vdc. If one or both of the supply voltages is low or absent, the supply may be undersized for the power load demanded by the system. You could try a larger supply. If power is adequate, make sure that the drive spins up.

- *Check the drive ID.* Inspect any jumpers or dip switches and make sure the drive is set properly for the type of controller being used. An ESDI drive must be set to drive 0 or drive 1, an EIDE/UDMA drive must be set as either a master or slave, and an SCSI drive must have a valid, unique ID (usually ID0 or ID1). If the drive is not configured properly, your system will not recognize the drive.

- *Check the termination.* For ESDI or SCSI drives, you should also check for the proper positions of terminating resistors.

■ *Low-level (LL) format the drive (if possible).* An ESDI drive may be LL formatted improperly. Check the LL drive parameters used in LL formatting. If any of the parameters are incorrect, correct the parameters and try reformatting the drive again.

Symptom 2.77. You install a drive that has already been formatted, but it does not operate after installation. Start by checking the controller and cable installation. Also check the system CMOS to be sure that the proper parameters are entered for the drive being used. This is especially important when using an IDE/EIDE/Ultra-ATA drive in translation mode. Find out if the DOS version used to partition and high-level format the drive is compatible with your current system. A hard drive with an incompatible format or partition table will not function in your system. Make sure that you are using the same drive controller board used by the dealer who prepared the drive. Also check that you are using the same type of cables. It may be necessary to repartition the hard drive from scratch to ensure compatibility.

Symptom 2.78. You see a "No SCSI device found" or some similar error. Check the installation of any SCSI adapter software. If you booted from a clean floppy, the SCSI drivers probably did not load, so the SCSI host adapter may not be available. If the host adapter is running properly, check that the SCSI cables are attached to each device. No cables should be pinched, scraped, or cut. Next, check the SCSI adapter to see that all jumper or DIP switch settings are configured properly. A hardware conflict can easily cause problems with the adapter. If problems persist, try a new SCSI adapter. On the other hand, if the drive shows a series of LED flashes when powered up, it may be the SCSI hard drive that is defective.

Symptom 2.79. While using FDISK, you see an error such as "Error reading fixed disk" or "No fixed disk present." Double-check the signal cable(s) connected to the drive and make sure that the drive select jumper is set properly. Try a different signal cable. Also check the drive adapter's installation. Next, try a fresh version of FDISK. The version you are using may be old or corrupted. If you are using a dual-drive system, try swapping the drive 0/drive 1 (master/slave) relationship. If the problem persists, remove one of the two drives; they may simply be incompatible together. Try a drive from another manufacturer.

Symptom 2.80. After running FDISK, you receive an error message indicating an "Invalid drive specification" or similar problem. FDISK failed to create a proper partition on your hard drive. Try running FDISK again and be sure to save the partition configurations. Try shutting down the system before attempting a DOS format. Try a fresh version of FDISK; the version you are using may be corrupted. In a dual-drive configuration, try reversing the drive 0/drive 1 (master/slave) relationship; the drives may be incompatible with one another. Try each drive individually. If problems continue on the offending drive when used alone, the drive's partition table may be damaged. Try a new drive.

Symptom 2.81. You see an error such as "Track 0 bad, disk unusable." This is perhaps the most serious indication of a drive failure. With track 0 damaged, no partition or boot sector information is available to the drive, so the system cannot use it. Check the CMOS setup to verify the drive parameters. If the drive is an ESDI-type, check the DEBUG command used for LL formatting, and try the LL format again. For IDE and SCSI drives, the drive is probably defective. If you have an LL format routing for the IDE drive, you might give that a try. Otherwise, replace the defective drive.

CD-ROM Drives

Originally designed as an audio recording medium, the CD quickly found a place in the PC with a CD-ROM drive. The CD provides two key advantages over other forms of media: each disc holds tremendous amounts of information and discs can be exchanged in the drive. Taken together, the CD offers PC users access to almost unlimited information. Although CD-ROM drives are still rather slow in comparison to contemporary hard drives, CDs have become particularly popular for holding data-intensive multimedia (sound, images, and programs).

CD-ROM Drive Interfaces

Two major interfaces are used with modern CD-ROM drives: IDE/EIDE and SCSI. The 40-pin IDE/EIDE interface is shown back in Figure 2.2. IDE/EIDE drives (including the more recent UDMA/33 and UDMA/66 drives) are extremely popular, and most end-user systems made since 1989 carry some vintage of the IDE-type CD-ROM drive. SCSI drives are outstanding in server or multitasking systems. Refer to Figure 2.3 for a standard 50-pin SCSI connection, and refer to Figure 2.4 for a 68-pin SCSI connection.

CD-ROM Drives and Device Drivers

A low-level device driver enables DOS to access the CD-ROM adapter properly at the register (hardware) level. Since most CD-ROM adapters are designed differently, they require different device drivers. If you change or upgrade the CD-ROM drive at any point, the device driver must be upgraded as well. A typical real-mode device driver uses a .SYS extension and is initiated by adding its command line to the PC's CONFIG. SYS file such as

```
DEVICE=HITACHIA.SYS /D:MSCD000 /N:1 /P:300
```

The DEVICE command can be replaced by the command DEVICE HIGH if you have available space in the *upper memory area* (UMA).

A real-mode CD-ROM device driver will typically have three command-line switches associated with it. These parameters are needed to ensure that the driver installs properly. In the example command-line shown previously, the /D switch is the name used by the driver when it is installed in the system's device table. This name must be unique and be matched by the /D switch in the MSCDEX.EXE command line (covered later). The /N switch is the number of CD-ROM drives attached to the interface card. The default is 1 (which is typical for most general purpose systems). Finally, the /P switch is the I/O port address where the CD-ROM adapter card resides. As you might expect, the port address should match the jumper settings on the adapter board. If there is no /P switch, the default is 0300h.

CD-ROM Drives and MSCDEX.EXE

MS-DOS was developed in a time when no one anticipated that large files would be accessible to a PC, and it is severely limited in the file sizes that it can handle. With the development of CD-ROMs, Microsoft created an extension to MS-DOS that enables software publishers to access 650-MB CDs in a standard fashion, through the *Microsoft CD-ROM Extensions* (MSCDEX). MSCDEX is loaded in AUTOEXEC.BAT. As with most software, MSCDEX offers some vital features (and a few limitations), but it is required by a vast majority of CD-ROM products. Obtaining MSCDEX is not a problem; it is generally provided on the same disk containing the CD-ROM's LL device driver. New versions of MSCDEX can be obtained from the Microsoft Download BBS, the Microsoft forum on CompuServe (GO MSL-1), or the Microsoft Web site at *www.microsoft.com*.

CD-ROM Drive Troubleshooting

This section covers CD-ROM drive problems and solutions for resolving them.

Symptom 2.82. The drive has trouble accepting or rejecting a CD. This problem is typical of motorized CD-ROM drives where the disc is accepted into a slot or placed in a motorized tray. Here are some possible solutions:

- *Try the tray manually.* Turn off the PC, eject the tray manually, and gently slide the tray back and forth to see if there are any obstructions. If the tray slides smoothly, the load/unload motor may be failing, so replace the CD-ROM drive. Remember to update your LL driver when installing a new CD-ROM model.

- *Check for obstructions.* If the tray feels stuck or jammed, open the mechanism and check for obstructions in the mechanics.

- *Replace the drive.* If you cannot find any obstructions, replace the CD-ROM drive.

Symptom 2.83. The optical head does not seek. The optical head must move very slowly and smoothly to ensure accurate tracking. DOS may report this as a drive failure or an `error reading from drive x` problem. The head is either jammed or the linear motor has failed. The following checks can narrow down the problem:

- *Check for obstructions.* Inspect the linear motor rails and see if any foreign matter is interfering with the travel of your optical head. Also remove any foreign matter.

- *Replace the CD-ROM drive.* If problems persist, replace the drive outright. Remember to update your LL driver when installing a new CD-ROM model.

Symptom 2.84. The disc does not turn. This is almost always a problem with the CD-ROM drive itself (the spindle motor fails). Thus, perform the following checks:

- *Check the disc itself.* Make sure the disk is seated properly and is not jammed or obstructed.

- *Check the power connector.* Make sure the four-pin power connector is inserted properly and completely. If the drive is being powered by a Y-connector, make sure any interim connections are secure. Use a voltmeter and measure the +5 volt (pin 4) and +12 volt (pin 1) levels, as shown in Table 1.3. If either voltage (especially the +12 volt supply) is unusually low or absent, replace the power supply.

- *Check the signal connector.* Make sure the drive's signal interface cable is connected securely at both the drive and controller. If the cable is visibly worn or damaged, try a new one.

- *Replace the drive.* If problems persist, try replacing the CD-ROM drive.

Symptom 2.85. The optical head cannot focus its laser beam. This may often manifest itself as DOS error messages indicating that the disc cannot be read, is not ready, and so on. In almost all cases, the drive has failed and the following checks will help spot the problem:

- *Check the compact disc.* Make sure the CD is the proper format (you can't start a program from an audio CD) and see that it is physically clean. Try a reliable CD.

- *Dust the optical head.* Dust can obstruct the optical head. Try lightly dusting the optical head with photography-grade compressed air.

- *Replace the drive.* If problems persist, try replacing the CD-ROM drive.

Symptom 2.86. No audio is being generated by the drive.
Audio CDs can often be played in available CD-ROM
drives through headphones or speakers. The following
areas will probably be where the problem lies:

- *Check the compact disc.* Make sure that the CD is
  an audio CD or contains at least one audio track.

- *Test the front jack.* Plug headphones and speakers
  into the CD-ROM audio jack, start your CD player
  application, and see that audio is being generated.
  You may need to adjust the front volume control.

- *Replace the drive.* If problems persist, try replacing the CD-ROM drive.

**Symptom 2.87. You cannot access the CD-ROM drive letter
in the real mode.** You may see an error message such
as `Invalid drive specification`. This is typically
a problem with the real-mode CD-ROM drivers. The following checks will help resolve the problem:

- *Check the CD-ROM drivers.* Run the `DOS MEM /C`
  command and check the detailed report for both the
  LL CD-ROM driver and MSCDEX. If either driver is
  missing, it did not load. Make sure that the
  command-line switches for your LL CD-ROM driver
  and MSCDEX match.

- *Check your version of MSCDEX.* You may need to
  use SETVER or update your version of MSCDEX.

- *Check the power connector.* Make sure the four-pin
  power connector is inserted properly and completely.
  If the drive is being powered by a Y-connector, make
  sure any interim connections are secure. Use a voltmeter and measure the +5 volt (pin 4) and +12 volt
  (pin 1) levels, as shown in Table 1.3. If either voltage
  (especially the +12 volt supply) is unusually low or
  absent, replace the power supply.

- *Check the signal connector.*   Make sure the drive's signal interface cable is connected securely at both the drive and controller. If the cable is visibly worn or damaged, try a new one.

- *Replace the drive.*   If problems persist, try replacing the CD-ROM drive.

Symptom 2.88. You see an error message when trying to load the LL CD-ROM driver.   This is usually the result of a real-mode driver mismatch or drive adapter failure. The following checks will tell you for sure:

- *Check the driver version.*   Make sure that you are using the proper LL device driver for your CD-ROM drive. If you're swapping the drive or adapter board, you probably need to load a new driver. The driver file may also be corrupted, so try reinstalling the driver.

- *Check the signal connector.*   Make sure the drive's signal interface cable is connected securely at both the drive and controller. If the cable is visibly worn or damaged, try a new one.

- *Replace the drive adapter.*   If problems persist, chances are that the drive adapter has failed. Try a reliable adapter. Keep in mind that many CD-ROM drives use the adapter integrated into the system's sound card.

- *Replace the drive.*   If problems persist, try replacing the CD-ROM drive.

Symptom 2.89. The CD-ROM drivers will not install properly on a drive using compression software.   This is usually because you booted from a floppy disk and attempted to install drivers without loading the compression software first. Check the loading order. Allow your system to boot from the hard drive before installing the drivers. This enables the compression software to assign all drive letters. Alternately, you can boot from a compression-aware floppy disk. If you must boot the system from a floppy disk, make sure the diskette is configured to be fully compatible with the compression software being used.

Symptom 2.90. You see an error message indicating that the CD-ROM drive is not found. This type of problem may also appear as loading problems with the LL driver, so make the following checks:

- *Check the power connector.* Make sure the 4-pin power connector is inserted properly and completely. If the drive is being powered by a Y-connector, make sure any interim connections are secure. Use a voltmeter and measure the +5 volt (pin 4) and +12 volt (pin 1) levels, as shown in Table 1.3. If either voltage (especially the +12 volt supply) is unusually low or absent, replace the power supply.

- *Check the signal connector.* Make sure the drive's signal interface cable is connected securely at both the drive and controller. If the cable is visibly worn or damaged, try a new one.

- *Check the drive adapter.* Make sure that the adapter's IRQ, DMA, and I/O address settings are correct, and that they match with the command line switches used with the low-level driver. If the adapter is for a CD-ROM alone, you may also try installing the adapter in a different bus slot.

- *Check the SCSI termination.* If your CD-ROM uses a SCSI interface, make sure that the SCSI bus is properly terminated at both ends.

- *Replace the drive adapter.* If problems persist, replace the drive adapter.

Symptom 2.91. After installing the CD-ROM driver software, the system reports significantly less available RAM. This is usually a caching issue with CD-ROM driver software, which would need to be adjusted. This type of problem has been documented with Teac CD-ROM drives and

CORELCDX.COM software. If the software offers a command-line switch to change the amount of XMS allocated, reduce the number to 512 or 256. Check with tech support for your particular drive for the exact command-line switch settings.

Symptom 2.92. In a new installation, the driver fails to load successfully for the proprietary interface card. In almost all cases, the interface card has been configured improperly and the following steps will help solve this problem:

■ *Check the drive adapter.* Make sure that the drive adapter is configured with the correct IRQ, DMA, and I/O address settings. In some cases, you may simply enter the drive maker (Teac) as the interface type. Make sure that the interface is set properly for the system and your particular drive.

■ *Check the driver.* Also make sure that the driver's command-line switches correctly reflect the drive adapter's configuration.

Symptom 2.93. You are having trouble setting up more than one CD-ROM drive. You must be concerned about hardware and software issues and must make the following checks:

■ *Check the drive adapter.* Make sure that the drive adapter will support more than one CD-ROM on the same channel. If not, you will have to install another drive adapter to support the new CD-ROM drive.

■ *Check the LL drivers.* You will need to have one copy of an LL driver loaded in CONFIG.SYS, one for each drive. Make sure that the command-line switches for each driver match the hardware settings of the corresponding drive adapter.

■ *Check MSCDEX.* You need only one copy of MSCDEX in AUTOEXEC.BAT, but the /D: switch must appear twice, once for each drive ID.

Symptom 2.94. Your CD-ROM drive refuses to work with an IDE port. It may very well be that the drive uses a non-standard port (other than IDE). You must connect the CD-ROM drive to a compatible drive adapter. If the drive is proprietary, it will not interface to an IDE port. It may be necessary to purchase a drive adapter specifically for the CD-ROM drive.

Symptom 2.95. You cannot get the CD-ROM drive to run properly when mounted vertically. CD-ROM drives with open drive trays cannot be mounted vertically; disc tracking simply will not work correctly. The only CD-ROM drives that can be mounted vertically are those with caddies, but you should check with those manufacturers before proceeding with vertical mounting.

Symptom 2.96. The LCD on your CD-ROM displays an error code. Even without knowing the particular meaning of every possible error message, you can be assured that most CD-based error messages can be traced to the following causes (in order of ease):

- *Bad caddy.* The CD caddy is damaged or inserted incorrectly. The CD may also be inserted into the caddy improperly.

- *Bad mounting.* The drive is mounted improperly or mounting screws are shorting out the drive's electronics.

- *Bad power.* Check the +12 and +5 volts powering the CD-ROM drive. Low power may require a new or larger supply.

- *Bad drive.* Internal diagnostics have detected a fault in the CD-ROM drive. Try replacing the drive.

- *Bad drive controller.* Drive diagnostics have detected a fault in the drive controller. Try replacing the drive controller.

Symptom 2.97. When a SCSI CD-ROM drive is connected to a SCSI adapter, the system hangs when the SCSI BIOS starts.   In most cases, the CD-ROM drive supports plug-and-play, but the SCSI controller's BIOS does not. Disable the BIOS through a jumper on the controller (or remove the SCSI BIOS IC entirely) and use a SCSI driver in CONFIG.SYS instead. You may need to download a LL SCSI driver from the adapter manufacturer.

Symptom 2.98. You see an error message such as "Unable to detect ATAPI IDE CD-ROM drive, device driver not loaded."   You have a problem with the configuration of your IDE/EIDE controller hardware, so make the following checks:

- *Check the signal cable.*   Make sure that the 40-pin signal cable is attached properly between the drive and controller.

- *Check your controller configuration.*   IDE CD-ROM drives are typically installed on a secondary 40-pin IDE port. Make sure that no device in the system is using the same IRQ or I/O address as your secondary IDE port.

- *Check the LL driver.*   Make sure that any command-line switches for the LL driver in CONFIG.SYS correspond to the controller's hardware settings.

Symptom 2.99. The CD-ROM drive door will not open once the 40-pin IDE signal cable is connected.   You should only need power to operate the drive door. If the door stops when the signal cable is attached, some possible problems must be checked:

- *Check the power connector.*   Make sure that both +5 and +12 volts are available at the power connector, and see that the power connector is attached securely to the back of the CD-ROM drive.

■ *Check the signal cable.*   The 40-pin signal cable is probably reversed at either the drive or controller. Try a different signal cable.

■ *Check the controller type.*   Make sure that the 40-pin IDE drive is plugged into an IDE port, not a proprietary (non-IDE) port.

■ *Replace the drive.*   Try a reliable CD-ROM drive.

Symptom 2.100. The CD-ROM drive will not read or run CD Plus or Enhanced CD titles.   This is a known problem with Acer CD-ROM models 625A, 645A, 655A, 665A, 525E, 743E, 747E, and 767E. The CD Plus (or Enhanced CD) titles use a non-standard data format released and supported by Sony. The new format is for interactive CD titles that incorporate video clips and music, and the data structures on these CDs cannot be recognized by these CD-ROM drive models. In this case, you'll need to upgrade the CD-ROM drive outright to a newer model that can accommodate newer file types.

Symptom 2.101. You notice that the LED indicator on the CD-ROM is always on.   The drive seems to be working properly. This is not necessarily a problem. Some CD-ROM drive models (such as the Acer 600 series) use the LED indicator as a Ready light instead of as a Busy light. Whenever a CD is loaded in the drive, the LED will be lit and will remain lit whether the drive is being accessed or not. This feature tells the user whether or not a CD-ROM disc is currently loaded in the drive by simply checking the LED. There may be a jumper on the CD-ROM drive that enables you to switch the indicator light from Ready mode to Busy mode.

Symptom 2.102. The system locks up when using a Panasonic Big 5 CD-ROM drive under Windows 95. This trouble is known to occur if you're using IDE bus-mastering drivers with the Panasonic Big 5 five-disc

CD-ROM changer (model SQ-TC510N). The Panasonic drive will require new firmware to overcome this problem, so contact Panasonic to update the device with the latest firmware revision. To avoid this problem in the mean time, remove the CD-ROM changer from your system.

CD-ROM Drives and Windows 95/98

The following section will cover problems related to CD-ROM drives in Windows 95/98 systems.

Symptom 2.103. The front panel controls of your SCSI CD-ROM drive do not appear to work under Windows 95. Those same controls appear to work fine in DOS. Windows 95 uses SCSI commands to poll removable media devices every two seconds in order to see if there has been a change in status. Since SCSI commands to the CD-ROM generally have higher priority than front panel controls, the front panel controls will appear to be disabled under Windows 95. Try pressing the front panel controls repeatedly.

Symptom 2.104. You cannot change the CD-ROM drive letter under Windows 95. You need to change the drive's settings under the Device Manager:

1. Open the Control Panel and select the System icon.

2. Once the System Properties dialog opens, click on the Device Manager page.

3. Locate the entry for the CD-ROM. Click on the + sign to expand the list of CD-ROM devices.

4. Double-click on the desired CD-ROM.

5. Once the CD-ROM drive's Properties dialog appears, choose the Settings page.

6. Locate the current drive letter assignment box and enter the new drive designation. Multiple letters are needed only when a SCSI device is implementing LUN addressing (that is, multidisc changers).

7. Click on the OK button to save your changes.

8. Click on the OK button to close the Device Manager.

9. A System Settings Change window should appear. Click on the Yes button to reboot the system so that the changes can take affect, or click on the No button so that you can make more changes to other CD-ROMs before rebooting system. Changes will not become effective until the system is rebooted.

Symptom 2.105. You installed Windows 95 from a CD-ROM disc using DOS drivers, but when you removed the real-mode CD-ROM drivers from CONFIG.SYS, the CD-ROM no longer works.   You need to enable protected-mode drivers by running the Add New Hardware wizard from the Control Panel.

Symptom 2.106. You see a message stating that the "CD-ROM can run, but results may not be as expected."   This simply means that Windows 95 is using real-mode drivers. If protected-mode drivers are available for the CD-ROM drive, you should use those instead.

Symptom 2.107. You cannot play CD audio on a particular CD-ROM under Windows 95.   Replacing the CD-ROM resolves the problem. This is a known incompatibility issue with Acer 525E CD-ROM drives and Windows 95 (this does not affect the integrity of programs and data). Windows 95 will mute the CD audio on this and many other brands of double-speed IDE CD-ROMs. If you cannot obtain a patch directly from Microsoft or the CD-ROM manufacturer, your only real alternative is to replace the CD-ROM drive.

Symptom 2.108. After upgrading to Windows 98, you notice multiple CD-ROM letters.   You may see up to four CD-ROM drives displayed in My Computer and/or Windows Explorer, even though you have only one CD-ROM drive in the computer. This problem is known to occur with NEC 4X4, 4X6, 4X8, or 4X16 CD-ROM drives if you've installed the NEC Single CD tool in your previous version of Windows. To correct the problem, simply reinstall the tool under Windows 98 using the disk included with your NEC 4X CD-ROM drive. You may also want to download and install the latest versions of that software (and the CD-ROM drivers).

Symptom 2.109. After upgrading to Windows 98, you encounter problems with the CD-ROM and hard drive.   Once the upgrade to Windows 98 is complete, you cannot access your CD-ROM drive, hard disks connected to the IDE-type controller are forced to use DOS Compatibility Mode, or another drive appears in My Computer and/or Windows Explorer that is about 13 MB in size. This is a known problem when Helix Hurricane for Windows 95 (by Helix Software) is installed on your computer. To correct this issue, you'll need to remove Hurricane using its Uninstall tool (you may be able to patch or update Hurricane, but you'll need to contact the program manufacturer). Restart your computer and use the Startup menu to boot to the Windows 98 Safe Mode Command Prompt Only. Run the Uninstall tool in the folder where Hurricane is installed.

Symptom 2.110. Your SmartCD Manager software does not work under Windows 98.   After upgrading to Windows 98, you may find that your Torisan (Sanyo) three-disc CD-ROM drive now has three separate drive letters assigned to it. This problem may occur even though the SmartCD Manager program has assigned only one drive letter to this device. The problem occurs because Windows 98 replaces the CDVSD.VXD and TORISAN3.

VXD files included with the SmartCD Manager program. The updated versions of these files are not compatible with your SmartCD Manager software. To correct this problem, simply reinstall the SmartCD Manager program.

Symptom 2.111. The auto insert notification feature prevents a system's automatic suspend modes from working. Many current computers include power management features that place the computer in a "suspended power state" (a "power-down mode") after a given period of inactivity. Thus, make the following checks:

- *Check the auto insert notification.* If the auto insert notification option is enabled for IDE-type CD-ROM drives when power management is also enabled, the computer may not suspend automatically. This typically occurs because some IDE-type CD-ROM drives use the ATA GET MEDIA STATUS command method for polling, but a power management system will detect the action as drive activity. Since a drive then appears to be in use, the power management system will not power-down the system (this is a known issue with Windows 95 OSR2). You can work around this issue by disabling the auto insert notification option for affected drives.

- *Update necessary files.* As a more permanent fix, you may also download and install the file REMIDEUP.EXE from Microsoft's Web site. This update will install the file update, ESDI_506.PDR version 4.00.956 (dated 5/14/96). Of course, later versions of the file should also work.

Symptom 2.112. The computer locks up while browsing a CD-ROM. This often occurs under Windows 95/98 after installing a Hewlett-Packard CD-RW drive in some Compaq Deskpro computers. Your computer may halt when you try to use My Computer or Windows Explorer to view the CD-RW drive. In most circumstances, this type of problem is driver-related. When dealing with Compaq systems, Compaq uses a custom device driver file named CPQDFVS.VXD. This file is located in the \Windows\System\Iosubsys folder and can lock up the computer when you try to read from the CD-RW drive. To work around this problem for the Compaq, delete or rename the CPQDFVS.VXD file. To correct this issue on a more permanent basis, contact Compaq for a patch or update to the CPQDFVS.VXD file.

Symptom 2.113. You cannot read Rock Ridge CD-ROM extensions under Windows. This occurs because Windows 95 and 98 are simply not designed to support the Rock Ridge CD-ROM extensions. Rock Ridge is a means of storing POSIX file system extensions on a CD-ROM, but Windows 95/98 uses the Joliet file system (which enables deep subdirectories and long file names) instead of the Rock Ridge CD-ROM format. If you need to read Rock Ridge-formatted CD-ROMs in Windows 95/98, configure real-mode driver support for the CD-ROM using the Windows 95/98 version of MSCDEX.EXE in AUTOEXEC.BAT and the DOS device drivers (provided by the CD-ROM drive manufacturer) in CONFIG.SYS.

Symptom 2.114. You cannot access a CD-ROM drive under Windows 95/98. When you try to access your CD-ROM drive in Windows, you cannot run executable (.EXE) files, you cannot view complete directory listings, or you get a `Device not found` error message. These problems will develop if you're using an older version of the MSCDEX.EXE file that is not compatible with Windows 95/98. This commonly occurs when you install certain real-mode CD-ROM drivers; an older version of the MSCDEX.EXE file is copied to the hard disk, and the AUTOEXEC.BAT file is updated to utilize this older file. Modify the AUTOEXEC.BAT file manually to address the correct version of MSCDEX.EXE:

Symptom 2.115. A Sony CD-ROM drive is not detected during Windows 95/98 Setup. This problem can occur when the Sony CD-ROM drive is attached to a Media Vision sound card. Setup will search for Sony CD-ROM drives at several base I/O addresses, but a Sony CD-ROM drive attached to a Media Vision sound card is not in the range of addresses that Setup checks. As a result, Setup retains the existing real-mode drivers for the CD-ROM drive, but this often reduces system performance. You can get around this problem by setting up the Sony CD-ROM drive in Windows manually.

Symptom 2.116. The system locks up while copying data from the CD-ROM under Windows 95/98. When you are copying a large directory structure from a CD-ROM drive to a local hard disk, your computer may lock up (forcing you to reboot). This problem is typically caused by the CD-ROM *read-ahead* feature. The feature can cause the CD-ROM drive controller to be driven faster than it was designed to be. To prevent this problem, reduce the read-ahead caching level for your CD-ROM.

Symptom 2.117. Two CD-ROM drive letters appear in My Computer under Windows 95/98. When you use My Computer or Windows Explorer, two CD-ROM drives may be displayed (even though you have only one CD-ROM drive in your computer). When you try to access either CD-ROM drive, your computer may lock up. This trouble can occur if you have both the real-mode CD-ROM device drivers and the Windows 95/98 CD-ROM device drivers installed. To resolve this problem, use the System Configuration Editor (SYSEDIT.EXE) to disable the real-mode CD-ROM device drivers.

Symptom 2.118. The CD-ROM refuses to run automatically under Windows 95/98 when a disc is inserted.   This may occur even when the auto insert notification feature is enabled. In most cases, the trouble is caused by an incorrect value in the registry. To resolve this problem, use Registry Editor to locate the following key:

```
HKEY_CURRENT_USER\Software\Microsoft\Windows\
CurrentVersion\Policies\Explorer\
NoDriveTypeAutoRun
```

Then modify the value for the NoDriveTypeAutoRun key to 0000 95 00 00 00 (or 0x95 in REGEDT32.EXE). After you make this change, quit the Registry Editor and restart your computer.

Symptom 2.119. A CD-ROM icon appears for a hard drive under Windows 95 OSR2 or Windows 98.   When you attempt to review your drives through My Computer, your hard disk icon may appear as a CD-ROM icon. If you double-click the CD-ROM icon in My Computer, you may receive an error message such as `Cannot find autorun.exe`. This problem can occur if the AUTORUN.INF file has been located in the root folder of your hard disk. To correct the problem, rename the AUTORUN.INF file to AUTORUN.OLD.

Symptom 2.120. You receive an error such as "CD-ROM cache acceleration file is invalid" under Windows 98. This kind of problem is typically encountered when using Quarterdeck SpeedyROM version 1.0 under Windows 98. Also, even though SpeedyROM may offer to reconstruct this file, you may continue to receive the same error message whenever you restart your computer. This trouble is generally caused when your computer's BIOS is configured to use a Fast Reboot feature. To correct this issue, disable the Fast Reboot feature in your computer's CMOS Setup.

NOTE: Your BIOS may use a term other than Fast Reboot to identify the feature, so refer to your system's documentation for more CMOS Setup details.

CD-R Drives

CD-Rs present some special problems for the typical PC. Many high-performance CD-R units use the SCSI interface in order to handle a more consistent data transfer from the system to the drive. Installing a CD-R may require the addition (and expense) of a SCSI host adapter and associated driver software. CD recording demands a substantial commitment of hard drive space, perhaps as much as one GB, in order to create an image file for recording (an image file basically converts the data to be recorded into the "pits" and "lands" that must be encoded to the blank disc). So if you're tight on drive space, you may also need another hard drive to support the CD-R. Finally, CD-Rs require a constant and uninterrupted flow of data during the recording process. If the CD-R data buffer empties, the recording process will halt, and your blank CD will be ruined. This means you'll need fast hard drives and a high-performance interface (PIO Mode 4 or UDMA). This part of the chapter explains some problems associated with installing and using a CD-R, and illustrates a series of troubleshooting symptoms and solutions.

CD Recording Issues

Writing data to a recordable CD is a complex process that demands a relatively great deal from your PC's hardware and software. Most of this complexity is hidden by the power of the CD authoring program, but you should be aware of a number of important factors that can influence the success of CD recording. This part of the chapter covers the principle issues involved in CD recording.

File Sizes.   The sheer amount of data being written to the CD is less important than the individual file sizes. The recorder may have trouble locating and opening small files quickly enough to send them smoothly to the CD-R where fewer large files are typically problem-free.

System Interruptions.   Any interruption in the flow of data is fatal to CD recording, so make sure that your CONFIG.SYS and AUTOEXEC.BAT files do not load any TSR utilities that may periodically interrupt the computer's drive operations. Utilities like screen savers, calendar alarms or reminders, and incoming faxes are just a few features that will interrupt disc writing. If the PC is part of a network, you should temporarily disable network sharing so that no one tries to access the files you're trying to write to the CD.

The Hard Disk.   The hard drive is a critical component of the CD-R system because you must transfer data from the HDD to the CD-R at a rate adequate to keep the recorder's buffer filled. Three major issues must be considered when dealing with your hard drive:

- *Speed.*   In order to write a virtual image file to a compact disc, the hard disk from which you are writing must have a transfer rate fast enough to keep the CD-R drive buffer full. This usually means an average hard disk access time of 19 milliseconds or less. It would also help to use a high-performance drive interface such as Ultra-DMA/33, Ultra-DMA/66, or SCSI-3.

- *Fragmentation.*   This issue is also related to speed. Searching all over a very fragmented hard disk for image file data can cause drive operations to slow down. In many cases, a badly fragmented hard drive cannot support CD-R operations. Be sure to defragment your hard drive before creating an image file.

- *Thermal calibration.* All hard disks periodically perform an automatic thermal calibration to ensure proper performance. Calibration interrupts hard disk operations for as much as 1.5 seconds. Some hard disks force a calibration at fixed intervals (even if the disk is in use), causing interruptions that are fatal to CD writing. This problem is worse when the image file is large, and the writing process takes longer. If you can select a new hard drive to support CD-R operations, choose a drive with intelligent thermal calibration (it postpones recalibration until the drive is idle).

CD-R Speed. Typical CD-Rs are capable of writing at two or four times the standard writing/playback speed of 150 KB/s (75 sectors/s). Recording speed is simply a matter of how fast the bits are inscribed by the laser on the disc surface. It has nothing to do with how fast you read them back or how much data you can fit on the disc. However, higher recording speeds can accomplish a writing process in a shorter period of time. Faster recording speeds are certainly a time saver, but it also means that larger recording buffers are required (and those buffers empty faster). As a consequence, faster recorders will demand a faster hard drive and interface to support data transfers. In most cases, buffer underrun type problems can often be corrected by slowing down the recording process rather than upgrading the drive system.

When you write a real ISO image file from a hard disk to CD, speed is rarely a problem because the image is already one gigantic file. The files and structures are already in order and divided into CD-ROM sectors, so it is only necessary to stream data off the hard drive to the CD-R. When you write from a virtual image, things get trickier because a virtual image is little more than a list. The CD authoring program must consult the virtual image database to find out where each file should go in the image and where each file is actually is stored on a hard disk. The authoring software must then open the file and divide it into CD-ROM sectors, all while sending data to the CD-R in a smooth, continuous stream. Locating and opening each file is often the more time-consuming part of the recording process (which is why on-the-fly writing is more difficult when you have many small files).

CD-R Buffer. All CD-Rs have a small amount of on-board buffer memory. The CD-R's buffer helps to ensure that there is always data ready to be written because extra data is stored as it arrives from the computer. The size of the buffer is critical to trouble-free writing. A slow-down or interruption in the transfer of data from the computer will not interrupt writing so long as the buffer is not completely emptied. The larger the buffer, the more safety margin you have in case of interruptions. If your CD-R has a small buffer and your hard disk is slow, you may find it difficult (or impossible) to write virtual images on the fly to CD. When this occurs, you can make a real ISO image file on the hard disk and record to CD from that, use a faster hard disk subsystem, or upgrade your CD-R's buffer (if possible).

> **NOTE**: If you want to write a virtual image on the fly to CD and you have a slow hard disk, it is generally safest to write at 1X speed. Otherwise, create a real ISO image file first and record from that. In most situations where your hardware configuration is adequate (a fast, defragmented hard disk, a few small files, and a good-sized CD-R buffer), you can successfully write virtual images straight to CD. However, it's always best to test first and create a real ISO image file only if necessary.

Typical Compatibility Problems

Even when CDs record perfectly, it is not always possible to read them correctly in other drives. The following notes highlight three common compatibility issues.

Problems Reading Recordable CDs. Recordable CDs frequently cannot be read in older CD-ROM drives. If the CD can be read when used on the CD-R but *not* on a standard CD-ROM drive, check the disc recording utility to make sure that the session containing the data you just wrote is closed. CD-ROM drives cannot read data from a session that is not closed.

If your recorded disc is ejected, if you receive an error message, or if you have any random problems accessing files from the recorded disc, the problem may be that your CD-ROM drive is not well calibrated to read recorded CDs. Try the disc on another CD-ROM drive, or upgrade the CD-ROM drive itself.

If you recorded the disc using DOS filenames, but you experience difficulties in reading back the recorded CD with DOS or Windows, it may be that you have an older version of MSCDEX (before version 2.23) on your system. Check your MSCDEX version and update it if necessary.

Problems Reading Multisession CDs. If you can only see data recorded in the first session on the CD but not in subsequent sessions, it may be that the disc was recorded in CD-ROM (Mode 1) format, while your multisession CD-ROM drive only recognizes CD-ROM XA (Mode 2) multisession CDs. If this happens, you may need to rerecord the disc in the correct mode. Of course, your CD-ROM drive must support multisession operations in the first place. If you can only see data recorded in the last session, you may have forgotten to link your new data with data previously recorded on the CD. Refer to the instructions for your CD-R and review the suggested steps required to create a multisession CD.

CD-ROM Drive Incompatibility with Recordable CDs. It may seem that you write a CD without trouble and can read it properly on your CD-R, but when you put the disc in a standard CD-ROM drive, the disc is ejected. You may also see error messages such as `No CD-ROM` or `Drive not ready`, or you have random problems accessing some files or directories. You may also find that the problems disappear when reading the CD on a different CD-ROM drive.

At first, you may suspect a problem with the original CD-ROM drive, but this may be due to compatibility problems with some CD-ROM drives (especially older ones) and recorded CDs. Some CD-ROM drive lasers are not calibrated to read recordable CDs (often the surface is different from that of factory-pressed CDs). If your CD-ROM drive reads mass-produced (silver) CDs but not recordable CDs, check with the CD-ROM drive manufacturer to determine whether this is the problem. In some cases, a drive upgrade may be available that will resolve the problem.

> **NOTE**:   The combination of a blank disc brand and a CD-R can also make a difference. Use blank CD media that has been recommended by the CD-R manufacturer.

Typical Multisession CD Issues

You may encounter older CD-ROM drives that have trouble reading multisession CDs. Multisession discs are recorded according to the Orange Book (Part II) standard that states that sessions can be written in either the CD-ROM or CD-ROM XA format. A fully compliant multisession CD-ROM drive should always be able to access at the LAST session on a disc *regardless* of its format.

Unfortunately, there have been misunderstandings and misinterpretations of the Orange Book standard, but to understand the problem, you need to know a bit of history. Multisession recording was first used by Kodak for their Photo CD initiative. Now one roll of film does not fill up a Photo CD disc, so when you take your disc and a new roll of film for new Photo CD processing, the new photos are added in a new session.

This new session is linked to previous sessions so that you can see all the photos on the disc no matter how many sessions they are recorded in.

Kodak chose the CD-ROM XA standard for its Photo CD disc format for reasons that had nothing to do with the Orange Book standard. But since Photo CD was the first reason that CD-ROM drive manufacturers had to create multisession drives, many assumed that the Kodak approach to multisession (CD-ROM XA) was the only way. They accordingly wrote software drivers that assume a multisession disc must also be XA. When one of these drivers sees a disc that is not XA, it assumes that the disc is also not multisession-capable, and it tells the CD-ROM drive to read only the first session on the disc. The result is that a multisession disc is read as if it were a single-session disc, and you see only the data in the first session.

CD-ROM drive manufacturers have generally resolved this glitch in newer drives and drivers (8X CD-ROM and later drives). But if you record a multi-session disc in CD-ROM format, you may find that some older drives, even if specified as a multisession drive, may not read beyond the first session on the disc. If you need to share multisession discs with others, you should test to see which format their CD-ROM drives can handle. To be on the safe side, write your disc in the CD-ROM XA format. A more permanent fix is to upgrade the older CD-ROM to a model that is fully multisession-compliant.

> **NOTE**: You cannot mix formats on the same disc. A multisession disc containing both CD-ROM and CD-ROM XA sessions would be unreadable on most drives.

Buffer Underruns

CD writing is a real-time process that must run constantly at the selected recording speed without interruptions. Most of the time, your computer will pass data to the CD-R faster than it is needed. This keeps

CD-R's buffer constantly filled with a reserve of data waiting to be written, so small slowdowns or interruptions in the flow of data from the computer will not interrupt the writing process. The CD-R's internal buffer stores this extra data as it arrives to help maintain a steady flow of data to the writing laser.

The size of the buffer is critical to trouble-free writing. Remember that a slowdown or interruption in the transfer of data from the computer will not stop a writing cycle so long as the buffer is not *completely* emptied. The larger the buffer, the more safety margin you have in case of interruptions. A *buffer underrun* error means that for some reason the flow of data from the hard disk to the CD-R was interrupted long enough for the CD-R's buffer to be emptied, and writing was halted. If this occurs during an actual write operation (rather than a pre-writing test), your recordable disc may be ruined. The following checklist covers many of the typical issues that may trigger a buffer underrun.

Hard Disk Issues. The problems that typically affect hard disks are as follows:

- *"Dumb" thermal recalibration.* Disable thermal recalibration on the drive before writing or enable one hour or so for the system temperature to stabilize before writing.

- *Excessive file fragmentation.* Defragment the drive with Defrag before burning a CD.

- *Insufficient free space.* The CD-R will almost certainly require some amount of temporary workspace on the hard drive. If insufficient free space is on the hard drive, you may need to free additional space by offloading unneeded files or upgrading the drive itself.

- *Too many small files.* When recording on the fly, many small files may present too much of a load on your data transfer system, so try making an ISO image file first.

- *Damaged files.* Files that are damaged or corrupted will often cause errors that will interrupt the flow of data. Run ScanDisk and Defrag to locate any possible file system problems before recording.

- *Recording files in use.* Make sure that no files to be recorded are currently in use by any application.

Hardware Issues. Typcial hardware problems consist of the following issues:

- *Slow hard drives.* Older hard drives may not support data transfer speeds high enough to keep the CD-R buffer filled. If you use slow hard drives, make an ISO image file first rather than writing on the fly.

- *Burst data transfers.* Source devices that operate in burst data transfer modes may have difficulty keeping the CD-R buffer filled. Try disabling the burst mode. This may slow the overall data transfer but may even out the flow of data, making it easier to keep the buffer filled.

- *CD-R controller configuration.* Verify that the IDE or SCSI controller operating the CD-R is configured for optimum performance (use bus master drivers for IDE controllers).

- *Sync problems.* Certain combinations of drives and controllers may not synchronize data properly. Check that you're using the recommended hardware devices for proper CD-R operations.

- *Outdated device drivers.* Verify that you're using the latest device drivers for the CD-R, controller, and other related devices in the system.

- *Slow computer speed.* Systems older than 486 platforms may simply be too old to support the data transfer needs of a CD-R. Verify that your system meets the minimum system requirements for your particular CD-R model.

- *CD-R quality.* Be sure to use good-quality CD-R discs that are recommended by the CD-R manufacturer. Dirty, old, or scratched discs may not function.

Memory-Resident Software Issues. CD-R systems may encounter buffer underrun problems when the following types of software are at work on your system. You may want to systematically disable the following software types:

- Anti-virus software
- Screen saver software
- System agent software
- Scheduler software
- TSR software
- Network software
- System sounds
- Animated icons or utilities
- Any program that may activate on its own

Windows 95/98 Issues. The following are some Windows 95/98 problems to watch for:

- *Insufficient virtual memory.* Adjust your Virtual Memory settings to use at least 32 MB of RAM for virtual memory.

- *Disable "auto insert notification."* If you have more than 16 MB of RAM, disable Auto Insert Notification for the CD-ROM.

- *Change the system's role.* If you have more than 16 MB of RAM, change the hard drive's Typical Role to Network Server.

Tips to Avoid Buffer Underruns

- Always set audio discs to write at 1X.

- Change the DMA transfer rate for the drive controller card being used (select the fastest data transfer rate available for your system and drives).

- Defragment your hard drives at least once a week to prevent files from being scattered across the hard drive.

- Disable or remove all software in the computer except the OS, the recording software, and the drivers for your source devices and CD-R.

- Disc-to-disc copying generally requires a SCSI-2, fully ASPI-compliant CD-ROM drive (at least 4X). Copying audio requires a source CD-ROM drive that supports digital audio extraction.

- Do not record across a network. Copy the desired files to your local hard drive first.

- Do not try to copy empty directories, zero-byte files, or files that may be in use by the system at the time.

- For best results, use SCSI-2 (or faster) source devices.

- In any OS, always use the newest drivers from your SCSI controller card manufacturer.

- Log out of any networks if possible (including Windows for Workgroups and/or Microsoft Network).

- Make sure your hard drive does Smart Thermal Recalibration. It won't recalibrate if the drive is being used.

- Make sure your SCSI controller card is fully ASPI-compliant.

- More than 10,000 very small files should be written to an .ISO image first or recorded at 1X if possible in order to ease data transfer demands.

- Record at a slower speed (2X rather than 4X).

- The temporary directory should always have free space at least twice the size of the largest file you are recording.

- Try a different hard disk and/or high-quality gold recordable disc.

- With DOS 6.22 or below and a source hard disk 1 GB or larger, partitions should be kept smaller than 1 GB so that the hard disk cluster size is 16 KB instead of 32 KB.

- Write an .ISO image to the hard disk first (if you have enough hard drive space).

CD-R Drive Troubleshooting

CD-Rs are subject to a large number of potential errors during operation. Many typical recording errors are listed next. In most cases, the error is not terribly complex and can be corrected in just a few minutes once the nature of the problem is understood. Keep in mind that the actual error message is dependent on the CD-R software in use, so your actual error messages may vary just a bit.

> **NOTE**:   For basic CD-ROM-related issues, refer to the CD-ROM troubleshooting information earlier in this chapter.

Symptom 2.121. Absorption control error <xxx>. This error most often means that there is a slight problem writing to a recordable disc, perhaps caused by a smear or speck of dust. It does not necessarily mean that your data has not been correctly recorded. A sector address is usually given so that you can (if you want) verify the data in and around that sector. When writing is completed, try cleaning the disc (on the non-label side) gently with a lint-free cloth. If the error occurs again, try a new disc.

Symptom 2.122. Application code error. This error typically occurs when you try to write Kodak recordable CDs (Photo CDs) on non-Kodak CD-Rs. These discs have a protection bit that is recognized only by the Kodak CD-R. All other recorders will not record these discs. In this case, you'll need to use standard blank CDs.

Symptom 2.123. Bad ASPI open. The CD-R ASPI driver is bad or missing, and the SCSI CD-R cannot be found. Check the installation of your CD-R drive and SCSI adapter, and then check the driver installation. Try reinstalling the SCSI driver(s).

Symptom 2.124. Buffer underrun at sector <xxx>. Once an image file is generated, CD writing is a real-time process that must run constantly at the selected recording speed without interruptions. The CD-R's buffer is constantly filled with data from the hard drive waiting to be written. This buffering action ensures that small slowdowns or interruptions in the flow of data from the computer do not interrupt the writing process. A buffer underrun message indicates that the flow of data from the hard disk to the CD-R was interrupted long enough for the CD-R's buffer to be emptied, and writing was halted. If this occurs during an actual write operation rather than a test, your CD may be damaged.

To avoid buffer underruns, you should remove as much processing load as possible from the system. For example, make sure that no screen savers or other TSR programs are active (they can momentarily interrupt operations). Close as many open windows as possible. See that your working hard disk cannot be accessed via a network.

For SCSI CD-R drives, the CD-R's position in the SCSI chain or the cable length between the computer and the CD-R may cause data slowdowns. Try connecting the CD-R as the first peripheral in the SCSI chain (if not done already) and use a shorter SCSI cable (if possible) between the CD-R and the SCSI host adapter.

Symptom 2.125. The current disc already contains a closed audio session.   Under the Red Book standard for audio CDs, all audio tracks must be written in a single session. If you add audio tracks in more than one session, playback results will be unpredictable. Most CD-ROM drives will playback all audio tracks on a CD even if they are recorded in several different sessions, but most home and car CD players can only playback the tracks in the first session. If you continue and record audio in a different session, you may have problems reading subsequent audio sessions.

Symptom 2.126. The current disc contains a session that is not closed.   In actual practice, CD-ROM drives can only read back one data track per session, so avoid recording another data track in an open session. Be sure to close the session before writing additional data to the disc.

Symptom 2.127. The currently selected source CD-ROM drive or CD-R cannot read audio in digital format.   This is more of a warning than a fault. Reading audio tracks in digital format is not the same as playing the music, and few CD-ROM drives can read audio tracks in digital format (only Red Book format). You may need to copy the music data from the CD to the hard drive first, and then post-process the digital audio data through the application used to make the new CD.

Symptom 2.128. Data overrun/underrun.   The SCSI host adapter has reported an error that is almost always caused by improper termination or a bad SCSI cable. Recheck the installation of your SCSI adapter, cabling, and termination. You may also need to reduce the processing overhead needed by unused applications. Refer to the "Buffer Underruns" section of this chapter for more details.

Symptom 2.129. The destination disc is smaller than the source disc. This error commonly occurs when you're trying to duplicate an existing CD to the CD-R. There is not enough room on the recordable CD to copy the source CD. Try recording to a blank CD-R disc. Use 74-minute media instead of 60-minute media. Some CDs cannot be copied due to the *Table of Contents* (TOC) overhead in CD-Rs and also due to the calibration zone overhead. You may need to break up the source CD between two or more different CD-R discs.

Symptom 2.130. The disc already contains tracks and/or sessions that are incompatible with the requested operation. This error appears if you are trying to add data in a format that is different from the data format already on the disc. For example, you'll see this type of error when trying to add a CD-ROM XA session to a disc that already contains a standard CD-ROM session. A disc containing multiple formats is unreadable, so you are not allowed to record the different session type.

Symptom 2.131. The disc is write-protected. You are attempting to write to a CD-R disc that has already been closed. Do not try writing to discs that are closed. Instead use a fresh blank disc for writing.

Symptom 2.132. Error 175-xx-xx-xx. This error code often indicates a buffer underrun. See the information about buffer underruns contained at the start of this CD-R section.

Symptom 2.133. Error 220-01-xx-xx. This error code often indicates that some of your software cannot communicate with a SCSI device, possibly because your

SCSI bus was reset. In many cases, this is caused by conflicts between real-mode and protected-mode SCSI drivers working in a Windows 95/98 system. Try REMming out any real-mode SCSI drivers in your file CONFIG.SYS (the protected-mode drivers provided for Windows 95/98 should be sufficient on their own). You may need to download and install updated protected-mode drivers for the SCSI host adapter and CD-R drive (as well as other SCSI devices that may be installed).

Symptom 2.134. Error 220-06-xx-xx. This error code often indicates a SCSI selection time-out error that suggests a SCSI setup problem, usually with the SCSI host adapter. Contact your SCSI host adapter manufacturer for detailed installation and testing instructions. You may need to adjust the SCSI BIOS Setup or update the SCSI drivers in your system.

Symptom 2.135. An error occurs reading the TOC or Program Memory Area (PMA) from the disc. This recordable disc is defective or has been damaged (probably during a previous write operation or the current write operation). Do not try and write to this disc. Unfortunately, you can do little here except to discard the defective disc. Try a fresh, good-quality disc instead.

Symptom 2.136. An invalid logical block address. This error message usually means that the CD mastering software has requested a data block from the hard disk that either does not exist or is illegal. This may suggest a corrupted hard disk or a damaged ISO file. Exit the CD mastering software and run ScanDisk and Defrag to check and reorganize your hard drive. You may need to rebuild an ISO file or reload damaged files from a backup.

Symptom 2.137. Last two blocks stripped. This message appears when copying a track to a hard disk if the track you are reading was created as multisession compliant (following the Orange Book standard). This is because a multisession track is always followed by two run-out blocks. These are included in the count of the total size (in blocks) of the track but do not contain data and cannot be read back. This message appears to alert you just in case you notice that you got two blocks fewer than were reported for the read length. Don't panic; you haven't lost any data.

Symptom 2.138. Read file error. A file referenced by the virtual image database cannot be located or accessed. Make sure that the suspect file is not being used by you or someone else on a network. The file may also be damaged or corrupt, so exit the CD-R application and run ScanDisk and Defrag to check the file system for problems. You may need to reload damaged files from a backup.

Symptom 2.139. The selected disc track is longer than the image file. The disc verify process fails immediately because the source ISO 9660 image file and the actual ISO 9660 track on the CD are not the same size. The disc track is actually longer than the image file and could indicate a defective CD-R drive. Retry the operation with a good-quality CD-R disc. If the problem persists, you might try replacing the CD-R drive.

Symptom 2.140. The selected disc track is shorter than the image file. The disc verify process fails immediately because the source ISO 9660 image file and the actual ISO 9660 track on the CD are not the same size. The disc track is actually shorter than the image file and could indicate a defective CD-R drive. Retry the operation with a good-quality CD-R disc. If the problem persists, you might try replacing the CD-R drive.

Symptom 2.141. Write emergency. This error occurs if the drive is interrupted during a write action. It is commonly seen when writing Red Book audio, but it can also occur with data recordings. For example, one typical reason for a write emergency is dust particles that cause the laser to jump off track. In most cases, the CD-R disc is ruined, and you'll need to retry the write process with a quality disc.

Symptom 2.142. You encounter buffer miscompare errors when using a SCSI host adapter diagnostic utility. In many cases, you likely have a DMA channel conflict with another card (or device) in the system. Check the settings of every card or device that uses an IRQ, DMA channel, or I/O port address, and compare these settings to the ones used for the SCSI host adapter. If there is a DMA conflict, change the DMA channel on the SCSI card to an unused channel.

Another possibility is that you're dealing with a motherboard that doesn't support bus mastering (not all PC's support bus mastering). For example, a Gateway 2000 P5-133 only has one bus mastering slot that is normally occupied by the video adapter. If the SCSI adapter (an Adaptec AHA-1535 card) is installed in a non-bus-mastering slot in this machine, the system may freeze when trying to access a CD from the CD-R drive. It may be necessary to upgrade the motherboard to access additional bus mastering slots.

Symptom 2.143. You cannot access a CD-R after upgrading to Windows 98. You may find this happens most frequently with Philips CDD200 or HO 4020I CD-R drives and is almost always due to problems with Corel CD Creator 2.0 being present on your system. Correcting this problem can be accomplished in two different ways. First, uninstall Corel CD Creator and install other CD authoring software (Adaptec Easy CD Creator Pro) that should be better able to support the CD-R drive. If you cannot replace the CD authoring software, check with the CD-R maker to see if a firmware upgrade is available for the CD-R drive.

Symptom 2.144. You receive an error when recording an audio track under four seconds.   If you try to record an audio track or .WAV file that is less than four seconds long, you will get a message indicating that a certain track cannot be written because it is less than four seconds long. Do not use .WAV files of less than four seconds. The audio standard for compact disc (red book) does not allow audio files of less than four seconds. Make the audio file longer and try recording it again.

CD-RW Drives

The ISO 9660 file system has long been the established standard in CD-ROM and CD recording (by comparison, Mac systems use the HFS approach). In fact, ISO 9660 is one of the key elements that propelled CD-ROM drives to the status of standard equipment on the PC by the early 1990s. With the broad introduction of CD-RW drives, however, ISO 9660 has been replaced by the *Universal Data Format* (UDF) file system. This part of the chapter offers some essential background on UDF and explains how the use of UDF affects the compatibility of CD-RW discs with existing CD-ROM and CD-RW drives.

Let's start with some perspective on ISO 9660. The ISO 9660 file system grew out of the original High Sierra file system of the late 1980s. All the files read on your CD-ROM or recorded on your CD-R use the ISO 9660 format. Both Windows and Mac OSs can read ISO 9660 discs because they provide built-in ISO 9660 readers; the reader is totally transparent to the end user. Although ISO 9660 is just fine for existing CD-ROM and CD-R drives, it is really not sufficient to support the new generation of CD-RW drives as well as the emergence of DVD drives. CD-RW drives require that files be added incrementally (one file at a time) without a waste of overhead space, and that individual files can be erased at will to make room on a disc. In addition, DVD drives require a file system that can support drives at least 4 GB in size. These demands are well beyond the scope of ISO 9660.

UDF addresses all of these concerns by providing a format that can add and erase individual files as needed as well as support the large disc space promised by DVD. Another advantage of UDF is its cross-platform compatibility. A UDF disc can be read by both Mac and Windows platforms. For example, a file could be written using a Mac and then be read back on a Windows PC. The UDF file format is also able to maintain Mac file attributes (such as icons, resource forks, and file types) while ISO 9660 cannot do this.

Working with UDF

The DirectCD technology used with CD-RW drives reads and writes to the CD-RW disc using the UDF format. If you're working on a PC with a CD-RW drive (or plan on installing one yourself), chances are that you'll be using a DirectCD applet to invoke UDF on that disc. Currently, two versions of UDF exist. UDF 1.02 is the version used on current DVD-ROM and DVD-video discs. UDF 1.5 is a superset of 1.02 that adds support for CD-R and CD-RW drives. If you're using DirectCD under Windows 95/98, chances are that you're using UDF 1.5.

Disc Capacity Under UDF. An important issue to keep in mind when using DirectCD is that you never get the same data capacity from a CD-RW disc that you do from a CD-R disc under ISO 9660. Traditional CD-Rs under ISO 9660 can provide a full 650 MB from a blank 74-minute disc. By comparison, UDF demands a certain amount of recording overhead that reduces the overall amount of data that can be recorded on a CD-R or CD-RW disc. In normal operations, you can fit up to 493 MB on a CD-RW disc under DirectCD. For a CD-R disc under DirectCD, you can generally fit up to 618 MB.

UDF and Disc Compatibility. There's only one little problem with UDF: Windows 95 does not support it natively. The DirectCD drivers installed with a CD-RW drive enable Windows 95 to read UDF discs in a CD-RW drive, but using DirectCD (UDF) discs in other drives is a little trickier. When DirectCD begins writing data to a disc, it opens a session. Before any CD-ROM drive can read a disc, the session must be closed. When you eject a disc from a CD-RW drive using the DirectCD applet, you can choose to close the disc to ISO 9660. If you do not close the disc to ISO 9660 when you eject it, you cannot read it on a CD-ROM drive. You must read it on a CD-R or CD-RW drive fitted with DirectCD. This is a limitation of CD-ROM drives, not the DirectCD software.

> **NOTE**: Windows 98 SE (and subsequent versions of Windows) with DVD support should fully support UDF.

If you close the disc to UDF, you can still read the UDF format, but you'll need a multi-read CD-ROM drive and a UDF reader utility. For example, when you install Adaptec's UDF reader in your system, you should be able to read your closed session CD-R and CD-RW discs on CD-ROM drives regardless of whether they are ISO 9660 or UDF.

Multi-Read CD-ROM Drives. UDF reader utilities are designed to support the new generation of multi-read CD-ROM drives. Multi-read is a specification developed and endorsed by the *Optical Storage Technology Association* (OSTA) and is accepted by the industry at large. Most new CD-ROM drives on the market today (manufactured after mid-1997) are multi-read-compatible. To be multi-read-compliant, a CD-ROM drive must be able to

- Read CD-RW discs
- Read packet-written discs (both CD-R and CD-RW)
- Support the OS to utilize UDF 1.5 (or later)

> **NOTE**: Some non-multi-read CD-ROM drives can read UDF-formatted CD-R media, but not CD-RW media using an appropriate UDF reader utility.

UDF Readers.   A UDF reader enables multi-read CD-ROM drives to read closed-session, UDF-formatted CD-R and CD-RW media under Windows 95/98 and the Macintosh OS. The UDF reader for Windows is called the *UDF Reader Driver* and the UDF Reader for Mac OS is called *UDF Volume Access*. UDF readers are particularly useful if you're using DirectCD to record data to a CD-RW disc because you will then be able to read the CD-RW disc in a multi-read CD-ROM drive. Without a UDF reader, you could only read the UDF disc in another CD-RW drive using DirectCD. Since UDF is designed to be a cross-platform file format, UDF readers also enable you to interchange UDF-formatted discs between Mac and Windows systems. Most companies that develop DirectCD software (such as Adaptec) already offer UDF reader utilities free of charge. You can download the Adaptec UDF reader from the Adaptec Web site at *www.adaptec.com* or specifically from their patch/upgrade Web page at *www.adaptec.com / support / files / upgrades.html*. For more information, you could also send an e-mail to Adaptec at *udfreader@adaptec.com*.

UDF Reader Compliance.   Since UDF is intended to provide a universal file interchange format, any UDF reader utility should be able to read all UDF 1.5 formatted media (media formatted with DirectCD). However, no independent third-party organization can test for UDF compliance, so there is no guarantee that all media claiming to be UDF-formatted will be readable by every UDF reader under all conditions. If you have trouble reading a UDF disc with one particular reader utility, you might want to try another reader utility.

UDF and Audio CDs. A popular use of CD-R and CD-RW discs is to record music for playback on an ordinary CD player (copying old vinyl LPs to CD). Although this is a tried and true process for CD-R discs recorded under ISO 9660, this will not work with UDF discs recorded with DirectCD. Audio files recorded under UDF will not work when played in a commercial CD player, but audio files played on a CD-R or CD-RW drive under DirectCD should work normally.

Windows 98 and UDF. Although Windows 95 does not provide direct support for UDF, information gleaned from Microsoft and Adaptec suggests that Windows 98 will support UDF 1.02 for DVD-ROM and DVD-video discs. However, preliminary results indicate that Windows 98 may not provide native support for UDF 1.5, so DirectCD software and UDF readers may still be required after Windows 98 is installed. Windows 98 SE may not require a separate UDF reader.

NOTE: Mac OS 8.1 already supports UDF 1.02.

Using DirectCD

Some simple rules must be followed when preparing and working with CD-RW drives. Preparing new discs, writing data, adding data, erasing data, ejecting the disc, and recovering damaged discs are the most typical procedures that you'll need to master. This part of the chapter outlines these essential steps though you should refer to your CD-RW user's manual for drive-specific information.

Preparing a Data CD. Use the following steps to start DirectCD and prepare a blank CD-RW disc for reading and writing data:

1. Start the computer and insert a blank CD-RW disc in the CD-RW drive. After a few seconds, a screen will appear and ask, `Please select the type of CD you wish to create.` If the DirectCD Disc Ready window appears, the disc has already been prepared and you can start writing data to it immediately.

   NOTE: If no screen appears after about 15 seconds, the disc may not be blank, it may have an unreadable format, or the Auto insert notification option may be disabled.

2. Select the option, `Click here to create a data CD that will be accessible through a drive letter` (as you would use a floppy drive). The Format Disc screen appears.

3. If you're formatting a CD-R disc, click Next on the Format Disc screen.

4. If you're formatting a CD-RW disc, you can choose between two formatting options. Click the Advanced button that appears on the Format Disc screen. When the next screen appears, select either Fast Format or Full Format and click OK.

   NOTE: It's often easier to select the Fast Format option that lets you start writing to the CD-RW disc almost immediately (while the disc is formatted in the background). A Full Format requires you to wait about an hour until the formatting is complete before you can write to the disc.

5. When the Name Your Disc screen appears, type a name for the disc and click Finish. Disc formatting then begins. When the DirectCD Disc Ready window appears, the formatting is complete.

6. Click OK. The DirectCD disc is ready for you to write data to it.

Writing Data to a DirectCD Disc. Once your CD is formatted as a DirectCD disc, you can write data to it in several different ways:

- Drag and drop files from Windows Explorer right onto the CD-RW icon.

- Select Save As from a Windows 95/98 /NT application File menu and select the drive letter of your CD-RW.

- Use the Send To command.

- Use the MS-DOS command prompts from a DOS window in Windows 95/98 /NT.

Ejecting a DirectCD Disc   DirectCD gives you several formatting options when you eject a DirectCD disc from the CD-RW drive. The options depend on what kind of disc DirectCD detects in the drive and how you want to use the disc. To eject a DirectCD disc, follow these steps:

1. Push the Eject button on the front of the CD-RW drive or right-click on the CD icon on the taskbar and select Eject from the drop-down list box. The Eject Disc screen appears.

2. Carefully read the text that appears on the screen and (if options are presented) select the option you require.

3. Click Finish to eject the disc from the CD-RW drive.

Erasing a DirectCD Disc.   If you're using CD-RW discs, you can actually erase files from the disc and use the recovered space to write new files. However, if you delete files from a CD-R disc, the files become invisible to the file system (that is, Windows Explorer), but the space they occupy is not made available for other files. So deleting files from a CD-R disc will not increase the available free space on the disc. To erase the contents of a DirectCD disc, follow these steps:

1. While in Windows Explorer, select the file(s) you want to erase.

2. Select Delete from the File menu.

3. Click Yes to confirm that you want to erase the files from the disc.

4. DirectCD erases the selected file(s) from the disc.

Fixing an Unreadable Disc. If no window appears on the screen (after about 15 seconds) when you insert a disc in the CD-RW drive, the disc may have an unreadable format. DirectCD has a ScanDisc application that may be able to recover data on the disc and enable you to write to it and read from it again. Follow these steps to use ScanDisc:

1. Double-click the CD icon on the right side of the Windows taskbar. If the disc is unreadable, the ScanDisc window will appear.

2. Read the text in the window and then click the ScanDisc button.

3. Wait while ScanDisc repairs the disc. A message will appear on the screen when ScanDisc is finished.

Caring for Rewriteable CDs

As a rule, rewriteable CDs are as rugged and reliable as ordinary pressed CDs. Still, you should exercise some rules in the careful handling and storage of rewriteable media:

- *Maintain a comfortable environment.* Don't expose rewritable discs to sunlight or other strong light for long periods of time. Also avoid high heat and humidity that can damage the physical disc. Always keep blank or recorded media in clean jewel cases for best protection.

- *Don't write on the disc.* Don't use alcohol-based pens to write on discs. The ink may eventually eat through the top (lacquer) surface and damage your data. Also don't use ball-point or other sharp-tipped pens because you may scratch right through the lacquer surface and damage the reflective gold layer (and ruin your data).

- *Don't use labels on the disc.* Don't put labels on discs unless they are *expressly* designed for rewritable CDs. The glue may eat through the lacquer surface just as some inks do, and/or the label may unbalance the disc and cause problems in reading it back or recording subsequent sessions. Never try to remove a label. You might tear off the lacquer and some of the reflecting surface.

- *Watch your media quality.* Many different brands of rewritable CD media are now available in the marketplace. Quality varies from brand to brand (and even from batch to batch within a given brand). If you have repeated problems that can be traced to the blank media you are using, try using a different brand or even a different batch of the same brand.

- *Don't use Kodak Photo CDs.* Avoid the use of Kodak Photo CDs on everyday CD-Rs. Kodak Photo CDs are designed to be used only with Kodak Photo CD professional workstations. Although the discs are inexpensive, they have a protection bit that prevents them from being written on many CD-Rs. When you attempt to write these discs on the recorders that recognize the protection bit, you will receive an error message.

- *Careful for power issues.* If you lose power while writing to your CD-RW (or if you exit an application or press Ctrl + Alt + Del) while writing to a CD, you may be able to salvage your rewritable CD if you follow the following steps:

  1. Leave the CD in the drive. Do not open the tray.
  2. Turn the machine off and then turn it back on.
  3. Re-enter the application you were using.

Once the application tries to access the CD-RW drive, the recovery operation will make it appear that the last session is there. However, only a part of the CD's directory may actually be included. Your rewritable CD is still usable if you can read that directory. Repeat the entire copy operation to make sure that your files are copied successfully.

CD-RW Drive Symptoms

Although UDF and CD-RW drives are now well-established industry standards, technicians may eventually need to address a number of compatibility problems and operating issues. This part of the chapter examines a selection of UDF issues and CD-RW problems.

> **NOTE**:   For basic CD and recording issues, refer to the previous parts of this chapter for CD-ROM and CD-R troubleshooting information.

Troubleshooting Tips

CD-RW drives are not terribly complicated devices to troubleshoot, but they can present some peculiar problems for technicians and do-it-yourselfers. Before you attempt to troubleshoot a CD-RW issue with your system, take a moment to work through the following checklist:

- Verify that your system meets the minimum requirements for your CD-RW drive. If not, the system may fail to run properly (if at all).

- Make sure the computer is plugged in and that each device has power. Connect any devices that are not receiving power.

- Turn off the computer's power, wait 15 to 20 seconds, and then reboot the system. This can clear some software conflicts.

- Repeat the operation with a different (reliable, good-quality) CD.

- Make sure you're using the right type of CD for the task at hand.

- Check the README file that came with the CD-RW drive for any last-minute compatibility or performance notes that might be present with your system. Also check the CD-RW drive maker's Web site for the latest drivers and firmware upgrades.

- If the problem(s) occur with power management, disable your PC's power management modes.

General Symptoms

This section will cover a variety of general problems and offer solutions for fixing them.

Symptom 2.145. A backup disc will not run properly. DirectCD is not suitable for making backup copies of game or application discs where the application must run from the CD. This is because DirectCD uses a different method of writing data to a disc (packet writing) than any discs produced with the ISO 9660 format. Packet-written (UDF) discs cannot be read by many standard CD-ROM drives or game machines. The only real way to work around this sort of problem is to use other recording software (such as Easy CD Creator for Windows 95/98 or Adaptec Toast for the Mac) to make a backup copy of the disc to CD-R.

> **NOTE**: Keep in mind that some games and commercial application discs use forms of copy protection that recording software cannot work around or break. Also remember that you cannot copy commercial software because of copyright restrictions.

Symptom 2.146. You receive an error such as "CD-RW is not under Direct CD control." You'll typically notice this problem under Windows 95/98 when you attempt to erase, format, or copy data to a CD-RW. This type of problem is most frequently encountered when using a

Ricoh CD-RW drive and Adaptec Direct CD software. The problem can occur when the CD-RW drive uses older firmware (a Ricoh CD-RW drive with v.2.03 firmware or earlier) or if you're using Adaptec DirectCD 2.0 or earlier. Try updating the drive's firmware and CD-authoring software.

Symptom 2.147. The CD-RW media cannot be used when the UDF format is interrupted.   If power is lost while formatting a CD-RW disc, the disc will become unusable in any application and fail if another format is attempted. To correct this issue, use the DirectCD Full Erase feature to wipe the disc and then try the format operation again.

Symptom 2.148. Files recorded in a second session do not appear.   If the files that you recorded in a second session do not appear when you try to read the disc in a CD-ROM drive, try the following tips:

- Try ejecting and reinserting the CD.
- Refresh the file list. Select the CD-RW icon in My Computer or Windows Explorer and then press F5.
- Check the drive. CD-RW discs can be used only in CD-RW drives or newer multi-read CD-ROMs.
- Try reading the CD in other CD-ROM drives. If other drives can read the disc, the problem is probably with the original CD-ROM drive.

Symptom 2.149. No DirectCD window appears after inserting a new CD-RW disc.   Verify that the CD-RW drive's DirectCD software and utilities have been installed properly. If the DirectCD window doesn't appear on the screen after you insert a new disc, follow these steps:

1. Wait a moment. It can take up to 15 seconds for the DirectCD window to appear.

2. If the rewriteable disc is already formatted, you can force the window by clicking Start on the taskbar, choosing Programs, and then selecting Create a CD.

3. To prepare a CD with Easy CD Creator or DirectCD, the disc must be blank (you may have inserted a disc that is already formatted). Remove the disc and insert a good-quality blank one.

4. The disc may have an unreadable format. DirectCD has a ScanDisk utility that may be able to recover data on the disc. Simply double-click the CD icon on the Windows taskbar. Start ScanDisk and allow the process to run. A message will appear when ScanDisk is finished.

Symptom 2.150. You receive an error message when double-clicking on the CD-RW icon. Several possible issues are typically caused by the drive's incapability to read the disc. Here are a few things to check:

- No CD is in the CD-RW drive. Insert a quality CD and try reading again.

- After inserting a CD, you need to wait a moment to let the CD-RW drive read the disc information. When the LED on the front of the drive stops flashing and stays green, click on the CD-RW drive's icon again.

- The CD may be in the tray upside-down or a little off-center. Try reinserting the CD with the disc label facing up.

- You may be trying to read from a blank recordable CD. Copy some information to the disc and try reading it again.

Symptom 2.151. Your CD-ROM drive cannot "see" a second session (or subsequent sessions) recorded on discs from a CD-RW drive. Several possible issues can occur when reading multisession discs created on a CD-RW drive with DirectCD software:

- *Reinsert the disc.*   Start by ejecting and reinserting the disc. This enables the drive to redetect the disc and try reading its sessions once again. You should also try refreshing the display. Select the My Computer icon in Windows Explorer and then press F5.

- *Check the drive.*   CD-RW discs can only be used in CD-RW drives or newer multi-read CD-ROMs (compatible with the UDF file system). If you're trying to read the disc on an older CD-ROM that is not multi-read compliant, you may need to upgrade the CD-ROM to a newer version.

- *Check your OS.*   Multi-session CDs created with DirectCD cannot be read in DOS or Windows 3.x. Make sure that you're in Windows 95, Windows 98, or some other UDF-compliant OS.

3

Input Device Troubleshooting

All computers require at least one input device, a means of getting commands and instructions into the system. Input devices present the technician with special problems. In order to translate physical keystrokes and movements into digital signals, a reliable mechanical mechanism must be at work. As a result, input devices eventually wear out with regular use. The environment of the "real world" can also damage an input device through accumulations of dust, debris, physical abuse, and liquid spills. This section examines the most common types of input devices: keyboards, mice, and joysticks. Other more exotic input devices are also covered at the end of the chapter.

Keyboard Issues

A keyboard is *the* classic input device. In spite of the advances that have taken place in the PC industry over the last 20 years, the keyboard remains a direct and reliable means of typing commands and text into an *operating system* (OS). The greatest problems with keyboards are their susceptibility to dust, spills, and foreign matter (such as staples or paper clips).

Keyboard Assembly

The keyboard assembly is remarkably straightforward. A single printed circuit board containing a matrix of keys is sandwiched between two plastic housings. To access the printed circuit, you must remove the screws holding the plastic housings together (located on the underside of the keyboard). You must then separate the two housings held together by plastic tabs. A single thin cable connects the keyboard assembly to the keyboard controller on the motherboard via a *keyboard connector*. When a key is pressed, circuitry in the keyboard generates a key code that is passed to the PC.

Keyboards and Key Codes

When a key is pressed, the row and column signals that are generated are interpreted by a *keyboard interface* IC (typically located on the keyboard assembly itself). The keyboard interface converts the row and column signals into a single-byte code (called a *key code* or *scan code*). Two unique scan codes are produced during a keystroke cycle. When the key is depressed, a *make code* byte is sent along to the system. When the key is released, a *break code* byte is generated. Both codes are transmitted to the host computer in a serial fashion. By using two individual codes, the computer can determine when a key is held down or when keys are held in combinations. Table 3.1 illustrates the make and break codes for conventional keyboards used in the domestic United States.

Dvorak Keyboards

Most technicians are familiar with QWERTY-style keyboards, the standard format for typewriters that

TABLE 3.1   Typical Make and Break Codes for U.S. Keyboards

Key	Make Code	Break Code	Key	Make Code	Break Code
A	1E	9E	B	30	B0
C	2E	AE	D	20	A0
E	12	92	F	21	A1
G	22	A2	H	23	A3
I	17	97	J	24	A4
K	25	A5	L	26	A6
M	32	B2	N	31	B1
O	18	98	P	19	99
Q	10	90	R	13	93
S	1F	9F	T	14	94
U	16	96	V	2F	AF
W	11	91	X	2D	AD
Y	15	95	Z	2C	AC
0/)	0B	8B	1/!	02	82
2/@	03	83	3/#	04	84
4/$	05	85	5/%	06	86
6/^	07	87	7/&	08	88
8/*	09	89	9/(	0A	8A
./>	29	A9	-/_	0C	8C
=/+	0D	8D	[	1A	9A
]	1B	9B	;/:	27	A7
'/"	28	A8	,/<	33	B3
//?	35	B5	L Sh	2A	AA
L Ctrl	1D	9D	L Alt	38	B8
R Sh	36	B6	R Alt	E0 38	E0 B8
R Ctrl	E0 1D	E0 9D	Caps	3A	BA
BK SP	0E	8E	Tab	0F	8F
Space	39	B9	Enter	1C	9C
ESC	01	81	F1	3B	BB
F2	3C	BC	F3	3D	BD
F4	3E	BE	F5	3F	BF
F6	40	C0	F7	41	C1
F8	42	C2	F9	43	C3
F10	44	C4	F11	57	D7
F12	58	D8	Up Ar	E0 48	E0 C8
Dn Ar	E0 50	E0 D0	Lt Ar	E0 4B	E0 CB
Rt Ar	E0 4D	E0 CD	Ins	E0 52	E0 D2
Home	E0 47	E0 C7	Pg Up	E0 49	E0 C9
Del	E0 53	E0 D3	End	E0 4F	E0 CF
Pg Dn	E0 51	E0 D1	ScrLk	46	C6

All make and break codes are given in hexadecimal (hex) values.
Alphabetic characters represent both upper and lower case.

was adopted in the late 1800s. A popular alternative to the QWERTY keyboard is the *Dvorak keyboard*. Mechanically and electronically, the Dvorak keyboard is identical to conventional keyboards. Only the key order is different. All of the vowels are located on the left side of your *home row* (the middle row of letters) in the following pattern: AOEUIDHTNS.

Dvorak keyboards claim several advantages over QWERTY models. Most letters typed (about 70 percent) are on the home row, so the finger and wrist strain can be reduced. With less reach to deal with, typing can be accomplished faster and with fewer errors. The vast majority of words use both hands for typing although thousands of words demand only one-handed typing on QWERTY keyboards. This spreads out the strain on your hands more evenly.

Converting to Dvorak Keyboards

A Dvorak keyboard can be implemented using one of two methods: buying a dedicated keyboard or using keyboard conversions. Dedicated keyboards are just as the name implies. You buy a ready-made keyboard and plug it in. Although the keys are located in different places, the key codes are the same, so your PC doesn't know the difference. As a result, you can interchange QWERTY and Dvorak keyboards at will without any changes to the PC or OS. You can also convert your existing QWERTY keyboard to Dvorak under Windows 95:

1. Open the Control Panel and double-click on the Keyboard icon.

2. Select the Language page and double-click on the English (United States) entry (or your own default entry).

3. Select United States (Dvorak) from the list that appears.

4. Save your changes. You may need to install a diskette with the proper drivers.

5. It may be necessary to reboot the system.

Under DOS, you will need a DOS *Terminate and Stay Resident* (TSR) to handle the conversion. For MS-DOS 5.0 through 6.22, you can find the Dvorak TSR on the MS-DOS Supplemental Disk. You can obtain the driver files from Microsoft's FTP or Web site, or from the Microsoft forum on CompuServe (GO MSDOS). Download the file DOS62S.EXE.

> **NOTE**: If you do download and extract these supplemental DOS files, make very sure to extract them to a new directory. Under no circumstances should you allow DOS files to overwrite files in the DOS directory or anywhere in your Windows directory.

Once the software conversion is made, you will need to exchange the keys on your QWERTY keyboard. Figure 3.1 illustrates the comparison between a QWERTY key layout and a Dvorak key layout. You can use a key pulling tool to physically exchange the key caps, or use key stickers or overlays from Hooleon Corporation at 602-634-7515 or Keytime at 206-522-8973. You can also obtain more detailed information directly from Dvorak International at 802-287-2434.

The actual transfer of scan codes between the keyboard and PC is accomplished *serially* using one of the interfaces shown in Figures 3.2a and 3.2b. Note the three important signals in a keyboard interface: the *keyboard clock* (KBCLOCK), the *keyboard data* (KBDATA), and the *signal ground*. Unlike most serial communication that is asynchronous, the transfer of data from keyboard to controller is accomplished synchronously. Data bits are returned in sync with the clock signals. It is also important for you to note that most XT-style systems are designed with a uni-directional data path

QWERTY

Q W E R T Y U I O P

A S D F G H J K L ; '

Z X C V B N M , . /

Dvoark

" , . P Y F G C R L /

A O E U I D H T N S -

; Q J K X B M W V Z

Figure 3.1   QWERTY and Dvorak keyboard layouts

(from keyboard to system). AT-style keyboard interfaces are bidirectional, enabling AT keyboards to be controlled and programmed from the PC.

Virtually all computer keyboards are open to the air. Over time, everyday dust, pet hair, air vapor, cigar/cigarette smoke, and debris from hands and ordinary use will settle into the keyboard. Eventually, accumulations of this foreign matter will cause keys to stick or will prevent keys from making proper contact (that is, a key does not work every time it is pressed). In either case, keyboard problems will develop. Fortunately, correcting a finicky keyboard is a relatively straightforward process:

- *Get a key removal tool.*   Your local computer store should carry inexpensive key removal tools. If you cannot find one (or need one in a hurry), bend an

a. IBM PC/XT/AT Configuration

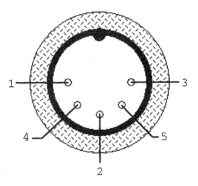

1	KBCLOCK
2	KBDATA
3	nc
4	Ground
5	+5 Vdc (or +3.0 or +3.3 Vdc)

b. 6 pin Mini DIN Connector

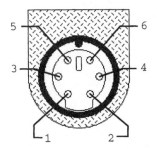

1	KBDATA
2	nc
3	Ground
4	+5 Vdc (or +3.0 or +3.3 Vdc)
5	KBCLOCK
6	nc

Figure 3.2a and b   AT and PS/2 keyboard interfaces

ordinary paper clip into the shape of a U and bend small tabs inward at the tips. Slip the tabs under the key and pull up gently. Do not struggle with the key cap and avoid removing the space bar unless absolutely necessary.

- *Remove the key cap of the offending key(s).*   Be sure to note the location of each key, as in Figure 3.1.

- *Dislodge foreign matter.*   Turn the keyboard upside down and rap on the case gently. This should dislodge staples, paper clips, and other stuff that might have dropped into the keyboard.

- *Sweep out the dust.*   Use a soft-bristled brush to sweep out any stubborn dust or debris. Use a can of compressed air and a thin nozzle to blow out any dust between the keys (you may want to do this in an open or outdoor area).

- *Clean the key contacts.*   Squirt a bit of good-quality electronic contact cleaner into the key switch and work the switch to distribute the cleaner. Enable the cleaner to dry completely and then test the key before reinstalling the key cap.

> **NOTE**:   If you choose to use a vacuum cleaner for keyboard cleaning, make sure that the vacuum is static-safe.

Keyboard Troubleshooting

The following section will cover some basic keyboard problems and possible solutions.

Symptom 3.1. During initialization, you see an error message indicating that no keyboard is connected. Virtually all keyboard problems are due to keyboard failures or connection problems, so several things must be checked:

- *Check the keyboard connection.*   Make sure that the keyboard connector is installed properly.

- *Check the keyboard switch setting.*   If the keyboard has a switch to select an XT or AT mode, make sure the switch is set properly. The switch is located underneath the keyboard (maybe under a small door). Most keyboards after around 1988 will not have this switch.

- *Replace the keyboard.*   Try a new keyboard and if it works, there is probably a fault in the original keyboard. Thus, simply replace the keyboard.

- *Check the motherboard.*   Inspect the keyboard connector in the PC itself. Make sure that any cable between the connector and motherboard is installed properly. If the keyboard connector is hard-soldered to the motherboard, check that none of the solder points are broken or "cold."

- *Replace the keyboard controller.*   In most cases, a keyboard controller fault manifests itself as a something other than a "no keyboard" problem, but it may be worth replacing the keyboard controller chip (if possible). Try using a POST board to isolate the error code. Otherwise, you should try replacing the motherboard.

Symptom 3.2. During initialization, you see an error message indicating that the keyboard lock is on. The detection of a locked keyboard will halt system initialization. This is usually just a simple oversight, so check the following areas:

- *Check the keyboard lock.*   Make sure that the keyboard switch is in the unlocked position. If the switch is unlocked, but the system detects it as locked, the switch may be defective. Check continuity across the switch in locked and unlocked positions. If the switch continuity does not respond, the switch is defective.

■ *Replace the motherboard.* If the switch continuity responds as expected, there is a fault on the motherboard. You may have to replace the motherboard.

Symptom 3.3. The keyboard is completely dead. No keys appear to function at all. All other computer operations are normal, but the keyboard does not respond when touched. Keyboard status *light-emitting diodes* (LEDs) may or may not be working properly. The problem could be spotted by doing one of the following:

■ *Replace the keyboard.* Try a reliable keyboard in the system. If it works, the original keyboard is probably defective and should be replaced. Also try the suspect keyboard on another system. If the keyboard works on another system, the fault lies on the motherboard.

■ *Check the motherboard.* Inspect the keyboard connector in the PC itself. Make sure that any cable between the connector and motherboard is installed properly. If the keyboard connector is hard-soldered to the motherboard, check that none of the solder points are broken or cold.

■ *Replace the motherboard.* If problems persist, you should replace the motherboard.

Symptom 3.4. The keyboard is acting erratically. One or more keys appear to work intermittently or are inoperative. The computer operates normally and most keys work just fine, but there seems to be one or more keys that do not respond when pressed. Extra force or repeated strikes may be needed to operate the key. Thus, peform the following steps:

- *Clean the keyboard.* Inspect the offending keys, clean out any accumulations of dust and debris, and then use contact cleaner to clean the key(s).

- *Replace the keyboard.* If you cannot clean the key(s), or problems persist, try replacing the keyboard with a reliable working keyboard.

Symptom 3.5. The keyboard is acting erratically. One or more keys may be stuck or repeating. A shorted or jammed key would be suspect and one of the following steps could lead to a solution:

- *Check for foreign objects.* Paper clips and keyboards that slide into the keyboard can easily short out keys and cause erratic keyboard operation.

- *Try some contact cleaner.* If you need to remove any key caps, clean the key contacts with good-quality electronic cleaner.

- *Replace the keyboard.* If problems persist, replace the keyboard outright.

Symptom 3.6. You see a message such as "KBC Error" displayed during system startup. Either the keyboard is not connected properly or the *keyboard controller* (KBC) chip has failed:

- *Check the keyboard connection.* Make sure that the keyboard connector is installed properly.

- *Replace the keyboard.* Try a new keyboard. If a new keyboard works, there is probably a fault in the original keyboard. Simply replace the keyboard. Try the keyboard on another system. If the keyboard works on another system, the fault lies on the motherboard.

- *Replace the keyboard controller.* If the KBC is mounted on a socket (like a BIOS), try replacing the KBC chip.

- *Replace the motherboard.* If you can't replace the KBC chip (or a new KBC fails to correct the problem), replace the motherboard outright.

Symptom 3.7. You cannot clear macros from a programmable keyboard. In most cases, you need to use the right key combination. Thus, take the following steps as needed:

- *Clear the keyboard programming.* If the keyboard has a Remap key, press that first (a program light will start blinking). Press the Ctrl key twice to map the key to itself. Press Alt twice to map the key to itself. Press the Suspend Macro key (the program light should stop blinking). Press the Ctrl and Alt keys while pressing Suspend Macro; this will clear all of the keyboard's programming. The key sequence used for your keyboard may be different, so be sure to check the procedure for your own keyboard.

- *Replace the keyboard.* If problems persist, replace the keyboard.

Symptom 3.8. The keyboard's keys are not functioning as expected. Pressing a key causes unexpected results or a series of operations that would ordinarily not be attributed to that key. Chances are that the keyboard has been programmed with macros, and you'll need to clear those macros to restore normal keyboard operation. If the keyboard has a Remap key, press that first (a program light or other LED will start blinking). Press the Ctrl key twice to map the key to itself. Press Alt twice to map the key to itself. Press the Suspend Macro key (the program light should stop blinking).

Press the Ctrl and Alt keys while pressing Suspend Macro; this will clear *all* of the keyboard's programming. The key sequence used for your keyboard may be different, so be sure to check the procedure for your own keyboard. If problems persist, replace the keyboard.

Symptom 3.9. Some keys on a programmable keyboard will not remap to their default state. This can happen with some Gateway 2000 (AnyKey) keyboards as well as other programmable keyboards. You may have to "force clear" the keyboard at boot time. To do so, power down the system. While holding down the Suspend Macro key, turn the system power back on. Continue booting with the Suspend Macro key depressed until the program light (or similar LED) quits flashing. This light will stay lit until you depress and release it.

> **NOTE**:   For Gateway 2000 AnyKey keyboards, if there is an *AnykeyXX T* line in the AUTOEXEC.BAT file, this will terminate any programming function of the keyboard. If there is an *AnykeyXX A* line in the file named AUTOEXEC.BAT, this will activate the programming function.

Symptom 3.10. A wireless keyboard types random characters. You'll need to reset both ends of the wireless system. First, take a look at the *Dual Inline Package* (DIP) switch settings controlling the *Radio Frequency* (RF) channel for the wireless transmitter and receiver (usually under the battery cover at the keyboard). Make sure that the transmitter and receiver modules are both set for the same channel. Find the Reset button on both the transmitter and receiver. Press the RF receiver Reset button first, and then press the RF Transmitter button immediately after (usually within 15 seconds of one another). If the problem persists, reboot the system and try the reset process again.

Symptom 3.11. The wireless keyboard beeps while typing.
In virtually all cases, the batteries in the wireless keyboard are running low. Replace the batteries and try
the wireless keyboard again; the beeping should stop.
Otherwise, the keyboard's transmitter or receiver modules may be dirty, obstructed, or defective.

**Symptom 3.12. Typed characters do not appear, but the
cursor moves.** This issue is a result of the color
scheme being used. Some of the applications reported
as suffering this problem are MSWORKS 4.0, CASH-
GRAF, MSBOB (the address book and letter writer),
and MSPUBLISHER. Check the color scheme selected
by right-clicking on the desktop. Click on Properties
and then the Appearance tab. Set the scheme to
Windows Standard. Click on OK to return to the desktop. The text should now appear normal. This solution
can generally be attempted with any application.

**Symptom 3.13. Some function keys and Windows keys may
not work for some PC configurations.** For example, this
is a known problem with Toshiba 8500 desktop systems and the Microsoft Natural Keyboard. In virtually
all cases (including the Toshiba 8500), the PC keyboard
controller BIOS recognizes the keyboard during the
Power-On Self Test (POST), but it does not recognize
some of the keys, including certain function keys and
Windows-specific keys. You'll need to try a generic keyboard or upgrade the system's keyboard controller
BIOS.

**Symptom 3.14. One or more Windows-specific keys don't
work.** This is almost always a limitation of the keyboard controller BIOS. For example, a Jetkey keyboard
controller BIOS (v.3.0) will not recognize the right
Windows key on a Microsoft Natural Keyboard. You'll
need to try a generic keyboard or upgrade the system's
keyboard controller BIOS.

Symptom 3.15. Remote control programs don't work after installing keyboard drivers. Many PC "remote control" programs (PC Anywhere, ReachOut, and Carbon Copy) use keyboard and mouse drivers that are simply not compatible with the keyboard's specific drivers. For example, the remote control programs listed previously will not work when IntelliType software is installed for the Microsoft Natural Keyboard. You'll need to disable the remote control software, install patches for the remote control software that will properly support the keyboard, or replace the keyboard with a more generic model.

Symptom 3.16. On a PS/2 system, you encounter keyboard errors, even though the keyboard driver loads successfully. Often, you'll see an error like `Keyboard error-keyboard not found`, and you cannot access the keyboard. This type of problem is known to occur on PS/2 systems when the IBM ROM BIOS patch file (DASDDRVR.SYS) is loaded *after* the keyboard driver in CONFIG.SYS. Rearrange the CONFIG.SYS file to load the DASDDRVR.SYS file before the keyboard driver. Make sure you are loading the patch driver (DASDDRVR.SYS) that is designed for your *specific* computer (for example, you cannot use the DASDDRVR.SYS file that ships with an IBM PS/2 Model 80 on a PS/2 Model 70 computer). This device driver can normally be found on the SETUP disk that you received with your IBM PS/2. Otherwise, you can obtain it from IBM (*www.ibm.com*).

Symptom 3.17. Assigned key sounds do not work. When you assign sounds to keystrokes (under the Options tab in the Keyboard tool in your Control Panel), the sounds may play when you press the assigned keys. This problem is known to occur with some programmable keyboards when HiJaak Pro or HiJaak 95 Graphics Suite is installed on your computer. These products may load a device driver named "Runner" that disables programmable keyboard sounds. You may be able to work around the problem by closing the Runner task. For example, press Ctrl+Alt+Del to open the Close Program dialog box. If Runner is listed, click Runner and then click End Task.

Symptom 3.18. You cannot use Windows-specific keys to start task-switching software other than TASKSW16.EXE. You *can* start the desired task-switching software using Ctrl+Esc or by double-clicking the desktop. Chances are that your Windows-specific key will not start any other task switching utility if TASKSW16. EXE can be found on the path. You'll need to update the task-switching program reference in SYSTEM.INI. Load SYSTEM.INI into any text editor and modify the line that reads

```
TASKMAN=TASKSW16.EXE
```

to read

```
TASKMAN=<task manager>
```

where `<task manager>` is the name of the executable file you want to start when you press the Windows key. Rename the TASKSW16.EXE file (TASKSW16.OLD) or move it to a directory that is not in the path. Save and close the SYSTEM.INI file and then restart the computer.

Symptom 3.19. The NumLock feature may not activate when the NumLock key is pressed. This can happen with some programmable keyboards when pen software is installed on the system. You should be able to correct the problem by disabling the pen device:

1. Click Start, select Settings, and then click Control Panel.

2. Double-click the System icon and select the Device Manager tab.

3. Double-click the Ports entry to expand it.

4. Double-click the port to which the pen (or touch-screen) device is connected.

5. In the Device Usage area on the General tab, click the Original Configuration (Current) check box to clear it (if you're using OSR2, click the Disable In This Hardware Profile check box to select it).

6. Click OK, then restart the system when prompted.

> **NOTE**: To enable your pen device again, repeat the steps above, but reselect (or reclear) the check box in Step 5.

Symptom 3.20. The Language section of the Keyboard tool is disabled under Windows 95/98. When you're using the Keyboard tool in Control Panel, you may encounter the following symptom(s): a message may say Old-Style Keyboard detected, pane disabled, or the language list may be blank (and you may not be able to change any language settings). This problem can occur if the keyboard registry key is damaged or missing:

```
HKEY_LOCAL_MACHINE\System\CurrentControlSet\
control\keyboard layouts
```

To resolve this problem, reinstall Windows 95 or Windows 98 into the same folder as the original installation.

Symptom 3.21. You encounter keyboard problems when using IE 4.0x/5 and an Adobe Acrobat (.PDF) file under Windows 98.   If you have an Adobe Acrobat (.PDF) file open in Internet Explorer, you may lose some keyboard functionality. Keys that may not work may include the Page Up, Page Down, and the arrow keys. To work around this problem, minimize and restore the IE window, use the Zoom buttons on the Adobe Acrobat toolbar, or use the mouse to scroll through the file.

Symptom 3.22. You have problems using a real-mode keyboard driver with an international code page.   If an international code page is installed in conjunction with a real-mode keyboard driver (such as KEYBOARD.SYS), you may find that console programs cannot detect extended character keystrokes (such as Insert, Delete, Home, and so on). Console programs that don't work directly with the console API may not recognize extended keystrokes. When a real-mode keyboard driver is installed, the current character in the keyboard buffer is sent to the console program. With an international code page loaded, the data returned through the console API is slightly different than that in Windows 95/98. This problem has been corrected in Windows 98 SE, but for older versions of Windows, you can download the patch (a new version of CONAGENT.EXE) from *www.microsoft.com/support/supportnet/overview/overview.asp*.

Symptom 3.23. You find two keyboards listed in the Windows 98 Device Manager.   When you restart your computer after installing a USB keyboard, both the USB keyboard device and the Standard 101/102 -Key or Microsoft Natural Keyboard device are listed in the Keyboard branch of your Device Manager. This occurs because USB keyboards may still require the Standard 101/102 -Key or Natural Keyboard driver to work properly (if your BIOS does not fully support USB in the real mode). This may seem awkward, but it's perfectly normal. If you disable the Standard 101/102 -Key or Microsoft Natural Keyboard device in Device Manager and restart your computer, the USB keyboard will not work; Windows 98 automatically installs the device again. You might try a system BIOS upgrade to better support the USB ports on your motherboard.

Symptom 3.24. The new USB keyboard does not operate properly under Windows 98 after installation. You know that your system should fully support USB devices. This problem can occur when you install a new USB keyboard while your system is off and when your computer is set up to have you to log on when you start it. USB keyboards are not enumerated until *after* you log on to your computer. To correct this problem, click Cancel when you're prompted to log on, click Start, click Log Off (user name), click Yes, and *then* log on to your computer.

Symptom 3.25. You notice that the keyboard language unexpectedly changes to a default language. When you start a program under Windows 95/98 (or when a program is started using OLE), your keyboard may revert to the default language, regardless of the language you're currently using. For example, when you start a program, you'll see the language icon on the taskbar change to indicate that the default language is being used (but when a program is started using OLE, the language icon may not change). To work around this problem, simply change the keyboard driver to the desired language *after* you start the program. Click the language icon on the taskbar, and then click the language that you want. Now press the appropriate short-cut key combination for switching keyboard layouts (by default, this is Left Arrow + Alt + Shift).

Symptom 3.26. The "automatic repeat" feature doesn't work for USB keyboards after returning from suspend mode under Windows 98 SE. This is a known problem with Windows 98 SE, but a patch is available from Microsoft at *www.microsoft.com/support/supportnet/overview/overview.asp*. The English version of this patch should have the following file attributes (or later):

```
KBDHID.VXD   10/04/99   05:32p   4.10.2223   16,666KB
```

Symptom 3.27. After upgrading to Windows 98, your custom keyboard layout may be lost. This problem occurs when user profiles are enabled in Windows 95 and a custom keyboard layout option is selected in a user profile (rather than the default profile). Since Windows 98 Setup only parses the settings for a default user during the upgrade to Windows 98, the keyboard setting changes to the default user profile during the upgrade. To correct this problem, log on to the computer using a user profile *other* than the default, and then modify the keyboard layout in Windows 98:

1. Click Start, highlight Settings, and then click Control Panel.

2. Click Keyboard, click Language, click Properties, and then click the layout you want to use in the Keyboard Layout box.

3. Click OK, click OK again, and then restart the computer.

Symptom 3.28.Your laptop does not detect a PS/2 keyboard. This is a known problem with configurations such as the IBM ThinkPad and a Natural Keyboard Elite. For example, when you connect the Natural Keyboard Elite to the PS/2 port on an IBM ThinkPad laptop, the keyboard may not be detected. This problem generally occurs because the PS/2 port on the IBM

ThinkPad does *not* detect any PS/2 keyboard without the correct adapter cable or docking station. To correct this problem, you must connect the keyboard to an appropriate docking station.

Symptom 3.29. Your particular keyboard doesn't work with a Compaq DeskPro 4000 system. For example, the Natural Keyboard Elite is known to have trouble with the Compaq DeskPro 4000. When you connect the keyboard to your computer, the keyboard may be detected the first time you start the system, but the keyboard may not be detected during subsequent starts. In virtually all cases, the keyboard device you're using will not operate on systems using the VIA UHCI chipset. Try a different (basic model) keyboard.

Symptom 3.30. You find that you cannot use the USB Natural Keyboard Elite in the DOS mode. For example, when you start the computer (or restart your computer) in DOS mode, the Natural Keyboard Elite may not function properly. You may also receive either of the following error messages:

```
Keyboard Error
```

or

```
Keyboard Not Present
```

This problem can occur if you connect the Natural Keyboard Elite to your computer using a USB adapter, but your computer's BIOS doesn't fully support USB keyboards. Your system BIOS *must* support USB devices for *any* type of USB keyboard to work in DOS. You should upgrade the system BIOS with a version that supports USB devices. To work around this issue temporarily, shut down Windows and turn off the computer. Disconnect the keyboard from the USB port, and then remove the USB adapter. Connect another keyboard to a PS/2 port on the computer and then restart the system normally.

Symptom 3.31. Keyboard lights do not illuminate in the DOS mode. This is a known problem when using the Natural Keyboard Elite with a Compaq Presario system under DOS. The LED lights on the keyboard may remain unlit in DOS but may work properly under Windows. This is an issue with the Compaq system (rather than the keyboard), but no features are lost in the DOS mode.

Symptom 3.32. Your keyboard does not work properly on an IBM Aptiva system. For example, when you connect a Natural Keyboard or Natural Keyboard Elite to an IBM Aptiva computer, the keyboard may not work properly. This problem may occur if you have IBM Rapid Access Keyboard software running on the Aptiva system. To correct this issue, remove the IBM Rapid Access Keyboard software (this software is not needed if you use another keyboard, such as the Natural Keyboard family):

1. Click Start, highlight Settings, and then click Control Panel.

2. Double-click the Add/Remove Programs icon.

3. In the list of installed programs, click IBM Rapid Access Keyboard and then click Add/Remove.

4. Follow the instructions on the screen to remove the IBM Rapid Access Keyboard software.

NOTE: The EZ-Button program is a component of the IBM Rapid Access Keyboard software, so this program is also removed when you remove the IBM Rapid Access Keyboard software.

Symptom 3.33. Your Natural Keyboard does not work properly on certain Toshiba laptops. For example, when you use a Natural Keyboard Elite attached to the PS/2 port on one of the following Toshiba laptops, the keyboard may not function properly:

- Satellite 110C

- Satellite Pro 400C

- Tecra 720CDT

- Tecra 500CDT

This problem can occur because plug-and-play hardware detection on the PS/2 port times out *before* the computer enumerates the keyboard; this is a problem with the keyboard. To get around this issue, use the USB adapter included with the keyboard to connect the keyboard to the USB port on the laptop (if one is available). If a USB port is not available on your computer, you'll need to return the keyboard for an updated model that *will* operate properly on the Toshiba family of laptops.

Mouse Issues

Although the keyboard is ideal for entering long sequences of text or instructions, it is very poor at designating selections. PC designers developed a pointing device that could streamline selections, thus paving the way for graphics-based operating systems like Windows 95. The development of computer pointing devices has been ongoing since the early 1970s, but the first commercial pointing devices for IBM-compatible systems was widely introduced in the early 1980s. The device's small size, long tail-like cord, and quick scurrying movements immediately earned it the label of *mouse*.

Mouse Assembly

A mouse consists of four major parts: the plastic housing, the mouse ball, the electronics PC board, and the signal cable. The *housing assembly* will vary a little, depending on the manufacturer and vintage of your particular mouse, but the overall scheme is almost always identical. The *mouse ball* is a hard rubber ball situated inside the mouse body just below a small *PC board*. When the mouse is positioned on a desktop, the ball contacts two actuators that register the mouse ball's movement in the X (left to right) and Y (up to down) directions. Both sensors generate a series of pulses that represent movement in both axis. Pulses equate to mouse movement; more pulses mean more movement. The pulses from both axis are amplified by the PC board and sent back to the computer along with information on the condition of each mouse button.

The *trackball* is basically an inverted mouse. Instead of using your hand to move a mouse body around on a desk surface, a trackball remains stationary. Your hand or fingertips move the ball itself that is mounted through the top of the device. For the purposes of this book, a mouse and a trackball are the same thing.

Mice and Device Drivers

All pointing devices require a device driver (usually loaded in the CONFIG.SYS or AUTOEXEC.BAT files during system startup). The device driver is responsible for interpreting the X and Y signals generated by a pointing device and then adding to (or subtracting from) the current cursor position. When an application queries the device driver, it can determine the exact position of the cursor as well as the state of any mouse buttons. Windows 3.1x and Windows 95/98 use their own protected-mode device drivers independent of any real-mode drivers loaded in the files CONFIG.SYS or AUTOEXEC.BAT.

Every mouse or trackball uses its own unique device driver. So when you install a new pointing device, you must update the driver also. However, virtually all pointing devices use similar program code to interrogate the cursor position and buttons. As a result, you may be able to use a mouse from one manufacturer and then use a driver from another, but this is not recommended, and you will invariably lose some functionality of the pointing device.

Cleaning a Pointing Device

Pointing devices are perhaps the simplest peripheral available for your computer. Although they are reasonably forgiving to wear and tear, trackballs and mice can easily be fouled by dust, debris, and foreign matter introduced from the ball. Contamination of this sort is almost never damaging, but it can cause some maddening problems when using the pointing device. A regimen of routine cleaning will help to prevent contamination problems. Turn your computer off before performing any of the following cleaning procedures:

- *Remove the ball.* A ball is held in place by a retaining ring. For a mouse, the retaining ring is on the bottom. For a trackball, the ring is in the top. Rotate the ring and remove it gently; the ball will fall out. Place the retaining ring in a safe place.

- *Clean the ball.* Wash the ball in warm, soapy water and then dry it thoroughly with a clean, lint-free towel. Place the ball in a safe place.

- *Blow out the dust.* Use a can of photography-grade compressed air to blow out any dust or debris that has accumulated inside the pointing device. You may want to do this in an open or outdoor area.

- *Clean the rollers.* Notice the three rollers in the mouse: an X roller, a Y roller, and a small pressure roller the keeps the ball pressed against the X and Y rollers. Use a cotton swab dipped in isopropyl alcohol to clean off any layer of gunk that may have accumulated on the rollers.

- *Reassemble and test.*   Allow everything to dry completely, and then replace the ball and retaining ring. You should then test the pointing device to be sure that it is performing as expected.

    NOTE: Do *not* use harsh solvents, wood alcohol, or chemicals inside the pointing device or on the ball. Chemicals can easily melt the plastic and result in permanent damage to the pointing device.

Mouse Troubleshooting

The following section covers a variety of mouse problems and solutions for resolving them.

Symptom 3.34. The cursor appears, but it only moves erratically as the ball moves (if at all).   This symptom may occur in either the horizontal or vertical axis and suggests that there is an intermittent condition occurring somewhere in the pointing device. Thus, perform the following checks:

- *Check the signal connector.*   Make sure the mouse cable is not cut or damaged anywhere, and see that it is attached securely to the serial or PS/2 port.

- *Clean the pointing device.*   Chances are that the X or Y roller (or both) are fouled. Use the procedure in the previous section to disassemble and clean the trackball or mouse.

- *Check for hardware conflicts.*   Make sure that no other devices in your system are using the same IRQ or I/O address range used by your COM port or PS/2 port. Also check that you are not using COM ports that share resources. For example, avoid using COM1 and COM3 (or COM2 and COM4) at the same time. Try the pointing device on a different port. Update the driver's command line switches if necessary.

- *Try a new pointing device.* If all else fails, try a reliable pointing device. You may have to update the drivers to accommodate the new pointing device.

Symptom 3.35. One or both buttons function erratically (if at all). Buttons are prone to problems from dust accumulation and general contact corrosion, and should have the following checks performed on them:

- *Check the signal connector.* Make sure the mouse cable is not cut or damaged anywhere, and see that it is attached securely to the serial or PS/2 port.

- *Clean the switch contacts.* It is possible that your switch contacts may have become fouled from dust accumulation or contact corrosion. Spray some good-quality contact cleaner into the switch contacts, work the cleaner around, let the cleaner dry, and then try the mouse again.

- *Check the driver.* Make sure that the driver is appropriate for your particular pointing device. If you have installed a new pointing device, see that the new driver is installed properly. If the driver uses command-line switches, see that the switches are configured properly. You might also check to see that the driver is the latest revision.

- *Try a new pointing device.* If all else fails, try a good pointing device. You may have to update the drivers to accommodate the new pointing device.

Symptom 3.36. The screen cursor appears on the display, but it does not move. If the cursor appears, the device driver has loaded correctly and the application program is communicating with the driver. In most cases, you have a connection problem and the following checks will help you spot the source:

- *Check the signal connector.*   Make sure the mouse cable is not cut or damaged anywhere, and see that it is attached securely to the serial or PS/2 port.

- *Clean the pointing device.*   Both the X and Y rollers are completely fouled. Use the procedure in the previous section to disassemble and clean the trackball or mouse.

- *Check for hardware conflicts.*   Make sure that no other devices in your system are using the same IRQ or I/O address range used by your COM port or PS/2 port. Also check that you are not using COM ports that share resources. For example, avoid using COM1 and COM3 (or COM2 and COM4) at the same time. Try the pointing device on a different port. Update the driver's command line switches if necessary.

- *Try a new pointing device.*   If all else fails, try a reliable pointing device. You may have to update the drivers to accommodate the new pointing device.

Symptom 3.37. The mouse or trackball device driver fails to load.   In most cases, the driver did not load because the pointing device was simply not detected. Perform the following checks to find the cause of the problem:

- *Check the signal connector.*   Make sure the mouse cable is not cut or damaged anywhere, and see that it is attached securely to the serial or PS/2 port.

- *Check the driver.*   If the driver is not written for your particular pointing device, it may not detect the device properly, so the driver will not load. If you see a "File not found" error when the device driver attempts to load, the driver may be corrupt or accidentally erased. You may try reinstalling the driver software.

- *Check the CMOS Setup.*   Many newer system BIOS versions provide an option in the CMOS Setup for a mouse port. Check the CMOS Setup and see that any entries for your mouse are enabled.

■ *Check for hardware conflicts.*   Make sure that no other devices in your system are using the same IRQ or I/O address range used by your COM port or PS/2 port. Also check that you are not using COM ports that share resources. For example, avoid using COM1 and COM3 (or COM2 and COM4) at the same time. Try the pointing device on a different port. Update the driver's command line switches if necessary.

■ *Try a new pointing device.*   If all else fails, try a reliable pointing device. You may have to update the drivers to accommodate the new pointing device.

Symptom 3.38. When installing a new mouse and driver, you see a "General protection fault" when trying to use the mouse with one or more applications under Windows.   In most cases, the new mouse driver is conflicting with one or more applications:

■ *Check the driver.*   Make sure the driver for your pointing device is the latest version that is the proper driver for your particular device. If a new driver is causing problems, try an older version if it is available.

■ *Try a new pointing device.*   If all else fails, try a reliable pointing device. You may have to update the drivers to accommodate the new pointing device.

Symptom 3.39. You see an error message such as, "This pointer device requires a newer version."   In virtually all cases, you have the wrong driver installed on the system. Make sure that the driver you are using is appropriate for the particular mouse. For example, a Logitech or Genius mouse selected in Windows Setup will cause this kind of problem if you have a Microsoft mouse on the system. Thus, change the mouse type under Windows.

Symptom 3.40. You see an error message such as, "Mouse port disabled or mouse not present." This is almost always a connection problem or a setup problem. Thus, perform the following checks:

- *Check the signal connector.* Make sure the mouse cable is not cut or damaged anywhere, and see that it is attached securely to the serial or PS/2 port.

- *Check the CMOS Setup.* Many newer system BIOS versions provide an option in the CMOS Setup for a mouse port. Check the CMOS Setup and see that any entries for your mouse are enabled.

Symptom 3.41. The mouse works for a few minutes and then stops. When the computer is rebooted, the mouse starts working again. This is a problem that often plagues cut-price mice and is almost always due to a buildup of static in the mouse. The static charges interfere with the mouse circuitry and cause the mouse to stop responding (though charges are not enough to actually damage the mouse). Generally, the problem can be solved in one of three ways: (1) spray the surrounding carpet and upholstery with a very dilute fabric softener to dissipate static buildup, (2) hire an electrician to ensure that the computer and house wiring are grounded properly, or (3) replace the mouse with a more static-resistant model.

Symptom 3.42. You attempt a double-click but get quadruple-click, or you attempt a single-click and get a double-click. This is a phenomenon called *button bounce* and is the result of a hardware defect (broken or poorly buffered mouse buttons). You may be able to clean the mouse buttons by spraying in some good electronic-grade contact cleaner. Otherwise, you'll need to replace the mouse outright.

Symptom 3.43. A single mouse click works, but double-click doesn't. When this problem occurs, it is almost always because the double-click speed is set too high in the Windows 95/98 mouse control panel. Try setting it lower. Click Start, select Settings, and then open the Control Panel. Double-click the Mouse icon and adjust the Double-click speed slider under the Buttons tab.

Symptom 3.44. A PS/2 mouse is not detected by a notebook PC under Windows 95. A known problem exists with PS/2 mouse detection on a Toshiba portable computer under Windows 95. You can usually correct the problem by taking the following steps:

1. Shut down the computer entirely and physically disconnect the PS/2 mouse from the PS/2 port.

2. Restart the PC to the DOS mode and create backup copies of the CONFIG.SYS and AUTOEXEC.BAT files.

3. Restart Windows 95 (reboot the PC if necessary).

4. Click Start, select Settings, open the Control Panel, and double-click on the System icon.

5. Select the Device Manager tab and double-click the Mouse entry.

6. Select the mouse entry that is not being detected (Toshiba AccuPoint) and click Remove.

7. Select and remove any other mouse entries.

8. Shut down the computer, reconnect the mouse, and then turn the PC back on.

9. When the system reboots, it should detect the mouse and attempt to reinstall the appropriate drivers.

If this doesn't fix the problem, a hardware issue could exist. Try a different PS/2 mouse (preferably from a manufacturer different than the current one). If a different make and model PS/2 mouse does not work, the PS/2 port may require service.

Symptom 3.45. Mouse pointer options are not saved.
This is a known problem when you use the Extra Points features in the Mouse Manager program included with the Microsoft Mouse driver. The pointer options are not saved or written to the MOUSE.INI file when you are running a virus-protection program such as *Microsoft Anti-Virus* (MSAV) or *Norton Anti-Virus* (NAV). To correct this problem, remove the files CHKLIST.MS or CHKLIST.CPS in the directory that contains the mouse files. To determine the location of that directory, type set at the MS-DOS command prompt, which will return a list of locations of various files and memory strings. Look for the MOUSE= line, then go to that directory, and delete the CHKLIST.MS or CHKLIST.CPS file. Reboot the system and try the saving options again.

Symptom 3.46. Clicking the right mouse button doesn't start the default context menus of Windows 95/98. If the mouse manager software you're running is using an assignment set for the right button, this assignment will override the Windows 95/98 default setting of "context menus." Open the mouse management software utility and change the assignment for the right button to "Unassigned." Save your changes and the right mouse button will now access the default context menus.

Symptom 3.47. The Packard Bell "Fast Media" device no longer functions after installing a pointing device under Windows 95/98. The Fast Media device is an infrared remote control device that enables you to control the mouse pointer as well as a CD player, TV tuner, modem, radio card, and other items. This device only works with native Microsoft drivers. When you install pointing device drivers, the Fast Media device no longer functions. This happens because the Fast Media software installs some virtual drivers that only communicate with the native Microsoft drivers.

Unfortunately, you may need to choose between the Fast Media system (and forego the advanced features of your new pointing device) or disable the Fast Media system in order to use all of the features of your pointing device. You may also check with Packard Bell to see if there is an update to the Fast Media drivers that are more compliant with other device drivers.

Symptom 3.48. Your Packard Bell only detects a basic two-button mouse after plugging it into a Media Select unit. The Packard Bell Media Select is a box that fits underneath the monitor and plugs into the PS/2 port of the computer system. This Media Select device also has a PS/2 port for a PS/2 style mouse. It seems that the Media Select unit uses a pass-through PS/2 port connection that causes detection problems for some pointing devices. In most cases, cleaning up the registry and removing unneeded entries can clear this problem:

> **NOTE**:   Do not attempt to edit your registry without first creating a complete registry backup on your boot diskette. Incorrectly editing the registry may prevent the system from booting.

1. Click Start and select Run.
2. On the Open line, type C:\WINDOWS\REGEDIT. EXE and press Enter.
3. Open the following key:

   ```
   Hkey_Local_Machine\System\CurrentControlSet\Ser
   vices\Class\Mouse\xxxx
   ```

   where xxxx is an incremental four-digit number starting at 0000.

4. Click on each folder under the Mouse folder and delete them until no 000X folders remain.
5. Save your changes and exit the Registry Editor.
6. Remove the FMEDIA reference from the Windows Startup group or the WIN.INI file as necessary.

7. Save any changes, shut down, and then restart the system normally.

8. Open the Properties dialog or applet for your pointing device to verify the correct detection.

If this does not correct the detection issue, you'll need to connect the pointing device directly to the computer system's PS/2 port (bypassing the Media Select box). You may also use the serial port if the pointing device is a PS/2-serial combination unit. This will enable you to keep the Media Select and achieve correct detection if the serial port is working properly.

Symptom 3.49. The mouse pointer does not move after installing a Logitech "First Mouse" on a Packard Bell system. Windows will generally *not* indicate any problems with mouse detection. A known compatibility problem exists with some Packard Bell computers and Logitech's two button "First Mouse" (version M/N:M34). You can use the keyboard to invoke a basic workaround:

1. Press Ctrl + Esc to open the Start menu.

2. Use the arrow keys to highlight Settings, then Control Panel, and press the Enter key.

3. Move the arrow key over to the Mouse icon and press the Enter key. This will open the Mouse Properties dialog box.

4. Using the Tab key, tab over to the Quick Setup tab, and then use the right arrow key to open the Devices tab.

5. Once on the Devices tab, tab over to the Add Mouse button and press the Enter key.

The pointing device applet should now detect the two-button serial mouse, and the pointer should now move properly. However, you'll need to perform this procedure each time you restart the system. If your

Packard Bell system has a dedicated PS/2 mouse port, another option is to contact the pointing device maker to see if you can exchange the serial version for a PS/2 version.

Symptom 3.50. After installing a three-button mouse, you receive an error such as "pointing device on unknown port." You may also find that the device is only shown as a two-button mouse. In most cases, older mouse traces in the registry must be removed before the new pointing device can be properly detected:

> **NOTE**: Do not attempt to edit your registry without first creating a complete registry backup on your boot diskette. Incorrectly editing the registry may prevent the system from booting.

1. Click Start and select Run.
2. On the Open line, type `C:\WINDOWS\REGEDIT.EXE` and press Enter.
3. Open the following key:

   ```
   Hkey_Local_Machine\System\CurrentControlSet\Ser
   vices\Class\Mouse\xxxx
   ```

   where `XXXX` is an incremental four-digit number starting at 0000.
4. Click on each folder under the Mouse folder and delete them until no 000X folders remain.
5. Save your changes and exit the Registry Editor.
6. Open the Properties dialog or applet for your pointing device to verify the correct detection.

Symptom 3.51. When installing a three- or four-button PS/2 pointing device on a laptop with its own pointing device, the new device only shows up as a two-button mouse. This issue has several possible solutions, depending on which laptop and pointing device you're using. Try disabling the internal pointing device. Some systems may require that you disable the internal pointing device *first* (usually through the CMOS Setup) in order to detect a new pointing device on the external mouse port. You may also want to contact the system manufacturer to see if a BIOS update is available or if any further information related to using external pointing devices is on the system.

Symptom 3.52. You receive a KBC error when connecting a pointing device to certain laptop PS/2 ports. This is a known compatibility issue between the Toshiba 400 series notebook and Logitech PS/2 "combo" pointing devices. These Toshiba systems have a single PS/2 connector on the back that may accept either a mouse or keyboard, and the problem is caused by a BIOS oversight. Toshiba has a BIOS upgrade that resolves this issue (version v.5.40 or later can be obtained by contacting Toshiba America). If a BIOS upgrade is not available, you may connect the Logitech combo pointing device to the serial port instead (use only Logitech adapters).

Symptom 3.53. After installing the applets for your pointing device, you receive an 0E Exception error on a blue screen. You may also find that you can press Enter and still access Windows, but this error appears on each boot. This problem is often encountered on IBM systems. IBM has found a problem with version 1.10 of their TrackPoint drivers. This error produces a blue screen on bootup *if* the mouse drivers are changed. The workaround for this trouble is to uninstall the IBM TrackPoint software through the Add/Remove Programs icon in the Windows Control Panel.

Symptom 3.54. The pointing device (or system) freezes when the system wakes from its suspend mode. Many current mouse drivers have the capability to perform a search for mice when a system wakes from its suspend mode (for Windows 95/98, this is defined by a key in the Windows registry). This registry setting defines the action that the driver will perform upon power management suspend/resume commands. If the mouse stops working after a resume, this parameter should be set to *Off*, as described next:

1. Click Start and select Run.

2. On the Open line, type REGEDIT.EXE and press Enter.

3. Click the plus sign next to HKEY_LOCAL_ MACHINE.

4. Click the plus sign next to SOFTWARE.

5. Click the plus sign next to your pointing device maker (Logitech).

6. Click the plus sign next to the software name (MouseWare).

7. Click the plus sign next to CurrentVersion.

8. Single-click on Technical folder and information should be displayed on the right side of the Registry Editor screen.

9. Under the Name column, double-click on the APMMode entry and an Edit String dialog box should appear.

10. Modify the *Value Data* line to read Off and click the *OK* button. The full line should now read:

```
HKEY_LOCAL_MACHINE\SOFTWARE\Logitech\MouseWare\
CurrentVersion\Technical\APMMode="Off"
```

Exit the Registry Editor and restart your system. Then test the computer again to see if it resumes without freezing. If you still experience APM issues, try uninstalling the mouse applet(s) using the Add/Remove Programs icon in the Control Panel. This will restore the system to the native drivers supplied by Windows.

Now test your system again to see it resumes correctly. If it still fails, try another mouse in the same port.

Symptom 3.55. When running a DOS program from Windows 95/98, the mouse cursor moves very slowly compared to native Windows applications. Several possible issues must be considered here. If the problem only occurs under one DOS application (and not in others), the problem may be with the particular application. You may need a patch or update for that application, or you may want to try installing the very latest mouse driver. Also try shutting down to DOS and running the program from the native DOS mode (rather than through a DOS window).

Symptom 3.56. The modem won't start after installing new mouse management software. This is a known problem when installing Logitech's MouseWare 6.60 or later under Windows 95. Sometimes the mouse drivers may detect the modem as a second mouse and try to initialize it. This can cause the modem to go into a busy state. However, you can prevent the mouse drivers from searching the serial port that the modem is using:

1. Download the current mouse driver for Windows 95.
2. Edit the Windows 95 registry by clicking on the Start menu and selecting Run.
3. Type `C:\WINDOWS\REGEDIT.EXE` on the Open line.
4. Click OK. The Registry Editor program will start.
5. Double-click on the HKEY_LOCAL_MACHINE folder.
6. Double-click on the SOFTWARE folder.
7. Double-click on the manufacturer's folder (Logitech).
8. Double-click on the manufacturer's driver folder (MouseWare).

9. Double-click on the CurrentVersion folder.

10. Click on the Global folder.

11. Let's assume the mouse is on COM1 and the modem is on COM2. On the right side of the screen, there will be a list of value data strings. Double-click on the PortSearchOrder string. An Edit String dialog box will appear. The Value Data line will read:

```
COM1, COM2
```

12. Remove the space, the comma, and COM2 so the line reads

```
COM1
```

13. If you only plan to use one mouse on the system, change the MaximumDevices value data line to 1 using the same previous steps. This will tell the driver to stop searching for additional mice after the primary mouse has been found.

    NOTE: If you are not using a serial mouse, remove Serial from the SearchOrder value data line so that no serial devices are searched for at all. In general, remove any reference to the port the modem is using.

14. Now click OK and the values under the data value section on the right side of the screen should change. Exit the registry editor (saving is automatic). Shut down the computer and reboot from a cold start so that your changes can take effect.

Symptom 3.57. The mouse pointer moves only vertically. The mouse is connected to a PS/2 port under Windows 95. If the mouse works along one axis but not the other, it's usually due to a hardware problem; either the mouse needs cleaning or repair. However, in some cases, a software configuration problem can occur when the mouse driver (Mouse Power v9.5) is installed on a system with plug-and-play BIOS running Windows 95 and the mouse is connected to the PS/2-style mouse port. As soon as you touch the mouse, the pointer darts over the right edge of the screen and then will move only up and down. To fix this problem, perform the following steps:

1. To regain control over your computer, reboot in Safe mode.

2. Click Start, then Run, then type REGEDIT, and press Enter.

3. Open HKEY_LOCAL_MACHINE\Enum folder and see if BIOS is listed under Enum. If it is, then you know the software configuration problem is causing the issue.

4. Open HKEY_LOCAL_MACHINE\Enum\BIOS\ *PNP0F13 and look for a key (usually 05 or 07) under *PNP0F13. Click on this key to highlight it. The key under *PNP0F13 should now be highlighted, and the corresponding values should be displayed on the right side of the window. Note the string values with an "ab" icon next to them and the binary values with a 011 icon next to them.

5. Compare your values to those shown below. Edit your entries until all your values shown on the screen match the following values shown:

   ```
   ab    Class          "Mouse"
   011   ConfigFlags    00 00 00 00
   ab    DeviceDesc     "Mouse Systems v2.18"
   ab    Driver         "Mouse\0000"
   ab    HardwareID     "*PNP0F0C"
   ab    Mfg            "Mouse Systems"
   ```

6. Open HKEY_LOCAL_MACHINE\System\Current ControlSet\Services\Class\Mouse. There should

be multiple keys under Mouse (such as 0000 and 0001). All but one are to be deleted. Carefully determine which one pertains to your current mouse (by looking at the values associated with each key) and delete all the keys under Mouse except the related one.

7. Make sure the one remaining key under Mouse is labeled 0000 (rename it if necessary).

8. Click on the X box in the far upper-right corner of the Registry Editor to close it.

9. Reboot the computer from a cold start. The computer should reboot in normal mode, and the problem with the mouse and keyboard should be gone.

Joystick Issues

One of the first game applications for the PC was flight simulation. However, keyboard and mouse controls did not lend themselves well to flight controls. PC designers later developed the *analog joystick* to provide both X and Y axis signals simultaneously. For game players, this translated to smooth left-right and up-down motions. Through the years, the joystick has become an enduring icon of computer entertainment.

Inside the Joystick

Each analog joystick is assembled with two separate potentiometers (typically 100k) arranged perpendicularly to one another. One potentiometer represents the X axis, while the other potentiometer represents the Y axis. Both potentiometers are linked together mechanically and attached to a movable stick. As the stick is moved left or right, one potentiometer is moved. As the stick moves up or down, the other potentiometer is moved. Of course, the stick can be moved in both the X and Y axis simultaneously with the proportions of resistance reflecting the stick's position. The wiring

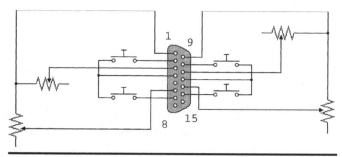

Figure 3.3 A standard 15-pin joystick wiring layout

scheme for a standard 15-pin dual joystick port is shown in Figure 3.3.

A joystick also has one or two buttons. The buttons are typically open, and their closed state can be detected by reading the byte at I/O port 201h. Since a game port is capable of supporting two joysticks simultaneously (each with two buttons), the upper four bits of 201h indicate the on/off status of the buttons.

Joystick Drift

The term *drift* (or *rolling*) indicates a loss of control by the joystick. There are three possible reasons for this:

- *Drift can be the result of a system conflict.* Since a game port does not generate an interrupt, conflicts rarely result in system crashes or lockups, but another device feeding data to port 201h can easily upset joystick operation. If you have sound boards or multi-port I/O boards in your system equipped with game ports, be sure to disable any unused ports (check with the user instructions for individual boards to disable extra game ports).

- *Drift can be due to heat.* Once PCs are started up, it is natural for the power used by most components to be dissipated as heat, and heating tends to change the value of components. For logic circuits, this is typically not a problem, but for analog circuits, the consequences can be much more pronounced. As heat changes the values of a game port's timing circuit, the joystick center values will shift. The circuit warms up, and error creeps into the joystick. It is interesting to note that the joystick itself is rarely the cause of drift. If you can compensate for drift by recalibrating the joystick, try a better quality game port adapter board.

- *Drift can also be a result of application problems.* A poor or inaccurate routine will tend to calibrate the joystick incorrectly. Try another application and if it can calibrate and use the joystick properly, you should suspect a bug in the particular application. Try contacting the application manufacturer to find if there is a patch or fix available.

Cleaning a Joystick

Ordinarily, the typical joystick should not require routine cleaning or maintenance. Most joysticks use reasonably reliable potentiometers that should last for the life of the joystick. The two major enemies of a joystick are wear and dust. Wear occurs during normal use as potentiometer sliders move across the resistive surface; it can't be avoided. Over time, wear will affect the contact resistance values of both potentiometers. Uneven wear will result in uneven performance. When this becomes noticeable, it is time to buy a new joystick.

Dust presents another problem. The open aperture at the top of a joystick is an invitation for dust and other debris. Since dust is conductive, it can adversely affect potentiometer values and interfere with slider contacts. This produces jumpy or non-linear responses.

To fix this problem, turn off the computer and disconnect the joystick. Open the joystick, which is usually held together by two screws in the bottom housing. Remove the bottom housing and locate the two (X and

Y axis) potentiometers. Most potentiometers have small openings somewhere around their circumference. Dust the joystick area with photography-grade compressed air, and spray a small quantity of quality electronic contact cleaner into each potentiometer. Move the potentiometer through its complete range of motion a few times and enable several minutes for the cleaner to dry. Reassemble the housing and try the joystick again. If problems persist, replace the joystick.

Joystick Troubleshooting

This section outlines common joystick problems and possible solutions for them.

Symptom 3.58. The joystick does not respond. In most cases, the joystick is not connected or installed properly. Numerous things can be checked:

- *Check the signal connector.* Make sure the joystick cable is not cut or damaged anywhere, and see that it is attached securely to the game port.

- *Check the application.* It is the application that interrogates the joystick port. Examine the Options or Setup sections of your application and see that the control method is set to "joystick" rather than "mouse" or "keyboard."

- *Check the game port.* Virtually all recent sound boards provide a 15-pin MIDI/joystick port in addition to the sound connections. If you are using the sound board port, make sure that the port is jumpered for use with a joystick (not MIDI). If you prefer to use a stand-alone joystick controller instead of the sound board's controller, see that the sound board's port is jumpered as a MIDI port or disable the port outright. Also be sure that the game port's I/O address is set properly (201h).

Symptom 3.59. The basic X/Y, two-button features of the joystick work, but the hat switch, throttle controls, and supplemental buttons do not seem to respond. In virtually all cases, the joystick is configured wrong, and the following checks will indicate where:

- *Check the application.* Many new applications provide several different joystick options and even enable you to define the particular use of each feature from within the application itself.

- *Check the joystick files.* Your joystick probably requires a supplemental definition file (an FCS file) in order to use all of the joystick's particular features.

- *Check the game port.* You may need a dual-port game port adapter. Some enhanced joysticks use *both* joystick positions (the XY axis and fire buttons make up one joystick, while the throttle and other buttons take up the other position). You may need to install a dual-port game port card.

Symptom 3.60. Joystick performance is erratic or choppy. This is usually a mechanical issue with the joystick itself, and the following checks could tell you more about this:

- *Check the signal connector.* Make sure the joystick cable is not cut or damaged anywhere, and see that it is attached securely to the game port.

- *Try a new joystick.* Test a good joystick on the system. If a new joystick works as expected, the original joystick is worn out or damaged internally.

- *Check the application.* Try recalibrating the joystick through the particular application. It may be necessary for you to upgrade the joystick's driver software.

- *Check the hardware setup.* Make sure that no other devices in the system using the I/O address assigned to your game port (201h).

- *Replace the game port.* It is possible that the game port may be too slow for your particular system. This frequently occurs when older game port boards are used in very fast computers. Try a `speed-adjusting` game port if you can.

Symptom 3.61. The joystick is sending incorrect information to the system and appears to be drifting. Either the application is not calibrating the joystick properly, or the game port is not adequate:

- *Check the application.* Try recalibrating the joystick using your particular application. If the problem persists, try calibrating the joystick through a different application. If calibration works through one application, but problems persist in another, you may have a buggy application that needs a patch to update.

- *Check the hardware setup.* Make sure that no other devices in the system use the I/O address assigned to your game port (201h).

- *Replace the game port.* If drift issues continue with different applications, you may need to replace the game port adapter with a low-drift or speed-adjusting model.

Symptom 3.62. You see an error such as "Joystick Not Connected" under Windows 95. Windows 95 does not recognize the game port hardware, so make the following checks:

- *Check the game port driver.* Use the Device Manager under Windows 95 to examine the resources assigned to the game port driver. Typically, the resource range should be set to 201h through

201h (only one address location). If the game port entry has a yellow icon next to it, there is a hardware conflict in the system, and other hardware is also trying to use the same I/O location.

■ *Check the game port hardware.* The game port card should be installed properly into its bus slot. Make sure that the game port is enabled (this is typical of game ports integrated onto sound cards or multi-I/O cards). If a sound card enables you to switch a 15-pin port between the MIDI and joystick, see that the jumper is set to the joystick position.

■ *Check the signal connector.* Make sure the joystick cable is not cut or damaged anywhere, and see that it is attached securely to the game port.

■ *Try a new joystick.* Test a good joystick on the system. If a new joystick works as expected, the original joystick is probably suffering from internal wiring damage.

Symptom 3.63. The joystick drifts frequently and requires recalibration. This type of symptom is usually the result of problems with the game port adapter. Here are two possible solutions:

■ *Replace the game port.* Try a different game port adapter and see if the problem persists. If problems disappear, you simply need a better quality or speed adjusting game port.

■ *Try a new joystick.* Test a good joystick on the system. If a new joystick works as expected, the original joystick is probably suffering from internal wiring damage.

Symptom 3.64. The joystick handle has lost tension. It no longer snaps back to the center. This problem may be accompanied by a rattling sound within the joystick. In most cases, a spring has popped out of place inside the joystick:

- *Check the joystick.*   Open the joystick and see if any springs or clips have slipped out of place. Replace any springs or clips (if possible).

- *Replace the joystick.*   If you cannot locate or correct the problem, simply replace the joystick outright.

Symptom 3.65. The joystick responds but refuses to accept a calibration.   In virtually all cases, the problem is with your game port adapter:

- *Check the hardware setup.*   Make sure that no other devices in the system use the I/O address assigned to your game port (201h). If more than one adapter in your system has game port capabilities, see that only one game port is enabled.

- *Replace the game port.*   If drift issues continue with different applications, you may need to replace the game port adapter with a low-drift or speed-adjusting model.

Symptom 3.66. The hat switch and buttons on a joystick work only intermittently (if at all). This problem also applies to stand-alone pedals.   In most cases, erratic behavior of a joystick's enhanced features is a symptom of game port speed problems. Here are some solutions:

- *Check the joystick.*   Before going too far, try a reliable joystick. If the problems disappear, the original joystick may in fact be defective. If the problems persist, you have a game port problem.

- *Check the hardware setup.*   Make sure that no other devices in the system use the I/O address assigned to your game port (201h). If more than one adapter in your system has game port capabilities, see that only one game port is enabled.

- *Replace the game port.*   If drift issues continue with different applications, you may need to replace the game port adapter with either a low-drift or speed-adjusting model.

Symptom 3.67. When downloading FCS (or calibration) files to a joystick, the line saying "put switch into calibrate" doesn't change when the download switch is moved. This is a typical problem with advanced joysticks. In most cases, the joystick needs to be "cleared:"

- *Clear the joystick.* Rock the download switch back to analog and then to calibrate. This should clear the joystick for a new calibration download.

- *Replace the joystick.* If problems persist, the actual switch may be defective. Try a good joystick instead.

Symptom 3.68. To download a calibration file, you need to rock the red switch back and forth a number of times (or hit the Enter key a number of times) to get it to 100 percent. This is virtually always the result of a keyboard controller (keyboard BIOS) problem.

Upgrade the keyboard controller (keyboard BIOS). Some advanced joystick products do not interact well with the host computer's keyboard controller. For example, Thrustmaster's Mark II experiences known microcode problems with a few of keyboard controller chips on the market. These include AMI versions (D, B, 8, 0), Acer, and Phoenix. You may need to replace the keyboard controller with a later version.

Symptom 3.69. You cannot use a joystick to a PC using a sound card with an ESS or OPTi chipset. The joystick may stop responding while using an application or report a "not connected" status the Game Controllers area of the Control Panel. This is a known problem with the ESS and OPTi sound chipsets. You'll need to set Single Mode DMA to use the joystick:

1. Click Start, select Settings, and then click Control Panel.

2. Double-click Multimedia.

3. On the Advanced tab, double-click the Audio Devices entry to expand it.

4. Click the Audio for ... entry that corresponds to your particular sound card and then click Properties.

5. Click Settings.

6. Click the Use Single Mode DMA check box to select it.

7. Click OK until you return to Windows. Then restart the PC.

Symptom 3.70. The joystick port is not removed when the sound card is removed. The entry for your game port will still be visible in the Windows 95/98 Device Manager. This is not really a problem. Windows 95/98 does not recognize the game port as being part of the sound card, so removing the sound card doesn't automatically disable the game port. Also, the *virtual joystick device driver* (VJOYD.VXD) cannot detect whether the game port or joystick are installed or not, so the driver is always active. You'll need to manually remove the game port in Device Manager:

1. Use the right mouse button to click My Computer, and then click Properties on the menu.

2. Click the Device Manager tab.

3. Double-click the Sound, Video, and Game Controllers entry to expand it.

4. Click the joystick port and then click Remove.

5. Return to Windows 95/98 and restart the system.

Symptom 3.71. You cannot disable a jumperless joystick port. This is an issue that frequently crops up with newer sound boards like the Ensoniq VIVO, and jumperless boards are controlled exclusively through drivers. The VIVO also uses drivers to disable certain functions like the joystick port. Use the following steps to disable the VIVO's joystick port (the specific command lines for your own sound board may be different, but the idea is very similar):

1. Leave Windows 95/98 and enter the DOS mode.

2. Edit the SNDSCAPE.INI file in the \Windows directory. Change the line *JSEnable*=true to *JSEnable*=false (check your particular sound board's documentation for the correct command line).

3. Save the file and reboot the system. The joystick will now be disabled.

Symptom 3.72. Your joystick doesn't work with a SoundBlaster Live card. This is an issue with the SoundBlaster Live card. It's an excellent sound card, but the game port on the card is very slow. This means any fast analog device that is used with the SoundBlaster Live card will have trouble being "seen" by Windows. In this instance, your best solution is to disable the sound card's game port and install a fast game port card instead.

Symptom 3.73. The cross-hair on your axis is off-center. This is a frequent issue with digital joysticks such as the Gravis Blackhawk Digital. Chances are that you're dealing with a Windows 95/98 "shadow driver" problem. Follow these steps to reach a resolution:

1. You'll need to restart your system in Safe mode.

2. Open your Control Panel, double-click the System icon, and then choose the Device Manager tab.

3. Click on the plus sign in front of the Sound, Video and Game Controllers entry to expand the list. You can only have one driver that contains the word "game port" or "joystick" in its name.

4. Make sure you have the Windows 95/98 CD or the disc containing your game port driver. Then remove all the listings that refer to your game port or joystick.

5. When you restart the computer, it should detect new hardware and may ask for the installation CD. If it recommends that you keep your newer driver, select No and install the drivers from your disc(s).

6. Save the changes and reboot the system if necessary. Your joystick should now be on center.

Symptom 3.74. You get a fatal exception error when you open the Gaming Devices wizard in the Control Panel. For example, you may see an error such as

```
A Fatal Exception Error 0E occurred at
0028:58C10F3F
```

This error can usually occur if the game port is conflicting with another device. Use the Device Manager to see whether another device is conflicting with the game port. If Device Manager reports that there's a problem with the configuration of the game port, reconfigure the game port so that it uses resources that are *not* already in use by another device. If the game port is a plug-and-play device and is conflicting with another device, you *must* disable the device *before* attempting to change the resource settings. Use the following steps under Windows 95:

1. Open the Control Panel and double-click the System icon.

2. Click the Device Manager tab and double-click Sound, Video and Game Controllers.

3. Double-click the Gameport Joystick entry.

4. In the Gameport Joystick Properties dialog box, click the General tab, click the Original Config-

uration check box to clear it, and then click OK. Under Windows 98, check the box `Disable  in this hardware configuration.`

Symptom 3.75. The joystick's throttle or slider control does not work in certain games. When you use the Side-Winder 3D Pro joystick, the throttle or slider control may not work in one or more of your games. This is because the throttle works only while the joystick is emulating a more basic model. For the SideWinder 3D Pro, the mode switch should be in position one, which causes the SideWinder 3D Pro to emulate a CH Flightstick Pro. Make sure that the switch is set in this position and calibrate the SideWinder as a CH Flightstick Pro joystick. This should correct the problem. You may also be able to correct the problem by patching or upgrading your offending game(s) to a version that supports your specific joystick type directly.

Symptom 3.76. The Game Controller switches between OK and Not Connected. When you use the Game Controllers tool in the Control Panel to check the status of a USB game controller, the game controller status may toggle between OK and Not Connected. In addition, you may see random buttons light up on the screen when you use the Game Controllers tool to test a USB game controller. This problem occurs when the USB game controller is connected to the game port on your computer, and the game port on your computer is not working correctly. To correct this problem, connect the USB game controller to the USB port on your computer or install a working game port in your computer. If no USB port is on your computer, you may be able to resolve this problem by contacting the manufacturer of your sound card to obtain updated drivers. This may correct problems or incompatibilities with the sound card's game port controller and enable the joystick to function properly.

Modem Troubleshooting

Although the PC has evolved tremendously over the last few years, few parts have undergone a more radical transformation than the modem. The plain, old 9600-*bits-per-second* (bps) workhorses of just a few years ago have progressed from 14.4 KB to 28.8 KB to 33.6 KB with ISDN/DSL capabilities seemingly overnight. The great advantage of this speed increase is that online sources such as the Internet can effectively offer content like graphics, animation, video, and audio, which has traditionally been far too data-intensive to be practical before. Along with these advances, however, some problems have also occurred. This section covers modem standards, initialization issues, and troubleshooting.

Understanding Modems

Basically, three types of modems exist: internal, external, and *Personal Computer Memory Card International Association* (PCMCIA). For this book, a PCMCIA modem should be regarded as an internal modem. The *internal* modem is a stand-alone board that plugs directly into a PC expansion bus, and each major modem function is detailed in Figure 4.1. The

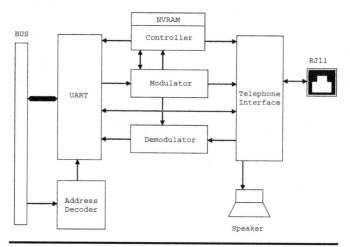

Figure 4.1   A block diagram of an internal modem

internal modem contains its own *Universal Asynchronous Receiver / Transmitter* (UART). It is the UART that manipulates data into and out of serial form. A UART forms the foundation of a serial port, and this can represent a serious hardware conflict for your PC. When installing an internal modem, be sure that the IRQ line and I/O address chosen for the UART serial port does not conflict with other serial ports already in the system. It may be necessary to disable conflicting ports.

Before being transmitted over telephone lines, serial data is converted into audio signals. This process is carried out by a *modulator* circuit. The modulated audio is then coupled to the telephone line using a circuit very similar to that used by ordinary telephones to couple voice. Audio signals are made available to a single RJ11-type (telephone line) connector at the rear of the modem. Internal modems often provide a second RJ11 jack for a separate telephone. Signals received from the telephone line must be translated back into serial data. The telephone interface separates received signals and passes them to the *demodulator*. After demodulation, the resulting serial data is passed to the UART, which in turn converts the serial bits into parallel words that are placed on the system's data bus.

Besides combining and separating modulated audio data, the *telephone interface* generates the *dual-tone multi-frequency* (DTMF) dialing signals needed to reach a remote modem, much the same way as a touch-tone telephone. When a remote modem dials in, the telephone interface detects the incoming ring and alerts the UART to begin negotiating a connection. Finally, the telephone interface drives a small speaker. During the first stages of modem operation, the speaker is often used to hear a dial tone, dialing signals, and audio negotiation between the two modems. Once a connection is established, the speaker is usually disabled.

A *controller* circuit manages the overall operation of the modem, but in a more general sense, it switches the modem between its control and data operating modes. The controller accepts commands from the modulator that enables modem characteristics and operating parameters to be changed. In the event of power loss or reset conditions, default modem parameters can be loaded from *Non-Volatile Random Access Memory* (NVRAM). Permanent changes to modem parameters are stored in NVRAM.

For all practical intents and purposes, the *external* modem (see Figure 4.2) provides virtually all of the essential functions offered by an internal modem. Many of the external modem's functions are identical to those of an internal modem. The major difference between modems is that the external modem does not include a built-in UART to provide a serial port. Instead, the external modem relies on a serial port already configured in the PC. A 9-pin or 25-pin serial cable often makes the external modem setup faster and easier than internal modems, since you need not worry about interrupt lines and I/O address settings. Hardware conflicts are rare with external modems.

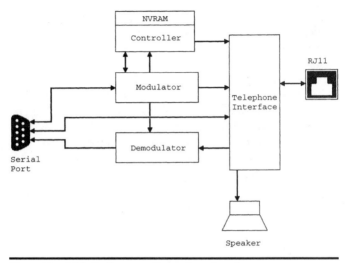

Figure 4.2   A block diagram of an external modem

The other practical difference in an external modem is the way it is powered. Although internal modems are powered from the expansion bus, external modems must be powered from a small AC adapter. In locations where AC outlets are scarce, this may be a problem. On the other hand, external modems provide a series of signal status *light-emitting diodes* (LEDs). The LEDs enable you to easily check the state of serial communications. One of the appealing attributes of external modems is the series of lights that typically adorns the front face. By observing each light and the sequence in which they light, you can often follow the progress of a communication or quickly discern the cause of a communication failure. The following markings are typical of many modems, but keep in mind that your particular modem may use fewer indicators (or be marked differently):

- High Speed *(HS)*.   When this indicator is lit, the modem is operating at its highest transfer rate.

- Auto Answer *(AA)*.   When illuminated, your modem will answer any incoming calls automatically. This feature is vital for unattended systems such as bulletin boards.

- Carrier Detect *(CD)*. This lights whenever the modem detects a carrier signal. This means it has successfully connected to a remote computer. This *light-emitting diode* (LED) will go out when either one of the modems drops the line.

- Off Hook *(OH)*. This LED lights anytime the modem takes control of the telephone line, the equivalent of taking the telephone off the hook.

- Receive Data *(RD)*. It is also marked Rx. This LED flickers as data is received by the modem from a remote modem.

- Send Data *(SD)*. It is also marked Tx. This LED flickers as data is sent from your modem to the remote modem.

- Terminal Ready *(TR)*. This light illuminates when the modem detects a *Data Terminal Ready* (DTR) signal from the communication software.

- Modem Ready *(MR)*. A simple power-on light that indicates the modem is turned on and ready to operate.

Modems and UART Types

Whether internal or external, the UART is clearly the heart of a modem. It is the modem that converts bus data into serial data (and vice versa). However, the UART must be able to keep pace with the modem's data transfer rate. As modem speeds have increased, UARTs have become faster also. When installing a new external modem on an older PC, the PC's serial port may simply not be fast enough to deal with the modem. The result is often limited modem performance (if the modem works at all). Today the 16550A UART is the device of choice. Table 4.1 compares the major UART types. When faced with an older UART, it is often possible to replace the UART IC outright. Otherwise, it is

TABLE 4.1   A Comparison of Popular UARTs

UART	Description
8250	This is the original PC/XT serial port UART. Several minor bugs can be found in the UART, but the original PC/XT BIOS corrected them. The 8250 was replaced by the 8250B.
8250A	This slightly updated UART fixed many of the issues in the 8250 but would not work in PC/XT systems because the BIOS was written to circumvent the 8250's problems. In either case, the 8250A will not work adequately over 9600 bps.
8250B	The last of the 8250 series reinserted the bugs that existed in the original 8250 so that PC/XT BIOS would function properly. The 8250B also does not run above 9600 bps.
16450	This higher speed UART was the desired choice for AT (i286) systems. Stable at 9600 bps, the 16450 laid the groundwork for the first high-speed modems. However, the 16450 will not work in PC/XT systems. This IC should be replaced by the 16550A.
16550	The 16550 was faster than the 16450, allowing operation above 9600 bps, but its performance was still limited by internal design problems. This IC should be replaced by the 16550A.
16550A	The fastest of the UARTs, a 16550A eliminates many of the serial port problems encountered when using a fast modem.

a simple matter to disable the existing serial port and install a newer serial adapter using a new UART.

The need for standards is no more acute than in communication. As modems have evolved, the United Sates and the international community has developed a suite of standards to outline the modem. Standards focus on three areas: data transfer, error correction, and data compression. Table 4.2 highlights Bell, *the International Telecommunication Union* (ITU, formerly the *International Telegraph and Telephone Consultative Committee* [CCITT]), and *Microcom Networking Protocol* (MNP) standards.

TABLE 4.2 **Modem Standards**

Bell Standards

BELL103	The first widely accepted modem standard using simple *Frequency Shift Keying* (FSK) modulation at 300 baud. This is the *only* standard where the data rate matches the baud rate. It is interesting to note that some modems today *still* support BELL103 as a lowest common denominator when all other modulation techniques fail.
BELL212A	A second widely accepted modem standard in North America using PSK modulation at 600 baud to transmit 1200 bps. Many European countries ignored BELL212A in favor of the similar (but not entirely identical) European standard called V.22.

ITU Standards

V.1	A very early standard that defines binary 0/1 bits as space/mark line conditions and voltage levels
V.2	Limits the power levels (in decibels or dB) of modems used on phone lines
V.4	Describes the sequence of bits within a character as transmitted (the data frame)
V.5	Describes the standard synchronous signaling rates for dialup lines
V.6	Describes the standard synchronous signaling rates for leased lines
V.7	Provides a list of modem terms in English, Spanish, and French
V.8	Describes the initial handshaking (negotiation) process between modems and forms the basis for call auto-detection or auto-switching (voice/fax/modem)
V.10	Describes unbalanced high-speed electrical interface characteristics (RS-423)
V.11	Describes balanced high-speed electrical characteristics (RS-422)
V.13	Explains simulated carrier control (with a full-duplex modem used as a half-duplex modem)
V.14	Explains the procedure for asynchronous to synchronous conversion

(continues)

TABLE 4.2   Continued.

ITU Standards

V.15	Describes the requirements and designs for telephone acoustic couplers. This is largely unused today since most telephone equipment is modular and can be plugged into telephone adapters directly rather than loosely attached to the telephone handset.
V.17	Describes an application-specific modulation scheme for a Group 3 fax that provides two-wire, half-duplex, trellis-coded transmission at 7200, 9600, 12,000, and 14,400 bps. In spite of the low number, this is a fairly recent standard.
V.19	Describes early DTMF modems using a low-speed parallel transmission. This standard is largely obsolete.
V.20	Explains modems with a parallel data transmission. This standard is largely obsolete.
V.21	Provides the specifications for 300-bps FSK serial modems (based upon BELL103)
V.22	Provides the specifications for 1200-bps (600-baud) PSK modems (similar to BELL212A)
V.22bis	Describes 2400-bps modems operating at 600 baud using *Quadrature Amplitude Modulation* (QAM)
V.23	Describes the operation of a rather unusual type of FM modem working at 1200/75 bps. That is, the host transmits at 1200 bps and receives at 75 bps. The remote modem transmits at 75 bps and receives at 1200 bps. V.23 is used in Europe to support some videotext applications.
V.24	This is known as EIA RS-232 in the United Sates. It defines *only* the functions of the serial port circuits. EIA-232-E (the current version of the standard) also defines electrical characteristics and connectors.
V.25	Defines automatic answering equipment and parallel automatic dialing. It also defines the answer tone that modems send.

TABLE 4.2   Continued.

ITU Standards

V.25bis	Defines serial automatic calling and answering, which is the ITU equivalent of AT commands. This is the current ITU standard for modem control by computers via a serial interface. The Hayes AT command set is used primarily in the United Sates.
V.26	Defines a 2400-bps PSK full-duplex modem operating at 1200 baud
V.26bis	Defines a 2400-bps PSK half-duplex modem operating at 1200 baud
V.26terbo	Defines a 2400/1200 bps switchable PSK full-duplex modem operating at 1200 baud
V.27	Defines a 4800-bps PSK modem operating at 1600 baud
V.27bis	Defines a more advanced 4800/2400 -bps switchable PSK modem operating at 1600/1200 baud
V.27terbo	Defines a 4800/2400 -bps switchable PSK modem commonly used in half-duplex mode at 1600/1200 baud to handle Group 3 fax rather than computer modems
V.28	Defines the electrical characteristics and connections for V.24 (RS-232). Although the RS-232 specification defines all necessary parameters, the ITU breaks the specifications down into two separate documents
V.29	Defines a 9600/7200 /4800-bps switchable PSK/QAM modem operating at 2400 baud. This type of modem is often used to implement a Group 3 fax rather than computer modems.
V.32	Defines the first of the truly modern modems as a 9600/4800-bps switchable QAM full-duplex modem operating at 2400 baud. This standard also incorporates trellis coding and echo cancellation to produce a stable, reliable, high-speed modem.

(continues)

TABLE 4.2 **Continued.**

ITU Standards

V.32bis	A fairly new standard extending the V.32 specification to define a 4800/7200 /9600/12000/ 14400-bps switchable TCQAM full-duplex modem operating at 2400 baud. Trellis coding, automatic transfer rate negotiation, and echo cancellation make this type of modem one of the most popular and least expensive for everyday PC communication.
V.32terbo	Continues to extend the V.32 specification by using advanced techniques to implement a 14400/16800/ 19200-bps switchable TCQAM full-duplex modem operating at 2400 baud. Unlike V.32bis, V.32terbo is not widely used due to the rather high cost of components.
V.32fast	The informal name to a standard that the ITU has not yet completed. When finished, a V.32fast modem will likely replace V.32bis with speeds up to 28,800 bps. It is anticipated that this will be the last analog protocol, eventually giving way to all-digital protocols as local telephone services become entirely digital. V.32fast will probably be renamed V.34 on completion and acceptance.
V.33	Defines a specialized 14,400-bps TCQAM full-duplex modem operating at 2400 baud
V.34	Defines the standard for modem communication at 2400 through 28,800 bps
V.34+	An update to V.34 outlining the enhancements needed for modem communication at 33,600 bps
V.36	Defines a specialized 48,000-bps group modem that is rarely (if ever) used commercially. This type of modem uses several conventional telephone lines.
V.37	Defines a specialized 72,000-bps group modem that combines several telephone channels

TABLE 4.2   Continued.

ITU Standards

V.42	The only ITU error-correcting procedure for modems using V.22, V.22bis, V.26ter, V.32, and V.32bis protocols. The standard is also defined as a *Link Access Procedure for Modems* (LAPM) protocol. ITU V.42 is considered very efficient and is about 20% faster than MNP4. If a V.42 connection cannot be established between modems, V.42 automatically provides fallback to the MNP4 error correction standard.
V.42bis	Uses a Lempel-Ziv-based data compression scheme for use in conjunction with V.42 LAPM (error correction). V.42bis is a data compression standard for high-speed modems that can compress data by as much as 4:1 (depending on the type of file you send). Thus, a 9600 baud modem can transmit data at up to 38,400 bps using V.42bis. A 14.4-kbps modem can transmit up to a startling 57,600 bps.
V.50	Sets standard telephony limits for modem transmission quality
V.51	Outlines the required maintenance of international data circuits
V.52	Describes the apparatus for measuring data transmission distortion and error rates
V.53	Outlines impairment limits for data circuits
V.54	Describes loop-test devices for modem testing
V.55	Describes impulse noise-measuring equipment for line testing
V.56	Outlines the comparative testing of modems
V.57	Describes the comprehensive test equipment for high-speed data transmissions
V.90	A standard for 56-Kbps modems approved by the ITU in February 1998
V.100	Describes the interconnection techniques between *Public Data Networks* (PDNs) and *Public Switched Telephone Networks* (PSTNs)

(continues)

TABLE 4.2 **Continued.**

MNP Standards

MNP class 1 *(block mode)*	An old data transfer mode that sends data in only one direction at a time, about 70 percent as fast as data transmissions using no error correction. This level is now virtually obsolete.
MNP class 2 *(stream mode)*	An older data transfer mode that sends data in both directions at the same time, about 84 percent as fast as data transmissions using no error correction
MNP class 3	The sending modem strips start and stop bits from a data block before sending it, while the receiving modem adds start and stop bits before passing the data to the receiving computer. About eight percent faster than data transmissions using no error correction. The increased throughput is realized only if modems on both ends of the connection are operating in a *split speed* (or *locked COM port*) fashion. That is, the rate of data transfer from computer to modem is *higher* than the data transfer rate from modem to modem. Also, data is being transferred in big blocks (one KB) or continuously (using the Zmodem file transfer protocol).
MNP class 4	A protocol (with limited data compression) that checks telephone connection quality and uses a transfer technique called *Adaptive Packet Assembly*. On a noise-free line, the modem sends larger blocks of data. If the line is noisy, the modem sends smaller blocks of data (less data will have to be resent). This means more successful transmissions on the first try, about 20 percent faster than data transmissions using no error correction at all, so most current modems are MNP4-compatible.
MNP class 5	A classical MNP data compression technique, MNP5 provides data compression by detecting redundant data and recoding it to fewer bits, thus increasing effective data throughput. A receiving modem decompresses the data before passing it to the receiving computer. MNP5 can speed data transmissions at twice the normal speed using no data compression or error correction (depending on the kind of data transmitted). In effect, MNP5 gives a 2400-bps modem an effective data throughput of as much as 4800 bps and a 9600-bps system as much as 19200 bps.

TABLE 4.2   **Continued.**

MNP Standards

MNP class 6	Uses *Universal Link Negotiation* to let modems get maximum performance out of a line. Modems start at low speeds and then move to higher speeds until the best speed is found. MNP6 also provides *statistical duplexing* to help half-duplex modems simulate full-duplex modems.
MNP class 7	Offers a much more powerful data compression process (Huffman encoding) than MNP5. MNP7 modems can increase the data throughput by as much as three times in some cases. Although more efficient than MNP5, not all modems are designed to handle the MNP7 protocol. Also, MNP7 is faster than MNP5, but MNP7 is still generally considered slower than the ITU's V.42bis.
MNP class 9	Reduces the data overhead (the housekeeping bits) encountered with each data packet. MNP9 also improves error correction performance because only the data that is in error has to be resent instead of resending the entire data packet.
MNP class 10	Uses a set of protocols known as *Adverse Channel Enhancements* to help modems overcome poor telephone connections by adjusting data packet size and transmission speed until the most reliable transmission is established. This is a more powerful version of MNP4.

Modern modems are programmable devices; that is, they can be highly configured in order to optimize their performance. Modem programming is accomplished by sending ASCII text strings during the initialization, dialing, and disconnect phases of the modem's operation. The codes used to program a modem are called the *command set*, and since a programming string is typically started by the term *AT*, the codes are usually referred to as the *AT command set* (not to be confused with the IBM PC AT). The advantage of a standard code set is software compatibility. Any generic communications software can work with almost any modem simply by using the correct AT command string. Table 4.3 provides an extensive listing of AT commands. This can be particularly helpful when trying to interpret command strings.

NOTE: Settings with an underline (such as <u>F0</u>) are the default settings for an entry.

TABLE 4.3   Index of the AT Command Set

Basic AT Commands	
(A/) Repeat Last Command.	
(A) Answer.	
(Bx) CCITT or Bell Modulation.	
B0	CCITT operation at 300 or 1200 bps
B1	BELL operation at 300 or 1200 bps
B2	V.23 originate mode, which receives 1200 bps and transmit 75 bps, or answer mode, which receives 75 bps and transmits 1200 bps
B3	V.23 originate mode, which receives 75 bps and transmits 1200 bps, or answer mode, which receives 1200 bps and transmits 75 bps
B15	Selects V.21 when the modem is at 300 bits/s
B16	Selects Bell 103J when the modem is at 300 bits/s (default)
(Cx) *Carrier Control*	The modem will accept the C1 command without error in order to assure backward compatibility with communications software that issues the C1 command. The C0 command may instruct some modems not to send a carrier (it puts them in a receive-only mode).
C0	Transmit carrier always off
C1	Normal transmit carrier switching
(Dx) *Dial*	The valid dial string parameters are described next. Punctuation characters may be used for clarity, with parentheses, hyphen, and spaces being ignored:
0–9, *DTMF digits*	The numbers 0 to 9
The star digit (*)	Tone dialing only

TABLE 4.3   Continued.

Basic AT Commands

The pound digit (#)	Tone dialing only
Flash (!)	The modem will go on-hook for a time defined by the value of S29.
Dial pause (,)	The modem will pause for a time specified by S8 before dialing the digits following ",".
Return to command state (;)	Added to the end of a dial string, this causes the modem to return to the command state after it processes the portion of the dial string preceding the ";". This enables the user to issue additional AT commands while remaining off-hook. The additional AT commands may be placed in the original command line following the ; or may be entered on subsequent command lines. The modem will enter call progress only after an additional dial command is issued without the ; terminator. Use "H" to abort the dial in progress and go back on-hook.
Enable calling tone (^)	Applicable to current dial attempt only. The calling tone is a 1800-Hz tone every three to four seconds that alerts the recipient of automatic calling equipment (as defined in CCITT V.25).
Ground pulse (>)	If enabled by a country-specific parameter, the modem will generate a grounding pulse on the EARTH relay output.
Wait for silence (@)	The modem will wait for at least five seconds of silence in the call progress frequency band before continuing with the next dial string parameter. If the modem does not detect these five seconds of silence before the expiration of the call abort timer (S7), the modem will terminate the call attempt with a NO ANSWER message. If busy detection is enabled, the modem may terminate the call with the BUSY result code. If the answer tone arrives during execution of this parameter, the modem handshakes.
List ($)	Displays a list of dial commands or the "Bong Tone" detection

(continues)

TABLE 4.3 **Continued.**

Basic AT Commands

(Dx) *Dial*

DTMF (A–D) *letters*	A, B, C, and D
Fastest speed (J)	Perform MNP 10-link negotiation at the highest supported speed for this call only
Power adjustment (K)	Enable power-level adjustment during MNP 10-link negotiation for this call only
Redial last number (L)	The modem will redial the last valid telephone number. This command must be immediately after the D with all the following characters ignored.
Select pulse dialing (P)	Pulse-dial the numbers that follow until a T is encountered. Affects current and subsequent dialing
Delay (R)	This command will cause the modem to wait 10 seconds after dialing and then go into answer mode. This command must be placed at the end of the dial string.
Select tone dialing (T)	Tone-dial the numbers that follow until a P is encountered. Affects current and subsequent dialing
Wait for dial tone (W)	The modem will wait for a dial tone before dialing the digits following W. If no dial tone is detected within the time specified by S6, the modem will abort the rest of the sequence, return on-hook, and generate an error message.

(Ex) *Command Echo.*

E0	Disables command echo
E1	Enables command echo

(Fx) *Select Line Modulation.*

F0	Selects auto-detect mode; all connect speeds are possible
F1	Selects V.21 or Bell 103 according to the B setting
F2	*Not supported* (some modems use this setting for 600 bps)

TABLE 4.3   Continued.

Basic AT Commands

(Fx) *Select Line Modulation.*

F0	Selects auto-detect mode; all connect speeds are possible
F1	Selects V.21 or Bell 103 according to the B setting
F2	*Not supported* (some modems use this setting for 600 bps)
F3	The originator is at 75 bps and the answerer is at 1200 bps.
F4	Selects V.22 1200 bps or Bell 212A according to the B setting
F5	Selects V.22bis as the only acceptable line modulation
F	Select V.32bis 4800 bps or V.32 4800 bps as the only acceptable line modulation
F7	Selects V.32bis 7200 bps as the only acceptable line modulation
F8	Selects V.32bis 9600 bps or V.32 9600 bps as the only acceptable line modulation
F9	Selects V.32bis 12000 bps as the only acceptable line modulation
F10	Selects V.32bis 14400 bps as the only acceptable line modulation

(Hx) *Disconnect [Hangup].*

H0	The modem will release the line if the modem is currently online and will terminate any test (AT&T) that is in progress.
H1	If on-hook, the modem will go off-hook and enter command mode. The modem will return on-hook after a period of time determined by S7.

(Ix) *Identification.*

I0	Reports product code
I1	Reports pre-computed checksum from ROM

(continues)

TABLE 4.3   Continued.

Basic AT Commands

(Ix) *Identification.*

I2	The modem will respond OK.
I3	Reports firmware revision
I4	Reports modem identifier string
I5	Reports Country Code parameter (such as 022)
I6	Reports modem data pump model and internal code revision

(Lx) *Speaker Volume.*

L0	Low speaker volume
L1	Low speaker volume
L2	Medium speaker volume
L3	High speaker volume

(Mx) *Speaker Control.*

M0	Speaker is always off.
M1	Speaker is on during call establishment but off when receiving the carrier.
M2	Speaker is always on.
M3	Speaker is off when receiving the carrier and during dialing but on during answering.

(Nx) *Automode Enable.*

N0	Automode detection is disabled.
N1	Automode detection is enabled.

(Ox) *Return to Online Data Mode.*

O0	Enters online data mode without a retrain
O1	Enters online data mode with a retrain before returning to online data mode
O3–14	Forces the modem to a new rate that is user-defined (defined in S62)

TABLE 4.3 **Continued.**

Basic AT Commands

(P) *Set Pulse Dial Default.*

(Qx) *Quiet Results Codes.*

Q0	Enables result codes to the DTE
Q1	Disables result codes to the DTE

(Sn) *Read/Write S-Registers.*

n=v	Sets S-register n to the value v
n?	Reports the value of S-register n

(T) *Set Tone Dial Default.*

(Vx) *Result Code Form.*

V0	Enables short-form (terse) result codes
V1	Enables long-form (verbose) result codes

(Wx) Error Correction Message Control.

W0	Upon connection, the modem reports only the DTE speed.
W1	Upon connection, the modem reports the line speed, the error correction protocol, and the DTE speed respectively.
W2	Upon connection, the modem reports the DCE speed.

(Xx) Extended Result Codes.

X0	Sends only OK, CONNECT, RING, NO CARRIER, ERROR, and NO ANSWER result codes
X1	Sends only OK, CONNECT, RING, NO CARRIER, ERROR, NO ANSWER, and CONNECT XXXX
X2	Sends only OK, CONNECT, RING, NO CARRIER, ERROR, NO DIAL TONE, NO ANSWER, and CONNECT XXXX

(continues)

TABLE 4.3   Continued.

Basic AT Commands

(Xx) *Extended Result Codes.*

X3	Sends only OK, CONNECT, RING, NO CARRIER, ERROR, NO ANSWER, CONNECT XXXX, and BUSY
X4	Enables monitoring of busy tones; sends all messages

(Yx) *Long Space Disconnect.*

Y0	Disables long space disconnect
Y1	Enables long space disconnect

(Zx) *Soft Reset and Restore Profile.*

Z0	Soft reset and restore stored profile 0
Z1	Soft reset and restore stored profile 1

AT & Commands

(&Bx) *Autoretrain.*

&B0	Hangs up on a poor received signal
&B1	Retrains on a poor received signal. Hangs up if the condition persists.
&B2	Does not hang up; does not retrain (tolerate any line)

(&Cx) *RLSD (DCD) Option.*

&C0	RLSD remains on at all times.
&C1	RLSD follows the state of the carrier.

(&Dx) *DTR Option.*

&D0	DTR drop is interpreted according to the current &Q setting as follows: (&Q0, 5, 6) DTR is ignored (assumed on). Enables operation with DTEs that don't provide DTR
	(&Q1, 4) DTR drop causes the modem to hang up. Auto-answer is not affected.

TABLE 4.3   Continued.

AT & Commands

(&Dx) *DTR Option.*

	(&Q2, 3) DTR drop causes the modem to hang up. Auto-answer is inhibited.
&D1	DTR drop is interpreted according to the current &Q setting as follows:
	(&Q0, 1, 4, 5, 6) DTR drop is interpreted by the modem as if the asynchronous escape sequence had been entered. The modem returns to asynchronous command state without disconnecting.
	(&Q2, 3) DTR drop causes the modem to hang up. Auto-answer is inhibited.
&D2	DTR drop is interpreted according to the current &Q setting as follows: (&Q0-6) DTR drop causes the modem to hang up. Auto-answer is inhibited.
&D3	DTR drop is interpreted according to the current &Q setting as follows:
	(&Q0, 1, 4, 5, 6) DTR drop causes the modem to perform a soft reset as if the Z command were received. The &Y setting determines which profile is loaded.
	(&Q2, 3) DTR drop causes the modem to hang up. Auto-answer is inhibited.

(&Fx) *Restore Factory Configuration.*

&F0	Restores factory configuration 0
&F1	Restores factory configuration 1

(&Gx) *Select Guard Tone.*

&G0	Disables Guard Tone
&G1	Disables Guard Tone
&G2	Selects 1800-Hz guard tone

(continues)

TABLE 4.3 Continued.

AT & Commands

(&Hn) *Sets Transmit Data (TD) flow control (see also &Rn).*

&H0	Flow control disabled
&H1	Hardware flow control, Clear to Send (CTS) (default)
&H2	Software flow control, XON/XOFF
&H3	Hardware and software flow control

(&In) *Sets Receive Data (RD) software flow control (see also &Rn).*

&I0	Software flow control disabled (default)
&I1	XON/XOFF signals to your modem and remote system
&I2	XON/XOFF signals to your modem only

(&Jx) *Telephone Jack Type.*

&J0	RJ11 telephone jack
&J1	RJ12 or RJ13 telephone jack

(&Kx) *Flow Control.*

&K0	Disables flow control
&K3	Enables RTS/CTS flow control
&K4	Enables XON/XOFF flow control
&K5	Enables transparent XON/XOFF flow control
&K6	Enables both RTS/CTS and XON/XOFF flow control

(&Lx) *Dial Up/Lease Line Option.*

&L0	Dial line
&L1	Leased line

(&Mx) *Asynchronous/Synchronous Mode Selection.*

&M0	Selects direct asynchronous operation
&M1	Selects synchronous connect mode with asynchronous offline command mode

TABLE 4.3 **Continued.**

AT & Commands

(&Mx) *Asynchronous/Synchronous Mode Selection.*

&M2	Selects synchronous connect mode with asynchronous offline command mode
&M3	Selects synchronous connect mode
&M4	Hayes AutoSync mode

(&Nn) *Sets connect speed.*

&N0	Variable rate (default)
&N1	300 bps
&N2	1200 bps
&N3	2400 bps
&N4	4800 bps
&N5	7200 bps
&N6	9600 bps
&N7	12,000 bps
&N8	14,400 bps
&N9	16,800 bps
&N10	19,200 bps
&N11	21,600 bps
&N12	24,000 bps
&N13	26,400 bps
&N14	28,800 bps
&N15	31,200 bps
&N16	33,600 bps
&N17	33,333 bps
&N18	37,333 bps
&N19	41,333 bps
&N20	42,666 bps
&N21	44,000 bps

(continues)

TABLE 4.3   Continued.

AT & Commands

(&Nn) *Sets connect speed.*

&N22	45,333 bps
&N23	46,666 bps
&N24	48,000 bps
&N25	49,333 bps
&N26	50,666 bps
&N27	52,000 bps
&N28	53,333 bps
&N29	54,666 bps
&N30	56,000 bps
&N31	57,333 bps

(&Px) *Dial Pulse Ratio.*

&P0	Make = 39%, break = 61% (at 10 pps for the United States).
&P1	Make = 33%, break = 67% (at 10 pps for Europe).
&P2	Make = 33%, break = 67% (at 20 pps for Japan).

(&Qx) *Sync/Async Mode.*

&Q0	Selects direct asynchronous operation
&Q1	Selects synchronous connect mode with async offline command mode
&Q2	Selects synchronous connect mode with async offline command mode
&Q3	Selects synchronous connect mode
&Q4	Select AutoSync operation
&Q5	The modem will try to negotiate an error-corrected link.
&Q6	Selects asynchronous operation in normal mode (speed buffering)

TABLE 4.3   Continued.

AT & Commands

(&Qx) *Sync/Async Mode.*

&Q8   MNP error control mode. If an MNP error control protocol is not established, the modem will fallback according to the current user setting in S36.

&Q9   V.42 or MNP error control mode. If neither error control protocol is established, the modem will fallback according to the current user setting in S36.

Starting AutoSync.   Set registers S19, S20, and S25 to the desired values before selecting AutoSync operation with &Q4. After the CONNECT message is issued, the modem waits the period of time specified by S25 before examining DTR. If DTR is on, the modem enters the synchronous operating state; if DTR is off, the modem terminates the line connection and returns to the asynchronous command state.

Stopping AutoSync.   AutoSync operation is stopped upon loss of carrier or the ON-to-OFF transition of DTR. The loss of the carrier will cause the modem to return to the asynchronous command state. An ON-to-OFF transition of DTR will cause the modem to return to the asynchronous command state and either not terminate the line connection (&D1 active) or terminate the line connection (any other &Dn command active).

(&Rx) *RTS/CTS Option.*

&R0   In Sync mode, CTS tracks the state of RTS; the RTS-to-CTS delay is defined by S26. In Async mode, CTS acts according to the V.25bis handshake.

&R1   In Sync mode, CTS is always on (RTS transitions are ignored). In Async, CTS will drop only if required by flow control.

&R2   Received data to computer only on RTS

(continues)

TABLE 4.3   Continued.

AT & Commands

(&Sx) *DSR Override.*

&S0	DSR will remain on at all times.
&S1	DSR will become active after the answer tone has been detected and inactive after the carrier has been lost.

(&Tx) *Test and Diagnostics.*

&T0	Terminates the test in progress. Clears S16
&T1	Initiates local analog loopback, V.54 Loop 3
&T2	Returns an Error message
&T3	Initiates local digital loopback, V.54 Loop 2
&T4	Enables digital loopback acknowledgment for remote request
&T5	Disables digital loopback acknowledgement for remote request
&T6	Initiates remote digital loopback
&T7	Remote digital with self-test and error detector
&T8	Initiates local analog loopback, V.54 Loop 3, with self test

(&Un) *Sets floor connect speed.*

&U0	Disabled (the default)
&U1	300 bps
&U2	1200 bps
&U3	2400 bps
&U4	4800 bps
&U5	7200 bps
&U6	9600 bps
&U7	12,000 bps
&U8	14,400 bps
&U9	16,800 bps

TABLE 4.3   Continued.

AT & Commands

(&Un) *Sets floor connect speed.*

&U0	Disabled (the default)
&U1	300 bps
&U2	1200 bps
&U3	2400 bps
&U4	4800 bps
&U5	7200 bps
&U6	9600 bps
&U7	12,000 bps
&U8	14,400 bps
&U9	16,800 bps
&U10	19,200 bps
&U11	21,600 bps
&U12	24,000 bps
&U13	26,400 bps
&U14	28,800 bps
&U15	31,200 bps
&U16	33,600 bps
&U17	33,333 bps
&U18	37,333 bps
&U19	41,333 bps
&U20	42,666 bps
&U21	44,000 bps
&U22	45,333 bps
&U23	46,666 bps
&U24	48,000 bps
&U25	49,333 bps
&U26	50,666 bps

(continues)

TABLE 4.3   Continued.

AT & Commands

(&Un) *Sets floor connect speed.*

&U27	52,000 bps
&U28	53,333 bps
&U29	54,666 bps
&U30	56,000 bps
&U31	57,333 bps

(&Vx) *Display Current Configuration and Stored Profiles.*

&V0	Views active file, stored profile 0, and stored phone numbers
&V1	Views active file, stored profile 1, and stored phone numbers

(&Wx) *Store Current Configuration.*

&W0	Stores the current configuration as profile 0
&W1	Stores the current configuration as profile 1

(&Xx) *Sync Transmit Clock Source Option.*

&X0	The modem generates the transmit clock.
&X1	The DTE generates the transmit clock.
&X2	The modem derives the transmit clock.

(&Yx) *Designate a Default Reset Profile.*

&Y0	The modem will use profile 0.
&Y1	The modem will use profile 1.

(&ZL?) *Displays the last executed dial string.*

(&Zn?)	Displays the phone number stored at position n (n = 0-3)
(&Zn=x)	Store Telephone Number
&Zn=x	(n = 0 to 3, and x = dial string)

TABLE 4.3   Continued.

AT % Commands

(%BAUD) *Bit Rate Multiplier.*

(%Cx) *Enable/Disable Data Compression.*

%C0	Disables data compression. Resets S46 bit 1
%C1	Enables MNP 5 data compression negotiation. Resets S46 bit 1
%C2	Enables V.42bis data compression. Sets S46 bit 1
%C3	Enables both V.42bis and MNP 5 data compression. Sets S46 bit 1

(%CCID) *Enable Caller ID.*

(%CD) *Carrier Detect Lamp.*

(%CDIA) *Display last DIAG.*

(%CIDS) *Store ID Numbers.*

(%CRID) *Repeat Last ID.*

(%CSIG) *Store SIG Numbers.*

(%CXID) *XID Enable.*

(%Dx) *V.42bis Dictionary Size.*

%D0	Dictionary set to 512
%D1	Dictionary set to 1024
%D2	Dictionary set to 2048
%D3	Dictionary set to 4096

(%Ex) *Enable/Disable Line Quality Monitor and Auto-Retrain Fallback/Fall Forward.*

%E0	Disables line quality monitor and auto-retrain
%E1	Enables line quality monitor and auto-retrain
%E2	Enables line quality monitor and fallback/fall forward
%E3	Enables line quality monitor and auto-retrain, but hang up when EQM reaches threshold

(continues)

TABLE 4.3   Continued.

AT % Commands	
(%Gx) *Auto Fall Forward/Fallback Enable.*	
%G0	Disabled
%G1	Enabled
(%L) *Line Signal Level.*	
(%Mx) *Compression Type.*	
%M0	Compression disabled
%M1	Transmit compression only
%M2	Receive compression only
%M3	Two-way compression

(%P) *Clear Encoder Dictionary.*

(%Q) *Line Signal Quality.*

(%Sx) *Set Maximum String Length in V.42bis.*

(%SCBR) *Call Back Reference Outgoing Calls.*

(%SKEY) *Store Authentication Key Outgoing Call.*

(%SPRT) *Security Mode, Outgoing Calls.*

(%SPNP) *Serial Plug and Play Control.*

(%SPWD) *Password Outgoing Calls.*

(%SSPW) *Supervisor Password Outgoing Calls.*

(%SUID) *User ID Outgoing Calls.*

(%TTx) *PTT Testing Utilities.*

%TT00–%TT09	DTMF tone dial digits 0 to 9
%TT0A	DTMF digit *
%TT0B	DTMF digit A
%TT0C	DTMF digit B
%TT0D	DTMF digit C
%TT0E	DTMF digit #
%TT0F	DTMF digit D

TABLE 4.3   **Continued.**

AT % Commands

(%TTx) *PTT Testing Utilities.*

`%TT10`	V.21 channel no. 1 mark (originate) symbol
`%TT11`	V.21 channel no. 2 mark symbol
`%TT12`	V.23 backward channel mark symbol
`%TT13`	V.23 forward channel mark symbol
`%TT14`	V.22 originate (call mark) signaling at 600 bps (not supported)
`%TT15`	V.22 originate (call mark) signaling at 1200 bps
`%TT16`	V.22bis originate (call mark) signaling at 2400 bps
`%TT17`	V.22 answer signaling (guard tone if PTT required)
`%TT18`	V.22bis answer signaling (guard tone if required)
`%TT19`	V.21 channel no. 1 space symbol
`%TT20`	V.32 9600 bps
`%TT21`	V.32bis 14400 bps
`%TT1A`	V.21 channel no. 2 space symbol
`%TT1B`	V.23 backward channel space symbol
`%TT1C`	V.23 forward channel space symbol
`%TT30`	Silence (online), go off-hook
`%TT31`	V.25 answer tone
`%TT32`	1800 Hz guard tone
`%TT33`	V.25 calling tone (1300 Hz)
`%TT34`	Fax calling tone (1100 Hz)
`%TT40`	V.21 channel 2
`%TT41`	V.27ter 2400 bps
`%TT42`	V.27ter 4800 bps
`%TT43`	V.29 7200 bps

(continues)

TABLE 4.3 Continued.

AT % Commands

(%TTx) *PTT Testing Utilities.*

%TT44	V.29 9600 bps
%TT45	V.17 7200 bps long train
%TT46	V.17 7200 bps short train
%TT47	V.17 9600 bps long train
%TT48	V.17 9600 bps short train
%TT49	V.17 12,000 bps long train
%TT4A	V.17 12,000 bps short train
%TT4B	V.17 14,400 bps long train
%TT4C	V.17 14,400 bps short train

AT \ Commands

(\Ax) *Select Maximum MNP Block Size.*

\A0	64 characters
\A1	128 characters
\A2	192 characters
\A3	256 characters
\A4	Max. 32 characters (for ETC-enhanced throughput cellular)

(\Bx) *Transmit Break to Remote.*

\B1–\B9	Break length in 100 milliseconds (ms) units (default is 3, non-error corrected mode only)

(\Cx) *Set Autoreliable Buffer.*

\C0	Does not buffer data
\C1	Buffers data on the answering modem for four seconds
\C2	Does not buffer data on the answering modem

TABLE 4.3 **Continued.**

AT \ Commands

(\Ex) *Optimize Local Echo.*

(\Gx) *Modem-to-Modem Flow Control (XON/XOFF).*

\G0	Disables modem-to-modem XON/XOFF flow control
\G1	Enables modem-to-modem XON/XOFF flow control

(\Jx) *Constant DTE Speed Option.*

\J0	DCE and DTE rates are independent.
\J1	DTE rate adjusts to DCE connection rate after online.

(\Kx) *Break Control.*

If the modem receives a break from the DTE when the modem is operating in data transfer mode:

\K0	Enter online command mode, no break sent to the remote modem
\K1	Clear data buffers and send break to remote modem
\K2	Same as \K0
\K3	Send break to remote modem immediately
\K4	Same as \K0
\K5	Send break to remote modem in sequence with transmitted data. If the modem is in the online command state (waiting for AT commands) during a data connection and the \B command is received in order to send a break to the remote modem:
\K0	Clear data buffers and send break to remote modem
\K1	Clear data buffers and send break to remote modem (same as \K0)
\K2	Send break to remote modem immediately
\K3	Send break to remote modem immediately (same as \K2)

(continues)

TABLE 4.3   Continued.

AT \ Commands

(\Kx) *Break Control.*

If the modem receives a break from the DTE when the modem is operating in data transfer mode:

\K4	Send break to remote modem in sequence with data
\K5	Send break to remote modem in sequence with data (same as \K4). If there is a break received from a remote modem during a non-error corrected connection:
\K0	Clears data buffers and sends break to the DTE
\K1	Clears data buffers and sends break to the DTE (same as \K0)
\K2	Sends a break immediately to DTE
\K3	Sends a break immediately to DTE (same as \K2)
\K4	Sends a break in sequence with received data to DTE
\K5	Sends a break in sequence with received data to DTE (same as \K4)

(\Lx) *MNP Block/Stream Mode Select.*

\L0	Uses stream mode for MNP connection
\L1	Uses interactive block mode for MNP connection

(\Nx) *Operating Mode.*

\N0	Selects normal speed buffered mode
\N1	Selects direct mode
\N2	Selects reliable (error correction) mode
\N3	Selects auto reliable mode
\N4	Selects LAPM error correction mode
\N5	Selects MNP error correction mode

TABLE 4.3 **Continued.**

AT \ Commands

(\O) *Originate Reliable Link Control.*

(\Qx) *DTE Flow Control Options.*

\Q0	Disables flow control
\Q1	XON/XOFF software flow control
\Q2	CTS flow control to the DTE
\Q3	RTS/CTS hardware flow control

(\S) *Report Active Configuration.*

(\Tx) *Set Inactivity Timer.*

n=0	Disables the inactivity timer
n51-90	Length in minutes

(\U) *Accept Reliable Link Control.*

(\Vx) *Protocol Result Code.*

\V0	Disables protocol result code (CONNECT 9600)
\V1	Enables protocol result code (CONNECT 9600/LAPM)

(\Xx) *Set XON/XOFF Pass-Through Option.*

\X0	If XON/XOFF flow control is enabled, does not pass XON/XOFF to remote modem or local DTE
\X1	Always passes XON/XOFF to the remote modem or local DTE

(\Y) *Switch to Reliable Operation.*

(\Z) *Switch to Normal Operation.*

AT - Commands

(-Jx) *Set V.42 Detection Phase.*

-J0	Disables the V.42 detection phase
-J1	Enables the V.42 detection phase

(continues)

TABLE 4.3   **Continued.**

AT - Commands

(-Kx) *MNP Extended Services.*

-K0	Disables V.42 LAPM to MNP 10 conversion
-K1	Enables V.42 LAPM to MNP 10 conversion
-K2	Enables V.42 LAPM to MNP 10 conversion; inhibits MNP Extended Services

---

(-Qx) *Enable Fallback to V.22 bis/V.22.*

-Q0	Disables fallback to 2400 bps (V.22bis) and 1200 bps (V.22). Fallback only to 4800 bps
-Q1	Enables fallback to 2400 bps (V.22bis) and 1200 bps (V.22)
(-SDR5n)	Distinctive Ring Reporting
-SDR51	Type 1 Distinctive Ring Detect
-SDR52	Type 2 Distinctive Ring Detect
-SDR53	Type 1 and Type 2 Distinctive Ring Detect
-SDR54	Type 3 Distinctive Ring Detect
-SDR55	Type 1 and Type 3 Distinctive Ring Detect
-SDR56	Type 2 and Type 3 Distinctive Ring Detect
-SDR57	Types 1, 2, and 3 Distinctive Ring Detect

Distinctive Ring Types

Type	On	Off	On	Off	On	Off	Sound
1	2.0	4.0					Rinnnnnnnnnng
2	0.8	0.4		0.8		4.0	Ring Ring
3	0.4	0.2	0.4	0.2	0.8	4.0	Ring Ring Rinnng

(-SEC=n) *LAPM and MNP Link Control.*

-SEC50	Disables LAPM or MNP10. EC transmit level set in register S91
-SEC51, 0-30	Enables LAPM or MNP10. EC transmit level set to value after comma (0 to 30)

TABLE 4.3   **Continued.**

AT - Commands

(-SKEY) *Program Key.*

(-SPRT) *Remote Security Mode.*

(-SPWD) *Program Password.*

(-SSE) *Simultaneous Voice Data.*

(-SSG) *Set DSVD Receive Gain.*

(-SSKY) *Program Supervisor Key.*

(-SSP) *Select DVSD Port.*

(-SSPW) *Supervisor Password.*

(-SUID) *Program User ID.*

(-V) *Display Root Firmware Version Number.*

AT " Commands

("Hx) *V.42bis Compression Control.*

"H0	Disables V.42bis
"H1	Enables V.42bis only when transmitting data
"H2	Enables V.42bis only when receiving data
"H3	Enables V.42bis for both directions

("Nx) *V.42bis Dictionary Size.*

"N0	512 bytes
"N1	1024 bytes
"N2	1536 bytes

("Ox) *Select V.42bis Maximum String Length.*

n56-64

n=32

AT ~ Commands

(~Dx) *Factory Configured Operating Profile.*

~D0	Disable (No error correction, no data compression)
~D0	Disable (No error correction, no data compression)

(continues)

TABLE 4.3 **Continued.**

AT ~ Commands

(~Dx) *Factory Configured Operating Profile.*

~D1	MNP4
~D2	MNP5
~D3	V.42
~D4	V.42bis

AT ~~ Commands

(~~Lx) *Digital Line Current Sensing On/Off.*

~~L0	Turn off digital line current sensing
~~L1	Turn on digital line current sensing

(~~S=m) *Digital Line Over-Current Sense Time Set.*

m=0 through 9

m=4

(~~S?) *Display Line Over-Current Sense Time Display.*

AT + Fax Commands

Some modems support fax commands conforming to EIA standard 578. These commands are given here with short descriptions. They also typically support error correction and V.17terbo at 19.2 KB.

(+FAA) *Auto Answer Mode Parameter.*

(+FAXERR=x) *Fax Error Value Parameter.*

(+FBOR=x) *Phase C Data Bit Order Parameter.*

(+FBUF?) *Read the Buffer Size.*

(+FCLASS?) *Service Class Indication.*

+FCLASS?   000 if in data mode; 001 if in fax class 1.

(+FCLASS-x) Service Class Capabilities.

TABLE 4.3 Continued.

AT + Commands

| +FCLASS=? | 0: modem is set up for data mode |
| | 0,1: modem is capable of data and fax class I services |

(+FCLASS=n) *Service Class Selection.*

+FCLASS=0 Select data mode

+FCLASS=1 Select fax class 1

(+FCR) *Capability to Receive.*

(+FDCC=x) *Modem Capabilities Parameter.*

(+FDCS=x) *Current Session Results.*

(+FDIS=x) *Current Session Negotiation Parameters.*

(+FDR) *Begin or Continue Phase C Receive Data.*

(+FDT=x) *Data Transmission.*

(+FET=x) *Transmit Page Punctuation.*

(+FK) *Terminate Session.*

(+FLID=x) *Local ID String Parameter.*

(+FMDL?) *Request Modem Model.*

(+FMFR?) *Request Modem IC Manufacturer.*

(+FPHCTO) *Phase C Time Out.*

(+FPTS=x) *Page Transfer Status.*

(+FREV?) *Request Modem Revision.*

(+FRH=?) *FAX SDLC Receive Capabilities.*

(+FRH=n) *Modem Accept Training (SDLC).*

(+FRM=?) *FAX Normal Mode Receive Capabilities.*

(+FRM=n) *Modem Accept Training.*

(+FRS=?) *FRS Range Capabilities.*

(+FRS=n) *Receive Silence.*

+FRS=4 Wait 40 ms for silence.

(continues)

TABLE 4.3 Continued.

AT + Commands

(+FTH=?) *FAX SDLC Mode Transmit Capabilities.*

(+FTH=n) *Modem Initiate Training (SDLC).*

(+FTM=?) *FAX Normal Mode Transmit Capabilities.*

(+FTM=n) *Modem Initiate Training.*

(+FTS=?) *FTS Range Capabilities.*

(+FTS=n) *Transmission Silence.*

+FTS=5	Fax transmission silence for 50 ms

(+VCID) *Caller ID Service.*

Other AT Commands

(_+BRC1_) *Remote Escape into BRC State (from Host Online Data Mode).*

($BRC) *Enable/Disable Host.*

(-CID) *Enable Caller ID Detection.*

(:E) *Compromise Equalizer Enable.*

:E0	Disables the equalizer
:E1	Enables the equalizer

($GIVEBRC) *Enter BRC State (from Target Online Command State).*

(*Hx) *Link Negotiation Speed.*

*H0	Link negotiation occurs at the highest supported speed
*H1	Link negotiation occurs at 1200 bps
*H2	Link negotiation occurs at 4800 bps

()Mx) *Enable Cellular Power Level Adjustment.*

)M0	Disables power level adjustment during MNP 10 link negotiation
)M1	Enables power level adjustment during MNP 10 link negotiation

TABLE 4.3   **Continued.**

Other AT Commands

()Mx) *Enable Cellular Power Level Adjustment.*

@M0	−26 bBm
@M1	−30 bBm
@M2	−10 bBm
@M26	−26 dBm

> **NOTE**:   Table 4.3 represents a compendium of commands compiled from a variety of modem manufacturers over several generations. Some modems may not be capable of every function or mode listed here.

Virtually all AT command strings start with the prefix AT (Attention). For example, the command string ATZE1Q0V1 contains five separate commands: attention (AT), reset the modem to its power-up defaults (Z), enable the command echo to send command characters back to the sender (E1), send command result codes back to the PC (Q0), and select text result codes that cause words to be used as result codes. Although this may seem like a mouthful, a typical modem can accept command strings up to 40 characters long. The term result codes are the messages that the modem generates when a command string is processed. Either numbers (default) or words (using the V1 command) can be returned. For example, when a command is processed correctly, a result code OK is produced, or CONNECT when a successful connection is established. Table 4.4 shows an index of modem result codes.

TABLE 4.4   Typical Modem Result Codes

Response Code		Definition
No.	*Verbose*	
0	OK	The OK code is returned by the modem to acknowledge execution of a command line.
1	CONNECT	Sent alone when speed is 300 bps
2	RING	The modem sends this result code when incoming ringing is detected on the line.
3	NO CARRIER	No modem carrier signal is detected.
4	ERROR	Generated from AT command string errors, if a command cannot be executed, or if a parameter is outside of range
5	CONNECT 1200	Connection at 1200 bps
6	NO DIAL TONE	No dial tone is received from the local line.
7	BUSY	A busy tone has been detected.
8	NO ANSWER	The remote modem does not answer properly.
9	CONNECT 600	Connection at 600 bps
10	CONNECT 2400	Connection at 2400 bps
11	CONNECT 4800	Connection at 4800 bps
12	CONNECT 9600	Connection at 9600 bps
13	CONNECT 14400	Connection at 14400 bps
14	CONNECT 19200	Connection at 19200 bps
15	CONNECT 16800	Connection at 16800 bps
16	CONNECT 19200	Connection at 19200 bps
17	CONNECT 38400	Connection at 38400 bps
18	CONNECT 57600	Connection at 57600 bps
22	CONNECT 1200TX/ 75RX	Connection at 1200 bps/75 bps

TABLE 4.4   Continued.

Response Code		Definition
No.	*Verbose*	
23	CONNECT 75TX/ 1200RX	Connection at 75 bps/1200 bps
24	CONNECT 7200	Connection at 7200 bps
25	CONNECT 12000	Connection at 12000 bps
26	CONNECT 1200/75	Connection at 1200 bps/75 bps (V.23)
27	CONNECT 75/1200	Connection at 75 bps/1200 bps (V.23)
28	CONNECT 38400	Connection at 38400 bps
29	CONNECT 21600	Connection at 21600 bps
30	CONNECT 24000	Connection at 24000 bps
31	CONNECT 26400	Connection at 26400 bps
32	CONNECT 28800	Connection at 28800 bps
33	CONNECT 115200	Connection at 115.2 Kbps
35	DATA	Modem data is present.
40	CARRIER 300	A V.21 or Bell 103 carrier has been detected on the line.
42	CARRIER 75/1200	A V.23 backward channel carrier has been detected on the line.
43	CARRIER 1200/75	A V.23 forward channel carrier has been detected on the line.
44	CARRIER 1200/75	A V.23 forward channel carrier has been detected on the line.
45	CARRIER 75/1200	A V.23 backward channel carrier has been detected on the line.
46	CARRIER 1200	The high or low channel carrier in either V.22 or Bell 212 mode has been detected on the line.
47	CARRIER 2400	The high or low channel carrier in V.22bis or V.34 mode has been detected on the line.

(continues)

TABLE 4.4 **Continued.**

Response Code		Definition
No.	*Verbose*	
48	CARRIER 4800	The channel carrier in V.32, V.32bis, or V.34 has been detected on the line.
49	CARRIER 7200	The channel carrier in V.32bis or V.34 has been detected.
50	CARRIER 9600	The channel carrier in V.32, V.32bis, or V.34 mode has been detected on the line.
51	CARRIER 12000	The channel carrier in V.32bis or V.34 mode has been detected.
52	CARRIER 14400	The channel carrier in V.32bis or V.34 mode has been detected.
53	CARRIER 16800	The channel carrier in V.32terbo or V.34 mode has been detected on the line.
54	CARRIER 19200	The channel carrier in V.32terbo or V.34 mode has been detected on the line.
55	CARRIER 21600	The channel carrier in V.34 mode has been detected on the line.
56	CARRIER 24000	The channel carrier in V.34 mode has been detected on the line.
57	CARRIER 26400	The channel carrier in V.34 mode has been detected on the line.
58	CARRIER 28800	The channel carrier in V.34 mode has been detected on the line.
66	COMPRESSION: CLASS 5	The modem has connected with MNP class-5 data compression.
67	COMPRESSION: V.42bis	The modem has connected with V.42bis data compression.
69	COMPRESSION: NONE	The modem has connected without data compression.
70	PROTOCOL: NONE	The modem has connected without any form of error correction.

TABLE 4.4 Continued.

Response Code		Definition
No.	Verbose	
76	PROTOCOL: NONE	The modem has connected without any form of error correction.
77	PROTOCOL: LAP-M	The modem has connected with V.42 LAPM error correction.
80	PROTOCOL: MNP	The modem has connected with MNP error correction.
81	PROTOCOL: MNP 2	The modem has connected with MNP error correction.
82	PROTOCOL: MNP 3	The modem has connected with MNP error correction.
83	PROTOCOL: MNP 2, 4	The modem has connected with MNP error correction.
84	PROTOCOL: MNP 3, 4	The modem has connected with MNP error correction.
100	CONNECT 28000 EC*	Connection at 28000 bit/s (V.90 mode) (Lucent Technologies)
101	CONNECT 29333 EC*	Connection at 29333 bit/s (V.90 mode) (Lucent Technologies)
102	CONNECT 30666 EC*	Connection at 30666 bit/s (V.90 mode) (Lucent Technologies)
103	CONNECT 33333 EC*	Connection at 33333 bit/s (V.90 mode) (Lucent Technologies)
104	CONNECT 34666 EC*	Connection at 34666 bit/s (V.90 mode) (Lucent Technologies)
105	CONNECT 37333 EC*	Connection at 37333 bit/s (V.90 mode) (Lucent Technologies)
106	CONNECT 38666 EC*	Connection at 38666 bit/s (V.90 mode) (Lucent Technologies)
107	CONNECT 41333 EC*	Connection at 41333 bit/s (V.90 mode) (Lucent Technologies)
108	CONNECT 42666 EC*	Connection at 42666 bit/s (V.90 mode) (Lucent Technologies)

(continues)

TABLE 4.4   Continued.

Response Code		Definition
No.	*Verbose*	
76	PROTOCOL: NONE	The modem has connected without any form of error correction.
109	CONNECT 45333 EC*	Connection at 45333 bit/s (V.90 mode) (Lucent Technologies)
110	CONNECT 46666 EC*	Connection at 46666 bit/s (V.90 mode) (Lucent Technologies)
111	CONNECT 49333 EC*	Connection at 49333 bit/s (V.90 mode) (Lucent Technologies)
112	CONNECT 50666 EC*	Connection at 50666 bit/s (V.90 mode) (Lucent Technologies)
113	CONNECT 53333 EC*	Connection at 53333 bit/s (V.90 mode) (Lucent Technologies)
114	CONNECT 54666 EC*	Connection at 54666 bit/s (V.90 mode) (Lucent Technologies)
151	CONNECT 31200	Connection at 31,200 bps
152	CONNECT 31200/ARQ	Connection at 31,200 bps with Automatic Repeat Request
153	CONNECT 31200/V34	Connection at 31,200 bps with fallback to 28.8 KB (V.34)
154	CONNECT 31200/ARQ/V34	Connection at 31,200 bps with ARQ and fallback to 28.8 KB
155	CONNECT 33600	Connection at 33,600 bps
156	CONNECT 33600/ARQ	Connection at 33,600 bps with Automatic Repeat Request
157	CONNECT 33600/V34	Connection at 33,600 bps with fallback to 28.8 KB (V.34)
158	CONNECT 33600/ARQ/V34	Connection at 33,600 bps with ARQ and fallback to 28.8 KB
180	CONNECT 33333	3COM, USR Modem
184	CONNECT 37333	3COM, USR Modem
188	CONNECT 41333	3COM, USR Modem
192	CONNECT 42666	3COM, USR Modem
196	CONNECT 44000	3COM, USR Modem

TABLE 4.4 **Continued.**

Response Code		Definition
No.	*Verbose*	
200	CONNECT 45333	3COM, USR Modem
204	CONNECT 46666	3COM, USR Modem
208	CONNECT 48000	3COM, USR Modem
212	CONNECT 49333	3COM, USR Modem
216	CONNECT 50666	3COM, USR Modem
220	CONNECT 52000	3COM, USR Modem
224	CONNECT 53333	3COM, USR Modem
228	CONNECT 54666	3COM, USR Modem
232	CONNECT 56000	3COM, USR Modem
236	CONNECT 57333	3COM, USR Modem

* EC only appears when the extended result codes configuration option is enabled. EC is replaced by one of the following symbols, depending upon the error control method used:

- *V42bis*   V.42 error control and V.42bis data compression

- *V42*   V.42 error control only

- *MNP 5*   MNP class 4 error control and MNP class 5 data compression

- *MNP 4*   MNP class 4 error control only

Besides simply selecting modem commands, many attributes of the modern modem are programmable. To accommodate this feature, each different parameter must be held in a series of memory locations (called *S-registers*). Each S-register is described in Table 4.5. For example, the default escape sequence for the AT command set is a series of three plusses: +++. You could change this character by writing a new ASCII character to S2. For the most part, default S-register values are fine for most work, but you can often optimize the modem's operation by experimenting with the register values. Since S-register contents must be maintained after power is removed from the modem, the registers are stored in NVRAM.

TABLE 4.5 Index of S-Register Assignments

Register	Function	Range	Units	Default
S0	Rings to auto-answer	0–255	Rings	0
S1	Ring counter	0–255	Rings	0
S2	Escape character	0–255	ASCII	43
S3	Carriage return character	0–127	ASCII	13
S4	Line feed character	0–127	ASCII	10
S5	Backspace character	0–255	ASCII	8
S6	Wait time for dial tone	2–255	Seconds	4
S7	Wait for carrier	1–255	Seconds	50
S8	Pause time for comma (,)	0–255	Seconds	2
S9	Carrier detect response time	1–255	1/10 sec	6
S10	Carrier loss disconnect time	1–255	1/10 sec	14
S11	Touch Tone (DTMF) duration	50–255	1/1000 sec	95
S12	Escape code guard time	0–255	2/100 sec	50
S13	*Reserved*	—	—	—

TABLE 4.5 Continued.

Register	Function	Range	Units	Default
S14	General bit-mapped options	—	—	138 (8Ah)
S15	*Reserved*	—	—	—
S16	Test mode bit map options (&T)	—	—	0
S17	*Reserved*	—	—	—
S18	Test timer	0–255	Seconds	0
S19	Auto-sync bit map register	—	—	0
S20	AutoSync HDLC address	0–255	—	0 or BSC sync character
S21	V.24/General bit map options	—	—	4 (04h)
S22	Speaker/results bit map options	—	—	118 (76h)
S23	General bit map options	—	—	55 (37h)
S24	Sleep inactivity timer	0–255	Seconds	1
S25	Delay to DTR off	0–255	1/100 sec.	5
S26	RTS-to-CTS delay	0–255	1/100 sec.	1
S27	General bit map options	—	—	73 (49h) with ECC 74 (4Ah) without ECC

(continues)

277

TABLE 4.5 Continued.

Register	Function	Range	Units	Default
S28	General bit map options	—	—	0
S29	Flash dial modifier time	0–255	10 ms	70
S30	Disconnect activity timer	0–255	10 sec.	0
S31	General bit map options	—	—	194 (C2h)
S32	XON character	0–255	ASCII	17 (11h)
S33	XOFF character	0–255	ASCII	19 (13h)
S34	*Reserved*	—	—	—
S35	*Reserved*	—	—	—
S36	LAPM failure control	—	—	7
S37	Line connection speed	—	—	0
S38	Delay before forced hangup	0–255	Seconds	20
S39	Flow control	—	—	3
S40	General bit map options	—	—	105 (69h) No MNP 10 107 (6Bh) MNP 10
S41	General bit mapped options	—	—	131 (83h)

TABLE 4.5 Continued.

Register	Function	Range	Units	Default
S43	Auto fallback character for	0–255	—	13 MNP negotiation
S44	Data framing	—	—	—
S46	Data compression control	—	—	136 (no compression), 138 (with compression)
S46*	Automatic sleep timer	0–255	100 ms	100
S47	Forced sleep timer with powerdown mode in PCMCIA	0–255	100 ms	10
S48	V.42 negotiation control	—	—	7
S49	Buffer low limit	—	—	—
S50	Buffer high limit	—	—	—
S50*	FAX/data mode selection	—	—	0 (data mode), 1 (fax mode)
S53	Global PAD configuration	—	—	—
S55	AutoStream protocol request	—	—	—
S56	AutoStream protocol status	—	—	—

(continues)

TABLE 4.5 Continued.

Register	Function	Range	Units	Default
S57	Network options register	—	—	—
S58	BTLZ string length	6–64	Bytes	32
S59	Leased line failure alarm	—	—	—
S60	Leased line failure action	—	—	—
S61	Leased line retry number	—	—	—
S62	Leased line restoral options	—	—	—
S62*	DTE rate status	0–17	—	16 (57600 bps)
S63	Leased line transmit level	—	—	—
S64	Leased line receive level	—	—	—
S69	Link layer k protocol	—	—	—
S70	Max. number of retransmissions	—	—	—
S71	Link layer timeout	—	—	—
S72	Loss of flag idle timeout	—	—	—
S72*	DTE speed select	0–18	—	0 (Last autobaud)

TABLE 4.5 Continued.

Register	Function	Range	Units	Default
S73	No activity timeout	—	—	—
S74	Minimum incoming LCN	—	—	—
S75	Minimum incoming LCN	—	—	—
S76	Maximum incoming LCN	—	—	—
S77	Maximum incoming LCN	—	—	—
S78	Outgoing LCN	—	—	—
S79	Outgoing LCN	—	—	—
S80	X.25 packet-level N20 parameter	—	—	—
S80*	Soft switch functions	—	—	1
S81	X.25 packet-level T20 parameter	—	—	—
S82	LAPM break control	—	—	128 (40h)
S84	ASU negotiation	—	—	—
S85	ASU negotiation status	—	—	—
S86	Call failure reason code	0–255	—	—

(continues)

TABLE 4.5 Continued.

Register	Function	Range	Units	Default
S87	Fixed speed DTE interface	—	—	—
S91	PSTN Xmit attenuation level	0–15	–dBm	10
S92	Fax Xmit attenuation level	0–15	–dBm	10
S92*	MI/MIC options	—	—	—
S93	V.25bis async interface speed	—	—	—
S94	V.25bis mode control	—	—	—
S95	Result code messages control	—	—	0
S97	V.32 late connecting handshake timing	—	—	—
S99	Leased line transmit level	0–15	–dBm	10
S101	Distinctive ring reporting	0–63	—	0
S105	Frame size	—	—	—
S108	Signal quality selector	—	—	—
S109	Carrier speed selector	—	—	—
S110	V.32/V.32bis selector	—	—	—

TABLE 4.5 Continued.

Register	Function	Range	Units	Default
S113	Calling tone control	—	—	—
S116	Connection timeout	—	—	—
S121	Use of DTR	—	—	—
S122	V.13 selection	—	—	—
S141	Detection phase timer	—	—	—
S142	Online character format	—	—	—
S143	KDS handshake mode	—	—	—
S144	Autobaud group selection	—	—	—
S150	V.42 options	—	—	—
S151	Simultaneous voice data control	—	—	—
S154	Force port speed	—	—	—
S157	Timeout result code	—	—	—
S201	Cellular transmit level (MNP 10)	10–63	—	58 (3Ah)
S202	Remote access escape character	0–255	ASCII	170

*The register may be used for different purposes by some modems.

(continues)

Modem Initialization Strings

One of the most difficult steps to configuring a new modem (or new modem software) is the proper use of initialization strings. These initialization strings (or *init strings* as they are sometimes called) are vital in order to set up the modem properly before each use. Otherwise, the modem will not behave as expected (if it works at all).

> **NOTE**: You may notice that a few of these AT command strings are so long that they run over into a second line. When you enter these strings into communication software, you should be sure to enter all of the commands without spaces or carriage returns on the same line.

At first glance, an initialization string may seem quite daunting. But if you take a moment to examine the string in detail (and refer to the AT Command set listed in Table 4.3), you should be able to decode even the latest command strings in just a few moments. Let's try a few more basic examples. The command string

```
ATS0=0&B1&H1&W
```

tells the modem to not answer an incoming call (S0=0), use CTS flow control (&B1), use a fixed DTE rate (&H1), and store this adjusted configuration in the modem's internal memory called NVRAM (&W). Similarly, the command string

```
ATS0=0&K3&W
```

tells the modem to not answer an incoming call (S0=0), use hardware flow control (&K3), and store this adjusted configuration in the modem's internal memory (&W). As you can see, an initialization string is merely a list of individual commands that enable, disable, or adjust specific operating parameters for a given modem. Most modem manufacturers attempt to use basic default values so that the modem will still operate without any alteration through the initialization string, but some amount of tailoring is usually required for optimum performance. If you cannot find the appropriate initialization string for your particular modem, you should check with the modem's manufacturer.

Initialization Strings and Windows 95/98

Modem initialization strings in Windows 95/98 and Windows Dial-Up Networking can be adjusted in the system registry or through the Modem icon in the Control Panel. When a modem is installed on a Windows 9x system, the default initialization string is written to the registry by the modem's .INF driver file. The key containing the default string is

```
HKEY_LOCAL_MACHINE\System\CurrentControlSet\
Services\Class\Modem\0000\Init
```

Systems with multiple modems may have modem IDs of 0000, 0001, 0002, and so on. You can use this entry in the registry to adjust the modem's initialization string manually using the *Registry Editor* (REGEDIT). However, most users are uncomfortable with editing the registry since serious errors can damage the registry and prevent Windows 95/98 from booting. The safer and faster method of adjusting the modem's initialization string is through the Modem icon. To do so, follow these steps:

1. Open your Control Panel and double-click the Modem icon.

2. Highlight your modem and click the Properties button.

3. Select the Connection tab, and then click the Advanced button.

4. The Advanced Connection Settings dialog appears.

5. Enter your new command string in the Extra Settings box. When using this box, you do *not* need to preface your new command string with AT.

You can try this yourself. Try entering S11=40 in the Extra Settings box. Click the OK button to save your changes and exit the Modem icon. Then try connecting to the Internet. Register S11 determines the amount of time (in milliseconds) between the tones of a phone number. The default setting is usually 70 milliseconds. By entering 40 milliseconds, you should hear a definite decrease in the time it takes to dial a number.

Just below the Extra Settings text box is the "Append to log" check box. If you select this option, Windows will keep a running log of the commands sent and received during a modem session. You can confirm that the correct commands are being sent. The combination of the Sent and Received commands may help you determine if a problem is caused by the system's software or hardware, or even by the service provider.

> **NOTE**: Be sure to check for an updated modem driver if you're experiencing modem problems, or when you check for driver updates for other system components. The new modem driver may contain a different (and better) default initialization string.

Modem Negotiation

The connection of two modems is not an instantaneous occurrence. Each connection is the result of a carefully planned process of *negotiation*. Modems must decide on their speed, data compression, error correction, and so on. Faster modems must recognize slower modems and revise their speed downward. The negotiation process is perhaps the most important part of a modem's operation (and the most prone to problems).

This part of the chapter outlines the negotiation sequence for a V.22bis (2400 bps) and a V.32 (4800/9600 bps) modem:

1. *Pickup.* The receiving modem picks up the ringing line (or goes off-hook). It then waits at least two seconds. This is known as a *billing delay* and is required by the telephone company to ensure that the connection has been properly established. No data transfer is allowed during the billing delay.

2. *Answer tone.* The receiving modem transmits an answer tone back to the network. A 2100-Hz tone lasts for about 3.3 seconds. An answer tone serves two purposes. First, you can hear this tone in the receiving modem's speaker, so manual modem users know when to place their modem into data mode. Even more important, the answer tone is used by the telephone network to disable echo suppressers in the connection in order to enable optimum data throughput. If echo suppressers remain active, the data transfer will be half-duplex (one direction at a time). The answering modem then goes silent for about 75 milliseconds to separate the answer tone from data.

3. *The USB1 signal.* The receiving modem then transmits alternating binary ones at 1200 bps (known as the *USB1* signal). This results in the static sound you hear just after the answer tone. The sending modem detects the USB1 signal in about 155 milliseconds and then falls silent for about 456 milliseconds.

4. *The S1 signal.* After the 456 milliseconds silence, the sending modem transmits double digits (such as 00 and 11) at 1200 bps for 100 milliseconds (the *S1* signal). An older Bell 212 or V.22 modem does not send the S1 signal, so if the S1 signal is absent, the receiving V.22bis modem will fall back to 1200

bps. The receiving modem (still generating a USB1 signal) receives the S1 signal. It responds by sending a 100 ms burst of S1 signal so that the sending modem knows the receiving modem can handle a 2400-bps operation. At this point, both modems know whether they will be operating in 1200-bps or 2400-bps mode.

5. *The SB1 signal.* At this point, the sending modem sends scrambled ones at 1200 bps (the SB1 signal). The scrambling creates white noise that checks power across the whole audio bandwidth. The receiving modem then replies with the SB1 signal for 500 ms.

6. *Ready to answer.* After 500 milliseconds, the receiving modem switches start sending scrambled ones at 2400 bps for 200 milliseconds. A full 600 milliseconds after getting the SB1 signal from the receiving modem, the sending modem also sends scrambled ones at 2400 bps for 200 milliseconds. After both modems have finished their final 200-millisecond transmissions, they are ready to pass data.

The negotiation process for a V.32 modem is remarkably similar to the V.22bis modem. However, the V.32 negotiation is more involved because of the error-correction elements that must be configured. Still, let's look at each step in the procedure:

1. *Pickup.* The receiving modem picks up the ringing line (or goes off-hook). It then goes through the billing delay required by the telephone company to ensure that the connection has been properly established. As with the V.22bis modem, no data transfer is allowed during the billing delay.

2. *Answer tone.* The receiving modem transmits an answer tone back to the network. A V.25 answer tone (a 2100-Hz tone with a duration of about 3.3

seconds) is returned to the calling modem. However, the V.32 modem uses a modified answer tone where the signal phase is reversed every 450 milliseconds. This sounds like little clicks in the signal. An answer tone serves two purposes. First, you can *hear* this tone in the receiving modem's speaker, so manual modem users know when to place their modem into data mode. Even more important, the answer tone is used by the telephone network to disable echo suppressers in the connection in order to allow optimum data throughput. The modems themselves will handle echo suppression.

3. *Signal AA.* The sending modem waits about a second after receiving the answer tone, and then generates an 1800-Hz tone (known as *Signal AA*). When the receiving modem interprets this signal, it knows (quite early on) that it is communicating with another V.32 modem.

4. *The USB1 fallback.* If the answering modem hears signal AA, it will immediately try establishing a connection. Otherwise, it will reply to the sending modem with a USB1 signal (alternating binary ones at 1200 bps). This causes the connection to fall back to a V.22bis connection. This fallback attempt will continue for three seconds. If the sending modem does not respond to the USB1 signal within three seconds, the receiving modem will continue trying the connection as a V.32.

5. *Signal AC and CA.* During a V.32 connection, the receiving modem sends Signal AC (a mixed 600-Hz and 3000-Hz tone signal) for at least 1/2400 th of a second. Then it reverses the signal phase, creating Signal CA.

6. *Signal CC.* When the sending modem detects the phase change in Signal AC/CA, it reverses the phase of its own Signal AA, creating a new signal (called *Signal CC*).

7. *Echo canceller configuration.*   Once the answering modem receives the phase-changed signal CC,
it again changes the phase of CA, returning it to
signal AC. This multitude of phase changes may
seem like a ridiculous waste of time, but this
exchange between the two modems is vital for
approximating the round-trip (propagation) delay
of the communication circuit so that the modem's
echo canceller circuitry may be set properly.

8. *Agreeing on specifics.*   Once the exchange of
phase changes sets the echo cancellers, both
modems exchange data in half-duplex mode in
order to set up adaptive equalizers, test the phone
line quality, and agree on an acceptable data rate.
In actual practice, the answering modem sends
first (from 650 milliseconds to 3525 milliseconds).
The sending modem responds but leaves the signal
on while the answering modem sends another
burst of signals (this is when the final data rate is
established).

9. *Passing data.*   Once the data rate is established,
both modems proceed to send scrambled binary
ones for at least 1/1200th of a second (a brief
white-noise sound), and then they are ready to
pass data.

Modem Troubleshooting Issues

Modems are some of the most versatile and diverse
devices in the PC market. As a result, it can be
extremely difficult and time-consuming to install and
configure a modem properly. Although installation
problems almost never damage a new modem, they can
seriously degrade the modem's performance (if the
modem works at all). The most common problems with
new installations are outlined:

- *Incorrect hardware resources.* An internal modem must be set with a unique IRQ line and I/O port. If the assigned resources are also used by another serial device in the system (such as a mouse), the modem, the conflicting device (or perhaps both) will not function properly. Remove the modem and use a diagnostic to check the available resources. Reconfigure the internal modem to clear the conflict. External modems make use of existing COM ports, so the COM port must be configured with the proper IRQ.

- *Defective telecommunication resources.* All modems need access to a telephone line in order to establish connections with other modems. If the telephone jack is defective or hooked up improperly, the modem may work fine, but no connection is possible. Remove the telephone line cord from the modem and try the line cord on an ordinary telephone. When you lift the receiver, you should draw a dial tone. Try dialing a local number. If the line rings, chances are good that the telephone line is working. Check the RJ11 jack on the modem. One or more bent connector pins can break the line even though the line cord is inserted properly. If the modem displays partial behavior (the fax features work, but the modem features do not), the two telephone wires may be reversed at the jack. Try reversing the red and green wires.

- *Improper cabling.* An external modem must be connected to the PC serial port with a cable. Traditional serial cables were 25-pin assemblies. Later, 9-pin serial connectors and cables became common. Out of those nine wires, only three are really vital. As a result, quite a few cable assemblies may be incorrect or otherwise specialized. Make sure that the serial cable between the PC and modem is a straight-through type cable. Also check that both ends of the cable are intact (or installed evenly, no bent pins, and so on). Try a new cable if necessary.

- *Improper power.* External modems must receive power from batteries or from an AC eliminator. Make sure that the batteries are fresh and installed completely. If an AC adapter is used, make sure it is connected to the modem properly.

- *Incorrect software settings.* Both internal and external modems must be initialized with an AT ASCII command string before a connection is established. If these settings are absent or incorrect, the modem will not respond as expected (if at all). Check the communication software and make sure that the AT command strings are appropriate for the modem being used. Different modems often require slightly different command strings.

- *Suspect the modem itself.* Modems are typically quite reliable in everyday use. If jumpers or DIP switches are on the modem, check that each setting is placed correctly. Perhaps their most vulnerable point is the telephone interface that is particularly susceptible to high-voltage spikes that might enter through the telephone line. If all else fails, try another modem.

Checking the Command Processor

The *command processor* is the controller that manages the modem's operation in the command mode. It is the command processor that interprets AT command strings. When the new modem installation fails to behave as it should, you should first check the modem command processor using the following outlined procedure. Make sure you have the modem's user guide on hand (if possible). When the command processor checks out, but the modem refuses to work under normal communication software operations, the software may be refusing to save settings such as COM port selection, speed, and character format:

- *Check the installation.*   Make sure the modem is installed properly and connected to the desired PC serial port. If the modem is internal, you should check the IRQ and I/O port settings.

- *Start your software.*   Open your communication software package and select a direct connection to establish a path from your keyboard to the modem. You will probably see a dialog box appear with a blinking cursor. If the modem is working and installed properly, you should now be able to send commands directly to the modem's command processor.

- *Check the command processor.*   Type the AT command and then press the Enter key. The modem should return an OK result code. When an OK is returned, chances are that the modem is working correctly. If you see double characters being displayed, try the ATE0 command to disable the mode echo command. If you do not see an OK, try issuing an ATE1 command to enable the mode echo command. If there is still no response, commands are not reaching the modem, or the modem is defective. Check the connections between the modem and serial port. If the modem is internal, check that it is installed correctly and that all jumpers are placed properly.

- *Reset the modem.*   Try resetting the modem with the ATZ command and the Enter key. This should reset the modem. If the modem now responds with OK, you may have to adjust the initialization command string in the communication software.

- *Try the factory defaults.*   Load the factory default settings by typing the AT&F command and then pressing the Enter key. This should restore the factory default values for each S-register. You may also try the AT&Q0 command and hit Enter to deliberately place the modem into asynchronous mode. You should see OK responses for each attempt that indicate the modem is responding as expected. It may be necessary to update the modem's initialization command string. If the modem still does not respond, the communication software may be incompatible or the modem is defective.

Checking the Dialer and Telephone Line

After you are confident that the modem's command processor is responding properly, you can also check the telephone interface by attempting a call. This also can verify an active telephone line. When the telephone interface checks out and the modem refuses to work under normal communication software operations, the software may be refusing to save settings such as COM port selection, speed, and character format. Make the following checks to find the solution:

- *Check the installation.* Make sure the modem is installed properly and connected to the desired PC serial port. If the modem is internal, you should check the IRQ and I/O port settings.

- *Start your software.* Open your communication software and select a direct connection to establish a path from your keyboard to the modem. You will probably see a dialog box appear with a blinking cursor. If the modem is working and installed properly, you should now be able to send commands directly to the modem.

- *Check the dialer.* Dial a number by using the DT (dial using tones) command followed by the full number being called, such as ATDT15088297683, followed by the Enter key. If your local telephone line only supports rotary dialing, use the modifier R

after the D. If calling from a PBX, be sure to dial
nine (or other outside-access codes). Listen for a dial
tone, followed by the tone dialing beeps. You should
also hear the destination phone ringing. When these
occur, they ensure that your telephone interface
dials correctly, and the local phone line is responding properly.

■ *Check the telephone interface.*   If there is no dial
tone, check the phone line by dialing with an ordinary phone. Note that some PBX systems must be
modified to produce at least 48 volts DC for the
modem to work. If there is no dial tone but the
modem attempts to dial, the telephone interface is
not grabbing the telephone line correctly (the dialer
is working). If the modem draws a dial tone but no
digits are generated, the dialer may be defective. In
either case, try another modem.

Modem Troubleshooting in Windows 98

Even with the versatility and support provided by
plug-and-play, many modem setups are still plagued by
installation, configuration, and performance problems,
especially when used under a Windows platform such
as Windows 98. This part of the chapter is intended to
offer a basic troubleshooting guideline when your
modem fails to dial-out under Windows 98.

Verifying Your Modem   Begin by checking the modem's
status in your Windows 98 system. It should be identified
correctly and installed with the proper device drivers:

1. Click Start, highlight Settings, and then click
   Control Panel.

2. Double-click the Modems icon.

3. Select the General tab and then verify that the
   modem listed in that entry is correct.

If no modem is listed or an incorrect modem is listed (even though Windows 98 reports that a modem was detected), you should download the very latest driver for your modem, remove the current modem reference(s), and then update the modem drivers:

1. Click Start, highlight Settings, and then click Control Panel.

2. Double-click the System icon.

3. Select the Device Manager tab.

4. If a modem entry exists, double-click the modem branch to expand it. If the entry does not exist, look for an Other Devices branch and then double-click it to expand that branch.

5. Double-click your modem entry, click the Driver tab, and then click the Update Driver button.

Your Windows 98 Update Device Driver wizard will then search for the best driver (or display a list from which you can select the appropriate driver). If you use the Update Device Driver wizard to search for a driver, you can also specify a location for the driver. Drivers for some additional modems are included in the \Drivers\Modem folder on the Windows 98 CD, but if you've downloaded a new set of modem drivers from the manufacturer's Web site, you may need to look for the new drivers in your Temp or Download directories. After the modem drivers are updated, reboot the system and verify that the correct drivers are listed. Then try using your modem again.

If the correct driver appears in your Device Manager, but the modem still refuses to operate properly, you may need to troubleshoot further. Follow these next steps depending on whether your modem is a Windows-only modem (a WinModem) or a standard modem.

WinModem Issues. A WinModem (also called a soft-ware modem) depends on drivers that are specific to the operating system in order to function. This means that your modem must be recognized by the operating system before any troubleshooting can be performed. Windows 98 should normally detect the presence of a WinModem and add it to the Device Manager properly. If a WinModem is not detected, you should expect one of three possible causes:

- The WinModem has previously been detected (even though the correct drivers may not have been installed for it). In this case, the WinModem should be listed in your Device Manager and the driver can be updated using the "Verifying Your Modem" procedure earlier.

- The WinModem drivers were installed and then removed, but some registry entries remain. The registry entries need to be removed before the WinModem can be detected again. For 3Com/US Robotics modems, use the WMREGDEL.EXE tool included on your Windows 98 CD to clear all WinModem-related registry entries and then restart your computer. The WMREGDEL.EXE tool is located in the \Drivers\Modem\3com-usr\Winmodem folder. If Windows 98 still does not detect your WinModem, the WMREGDEL.EXE tool may not have removed all the necessary registry entries. If this occurs, you may need to contact the particular modem maker in order to obtain a specific fix or workaround instructions (there may be a specific registry entry that needs to be deleted manually).

- The last option is to consider an actual WinModem defect; something may be wrong with the actual WinModem device. Try another WinModem (perhaps one from a different manufacturer) or check with your WinModem maker for specific testing instructions.

WinModem Driver Notes. If there are no default Windows 98 drivers for your WinModem, Windows 98 prompts you to search for drivers. Suitable drivers may exist in the \Drivers\Modem folder on your Windows 98 CD. If no drivers are located for your particular WinModem, Windows 98 adds the device under the Other Devices branch of your Device Manager. You can then use the Device Manager to update the existing drivers with new drivers provided by your WinModem manufacturer.

If your WinModem still does not work after installing and/or updating the drivers, there may be a resource conflict or an issue specific to your particular WinModem. Use the following sections of this discussion to troubleshoot further.

> **NOTE**: Given the dependence of a WinModem on operating system drivers, you cannot perform any troubleshooting outside of the operating system. For example, you cannot test a Windows 98 WinModem at a command prompt in the DOS mode.

Fax/Modem Issues. A standard fax/modem does not offload important tasks to the host system or rely on the operating system for direct support. This means you can test the modem in DOS even if it isn't detected by Windows. One of the easiest means of modem testing is to check direct communications with the modem port (COM port). Open a DOS windows under Windows 98, type the following command and then press Enter:

```
echo ATM1L3X0DT12345 > COM1
```

or replace COM1 with the serial port number to which the modem is connected (COM2 or COM3). The first command, AT (attention), signals that the modem is about to receive information. M1 is a universal command to turn the modem's speaker on (if it is off by default). L3 is a universal command to raise the modem's speaker volume to the maximum level (if it is at the lowest by default). X0 signals the modem to run the command without waiting for a dial tone. This is useful if modem and voice calls use the same phone line. Finally, the DT12345 command instructs the modem to dial the digits "12345." To hang up the modem again, simply type

```
echo ATH0 > COM1
```

and then press Enter. If your modem is on a port other than COM1, replace COM1 with the serial port number to which the modem is connected (COM2 or COM3).

> **NOTE**: To place your computer in DOS mode, click Start, click Shut Down, click Restart In MS-DOS Mode, and then click OK. To quit MS-DOS mode, type exit at the command prompt and then press Enter.

If the modem does not respond with a dial tone or communication signal in DOS mode, something may be physically wrong with either the modem or the COM port. Verify that the modem's COM port is configured as expected or reconfigure the modem manually. If there is a resource conflict between the COM port and another device in the system, you may need to resolve the conflict in order to enable the modem. Otherwise, try a new modem.

If the modem does not respond with a dial tone or communication signal in Windows 98 but does respond in DOS mode, Windows 98 itself may not be communicating correctly with your COM port. This trouble can occur for several reasons:

- The COM port has not been detected. Click Start, highlight Settings, click Control Panel, double-click Add New Hardware, and then follow the instructions on your screen to detect and install the COM port.

- The serial port device drivers are corrupt. Use the *System File Checker* (SFC) tool to verify the integrity of the SERIAL.VXD, VCOMM.VXD, and SERIALUI.DLL serial port drivers. To access the SFC, click Start, highlight Programs, highlight Accessories, point to System Tools, and then choose the System Information utility. Once the System Information utility starts, click Tools on the main menu and then select the System File Checker. You may need to reinstall or update any damaged files.

- Finally, there is a resource conflict between your COM port and another device in the system. You'll need to resolve the conflict using the Device Manager as shown in the next section of this article.

Resolving Resource Conflicts. A COM port requires the use of an interrupt (or IRQ) signal and an I/O port address. If you're using a WinModem, you should also plan on using a *Direct Memory Access* (DMA) channel. Normally, devices should use unique resources, and no two devices in the system can share the same resources. When the same resources are used by two or more devices, a resource conflict is said to occur. Conflicts may prevent one or both conflicting devices from functioning until the conflict is identified and resolved. In virtually all cases, you can manage resources and resolve conflicts using the Device Manager:

1. Click Start, highlight Settings, and then click Control Panel.

2. Double-click the System icon and then select the Device Manager tab.

If a resource conflict prevents one device from working, an exclamation point in a yellow circle is displayed for the device. However, a WinModem that conflicts with another device may not have an exclamation point in a yellow circle. In this case, you must determine if there is a conflict yourself. Follow these steps to view the resource settings used by your modem:

1. On the Device Manager tab, double-click the Modem branch to expand it.

2. Double-click your modem and then click the Resources tab.

   NOTE: If a Resources tab does not exist, your modem's resources cannot be configured by Windows 98. To determine the resources your modem is using, consult the documentation included with your modem.

3. Write down the resource settings used by your modem and then click OK.

4. Double-click Computer (at the top of your Device Manager hardware list) to view all the resource settings in use on your computer. Click each resource setting to determine if another device is using any of the same settings your modem is using.

   NOTE: Any hardware using the IRQ Holder for PCI Steering setting can be disregarded. This does not cause a resource conflict.

If another device is using any of the settings in use by your modem, you'll need to change the setting for that device (or your modem). If the device is plug-and-play-compliant, you may be able to do this through the Resources tab in Device Manager (although some devices may require you to change jumper pins or dip switches on the device itself). Since WinModems are invariably plug-and-play devices, you should be able to change the settings for the modem through your Device Manager:

1. Double-click the Modem branch to expand it and then double-click your WinModem entry.

2. On the Resources tab, click the Use Automatic Settings check box to clear it.

3. In the Setting Based On box, click a basic configuration with settings that do not conflict with any other device.

If none of the available basic configurations have settings that do not conflict with any other device, you may need to change some resource settings manually. Click the last available basic configuration and then double-click the resource setting you need to change. If you still cannot clear the conflict, you may need to remove the other conflicting device (at least temporarily).

Dealing with Other Issues. The general instructions covered previously are designed to provide the essential troubleshooting guidelines for most common modem problems. Still, a technician should be aware of many other specific modem issues under Windows 98.

U.S. Robotics WinModems. Some U.S. Robotics WinModems may not be detected properly during the Windows 98 upgrade process. This may occur even if the WinModem is working perfectly under Windows 95. If your U.S. Robotics WinModem is not detected when Windows 98 starts and is not listed in the Device Manager (either under the Modem or Other Devices branch), use the WMREGDEL.EXE tool included on the Windows 98 CD-ROM to clear all WinModem-related Registry entries and then restart your computer. The WMREGDEL.EXE tool is located in the \Drivers\Modem\3com-usr\Winmodem folder on the Windows 98 CD.

If Windows 98 still does not detect your U.S. Robotics WinModem, the WMREGDEL.EXE tool may not have removed all the necessary Registry entries. Try an updated version of the WMREGDEL.EXE tool from the 3Com/US Robotics FTP site.

Sound4 WinModems. Packard Bell systems typically incorporate the Sound4 WinModems, but these modems may not be detected properly during the Windows 98 upgrade process. If the WinModem stops working properly after upgrading to Windows 98, you'll need to contact Packard Bell technical support for a suitable workaround (depending on your system model).

WinModem Not Found. After you upgrade to Windows 98, double-click the WinModem icon in your Control Panel. You may receive an error such as the following:

```
Error: There is no WinModem found in your
computer, but some corrupted files were found
and they have been cleaned.
```

If you view your WinModem in Device Manager, you may also notice multiple WinModem entries. This problem will typically occur if your WinModem is not using the most current setup information (.INF) file or device driver. You'll need to delete all your WinModem entries, erase any WinModem references from the registry, and then redetect/reinstall the WinModem using the very latest .INF and driver files available from the modem maker.

Port Errors. When you try to use your modem, you may receive an error message such as

```
Could not open port
```

This type of hardware error message is generally the result of a resource conflict between the modem and another device (or a program is loading in the Startup folder that opens a COM port for some other use other than the modem). If you'd like to weed out any possible resource conflicts, refer to the guidelines covered in

"Resolving Resource Conflicts." If you'd like to check for possible Startup folder issues, you can use the following steps to temporarily disable programs in the Startup folder:

1. Click Start, highlight Programs, select Accessories, highlight System Tools, and then click System Information.

2. On the Tools menu, select the System Configuration Utility.

3. Click the Startup tab.

Identify any programs that may control your modem and then click that program's check box to clear it. If you're unsure whether or not a specific program should be disabled, clear all of the check boxes *except* for the following utilities:

- ScanRegistry
- SystemTray
- LoadPowerProfile
- TaskMonitor

After you save your changes, you'll need to reboot the system and see if your changes have cleared the problem. If not, try disabling other non-essential files in the Startup folder.

DUN Error 630. When you attempt to use *Dial-Up Networking* (DUN) services, you may receive an error message such as

```
Error 630: The computer is not receiving a
response from the modem. Check that the modem is
plugged in. Turn the modem off, and then turn it
back on.
```

This error message will occur if the modem is using an adjusted serial port assignment caused when new devices are installed by Windows 98 hardware detection. In these cases, change the properties of your DUN connection to use the new modem settings rather than wrestle with tweaking the modem's settings.

> **NOTE**: Certain programs in the Startup folder can also cause this error message. Systematically disable programs in the Startup folder as outlined in the "Port Errors" section.

DUN Error 633. When you attempt to use DUN services, you may receive an error message such as

```
Error 633: The modem is not installed or
configured for Dial-Up Networking. To check your
modem configuration, double-click the Modems icon
in Control Panel.
```

In many cases, you may need to delete and reconfigure the DUN settings for your modem. In other cases, this error message can occur if the TELEPHON.INI file is missing or damaged.

DUN Error 745. When you attempt to use DUN services, you may receive an error message such as

```
Error 745: An essential file is missing.
Re-install Dial-Up Networking.
```

This error message typically occurs when a DUN dynamic-link library (.DLL) file is missing or damaged. You may need to remove DUN support from Windows 98 Setup and then reinstall the support from the Windows 98 CD.

TAPI Issues. Check the modem's diagnostics by clicking Start, highlighting Settings, and then clicking Control Panel. Double-click the Modems icon and then select the Diagnostics tab. Click the More Info button to test the modem. When the modem passes its diagnostic tests but is not available in HyperTerminal, Phone Dialer, or DUN, there may be a problem with the computer's *Telephony Application Programming*

Interface (TAPI) setup or the TELEPHON.INI file may be missing or damaged. You may need to reinstall TAPI support or remove and reinstall the damaged file named TELEPHON.INI.

Checking Modem Firmware

Today it is common for modems to sport a Flash *Basic Input/Output System* (BIOS) or firmware, which can be updated as new firmware versions are made available. Many late-model 33.6-Kbps, x2 56-Kbps, and K56flex 56-Kbps modems offer such upgradeable firmware in preparation for the V.90 standard. If you're considering a modem firmware upgrade, you'll need to check the current firmware version on your modem. You can use HyperTerminal to interrogate the firmware version of your modem by performing the following steps:

1. Click Start, highlight Programs, select Accessories, and choose HyperTerminal.

2. Double-click the Hyperterm icon.

3. When the program starts, type TEST for a name and proceed.

4. When you're asked for a telephone number, just type 1234 and make sure that the correct modem device is selected from the Connect Using drop-down menu. Click OK to proceed.

5. Now click Cancel (don't actually try connecting). This will bring you to the terminal window.

6. Type in ATE1 (even if you don't see it appear on the screen) and press Enter. The modem should respond with OK.

Now you can type any AT commands you want. Try typing ATi3 or ATi92; these two AT commands will tell you the exact firmware version and type of modem that you're using. For example, my modem responds

U.S. Robotics Sportster 33600 Fax V4.3.185

Once you find the firmware version, you can compare it with the new version available for download and upgrade your firmware if the online version is newer. To determine if your modem supports the V.90 standard, follow these steps:

1. Click Start, select Settings, click Control Panel, and then double-click the Modems icon.

2. On the Diagnostics tab, click the correct modem and then click More Info.

3. After a few moments, a series of AT commands and responses will appear in the information box.

4. Locate the line that begins with ATI7. If your modem supports the V.90 standard, V.90 should be listed beside that command.

5. Click OK.

Modem Symptoms

The following section will cover some typical symptoms of modem problems and will outline the necessary steps for solving them.

Symptom 4.1. The PC (or communication software) refuses to recognize the modem. First, verify that the modem is turned on (external modems only). For internal modems, see that the modem is installed correctly and completely in its expansion slot. Check your *Complementary Metal Oxide Semiconductor* (CMOS) settings and verify that the COM port for your external modem is even enabled. A COM port (IRQ) conflict may exist in the system. Check the configuration of your internal modem (try the Windows 95 Device Manager) and verify that no hardware conflicts exist. If you have trouble running the modem in Terminal mode (the modem doesn't respond to AT commands), make sure that you're entering everything in either upper-case (AT) or lower-case (at) format. Mixing cases can sometimes confuse a modem.

Symptom 4.2. Your 33.6-Kbps modem is detected as a 28.8-Kbps modem. This can happen if your version of Windows 95/98 doesn't supply hardware information about the faster modem that you're trying to use. In virtually every case, you'll need to supply a suitable Windows 95/98 driver for the modem in the form of an .INF file that accompanies the modem device or is available for download from the modem manufacturer's Web site.

Symptom 4.3. The modem appears to be functioning properly, but you can't see what you are typing. Two types of duplex exist: *full* and *half*. Half-duplex systems simply transmit to and receive from each other. Full-duplex systems do that, plus they "receive" what they transmit, echoing the data back to the sender. Since half-duplex systems do not echo, what is being sent is typically not shown on the screen. Most terminal programs have an option to enable LOCAL ECHO so that what is transmitted is also displayed. You can often enable the modem's local echo by typing the ATE1 command during a direct connection, or add the E1 entry to the modem's initialization string. When local echo is not an option, switching to full-duplex mode will often do the same thing. Customer complaints that they can't see what they are typing are solved by turning on local echo or switching to full-duplex.

Symptom 4.4. The modem appears to be functioning properly, but you see double characters print while typing. By their nature, full-duplex modem connections produce an echo. If local echo is enabled in addition, you'll see not only what you are transmitting, but also that character being echoed, creating a double display. For example, when you hit A, you'll see AA. This can be annoying but is totally harmless. Customer complaints of double letters are solved by turning off local echo by entering the ATE0 command during direct connection or adding the E0 command to the modem's initialization string.

Symptom 4.5. Your 32-bit TAPI-compliant programs cannot detect your modem. Even though you have a modem installed under Windows 95/98 /SE, a 32-bit TAPI program may not be able to access the modem. The TAPI program may even start the Install New Modem wizard. For example, the Install New Modem wizard may start when you launch the Make New Connection wizard in DUN, even though a modem is already installed. The following error message may appear after you attempt to dial a connection:

```
Error 633 The modem is not installed or configured
for dial-up networking. To check your modem
configuration, double-click on the Modems icon
in the Control Panel.
```

In virtually all cases, this fault will occur if the Unimodem TAPI Service Provider file (UNIMDM.TSP) is missing or damaged. To correct the fault, extract a new copy of the UNIMDM.TSP file from your original Windows disks or CD to the \Windows\System folder. For Windows 95, the UNIMDM.TSP file is located in the WIN95_03.CAB cabinet file. For Windows 98, the UNIMDM.TSP file is located in the WIN98_63.CAB cabinet file. For Windows 98 Second Edition, the UNIMDM. TSP file is located in the WIN98_69.CAB cabinet file.

Symptom 4.6. Your modem diagnostics feature cannot access the modem under Windows 98. When you attempt to run modem diagnostics on the modem (a 3Com Megahertz 10/100 LAN+56K Modem PC card) after resuming your laptop from standby mode, you may receive the following error:

```
Couldn't open port.
```

This problem can occur if you try running the modem diagnostics before the computer goes into standby mode. Modem diagnostics leave the modem's communication port open. If the port is open when your computer goes into standby mode, it remains open after you resume your computer. This is a problem with Windows 98, and a patch is now available from Microsoft. The English version of this patch contains the following attributes:

```
VCOMM.VXD   6/25/99  12:51:29p
4.10.2017   Windows 98
```

Symptom 4.7. You have trouble with a Sierra Semiconductor 33.6-Kbps modem. When you try to use a Sierra Semiconductor 33.6-Kbps modem under Windows 98, you may encounter an Error 630 message, and your modem may not connect successfully. This problem may not occur with every program that uses your modem. This trouble can occur because the Sierra Semiconductor 33.6 modem driver is not fully compatible with Windows 98. To correct this issue, update the modem driver to a version that's fully compliant with Windows 98. To work around this issue, you can configure your modem to use the Sierra 28800 PnP SQ3456 modem driver (though this will operate the modem at a slower speed than normal):

1. Click Start, highlight Settings, click Control Panel, and then double-click the System icon.

2. Click the Device Manager tab, double-click the Modem entry, click your Sierra modem, and then click Properties.

3. Click the Driver tab, click Update Driver, and then click Display a list of all the drivers in a specific location, so you can select the driver you want.

4. In the Manufacturer's box, click Sierra Semiconductor.

5. In the Models box, click Sierra 28800 PnP SQ3456.

6. Click Next and then follow the instructions on the screen to finish installing the driver.

Symptom 4.8. When creating a connection, your modem is missing from the Select A Device box. If you try to use an existing connection under Windows 98, you may receive an error such as:

```
Error 633: The modem is not installed or
configured for Dial-Up Networking. To check
your modem configuration, double-click the
Modems icon in Control Panel
```

If you test your modem by clicking More Info on the Diagnostics tab under the Modems icon in your Control Panel, your modem may respond normally and appear to be working correctly. This problem can occur if the TAPI Service Provider entry in your registry is missing (or corrupted) or if the TELEPHON.INI file is missing or damaged. Access the system registry and use REGEDIT to view the following key:

```
HKEY_LOCAL_MACHINE\Software\Microsoft\Windows\
Current Version\ Telephony\Providers
```

1. Set the value of the ProviderFilename0 value to TSP3216L.TSP. Save the changes, quit the Registry Editor, and then restart your computer. If the TELEPHON.INI file is missing or damaged, you'll need to recreate it. Click Start, highlight Find, and then click Files Or Folders.

2. In the Named box, type `telephon.ini` and then click Find Now.

3. If you do not find the TELEPHON.INI file, skip the next step. If you do find the file, right-click the file, click Rename, type `telephon.old`, and then press Enter.

4. Quit the Find tool, click Start, click Run, type `tapiini.exe`, and then press Enter.

5. Restart your computer.

Symptom 4.9. You encounter trouble with a PhoebeMicro 56-Kbps modem under Windows 98/SE. The modem may refuse to dial out. It may also hang up and crash the communication software with an error such as

```
The modem failed to respond. Make sure it is
properly connected and turned on. If it is an
internal modem or is connected, verify that the
interrupt for the port is properly set.
```

In virtually every case, the problem is due to faulty or outdated modem drivers accompanying the device. Contact the modem manufacturer to obtain the very latest drivers, or try default drivers on the Windows 98/SE CD.

Symptom 4.10. Your modem refuses to dial out when using a TAPI program. When you use a TAPI program under Windows 95/98 (such as DUN, Phone Dialer, or HyperTerminal), you may receive an error message such as

```
There is no dialtone. Make sure your modem is
connected to the phone line.
```

In most cases, this error occurs when you're trying to dial using a calling card, and you have enabled the Wait for dial tone before dialing option. You must disable this option by doing the following:

1. Click Start, highlight Settings, and then click Control Panel.

2. Double-click the Modems icon.

3. Select your modem and then click Properties.

4. On the Connection tab, click the Wait for dial tone before dialing check box to clear it.

5. Click OK, and then click OK again.

6. It may be necessary to restart the computer.

Symptom 4.11. Your modem properties are not available through the Modems icon in your Control Panel. When you modify your modem's properties under Windows 95/98, the Configure button may be unavailable in HyperTerminal or DUN. Also, when you click your modem and then click Properties in the Modems tool under the Control Panel, you may receive an error message such as:

```
The modem properties cannot be displayed because
the modem information is corrupt. Remove this
modem by clicking Remove and add it again.
```

However, you find that removing and reinstalling the modem does not correct the problem. In a few cases, this problem can occur if an incorrect version of the UMDM16.DLL file is installed in the \Windows\ System folder. If this occurs, rename the UMDM16.DLL file and extract a new copy of the file from your original Windows CD. In the vast majority of cases, this problem will occur if the MODEMUI.DLL file is damaged. To correct this problem, use Windows Explorer or My Computer to rename the MODEMUI.DLL file in the \Windows\System folder to MODEMUI.OLD. Then extract a new copy of the file MODEMUI.DLL file from your Windows CD to your \Windows\System folder.

Symptom 4.12. Your faxes are garbled when using a class-two fax/modem. When you open the fax in a Windows 95/98 application such as Fax Viewer, the output may resemble a bar code or contain blank pages. This is almost always a problem with the fax/modem, since some class-two fax/modems reverse the bit order of incoming faxes. To correct this problem, switch the bit order of incoming faxes for each of your affected fax/modems by editing the registry:

1. Exit your fax/modem software and then launch your *Registry Editor* (REGEDIT).

2. Locate the following registry key:

```
Hkey_Local_Machine\Software\Microsoft\At Work
Fax\Local Modems\TAPI0001<xxxx>
```

where <xxxx> is a unique TAPI identifier for the fax/modem and then add the string value CL2SWBOR to that registry key.

3. Set the string value for CL2SWBOR to 1.

4. Save your changes, quit the Registry Editor, and then restart your computer.

Symptom 4.13. Your V.34 internal 28.8-Kbps modem is not detected properly. When you run the Add New Hardware wizard under Windows 95/98, the V.34 modem may be detected as a standard modem, even though the modem is included in the hardware list. This problem occurs since the V.34 modem included in the hardware list is not a 28.8-Kbps modem, but the actual installed modem is a 28.8-Kbps modem. To install the modem correctly, you'll need to provide the manufacturer's drivers:

1. Click Start, highlight Settings, and then click Control Panel.

2. Double-click the Modems icon.

3. Click Add.

4. Click the Don't detect my modem; I will select it from a list check box to select it, and then click Next.

5. Click Have Disk.

6. In the Copy Manufacturer's File From box, type the path to the disk containing the manufacturer's driver files and then click OK.

7. Follow the instructions on the screen to complete the installation.

Symptom 4.14. You cannot dial phone numbers over 32 characters long. When you try to dial a long phone number (over 32 characters) under Windows 98, your modem may not respond or dial out. This is typically a driver issue and is usually caused when using a controller-less modem with a standard (or generic) modem driver instead of the driver that is specifically designed for your particular modem. To resolve this issue, you should obtain and install the most current modem driver for your particular modem.

Symptom 4.15. You cannot initialize your modem properly when using pcANYWHERE under Windows 98. When you use Symantec's pcANYWHERE 7.0 to dial out by modem and establish a connection, you may receive an `Error initializing modem` error message. The modem then continues to dial out, and the connection is established. The performance of pcANYWHERE is not affected, but the error message may appear every time you dial out with a modem to establish a pcANYWHERE connection. This problem is known to occur with version 7.0 of this software, and you will need to upgrade to pcANYWHERE 7.5 or later in order to correct the problem.

Symptom 4.16. The modem is detected on the wrong COM port on your PC. The modem may not respond or work correctly, and the modem may appear to be using COM3 even if you've configured your modem to use COM1. This is a known issue with systems such as the Acer Aspire and is caused by an issue with the system's BIOS. For example, this problem can occur if COM1 is disabled in your computer's BIOS, but the system incorrectly reports the disabled status of COM1. Windows 95/98 still detects COM1 and may assign your modem to COM3 to avoid resource conflicts. The proper long-term fix is to upgrade the system BIOS, but you may work around the issue by disabling COM1 in the Device Manager:

1. Right-click My Computer, click Properties, and then click the Device Manager tab.

2. Double-click the Ports (COM and LPT) branch to expand it, click Communications Port (COM1), and then click Properties.

3. Click to select the `Disable in this hardware profile` check box and then click OK.

4. Double-click the Modems branch to expand it, click your modem, click Remove, and click OK. Then restart your computer.

5. When your computer restarts, follow the instructions on the screen to reinstall your modem.

Symptom 4.17. You encounter an "Error 630" when dialing out with your modem. When you attempt to dial out under Windows 98, you may receive an error message such as

```
Error 630: The computer is not receiving a
response from the modem. Check that the modem is
plugged in, and if necessary, turn the modem off,
and then turn it back on.
```

You may also see an error indicating that the communication port is invalid or busy. This fault can occur if you have the Support SerialKey devices accessibility option configured to use the same COM port where your modem is connected. You'll first need to disable or reconfigure the Support SerialKey devices option:

1. Click Start, highlight Settings, click Control Panel, and then double-click Accessibility Options.

2. On the General tab, either click to clear the Support SerialKey devices check box or click Settings. Click a different COM port in the Serial port box and then click OK.

3. Click OK.

Symptom 4.18. You cannot get CU-SeeMee videoconferencing to work with ADSL under Windows 98/SE. When you try to establish a CU-SeeMe video conference with an *Internet Connection Sharing* (ICS) host over an *Asymmetric Digital Subscriber Line* (ADSL) connection, you may be unable to connect to any Internet conference site. If you are able to initialize a conference, it may time out. You should disable ICS on the host computer:

1. Click Start, highlight Settings, click Control Panel, and then double-click Internet Options.

2. Click the Connections tab and then click Sharing.

3. Click to clear the Enable Internet Connection Sharing check box and then click OK.

4. Use CU-SeeMe on the ICS host.

Symptom 4.19. The modem will not answer at the customer's site, but it works fine in the shop. Since deregulation of the original Bell Telephone company, customers have been allowed to attach devices to phone lines with the proviso that they notify the phone company of each device's FCC registration and *ringer equivalence number* (REN). Although few customers make it a point of informing their local telephone company how many phones and gadgets are connected to the telephone line, there is a good reason for having it. You see, the amount of *ringing voltage* supplied to a site is fixed. If you load down the line beyond its maximum rating, not enough voltage will be available to ring all of the bells. The *ringer equivalence* is the amount of load that the device will place on the line. Modems must be able to detect a ring signal before they know to pick up. If the ringing signal is too weak, the modem will not detect it properly and initiate an answer sequence.

Have the customer remove some other equipment from their phone lines and see if the problem disappears. With today's fax machines, modems, multiple extension phones, and answering machines all plugged into the same line, it would be easy to overload the ringing voltage. The customer should also take a listing of the registration numbers and ringer equivalence numbers on *all* devices connected to phone lines and notify the local phone company of them. The phone company can then boost the ringer voltage to compensate for the added loads.

As a precaution, make sure that your customer is starting the communication software properly before attempting to receive a modem call. The modem will not pick up a ringing line unless the proper software is running, and the modem is in an auto-answer mode.

Symptom 4.20. Your modem is receiving or transmitting garbage or is having great difficulty displaying anything at all. Serial communication is totally dependent on the data frame settings and transfer rate of the receiver and the transmitter being an exact match. The baud rate, word bits, stop bits, and parity must all match exactly or errors will show up. These errors can show as either no data or as incorrect data (garbage) onscreen. You'll see this one crop up a lot when customers switch from calling a local *Bulletin Board Service* (BBS) to CompuServe. Local BBSs are usually set for eight-bit words, no parity, and one stop bit. CompuServe, on the other hand, uses seven-bit words, even parity, and two stop bits. The terminal software must be reconfigured to match the settings of each service being called. Most programs allow for these differences by letting you specify a configuration for each entry in the dialing directory. Also check the method of flow control being used (XOFF/XON, DTR/DSR, CTS/RTS) and make sure that it is set properly.

Baud rate mismatches most often result in what looks like a dead modem. Often, nothing is displayed on either end. Modems will automatically negotiate a common baud rate to connect at without regard to the terminal settings. The modems will normally connect at the highest baud rate available to the slowest modem, so if a 14400-bps modem connects to a 2400-bps modem, both will set themselves to 2400 bps. If the software on the higher speed modem is still set for the higher speed, you'll typically get large amounts of garbage or nothing at all.

If the problem is a result of being connected to a service such as a BBS, call the SYSOP and find out the settings. You can also let the modem tell you its transfer rate. Before dialing, set a direct connection and send the ATQ0V1 command to the modem. This tells the modem to send result codes in plain English. When connected, you'll see a message similar to CONNECT 2400. The actual number you see is the bps rate, and you can reconfigure your software accordingly. Working out the word, stop, and parity bits may be a process of trial and error, but almost all BBS installations use eight data bits, no parity, and one stop bit. If you are forced to attempt trial and error, target one item to get right at a time. First, get the baud rates to match. Next, get the word bits settled down and then go for parity and stop bits. If you make more than one change, you'll never know which change made the difference. It may seem slower, but your overall service time will be cut.

Symptom 4.21. The modem is connected and turned on, but there is no response from the modem. The communication software's configuration must match the port settings of the modem. Check to make sure that any modem parameters are entered and saved properly. Establish a direct connection with the modem and enter the ATZ command. This will reset the modem. The modem should respond with OK or 0 (the numerical equivalent of OK). If that doesn't work, change to COM2 and try again. Then try COM3 and COM4. If none of the combinations work, check the DIP switches or jumpers on the modem for the correct configuration. Finally, try the modem on another PC or replace the suspect modem outright.

Symptom 4.22. The modem will not pick up the phone line. The modem is unable to initiate a call or answer an incoming call. Most modems today come with two RJ11 telephone line connectors for the phone lines, one labeled LINE (where the outside line enters the modem) and the other labeled PHONE (where an extension telephone can be plugged in). Check that the outgoing telephone line is plugged into the LINE jack. Leave the PHONE connector disconnected while the modem is in use.

Test the modem manually by establishing a direct connection and typing a dial command such as `ATDT15083667683`. When you enter this command string, the modem should go off hook, draw a dial tone, and dial the numbers. If this happens as expected, you can be reasonably sure that the modem is working properly and the communication software is at fault. Check the modem initialization strings or try a new communication package. If the modem does not respond during a direct connection, check that the modem is installed and configured properly. You may need to try a new modem.

Symptom 4.23. The modem appears to work fine but prints garbage whenever it's supposed to show IBM text graphics such as boxes or ANSI graphics. Your terminal emulation mode is wrong. The communication software is probably set for seven-bit words. The IBM text graphic character set starts at ASCII 128 and has to have the eighth bit. Adjust the communication software configuration to handle eight-bit words. You may also be using an unusual ASCII character set during the connection. Try setting the character set emulation to ANSI BBS or TTY.

Symptom 4.24. You frequently see strange character groups like "[0m" appearing in the text.   These are ANSI control codes attempting to control your display. Popular among BBS software, ANSI codes can be used to set colors, draw ASCII boxes, clear the screen, move the cursor, and so on. DOS provides an ANSI screen driver called ANSI.SYS that can be loaded into the CONFIG.SYS when the computer is rebooted. Most of today's terminal software will offer a setting for this as well. If you are able to select character set emulation in your communication software, try setting to ANSI BBS.

Symptom 4.25. The modem makes audible clicking noises when hooked to a phone line.   There is probably a short in the phone line. The clicking is the noise of the modem trying to pick up when it finds the short and hang up when the short clears. Try replacing the line cord going from the modem to the telephone wall jack. Line cords don't last very long under constant use and abuse. If problems continue, try using a different telephone line. The physical wiring may be defective between the wall jack and telephone pole. Contact your local telephone company if you suspect this to be the case. Next, try establishing a direct connection to the modem and enter an AT&F command that will restore the modem's factory default settings. If that clears the problem, the modem's initialized state may not be fully compatible with the current telephone line characteristics. Check each modem setting carefully and adjust the parameters to try and settle its operation down. If factory default settings do not help and the telephone line seems reliable, there may be a problem with the modem's telephone interface circuit. Try replacing the modem.

Symptom 4.26. The modem is having difficulty connecting to another modem.   The modem is powered and connected properly. It dials the desired number and you can hear the modems negotiating, but they never quite seem to make a connection. This is a classic software configuration problem. You may often see a No Carrier message associated with this problem. Check each parameter in your communication software, especially the modem's AT initialization string. Make sure that each entry in the string is appropriate for your modem. If the string looks correct, try disabling the modem's MNP5 protocol. You will have to refer to the modem's manual to find the exact command, but many modems use AT\N0. If your modem is using MNP5 and the destination modem does not support it, the negotiation can hang up. If problems persist, try lowering the modem's data transfer rate. Although most modems can set the proper transfer rate automatically, some modems that do not support it may also cause the negotiation to freeze.

Another problem may be that your modem is not configured to wait long enough for a carrier from the remote modem. You can adjust this delay by entering a larger number for S-register S7. Start the communication software, establish a direct connection (terminal mode), and type ATS7? followed by the Enter key. This will return the current value of register S7. You can then use the ATS7=10 command to enter a larger delay (in this case, 10 seconds). This should give the destination modem more time to respond. If all else fails, try a modem from a different manufacturer.

Symptom 4.27. The modem starts dialing before it draws a dial tone.   As a result, one or more of the numbers are lost during dialing, making it difficult to establish a connection. Chances are that the modem is working just fine, but the modem does not wait long enough for a dial tone to be present once it goes off hook. The solution is to increase the time delay *before* the modem starts dialing. This can be done by changing the value in S-register S6. To find the current value, start the communication software and establish a direct connection (terminal mode). Then type ATS6? followed by the

Enter key. This queries the S-register. You can then enter a new value such as ATS6=10 to provide a 10-second delay.

Symptom 4.28. The modem has trouble sending or receiving when the system's power saving features are turned on. This type of problem is most prevalent with PCMCIA modems running on a notebook PC. The power conservation features found on many notebook systems often interferes with the modem's operation. Proper modem operation typically relies on full processing speed, which is often scaled back when power conservation is turned on. Ultimately, the most effective resolution to this problem is simply to turn the power conservation features off while you use the modem (you can reset the power features later). However, it may be possible to correct these types of problems using a BIOS upgrade for the mobile PC or an updated modem driver.

Symptom 4.29. You see an error such as "Already online" or "Carrier already established." These types of errors often arise when you start a communications package while the modem is already online. You might also find this problem when the *Carrier Detect* (CD) signal is set to "always on" (using a command string such as AT&C0). To make sure that the CD signal is on only when the modem makes a connection, use a command string such as AT&C1&D2&W. The &W suffix loads the settings into *non-volatile RAM* (NVRAM). If this problem arises when you hang up the connection without signing off the modem, you will have to reboot the system to clear CD. AT&F and ATZ will not clear the signal.

Symptom 4.30. The modem refuses to answer the incoming line. First, be sure to set the communication software to answer the calling modem or set the modem to auto-answer mode (set S-register S0 to one or more). On external modems, you will see the AA LED lit when the

auto-answer mode is active. Problems can also occur if
your external modem does not recognize the DTR signal generated by the host PC. The AT&D command controls how the modem responds to the computer's DTR
signal. An external modem turns on the TR light when
it is set to see the DTR signal. If the TR light is out, the
modem will not answer (regardless of whether the auto-
answer mode is enabled or not). Use the AT&D0 command if your serial port does not support the DTR
signal, or if your modem cable does not connect to it.
Otherwise, you should use the AT&D2 command.

**Symptom 4.31. The modem switches into the command
mode intermittently.**   When this problem develops, you
may have to tweak the DTR arrangement. To correct
this fault, try changing the modem's DTR setting using
the AT&D2&W command.

**Symptom 4.32. Your current modem won't connect at 2400
bps with a 2400-bps modem.**   This is a compatibility
issue between vastly different generations of hardware. The modem you're trying to connect with is
almost certainly an older model that doesn't support
error control (that is, MNP protocols). You can disable
error control on your modem with the AT&M0 command, pressing Enter, and placing the call to the modem
again. When you're finished, reset your modem with
ATZ to re-enable the error control features.

**Symptom 4.33. The communications software is reporting
many cyclic redundancy check (CRC) errors and low characters per second (CPS) transfers.**   This may simply be
a matter of a poor phone connection established
through the telephone network. Try making the call
again. Chances are that the call will be routed differently and result in a more reliable connection. Next,
check the flow control scheme (XOFF/XON, CTS/RTS,
and so on) to verify that it is optimum or type AT&F1
from the terminal mode to load the optimum flow con-

trol setting. The serial port rate in your communications software may be set too high for your modem's UART or your area's phone lines. Try lowering the serial port rate in your communications software to 38,400 bps or 19,200 bps (or lower for slower modems). The remote site you are dialing into may have trouble with the *file transfer protocol* (FTP) you've selected. Try using a different FTP (such as Ymodem-g rather than Zmodem). Do not use Xmodem if other protocols are available. Finally, a TSR program may be running in the background and interfering with data communications. Disable any TSR programs running in the background and try the communication again.

Symptom 4.34. Errors are constantly occurring in your V.17 fax transmissions. As a rule, sending fax transmissions over a modem should present no special problems for a PC, but certain issues should be kept in mind. First, your modem initialization string could be insufficient or incomplete for fax transmissions. Enter the correct initialization string for fax support (such as `AT&H3&I2&R2S7=90`). You could also have a disruptive TSR program running in the background. Disable any TSR programs and try the communication again. There could be an outdated communications driver on your system. Load the communications driver that came with your fax software (this may require you to reinstall your internal modem). Finally, your baud rate may be set too high. Try a lower baud rate of 9600 bps.

Symptom 4.35. Your 32-bit communications programs may report a slower speed than your 16-bit communications programs. For example, if your 16-bit programs report that they are communicating at 38,400 bps, your 32-bit Windows 95/98 programs may report that they are communicating at 14,400 bps. The problem here is a difference in the way 16-bit and 32-bit programs report communication speeds.

A 32-bit communication program designed for Windows 95/98 /NT reports the modem line speed when reporting the speed at which the program is communicating. The modem line speed is the speed between your modem and the modem you're connected to (the speed at which data is transmitted over the telephone line). By comparison, most 16-bit communications programs that are designed for DOS/Windows 3.x report the port speed when reporting the speed at which the program is communicating. The port speed is the speed between your modem and your computer (the speed between the serial port that your modem is connected to and your computer). Since port speed is typically faster than modem line speed, 16-bit programs generally report a faster speed than 32-bit programs. You can use the following workaround to correct the issue:

1. Click Start, highlight Settings, and then click Control Panel.

2. Double-click Modems.

3. Click your modem and then click Properties.

4. On the Connection tab, click Advanced.

5. In the Extra Settings box, type S95=0 and then click OK.

6. Click OK and then click Close.

Symptom 4.36. During installation, a modem setup program cannot find the internal modem. In virtually all cases, you have a hardware conflict between the modem and another device in the system. Check the hardware installation first. For internal modems, make sure the IRQ and I/O address are set correctly, and check that no other devices are using the same

IRQ or I/O space as your modem. Under Windows 95/98, the Device Manager can usually display any conflicting devices with yellow icons (exclamation marks). Next, make sure that the modem is inserted properly into its bus slot. If any of the card's gold "fingers" appear corroded or soiled, clean the fingers gently with a pencil eraser. Try the modem in another bus slot. Finally, check the modem switches. Most external modems use a series of DIP switches to configure its various features. Refer to the modem's documentation and see that any modem switches are set properly.

Symptom 4.37. After installing a new internal modem, the system mouse driver no longer loads or the mouse behaves erratically. In virtually all cases, there is a hardware conflict between the new modem and the existing mouse port. Check the hardware installation. If the mouse is connected to a COM port, make sure that your internal modem is set to use a different COM port. You may need to disable COM2 on the motherboard or I/O controller and set up the modem as COM2. Under Windows 95/98, the Device Manager can usually display any conflicting devices with a yellow icon (exclamation mark).

Symptom 4.38. After installing modem driver software, Windows locks up or crashes. This is almost always the result of a defective or outdated modem driver. Check the software installation. Make sure that the modem driver software you have installed is the proper version for the particular modem *and* your version of Windows (3.1, 3.11, 95, or 98). You can usually check the driver version on the modem manufacturer's Web site. If you do find that the modem driver is incorrect, run any uninstall utility that accompanied the software in order to remove the driver cleanly. Otherwise, you'll have to remove the modem driver references from SYSTEM.INI manually. Under Windows 95/98,

you can often remove a device from the Device
Manager and then enable Windows to redetect the
modem during the next boot (and reinstall the new drivers at that point).

**Symptom 4.39. DOS communication software works fine,
but Windows communication software will not.** You may
also see Windows error messages suggesting that certain files are missing. In most cases, the modem drivers (and any required parameters) have not been
loaded properly. Check the software installation and
make sure that the modem driver software you have
installed is the proper version for the particular
modem and your version of Windows. Try uninstalling
the modem drivers (if possible) and then reload the drivers from scratch, making sure that they are set up
properly for your system configuration. Next, check the
manufacturer's Web site for any adjustments or
workarounds that may be required for your particular
modem and drivers. You may need to make manual
adjustments to SYSTEM.INI and WIN.INI files as well
as the Windows 95/98 registry files.

**Symptom 4.40. You cannot get the modem's distinctive
ring feature to work.** Some new modems support the
distinctive ring service provided by many telephone
companies. This enables the modem to reside on the
same physical telephone line as other devices but only
answer when the proper ringing pattern is received.
Improper modem configuration is the most common
problem. Try calling the distinctive ring numbers associated with your telephone line and see that each number rings with the required pattern. Note that the
distinctive ring service is not available from all telephone companies and service areas. Next, check the
initialization string for S101. Modems supporting distinctive ring usually control the feature through register S101. A typical AT command string may appear,
such as AT&FS101=60. A typical setting list is shown:

- S101=0 detects all ringing cadences and reports them with the RING result code.

- S101=1 enables the RING result codes; all ringing types will be reported.

- S101=30 reports only unidentified ring types.

- S101=46 reports only ring type D.

- S101=54 reports only ring type C.

- S101=58 reports only ring type B.

- S101=60 reports only ring type A.

- S101=62 disables *all* ringing detections. The modem will not answer any ring.

> **NOTE:** To specify a particular ring type, you must disable the other ring types with this register.

Next, check the initialization string for -SDR. Rather than using S-register 101, some modems use the -SDR command to configure distinctive ring operations. A typical AT command string may appear such as AT&F-SDR=1. A setting list is shown:

- -SDR=0 disables the distinctive ring function.

- -SDR=1 enables distinctive ring type 1.

- -SDR=2 enables distinctive ring type 2.

- -SDR=3 enables distinctive ring type 1 and 2.

- -SDR=4 enables distinctive ring type 3.

- -SDR=5 enables distinctive ring type 1 and 3.

- -SDR=6 enables distinctive ring type 2 and 3.

- -SDR=7 enables distinctive ring type 1, 2, and 3.

Symptom 4.41. You cannot get the modem's caller ID feature to work. Some new modems support the caller ID service provided by many telephone companies. This enables the modem to identify the telephone number and caller to the computer's communication software when the ringing line is answered. Improper modem configuration is the most common problem. Before you do anything else, check the caller ID service. Connect any caller ID-compatible telephone or phone box to the telephone line and make sure that the ID service is working properly. Note that the caller ID service is not available from all telephone companies and service areas. Also, remove other caller ID devices. It is possible that other caller ID-compatible telephones of phone boxes may be interfering with the modem. Try removing any other devices from the phone line. Check the initialization string for %CCID. Modems supporting caller ID usually control the feature through a %CCID command. A typical AT command string may appear, such as AT&F%CCID=1. A setting list is shown:

- %CCID=0 turns caller ID off.
- %CCID=1 gives caller ID data using a formatted output.
- %CCID=2 gives caller ID data using an unformatted output.

Finally, check the initialization string for aCID. Rather than using the %CCID command, some modems support caller ID using the #CID command. A typical command string may appear, such as AT&F#CID=1. A setting list is shown:

- AT#CID=0 turns caller ID off.
- AT#CID=1 gives caller ID data using a formatted output.
- AT#CID=2 gives caller ID data using an unformatted output.

NOTE: Two special messages may be sent instead of caller ID information. *O* means that the caller is out of the caller ID service area, usually a long distance call. *P* is for Private and will be displayed for callers who have made arrangements with their phone company to have their numbers blocked.

Symptom 4.42. You cannot recall previous caller ID data. This assumes that normal caller ID features are proven to be working correctly. In most cases, your communication software is not sending the correct AT command to your modem. Check the caller ID feature and make sure that caller ID is enabled using the %CCID or #CID commands, as in the previous symptom. Caller ID must be enabled first before data can be recalled. Check the initialization string for %CRID. Caller ID data can typically be recalled using the %CRID command, such as AT%CRID=0 (recall formatted data) or AT%CRID=1 (recall unformatted data).

Symptom 4.43. The modem appears to be set up and configured properly, but it is experiencing data loss. Such symptoms may appear as excessive file transfer errors, missing text or characters, and jumbled ASCII text. Though modern modems are capable of data rates up to 230,400 bps, data rates over 19,200 bps can cause problems for older PCs due to inadequate serial port hardware. Check the UART first. Your serial ports should be using 16550A UARTs for optimum performance. If the UART is older, data throughput will be limited. If you cannot upgrade the UART chip directly, you can often disable the existing serial port and install an upgraded I/O board. Any diagnostic program such as MSD can identify the UARTs in your system. Check your modem drivers and make sure that the modem driver software is up to date and optimized for your particular version of Windows (3.1, 3.11, 95, or 98). Finally, reduce your data rates. If you cannot resolve the problem through a driver or new UART, try reducing the modem's data rate in your communication software.

Symptom 4.44. When running modem software, you see an error such as "Can't run on a plug-and-play-ready system." In most cases, the PCMCIA modem is incompatible with a PC's plug-and-play architecture. Check your plug-and-play driver. You may need to load an alternative plug-and-play driver for your modem. Check with the modem manufacturer's BBS, CompuServe forum, or Web site to obtain any updated driver software. You may need to disable the existing DOS plug-and-play driver in CONFIG.SYS.

Symptom 4.45. The modem appears to be set up and configured properly, but it regularly connects at slower speeds than it is capable of. Several different factors can account for such a problem. First, modems can only connect at the maximum speed of the slowest modem. If the remote modem is slower than yours, your connection speed will be limited. Try connecting to a faster BBS or other online connection. Check the modem initialization string next. One or more important commands may be missing from the command string. Look for the recommended initialization string in the modem's documentation. Also check that the correct modem is selected in the communication software and check the modem's firmware version. Use the ATI3 command to check the modem's ID information (including the firmware revision). If the firmware is old, it may need to be updated. If the firmware is new, it may contain a bug that the manufacturer should be made aware of. Finally, try a different phone line. Faulty, noisy telephone connections can reduce effective communication speeds. Try the call at an off time or try calling on a different phone line.

Symptom 4.46. Windows 95/98 insists on assigning the modem to COM5. You will need to reconfigure the modem's port assignment through the Control Panel. First, you'll need to remove any unused modem entries. Software that has been loaded for previous modems may interfere with the current modem's software. Remove unused modem hardware references through the Device Manager:

1. Select My Computer, double-click on Control Panel, and then choose Modems.

2. Highlight any modems that are no longer in the system and press the Remove button.

3. If the same modem has multiple entries, remove all entries for the modem, restart the system, and then reinstall the software.

Next, verify the modem on COM5. Check to see that the modem is identified and checks properly before continuing:

1. Select My Computer, double-click on Control Panel, and then choose Modems.

2. Select the Diagnostics tab.

3. Highlight COM5 and press the More Info button.

4. Verify that the modem responds to the ATI3 command with its proper ID information.

5. Click OK.

Now find an unused COM port. Check the Diagnostics screen and examine the COM ports in use; any ports not in use are available. Next, use REGEDIT.EXE to edit the Windows 95/98 registry. You can change the COM port assignment by adjusting the registry:

1. Click on the Start button and then select Run.

2. Type regedit and click OK.

3. Select the Edit/Find option and then type COM5.

4. Click Find Next. This should highlight PORTNAME under a Registry key.

5. Double-click on PORTNAME.

6. Enter the new COM port such as COM2.

7. Click OK and then close REGEDIT.

8. Shut down and restart Windows 95/98.

> **NOTE**: Before attempting to edit a Windows 95 reg-
> istry file, make sure to have a complete backup of the
> registry files SYSTEM.DAT and USER.DAT.

Finally, check the updated configuration and verify
that modem now works on a new COM port:

1. Select My Computer, double-click on Control
   Panel, and then choose Modems.

2. Select the Diagnostics tab.

3. Select the new COM port that you selected for the
   modem.

4. Press the More Info button.

5. Verify that the modem responds to the ATI3 command with its proper ID information.

6. Click OK.

**Symptom 4.47. You cannot get the modem to work with a
Winsock, but conventional BBS or CompuServe connections work fine.** In almost all cases, one or more command strings in your Internet connection configuration
files are causing an error with the modem. First, make
sure that you are using the Winsock version that is
appropriate for your particular Internet connection
software. Next, check the configuration file. Contact
your modem manufacturer to check on any fixes or
workarounds, but some modems may not work with
the default command strings provided with their
Internet software. For example, the Motorola Power
14.4 PCMCIA modem will not work with Trumpet
Winsock because of an error in the LOGIN.CMD file;
the $modemsetup = string is wrong.

Symptom 4.48. You are having trouble configuring the modem for hardware and software flow control. This is usually due to invalid command strings. Try some generic command strings. The following two AT command strings can configure most Hayes-compatible modems for hardware or software flow control. Keep in mind that you may need to add some additional commands in order to configure the modem completely:

- Software flow control (XON/XOFF): AT&F1&C1&D2\

- Hardware flow control (CTS/RTS): AT&F1&C1& D2\Q3\

Symptom 4.49. The modem will not establish a connection through a cellular telephone. In most cases, the modem is not configured properly. Check the *Station Class Mark* (SCM) setting first and make sure that the SCM level is set correctly. Try resetting the modem with an AT&F1 command. Check the phone type. Make sure that the telephone is set to analog mode. The digital mode may interfere with modem operation.

Symptom 4.50. The modem will not fax properly through a cellular telephone. In most cases, the modem is not configured properly. Check the modem's initialization string first and make sure that the initialization string is set correctly. A basic command string may be AT&F1E1V1&C1&D2\Q3S7=90S10=60 (though this may not work on all modems). Check the data rate next. For faxing, see that the data rate is set to 4800. You may use the AT%B4800 command.

Symptom 4.51. Windows 95/98 recognizes the modem, but 16-bit communications software will not see it. Windows 95/98 may not have updated the SYSTEM.INI file to reflect changes to the COM port settings. Check the SYSTEM.INI file. Your COM port base address and IRQs are defined in the [386Enh] section of the file SYSTEM.INI. Check these settings to make sure that

they match your modem settings. The following lines
need to be added to your SYSTEM.INI file in the
[386enh] section:

```
com1irq=4
com1base=03f8
com2irq=3
com2base=02f8
com3irq=4
com3base=03e8
com4irq=3
com4base=02e8
```

**Symptom 4.52. DOS ICU software is installed, but it will not
enable configuring the modem on COM1 or COM2.** The
ICU software may be inappropriate for your particular
modem and system configuration. Check with the
modem manufacturer and see if there is a replacement
DOS plug-and-play driver or other workaround. If alternate plug-and-play software is available, you may need
to remove the installation of ICU before proceeding:

1. Delete the ESCD.RF file from the root directory
   of c:\.

2. In the CONFIG.SYS file, delete the line that says
   device=c:\plugplay\ . . . and then save
   your changes.

3. In the [386Enh] section of SYSTEM.INI, delete the
   lines that start with device=c:\plugplay\
   . . . and then save your changes.

4. In the [windows] section of WIN.INI, the RUN= entry
   should have no reference to ICU or PLUGPLAY
   after the equal sign. Save your changes if any were
   made.

5. Delete the c:\plugplay directory.

6. Exit windows and reboot your system.

Symptom 4.53. The modem's flash ROM update will not install because it cannot recognize the modem's current firmware version. This is invariably a problem with the flash ROM update software itself. Check the software source. Contact the manufacturer to see if a corrected update is available or see if there is a workaround to the problem. One or more command-line switches may override the update's firmware auto-detection.

Symptom 4.54. The modem establishes connections properly, but it frequently drops connections. Both hardware and software issues can cause this kind of trouble. Problems with the telephone connection itself can cause connection problems. Try connecting to various different places. If problems seem to occur more frequently in one connection over another, the remote location may be suffering from communication problems. Also try using a different local telephone line. Next, check the modem's initialization string and make sure that the modem is set up properly for data compression and error correction. Finally, check the Windows driver. If you are using Windows-based communications software, it must be able to support high speeds. The standard Windows drivers will not support 28.8-KB operations unless third-party communications software modifies it (though Windows 98 drivers are more current). To find out which communications driver you are currently using, review the [Boot] section of your SYSTEM.INI file.

Symptom 4.55. When selecting a modem in your communication software, your particular modem is not listed. You will need to obtain the proper driver supplements from the modem manufacturer (or software maker). Try running the modem as a Hayes-compatible. Virtually all modems will function as generic Hayes-compatible modems using `AT&F&C1&D2`.

Symptom 4.56. It seems to take the modem an unusually long time to hang up. The carrier delay time is probably set too long. Check the carrier delay time. Modems can be set to wait (often as long as 25 seconds) after a carrier is lost to see whether it comes back. If you frequently encounter poor signal quality, this can be quite convenient. After a legitimate hang-up, however, the modem may continue to wait. In this case, you may want to set the value of the S10 register to a low number, for example, 10 or less.

Symptom 4.57. The modem is configured as COM4 (IRQ3) under Windows 95/98, but the modem refuses to work. A hardware acceleration issue may be the problem. Go into the Windows 95/98 Control Panel, double-click the System icon, select Performance, and then click Graphics. Set Hardware Acceleration to None and try the modem again. Some advanced modem manufacturers have found there to be an addressing conflict with certain graphic accelerator cards. If you configure your Windows 95 graphic driver to a basic *Variable Graphics Array* (VGA) and find the modem now works at that setting, then the problem is probably an addressing conflict with your graphics card. You may want to try using one of the more commonly used COM port and IRQ settings such as

- COM 1, IRQ 4
- COM 2, IRQ 3
- COM 3, IRQ 5 (if not used by your sound card)

Symptom 4.58. When auto-detect tries to add a new modem at COM2, Windows 95/98 locks up. Open the Control Panel (System Settings) and deselect COM2. This can be accomplished by selecting COM2 under System Settings and then choosing Properties. A red X should be in a box towards the bottom of the Properties screen. Click once on the X and it should clear. This disables the COM port in Windows 95. Click OK and then restart the machine. When Windows 95/98 restarts, it should now find the COM port. This technique can apply to all available COM ports.

Symptom 4.59. HyperTerminal works using PCMCIA support under Windows 95/98, but no 16-bit communication programs work. Using a text editor, edit the file SYSTEM.INI in your Windows directory. Under the [386Enh] section of your SYSTEM.INI file, change the COMM.DRV line back to its original COMM.DRV. This line should read `comm.drv=comm.drv`. Also check that a line says `device=*vcd`. If your SYSTEM.INI has a line that reads `device=*vrdd`, place a semicolon in front of it. Your 16-bit applications should now work.

Symptom 4.60. A Winmodem installed correctly responds to AT commands fine, but whenever you call out, the modem makes a 9600 V.34 connection. This is typically due to a problem with the current communications driver. Adding the following line

```
ForceBridgeOrRouter=TRUE
```

to the SYSTEM.INI file may correct this problem by bypassing the current communications driver and going directly to the Winmodem driver. You should also make sure that your port rate is set to 19,200 in your Control Panel (Port Settings) in Windows 3.1x and that it is set to 38,400 or higher under Windows 95/98.

Symptom 4.61. Windows 95/98 doesn't detect the WinModem. First, make sure that the system has a free COM port or IRQ to use. If the WinModem was previously installed on the system with Windows 3.1x running, you'll need to search the SYSTEM.INI and WIN.INI files and remove all WinModem settings so that Windows 95/98 can detect the WinModem properly. Under Windows 95/98, make sure that the modem is not listed in the Device Manager under Other

Devices. If it is, delete the reference and reinstall. Next, make sure the WinModem's key (USR1001 for the USR WinModem) is not in the registry. If it is, remove the reference(s) from the registry.

Symptom 4.62. You have difficulty using a WinModem after upgrading to Windows 98. If you double-click the WinModem icon in Control Panel, you may receive the following error message:

```
Error: There is no WinModem found in your
computer, but some corrupted files were found
and they have been cleaned.
```

If you view your modem in the Device Manager, you may also notice more than one WinModem entry. This problem generally occurs because your WinModem is not using the most current .INF file or device driver. To correct this problem, uninstall the WinModem drivers, remove the multiple WinModem entries in Device Manager, and then reinstall the most current Win-Modem drivers:

1. Click Start, highlight Settings, click Control Panel, double-click the WinModem icon, and then click Uninstall. This should uninstall the WinModem drivers.

2. See if the WinModem icon is still in the Control Panel. If the WinModem icon is gone, the uninstall process is successful. If the WinModem icon is still available, the uninstall process is not successful, and you will need to contact the modem manufacturer for detailed removal instructions.

3. Now remove the WinModem entries in Device Manager. Right-click My Computer, click Properties, and then click the Device Manager tab.

4. Double-click the Modem branch to expand it, click a WinModem entry, and then click Remove. Repeat this until all WinModem entries are removed. Then click OK.

5. Reinstall the most current WinModem drivers.

Symptom 4.63. The WinModem is repeatedly detected when you start Windows 98. For example, after you uninstall a WinModem and restart your computer, Windows 98 may try to install the modem and prompt you to restart your computer. After you restart your computer, Windows may prompt you to restart your computer again, and this behavior may continue indefinitely. This problem can occur if you uninstall the WinModem by using Device Manager (or the Modems tool in your Control Panel) instead of using the WinModem utility provided by the modem's manufacturer. To fix this problem, use the WinModem utility to uninstall your WinModem instead of using the Device Manager or the Modems tool:

1. Restart your computer and start Windows 98 in the Safe mode.

2. Click Start, highlight Settings, and then click Control Panel.

3. Use the WinModem utility to uninstall your WinModem. For detailed information about how to use the WinModem utility to uninstall your WinModem, review the documentation included with your particular modem.

4. Restart your computer normally.

5. If you're prompted to install your WinModem again, use the software included with your modem to do so.

5

Motherboard Troubleshooting

The *motherboard* is the heart of any personal computer. It is the motherboard that handles system resources such as IRQ lines, *Direct Memory Access* (DMA) channels, *input/output* (I/O) locations, and core components such as the processor, chipset, and all system memory, including SDRAM, *Basic Input-Output System Read-Only Memory* (BIOS ROM), cache, and *Complimentary Metal Oxide Semiconductor Random Access Memory* (CMOS RAM). Indeed, most of a PC's capabilities are defined by the motherboard components. This chapter shows you how to recognize symptoms and translate error information into motherboard repairs.

Motherboard Issues

Now it's time to actually look at a current motherboard up close and identify the critical parts that you should expect to find. For the purposes of this book, we'll examine the Intel VC820 ATX Slot 1 motherboard,

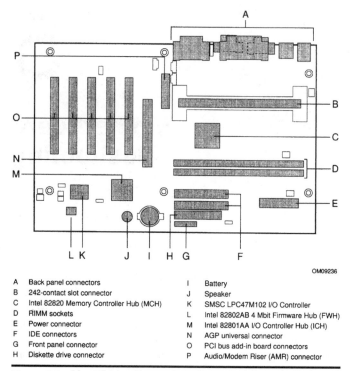

OM09236

A	Back panel connectors	I	Battery
B	242-contact slot connector	J	Speaker
C	Intel 82820 Memory Controller Hub (MCH)	K	SMSC LPC47M102 I/O Controller
D	RIMM sockets	L	Intel 82802AB 4 Mbit Firmware Hub (FWH)
E	Power connector	M	Intel 82801AA I/O Controller Hub (ICH)
F	IDE connectors	N	AGP universal connector
G	Front panel connector	O	PCI bus add-in board connectors
H	Diskette drive connector	P	Audio/Modem Riser (AMR) connector

Figure 5.1 Identifying the major elements of a motherboard. Courtesy of Intel Corporation.

shown in Figure 5.1. Other motherboards and form factors will appear a bit different, but the basic parts are all the same.

> **NOTE**:   The chipset components discussed in the following section are presented for example purposes only. Your motherboard will undoubtedly use different chips (and chipsets), each offering their own set of characteristics.

I/O Panel Connections

These are the serial, parallel, USB, and PS/2 ports that you'll use to connect peripheral devices to the system.

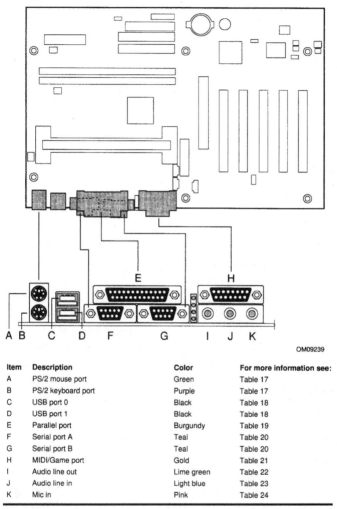

Item	Description	Color	For more information see:
A	PS/2 mouse port	Green	Table 17
B	PS/2 keyboard port	Purple	Table 17
C	USB port 0	Black	Table 18
D	USB port 1	Black	Table 18
E	Parallel port	Burgundy	Table 19
F	Serial port A	Teal	Table 20
G	Serial port B	Teal	Table 20
H	MIDI/Game port	Gold	Table 21
I	Audio line out	Lime green	Table 22
J	Audio line in	Light blue	Table 23
K	Mic in	Pink	Table 24

Figure 5.2 View of ATX back panel connections. Courtesy of Intel Corporation.

Figure 5.2 illustrates the I/O port layout for a VC820 motherboard. The number of ports and their relative location may vary from model to model, but this figure is a good overall example.

The ports in the back panel are as follows:

- A: PS/2 mouse port
- B: PS/2 keyboard port
- C: USB port 0
- D: USB port 1
- E: Parallel port
- F: Serial port 0
- G: Serial port 1
- H: MIDI/game port
- I: Audio line output
- J: Audio line input
- K: Microphone input

Slot 1 Connector.   This is the 242-pin connector for your Intel Pentium II/III processor. For an AMD Athlon processor, you'd have a Slot A connector that looks almost identical. Be sure that the retention mechanism is secure and attaches properly to the CPU cartridge.

82820 Memory Controller Hub Chip.   This is the core processing chip that interfaces the *Central Processing Unit* (CPU), memory, and AGP bus.

RIMM Sockets.   These sockets support up to two *Rambus memory modules* (RIMMs). If these were *Dual Inline Memory Modules* (DIMMs) sockets, you'd probably be using 168-pin PC100 (100-MHz) or PC133 (133-MHz) SDRAM DIMMs.

ATX Power Connector.   This is the standard 20-pin ATX power connector provided by the power supply.

Integrated Development Environment (IDE) connectors. These are the primary and secondary 40-pin IDE controller ports for your hard drives and other *AT*

Attachment Packet Interface (ATAPI) devices like CD-ROM or DVD-ROM drives. This system supports Ultra-DMA/66 drives for peak performance.

Front Panel Connector.   This header provides the pins that connect to the case wires (such as the power's *light-emitting diode* (LED), power switch, key lock, and so on).

Floppy Connector.   This is the standard 34-pin floppy controller port.

CMOS Battery.   This is the coin cell that maintains your CMOS RAM contents. Be sure to replace the battery every few years with an identical battery type.

Speaker.   Normally, the speaker serves little purpose except to handle beep codes generated by the BIOS *power-on self-test* (POST).

LPC47M102 I/O Controller Chip.   This chip handles all of the I/O ports in the system as well as the floppy controller function.

82802 Firmware Hub Chip.   This is the four-Mb controller that handles your BIOS and CMOS RAM.

82081 I/O Controller Hub Chip.   This is a highly integrated controller that supports your *hard disk drive* (HDD) controller channels, USB ports, PCI bus, and audio system.

AGP Bus Connector.   This is your AGP bus slot for the installation of your video adapter card. If you use a PCI video card instead, you may need to disable the AGP slot in the CMOS Setup.

PCI Bus Connectors.   These are your main expansion slots for other devices in the system.

Audio/Modem Riser (AMR) Connector. This connector supports the relatively new Intel standard interface for audio/modem devices. Also, you should be familiar with numerous smaller connectors on the motherboard, and several of them are illustrated in Figure 5.3. Your particular motherboard may offer more or different connectors, but the VC820 motherboard supplies the following:

A. "Legacy" CD Audio Connector. This is the conventional audio connector found on most sound cards. Since the VC820 offers on-board sound support, you can feed the audio from a CD to this connector. The Legacy pinout is as follows:

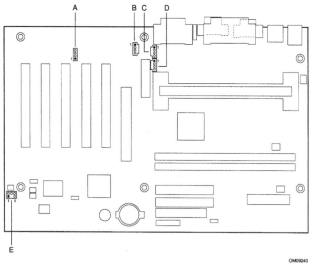

OM09240

Item	Description	Color	Style	Reference Designator
A	CD-ROM (see Table 25)	N/A	Legacy-style, 2 mm	J2C1
B	CD-ROM (see Table 26)	Black	ATAPI	J1F1
C	Telephony (see Table 27)	Green	ATAPI	J2F1
D	Auxiliary line in (see Table 28)	Tan	ATAPI	J2F2
E	PC/PCI (see Table 29)	N/A	2x3	J7A2

Figure 5.3 Identifying audio-based motherboard connectors. Courtesy of Intel Corporation.

- *Pin 1*   CD ground
- *Pin 2*   Audio left channel
- *Pin 3*   CD ground
- *Pin 4*   Audio right channel

B. ATAPI CD Audio Connector.   This is a slightly different CD audio connector scheme using differential signaling. The presence of this second connector also lets you mix audio from a second compliant CD-ROM drive. The pinout is as follows:

- *Pin 1*   Left audio signal
- *Pin 2*   Differential ground
- *Pin 3*   Differential ground
- *Pin 4*   Right audio signal

C. Telephony Connector.   This is the connector that you would use to attach telephony devices to the system. The telephony connector pinout is as follows:

- *Pin 1*   Analog audio mono input
- *Pin 2*   Ground
- *Pin 3*   Ground
- *Pin 4*   Analog audio mono input

D. Auxiliary Line Input.   This is a sound channel that enables you to mix in an auxiliary audio signal. The pinout is as follows:

- *Pin 1*   Left auxiliary signal
- *Pin 2*   Ground
- *Pin 3*   Ground
- *Pin 4*   Right auxiliary signal

E. PC/PCI Connector. This is a serial interface to the PCI bus that can be used with several PCI-based devices that do not necessarily use a PCI bus. The pinout for this connector is listed:

- *Pin 1*   PCI data in
- *Pin 2*   Ground
- *Pin 3*   No connection
- *Pin 4*   PCI request out
- *Pin 5*   Ground
- *Pin 6*   Serial IRQ out

Numerous hardware control and power connections can be found on the motherboard, as shown in Figure 5.4. These connectors are used to attach the power supply, operate fans, and manage wake devices. These features are vital for proper cooling and effective power management, and the VC820 motherboard offers the following connections:

A. Power Supply Fan. This is a three-wire fan cable that provides power to the +12Vdc supply fan. The third wire provides a tachometer signal to the motherboard that the motherboard can use to monitor the fan's performance.

B. Processor Cooling Fan. This is a three-wire fan cable that powers the processor's +12Vdc cooling fan. The third wire provides a tachometer signal to the motherboard that the motherboard can use to monitor the fan's performance.

C. Power Connector. This is the 20-pin ATX cable that powers the motherboard. It is vital that this cable be securely attached to the motherboard connector. Otherwise, power may cut out erratically. Data loss and damage to the motherboard may result. Table 5.1 lists the pinout for the ATX power cable.

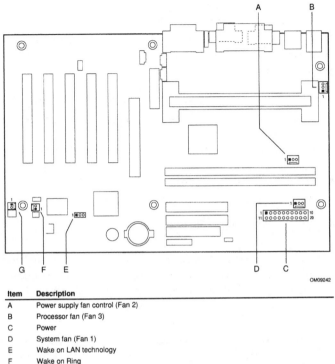

OM09242

Item	Description
A	Power supply fan control (Fan 2)
B	Processor fan (Fan 3)
C	Power
D	System fan (Fan 1)
E	Wake on LAN technology
F	Wake on Ring
G	Chassis intrusion

Figure 5.4 Identifying power and power management connections. Courtesy of Intel Corporation.

TABLE 5.1 The ATX Power Connector Pinout

Pin 1	+3.3Vdc	Pin 12	− 12Vdc
Pin 2	+3.3Vdc	Pin 13	Ground
Pin 3	Ground	Pin 14	PS-ON ("Soft" power
Pin 4	+5Vdc		control signal)
Pin 5	Ground	Pin 15	Ground
Pin 6	+5Vdc	Pin 16	Ground
Pin 7	Ground	Pin 17	Ground
Pin 8	Power good	Pin 18	− 5Vdc
Pin 9	+5Vdc (Standby)	Pin 19	+5dc
Pin 10	+12Vdc	Pin 20	+5dc
Pin 11	+3.3Vdc		

D. System Fan. This is a three-wire fan cable that powers the system's +12Vdc chassis cooling fan. The third wire provides a tachometer signal to the motherboard that the motherboard can use to monitor the fan's performance.

E. Wake On LAN Connector. This connector enables you to attach a device that will wake the system from a *Local Area Network* (LAN) when a system is in the power-down state. The three pins are listed as follows:

- *Pin 1*   +5Vdc (standby)
- *Pin 2*   Ground
- *Pin 3*   Wake On LAN signal

F. Wake On Ring Connector. This two-pin connector enables you to attach a device that will wake the system from a modem when an incoming ring is detected. The two signals are Ground and Ring.

G. Chassis Intrusion Connector. This two-pin connector is usually wired to a switch on the chassis that will alert the system when the cover is opened. This is often done as a safety interlock to prevent users from opening the system and interrupting mission-critical processes. The two signals are Ground and Open.

Ultimately, you'll need to connect front-panel cables to the motherboard to control power, reset, and so on. Figure 5.5 highlights the front-panel connector used on the VC820 motherboard, and Table 5.2 lists the pin assignments for the front-panel connector.

Motherboard Resources

One of the important advantages of any PC motherboard is its capability to accept expansion devices such as sound boards, network cards, modems, and so on. It is exactly this kind of versatility that made the origi-

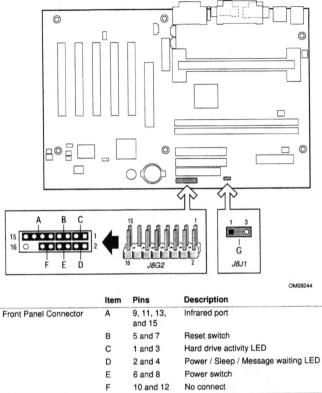

OM09244

	Item	Pins	Description
Front Panel Connector	A	9, 11, 13, and 15	Infrared port
	B	5 and 7	Reset switch
	C	1 and 3	Hard drive activity LED
	D	2 and 4	Power / Sleep / Message waiting LED
	E	6 and 8	Power switch
	F	10 and 12	No connect
Auxiliary Front Panel Power LED Connector	G	1 and 3	Auxiliary Power LED connector (Pin 2 keyed)

Figure 5.5 Identifying front panel connections. Courtesy of Intel Corporation.

TABLE 5.2 Front-Panel Connector Pinout

Pin 1	HDD power	Pin 2	Front-panel LED (green)
Pin 3	HDD active LED	Pin 4	Front-panel LED (yellow)
Pin 5	Ground	Pin 6	Power switch
Pin 7	Reset switch	Pin 8	Ground
Pin 9	+5Vdc (IR power)	Pin 10	No connection
Pin 11	IR serial input	Pin 12	Ground
Pin 13	Ground	Pin 14	No connection

nal PC so popular. However, each expansion device requires certain resources from the system. Typically, three types of resources are provided for expansion devices: interrupts (IRQs), DMA channels, and I/O port addresses. As expansion devices are added to a PC, resources are assigned to the particular device, and no two devices may use the same resources. Otherwise, a hardware conflict will result. Table 5.3 illustrates typical IRQ assignments for the PC, Table 5.4 shows you the standard DMA assignments, and Table 5.5 lists conventional I/O port addresses.

TABLE 5.3   Standard Interrupt (IRQ) Assignments for IBM PC/AT-Type Systems

IRQ	Function
0	System timer IC
1	Keyboard controller IC
2	Second IRQ controller IC
3	Serial port 2 (COM2: 2F8h–2FFh and COM4: 2E8h–2EFh)
4	Serial port 1 (COM1: 3F8h–3FFh and COM3: 3E8h–3EFh)
5	Parallel port 2 (LPT2: 378h or 278h)
6	Floppy disk controller
7	Parallel port 1 (LPT1: 3BCh [mono] or 378h [color])
8	Real-Time Clock (RTC)
9	Unused (redirected to IRQ 2)
10	USB (on systems so equipped and can be disabled)
11	Windows sound system (on systems so equipped and can be disabled)
12	Motherboard mouse port (PS/2 port)
13	Math coprocessor
14	Primary AT/IDE hard disk controller
15	Secondary AT/IDE hard disk controller (on systems so equipped and can be disabled)

TABLE 5.4   Standard DMA Assignments for IBM PC/AT-Type Systems

DMA	Traditional Function	Current Function(s)
0	Dynamic RAM refresh	Audio system
1	Unused	Audio system or parallel port
2	Floppy disk controller	Floppy disk controller

TABLE 5.4   Continued.

DMA	Traditional Function	Current Function(s)
3	Unused	ECP parallel port or audio system
4	Reserved (used internally)	Reserved (used internally)
5	Unused	Unused
6	Unused	Unused
7	Unused	Unused

TABLE 5.5   Modern AT I/O Assignments

0000h–000Fh	PIIX4, DMA 1
0020h–0021h	PIIX4, Interrupt Controller 1
002Eh–002Fh	Super I/O Controller configuration registers
0040h–0043h	PIIX4, Counter/Timer 1
0048h–004Bh	PIIX4, Counter/Timer 2
0060h	Keyboard Controller (KBC) byte, Reset IRQ
0061h	PIIX4, NMI, speaker control
0064h	KBC, CMD/STAT byte
0070h	(Bit 7) PIIX4, Enable NMI
0070h	(Bits 6-0) PIIX4, RTC, address
0071h	PIIX4, RTC, data
0078h	Reserved, board configuration
0079h	Reserved, board configuration
0081h–008Fh	PIIX4, DMA page registers
00A0h–00A1h	PIIX4, Interrupt Controller 2
00B2h–00B3h	*Advanced Power Management* (APM) control
00C0h–00DEh	PIIX4, DMA 2
00F0h	Reset numeric error
0170h–0177h	Secondary IDE Controller channel
01F0h–01F7h	Primary IDE Controller channel
0200h–0207h	Audio/game port
0220h–022Fh	Audio (Sound Blaster-compatible)
0240h–024Fh	Audio (Sound Blaster-compatible)
0278h–027Fh	LPT2
0290h–0297h	Management extension hardware
02E8h–02EFh	COM4/Video (8514A)
02F8h–02FFh	COM2
0300h–0301h	MPU-401 (MIDI)
0330h–0331h	MPU-401 (MIDI)
0332h–0333h	MPU-401 (MIDI)
0334h–0335h	MPU-401 (MIDI)
0376h	Secondary IDE channel command port
0377h	Secondary floppy channel command port
0378h–037Fh	LPT1
0388h–038Dh	AdLib (FM synthesizer)

(continues)

TABLE 5.5   Continued.

03B4h–03B5h	Video (VGA)
03BAh	Video (VGA)
03BCh–03BFh	LPT3
03C0h–03CAh	Video (VGA)
03CCh	Video (VGA)
03CEh–03CFh	Video (VGA)
03D4h–03D5h	Video (VGA)
03DAh	Video (VGA)
03E8h–03EFh	COM3
03F0h–03F5h	Primary floppy channel
03F6h	Primary IDE channel command port
03F7h	Primary floppy channel command port
03F8h–03FFh	COM1
04D0h–04D1h	Edge/level-triggered PIC
0530h–0537h	Windows sound system
0604h–060Bh	Windows sound system
LPT n + 400h	ECP port, LPT base address + 400h
0CF8h–0CFBh	PCI configuration address register
0CF9h	Turbo and reset control register
0CFCh–0CFFh	PCI configuration data register
0E80h–0E87h	Windows sound system
0F40h–0F47h	Windows sound system
0F86h–0F87h	Yamaha OPL3-SA configuration
FF00h–FF07h	IDE bus master register
FFA0h–FFA7	Primary bus master IDE registers
FFA8h–FFAFh	Secondary bus master IDE registers

Motherboard Checks

Since motherboard troubleshooting does represent a significant expense, you should be sure to start any motherboard repair by inspecting the following points in the PC. Remember to turn all power off before performing these inspections:

- *Check all connectors.* This can happen easily when the PC is serviced or upgraded, and you accidentally forget to replace every cable. Start with the power connectors, and inspect each cable and connector attached to the motherboard. Frayed cables should be replaced. Loose or detached cables should be reattached properly.

- *Check all socket-mounted ICs.*   Many chips in the computer (especially the CPU) get hot during normal operation. It is not unheard of for the repetitive expansion and contraction encountered with everyday use to eventually "rock" a chip out of its socket. The vibrations of physical shipping can also shake chips loose. The CPU, the math coprocessor (if used), BIOS ROM, and often the CMOS/RTC module are socket mounted, so check them carefully.

- *Check power levels.*   Low or erratic AC power levels can cause problems in the PC. Use a voltmeter and check the AC at the wall outlet. Be very careful whenever dealing with AC. Take all precautions to protect yourself from injury. If the AC is low or is heavily loaded by motors, coffee pots, or other highly inductive loads, try the PC in another outlet running from a different circuit. If the AC checks properly, use your voltmeter (or a measurement tool such as PC Power Check from Data Depot) to check the PC power supply outputs. If one or more outputs is low or absent, you should replace the supply.

- *Check the motherboard for foreign objects.*   A screw, paper clip, or free strand of wire can cause a short circuit that may disable the motherboard.

- *Check that all motherboard* Dual Inline Package *(DIP) switches / jumpers are correct.*   For example, if the motherboard provides a video port, and you have a video board plugged into the expansion bus, the motherboard video circuit will have to be disabled through a switch or jumper. Otherwise, a conflict can result that may interfere with motherboard operation. You will need the user manual for the PC in order to identify and check each jumper or switch. Today, virtually all jumperless motherboards are configured through the CMOS Setup.

- *Check for intermittent connections and accidental grounding.*   Inspect each of the motherboard's mounting screws, and see that they are not touching nearby printed traces. Also check the space under the motherboard and see that nothing might be grounding the motherboard and chassis. As an experiment, you may try loosening the motherboard's mounting screws. If the fault goes away, the motherboard may be suffering from an intermittent connection. When all the screws are tight, the board is bent just enough to let the intermittent appear. Unfortunately, intermittent connections are almost impossible to find.

Motherboard Symptoms

This section will cover a variety of symptoms regarding motherboard problems and offer solutions for fixing them.

Symptom 5.1. The Slot 1 retention mechanism is not holding the Slot 1 processor securely in place. You find that there is "play" that enables the processor to move (and possibly fall out of its slot). In virtually all cases, this means the retention mechanism is not mounted securely on the motherboard. It's probably sitting too high and allowing the CPU to float. You'll need to check the installation of that retention mechanism. Support the motherboard so that it will not bend while the retention mechanism is being pressed into the mounting holes (but do not place the motherboard on a hard surface to install the retention mechanism). If the retention mechanism push pins are not secured properly, the retention mechanism can become loose, causing the processor to fall out of the motherboard. To install a retention mechanism with captive brass fasteners, simply use a medium Phillips screwdriver to screw the fasteners into the pre-installed brass Pemstuds. To install the retention mechanism with plastic fasteners, perform the following steps:

1. Leave space below each mounting hole so that the fastener can protrude through the hole.

2. Find the Slot 1 connector on the motherboard.

3. Position the retention mechanism on the motherboard next to the Slot 1 connector.

4. Push down on the retention bracket until the black plastic fasteners are correctly seated and the retention mechanism fits snugly against the board.

5. Push each white retainer pin into its respective black fastener until the head of each pin is seated onto the head of each fastener. This should keep the retention mechanism securely in place.

Symptom 5.2. After removing a hard drive or other IDE-type device, the system seems to boot slowly but seems fine otherwise.   Chances are that the BIOS still expects an IDE device to respond, and it is waiting for the device that you removed. This is where the delay is coming from. If you remove a secondary drive on the primary channel, or any drive on the secondary channel, you should check the CMOS Setup and set that corresponding drive position to "none" or "not installed." Save your changes and reboot the system. You should see that the BIOS is no longer waiting for devices that you marked out in the CMOS Setup.

Symptom 5.3. You notice that your system automatically powers back on after a power failure.   This is probably the result of a CMOS Setup configuration rather than a hardware fault, and it occurs on standard Intel-manufactured motherboard products that use a Phoenix BIOS and use either the Intel 430TX PCIset or the Intel 440LX PCIset (or a later chipset). You'll probably find a feature in the BIOS setup utility (usually under the Boot menu) that controls the action of the computer following a power failure. The options are usually Stay Off, Last State (to restore the previous power state before AC power was lost, either on or off), and Power On (so the system will always power back on). If you check this setting in the CMOS Setup, you'll probably notice that it's set to Power On or Last State. If you'd prefer the system to remain off after a power failure, set this entry to Stay Off.

> **NOTE**:   In all cases, the computer powers up for 300 milliseconds when AC power is restored, reads the current setup boot values, and goes to the appropriate state (on or off).

Symptom 5.4. You receive a "static device resource conflict" error message.   This warning message while booting Windows 95/98 can be generated from numerous (and often unrelated) situations. The majority of technicians reporting this problem have a Pro Audio Spectrum 16 card installed. The Windows 95/98 registration for this card includes both 10-bit I/O addresses (201H and 388H) and 16-bit aliases to these addresses (A201H and F388H). The BIOS detects that the 10-bit address will also overlap with the 16-bit address and flags this as a resource conflict. Since it is a single card requesting both these resources, the warning can be ignored if this is the case. Also, reports inform you of other configurations causing "static resource conflict" warnings. Some of these instances appear to be corrected by clearing the ESCD area in NVRAM, which can be accomplished by performing a CMOS clear:

1. Note your current settings.

2. Turn power off.

3. Set the CMOS Clear jumper or switch to the CLEAR position (see the product documentation).

4. Turn power on.

5. After approximately 30 seconds, turn the power off.

6. Set the CMOS Clear jumper or switch to the OFF or NORMAL position.

7. Turn your system on and enter the CMOS setup to change settings as you require (to the hard drive and so on).

Symptom 5.5. You cannot operate or boot from an LS-120 "floptical" drive.   In virtually all cases, this is a limitation of the motherboard's BIOS. For example, Intel motherboards that have a Phoenix BIOS and use either the Intel 430TX, 440LX, 440BX, or 440EX chipsets support booting from an LS-120 floppy drive. Most other motherboards with a Pentium MMX-compliant (or later) chipset will support LS-120 drives. If you have trouble recognizing or booting from the LS-120, check with the motherboard or system maker for a BIOS upgrade.

Symptom 5.6. When upgrading the motherboard, the system won't boot when using an older CPU, but it boots fine with a newer CPU.   You find that the older CPU runs fine on another system. This generally means that the newer motherboard contains a "lockout" that prevents 66-MHz bus speeds. This forces the motherboard to use 100-MHz or 133-MHz bus speeds. If a 66-MHZ host bus processor is installed, the motherboard will not boot. If this is the case, there is no way around the problem except to use an appropriate processor model.

Symptom 5.7. The system displays PC100 memory even though PC133 memory is installed.   First, verify that your system bus is actually set to 133 MHz. If the bus is set to 100 MHz, the memory speed may be reported incorrectly. This error may also sometimes occur when the DRAM Clock entry in your CMOS Setup is set incorrectly. Try setting the DRAM Clock to Host CLK in the Chipset features section of your CMOS Setup.

Symptom 5.8. The motherboard's COM port(s) won't work.   In almost every case that I've ever heard of, an inability to use a COM port is a result of not using the supplied header cables, or the COM ports are disabled in the CMOS Setup.

Symptom 5.9. The system halts during boot and displays an "Incompatible ATAPI Device" error. This may occur after installing a new ATAPI device or upgrading the motherboard with existing ATAPI device(s). This is a known issue with the Pioneer 32X CD-ROM and an AMI BIOS, and this can also occur with other incompatible BIOS versions and ATAPI devices. In almost every case, the solution is to upgrade the motherboard's BIOS to a newer version. Of course, you could also try a different ATAPI device instead.

Symptom 5.10. The system will not turn off when you press the power button. This is an issue with the motherboard's power management settings. In many cases, the power button is designed to turn off the system only when you press and hold the power button for more than five seconds. You may be able to reconfigure the power button for an "instant off" through the CMOS Setup. If you cannot reconfigure the power button for this, you may need a BIOS upgrade.

Symptom 5.11. You discover the "Wake On LAN" device has damaged your power supply. This is probably because your power supply did not provide an adequate standby current. You need to use a power supply with 800mA provided through the +5Vsb (standby) power line. This is required by most Wake On LAN network cards that require +5V@750mA in sleep mode. Try an ATX power supply with minimum 800mA at the +5Vsb output to avoid overcurrent damage to the power supply.

Symptom 5.12. You encounter a "Serial Presence Detect" error at boot time. This is a problem with the system RAM being properly identified to the BIOS. If non-SPD memory is detected during the POST or the BIOS cannot determine that the memory installed meets SPD 100-MHz requirements, the BIOS will display this error message:

```
SERIAL PRESENCE DETECT (SPD) device data missing or
inconclusive

Properly programmed SPD device data is required for
reliable operation

Do you wish to continue?

Y/N Type [Y] to continue, [N] to shut down
```

While non-SPD memory remains present on the system, subsequent boots will display the following message:

```
SERIAL PRESENCE DETECT (SPD) device data missing or
inconclusive

100MHz memory assumed
```

If SPD 100-MHz memory cannot be confirmed during POST, the BIOS will provide this information to the user and offer the option to run the system with memory that may not meet the full 100-MHz operating requirements. If the system will be used in a mission-critical application where data integrity is vital, the system should be shut down, and SPD 100-MHz memory should be installed prior to operation.

Symptom 5.13. After installing one or more RIMM modules in the system, you get a repeating beep code and no video. This is often a problem with the way you installed your new Rambus DRAM. Chances are that the beep code indicates a problem during detection of the RIMM modules. If a RIMM socket is not populated with memory, ensure it is populated with a continuity RIMM. Also check to ensure that system memory is securely installed, and that any RIMMs in use have been specifically recommended by the motherboard manufacturer.

Symptom 5.14. You find that IRQ9 is not available to assign an ISA device. Chances are that this is an issue related to your particular motherboard's power management system. For example, IRQ9 is not available to ISA devices on the Intel JN440BX motherboard because it is dedicated to the power management function on the motherboard's PIIX4 controller. This is also true for other motherboards that utilize the PIIX4 controller. You can free the IRQ by disabling the motherboard's power management features, or select another available IRQ for the device.

Symptom 5.15. Windows 98 reports insufficient memory with 32 MB installed. This is a known issue on motherboards that use the VIA MVP4 chipset (such as the AOpen MX59 Pro motherboard). The MVP4 chipset supports shared memory between system RAM and the video system; 8 MB of system RAM is assigned to the onboard graphics controller by default. If this is the case, you may actually only have 24 MB of RAM for Windows 98, and this may not be enough. You can add more RAM to the system. You may also enter the CMOS Setup and reduce the Frame Buffer Size value from 8 MB to 2 MB in order to keep more of the 32 MB available for Windows 98. If you do reduce the Frame Buffer Size, be sure to also reduce the color depth and resolution under Windows 98.

Symptom 5.16. The system runs fine with Setup Defaults but is unstable with Turbo Defaults. This is because the Turbo defaults generally use more aggressive settings that wringing more performance out of the motherboard. In some cases, certain hardware combinations may not respond well to Turbo settings and result in system instability. Check your hardware list against the requirements for the Turbo default settings. If you identify an item that is not appropriate (such as slow RAM), you can upgrade that hardware. Otherwise, you may simply need to select the Setup defaults and stick with an acceptable level of system performance.

Symptom 5.17. A motherboard failure is reported but goes away when the PC's outer cover is removed. There is likely an intermittent connection on the motherboard. When the housing is secured, the PC chassis warps just slightly. This may be enough to precipitate an intermittent contact. When the housing is removed, the chassis relaxes and hides the intermittent connection. Replace the outer cover and gently retighten each screw with the system running. Chances are that you will find one screw that triggers the problem. You can leave that screw out, but it is advisable to replace the motherboard as a long-term fix.

Symptom 5.18. The POST (or your software diagnostic) reports a CPU fault. This is a fatal error, and chances are that system initialization has halted. CPU problems are generally reported when one or more CPU registers do not respond as expected or have trouble switching to the protected mode. In either case, the CPU is probably at fault. Fortunately, the CPU is socket/slot-mounted and should be very straightforward to replace. Be sure to remove all power to the PC, and make careful use of static controls when replacing a CPU. Mark the questionable CPU with indelible ink *before* replacing it. *Zero-insertion force* (ZIF) sockets are easiest, since the chip will be released simply by lifting the metal lever at the socket's side. Slide out the original CPU and insert a new one. Then secure the metal lever and try the PC again. However, many CPUs are mounted in *pin grid array* (PGA) sockets, and a specialized PGA removal tool is strongly suggested for proper removal. You should also be able to use a small, regular screwdriver to gently pry up each of the four sides of the CPU, but be very careful to avoid cracking the chip, the socket, or the motherboard. Never use excessive force. When the chip is free, install the new CPU with close attention to pin alignment. Then gently press the new CPU into place. If you're working with Slot 1/Slot A processors, you'll need to release the processor's retention mechanism before removing the processor from its slot.

Symptom 5.19. The POST (or your software diagnostic) reports a "BIOS ROM checksum" error.   The integrity of your system BIOS ROM is verified after the CPU is tested. This is necessary to ensure that no unwanted instructions or data might easily crash the system during POST or normal operations. A checksum is performed on the ROM contents, and that value is compared with the value stored in the ROM itself. If the two values are equal, the ROM is considered good and initialization continues. Otherwise, the BIOS is considered defective and should be replaced.

Symptom 5.20. The POST (or software diagnostic) reports a timer (PIT) failure, an RTC update problem, or a refresh failure.   The PIT is often an 8254 or compatible device. Ultimately, one or more of its three channels may have failed, and the PIT should be replaced. It is important to realize that many modern motherboards incorporate the PIT functions into a system controller or other chipset device (refer to the chipset chapter for a listing of chipsets and functions). Since the PIT is typically surface-mounted, you can attempt to replace the device or replace the motherboard entirely.

Symptom 5.21. The POST (or software diagnostic) reports an interrupt controller (PIC) failure.   The PIC is often an 8259 or compatible device, and two PICs can be found on a typical AT motherboard (PIC#1 handles IRQ0 through IRQ7, and PIC#2 handles IRQ8 through IRQ15). Of the two, PIC#1 is more important since the lower interrupts have a higher priority, and the lowest channels handle critical low-level functions such as the system timer and keyboard interface. Generally, a diagnostic will reveal which of the two PICs have failed. Make sure that no interrupt conflicts take place between two or more system devices. You can then replace the defective PIC. In virtually all current systems, both PICs are integrated into a system controller chip or chipset device. You can replace the defective chip if you have the appropriate surface-mounted equipment available or replace the motherboard entirely.

Symptom 5.22. The POST (or software diagnostic) reports a DMA controller (DMAC) failure. The DMAC is often an 8237 or compatible device, and two DMACs can be found on a typical AT motherboard (DMAC#1 handles channel 0 through channel 3, and DMAC#2 handles channel 4 through channel 7). Of the two, DMAC#1 is more important since channel 2 runs the floppy disk controller. Generally, a diagnostic will reveal which of the two DMACs have failed. Make sure that no DMA conflicts take place between two or more system devices. You can then replace the defective DMAC. In many current systems, both DMACs are integrated into a system controller chip or chipset device. You can replace the defective chip if you have the appropriate surface-mounted equipment available or replace the motherboard entirely.

Symptom 5.23. The POST (or software diagnostic) reports a KBC fault. The *Keyboard Controller* (KBC) is often either an 8042 or an 8742. Since the KBC is a microcontroller in its own right, diagnostics can usually detect a KBC fault with great accuracy. The KBC may either be a socket-mounted PLCC device or (in rare cases) a surface-mounted chip. Remember to remove all power and mark the old KBC before you remove it from the PC. You'll probably need a PLCC removal tool to take out the old KBC. If you cannot exchange a defective KBC, you'll need to replace the motherboard.

Symptom 5.24. A keyboard error is reported, but a new keyboard has no effect.   The keyboard fuse on the motherboard may have failed. Many motherboard designs incorporate a small fuse (called a *pico-fuse*) in the +5Vdc line that drives the keyboard. If this fuse fails, the keyboard will be dead. Use your multimeter and measure the +5Vdc line at the keyboard connector. If this reads 0Vdc, locate the keyboard fuse on the motherboard and replace it (you may have to trace the line back to the fuse that looks almost exactly like a resistor).

Symptom 5.25. The POST (or software diagnostic) reports a CMOS or RTC fault.   With either error, it is the same device that is usually at fault. The CMOS RAM and RTC are generally fabricated onto the same device. RTC problems indicate that the RTC portion of the chip has failed or is not being updated. CMOS RAM failure can be due to a dead backup battery or a failure of the chip itself. When dealing with a CMOS or Setup problem, try the following protocol. First, try a new backup battery and reload the CMOS Setup variables. If a new battery does not resolve the problem, the CMOS/RTC chip should be replaced. Often, the CMOS/RTC chip is surface-mounted and will have to be replaced (or the motherboard will have to be replaced). However, there is a growing trend toward making the chip socket-mounted and including the battery into a single replaceable module (such as the Dallas Semiconductor-type devices). Modules are typically replaceable DIP devices.

Symptom 5.26. The POST (or software diagnostic) reports a fault in the first 64 KB of RAM.   The first RAM page is important since it holds the *BIOS data area* (BDA) and interrupt vectors, and the system will not work without it. When a RAM error is indicated, your only real recourse is to replace the motherboard RAM. On older motherboards, if the diagnostic indicates which bit has failed and you can correlate the bit to a specific memory chip, you can sometimes replace the defective chip (typically surface-mounted). Otherwise, you'll need to systematically locate and replace all the motherboard RAM or replace the motherboard entirely. Newer motherboards utilize DIMMs (and sometimes RIMMs) for *all* system memory, so it should be a relatively simple matter to cycle through each memory module with a reliable unit to isolate the defective memory.

Symptom 5.27. A jumperless motherboard receives incorrect CPU Soft Menu settings and now refuses to boot. This may occur on a motherboard such as the Abit IT5V and is usually due to accidental settings during system configuration. Fortunately, this type of problem can be corrected by removing power from the motherboard. Try turning off the system and unplugging it for several minutes. When you restore power to the system, the CPU Soft Menu will automatically reset the CPU frequency for the lowest setting and enable the motherboard to boot. You can then go back into the CPU Soft Menu and correct any speed-setting errors. If this were a jumpered motherboard, you would need to find the CPU speed jumper and set it correctly.

Symptom 5.28. You see the error message "System Resource Conflict" on the AMI BIOS POST display. This is an error generated by AMI plug-and-play BIOS (though other plug-and-play BIOSs may produce similar errors) and is generated when the BIOS detects a resource conflict during initialization. You may try to force the BIOS to reconfigure the conflicting resource by pressing the Insert key during POST. If problems continue, you may need a BIOS update that may be able to resolve assignment conflicts more intelligently. Otherwise, you may need to reconfigure the conflicting resource manually (disabling its plug-and-play support) or remove the offending device entirely.

Symptom 5.29. Your Power Management icon does not appear in the Windows 95/98 Control Panel. This occurs even though the APM parameter under the BIOS Power Management Setup is enabled. This problem occurs if you do not enable the APM function before you install Windows 95/98. If you have already installed Windows 95/98, you should reinstall it. Before doing so, however, make sure that the APM function is enabled.

Symptom 5.30. Systems with a Western Digital 1.6-GB HDD fail to boot even through BIOS recognized the presence of HDD.   This is a typical problem with large hard drives that often need additional time to start up after powering the system. Check your BIOS Advanced Setup and increase the Power-on Delay time. This should correct the problem. This problem may reoccur if CMOS default values are reloaded or CMOS contents are lost.

Symptom 5.31. After installing Windows 95, the system can no longer find the CD-ROM drive on the secondary IDE channel.   You may also find that the IDE drives are running in MS-DOS compatibility mode. This problem occurs often with motherboards using the Intel 430HX chipset. Windows 95 does not recognize the Intel 82371SB drive controller on the motherboard, and this causes BIOS to disable the secondary IDE channel. Devices on the secondary channel are not being detected after the system is rebooted. In most cases, you can upgrade the BIOS to correct this problem or move the IDE devices to a separate IDE controller. You may also be able to find and download a patch to update the MSHDC.INF file, which will force Windows 95 to recognize the 82371SB controller.

Symptom 5.32. The system hangs up or crashes when the chipset-specific PCI-IDE DOS driver is loaded.   This is a known problem with Micro-Star motherboards using a VIA VP1 chipset and Award BIOS 4.50PG. The problem is with the BIOS version and its interaction with the PCI controller portion of the VIA chipset. Upgrading the BIOS version should resolve the problem.

Symptom 5.33. You notice that your motherboard is unusually picky about which memory modules it will accept. This problem is most notable with Pentium-vintage motherboards and SIMMs, and this may occur even though the modules are all within the proper type and rating. Several possible problems must be considered. First, Intel chipsets (especially older chipsets) are very discriminating when it comes to memory speed, so make sure that the memory speed is well within the required range (usually 70 nanoseconds or faster). Next, try changing the Wait States in the CMOS Setup to a lower speed (4-4-4-4). If your system works under this low speed, then increase the speed (3-3-3-3, 3-2-2-2, 3-1-1-1, and so on) and keep trying until the best number has been reached. Finally, the memory itself may be of questionable quality. Try good-quality memory bought from a reputable vendor. Make sure the vendor offers a liberal return policy so that you can return questionable memory easily.

Symptom 5.34. You experience a problem with the pipeline burst cache. This is a recognized problem with UMC *pipeline burst* (PB) cache (especially on an Amptron motherboard). The problem can usually be solved by adjusting the cache control to 4-4-4-4 (the default in CMOS is typically 2-3-3-3). This will reduce performance somewhat but should stabilize cache operations.

Symptom 5.35. You encounter problems with Western Digital hard drives (the drives work on other systems). This type of problem has been identified with Asus motherboards using Award BIOS with older Western Digital (1.6GB) drives. Note that problems do not appear in newer Western Digital drives. Perform the following steps to find a solution:

- *Check the CMOS Setup.* Disable the "Quick Power-on Self Test" in your CMOS Setup and enable the Floppy Seek option. This will increase the time that the drive gets to spinup. If your CMOS offers a Power-on Delay Time instead, try increasing that time.

- *Avoid the use of software tools.* Also avoid using DEFRAG or the Disk Surface Scan feature of ScanDisk with Western Digital drives. Both have been reported to increase the number of bad blocks on the disk.

- *Check for BIOS upgrades.* Consider a BIOS upgrade (especially if you're using a motherboard with the Intel 430FX chipset). Some BIOS versions use a park head command that can cause problems with Western Digital hard drives.

- *Check for drive patches.* Review the Western Digital Web site (*www.wdc.com*) for any drive patches that might be currently available. If all else fails, you might replace the drive outright.

Symptom 5.36. You encounter memory parity errors at bootup. If you're using non-parity memory devices (a 32-bit device instead of a 36-bit device), you will need to disable ECC or Parity checking through the CMOS Chipset Features settings. This problem can occur if you reload default CMOS settings; this restores parity/ECC on a system with non-parity memory. Also keep in mind that the Triton chipset does not support parity, so even if you use parity RAM, you should try disabling parity checking. If the system is configured properly, you may actually have a memory failure, and you'll need to isolate the memory fault.

Symptom 5.37. You flash a BIOS, but now you get no video. When you flash a BIOS, the old CMOS settings are usually left useless. This means you'll have to clear and restore the proper CMOS settings before the system may run properly. Clear your CMOS RAM and reload the proper settings (or choose the BIOS Defaults for a good system baseline). The BIOS chip itself may also be troublesome. Some problems occur when flashing an

Intel flash ROM chip. Make sure that there are no warnings or cautions in the system documentation or from the manufacturer's Web site before flashing a particular BIOS chip. Try restoring the original BIOS (if possible) or contact the manufacturer for a replacement BIOS.

Symptom 5.38. You're trying to use a plug-and-play sound card and a plug-and-play modem together on the same system, but you're getting hardware conflicts. This is an all-too-common problem with plug-and-play systems. In general, the modem should take COM2 (2F8h and IRQ3), and the sound card should take 220h, IRQ5, and DMA 1. Try adding the cards one at a time. Install the sound card first and let Windows 95/98 detect it. Add the modem next. If problems persist, configure the cards manually (disable their plug-and-play support) if possible or try alternative cards.

Symptom 5.39. I have 32 MB (or more) of memory, and the BIOS counts it all during POST, but you only see 16 MB in the CMOS Setup screen. This is a problem that has been identified with some Award BIOS versions. To correct the problem, make sure that the Memory Hole option in the Advanced Chipset Setup area is disabled. This option assumes a maximum of 16 MB of physical RAM in the system. You may also try disabling the system's Shadow RAM or BIOS Shadow options.

Symptom 5.40. You move a working IDE drive from an older 386/486 system to your new system, but the drive is inaccessible. In most cases, the data transfer mode is set improperly for the old IDE hard drive (you're using LBA mode when the IDE drive requires CHS mode). Find the Peripheral Setup screen in your CMOS Setup and make sure to change all the PIO mode settings to Mode 0 (chances are the settings are currently at Automatic and are configuring the data transfer incorrectly). The idea is to ensure that the drive is configured exactly the same way as it was on its original system. If you cannot duplicate the original BIOS configuration, get the settings as close as you can. Then repartition and reformat the drive in order to use it on a different controller.

Symptom 5.41. The system frequently locks up or crashes after installing a Cyrix 6x86 CPU. In most cases, the Cyrix 6x86 is not being cooled properly and is overheating. Make sure that you have an ample heat sink/fan assembly attached properly to the Cyrix, and see that the fan is running. Also, the Cyrix 6x86 P166+ is a 3.52V CPU. Check your voltage regulator and see that it is set to provide 3.45 to 3.6 volts. A lower voltage setting may result in system instability.

Symptom 5.42. After installing a motherboard, you get registry corruption or "out of memory" errors from Windows 95/98. This type of symptom occurs most frequently with older Pentium motherboards (100–120 MHz) and is almost always a BIOS version problem that causes the motherboard to misbehave under Windows 95/98, resulting in registry corruption. You'll need to update the BIOS version for your particular motherboard, and it may be necessary to reinstall Windows 95/98 after the BIOS is updated.

Symptom 5.43. The motherboard refuses to detect the SCSI controller during bootup. This problem has been identified with the Dataexpert EXP8551 motherboard, but it may occur on many different types of PCI-based motherboards. In most cases, you will have to change the configuration of your PCI slots on the motherboard. For example, if the SCSI controller is installed on slot 2, you will need to configure the PCI slot 2 in the CMOS Setup or move the SCSI controller to a higher priority PCI slot.

Symptom 5.44. You find that you cannot run a Cyrix 6x86 CPU on a particular motherboard. This is a problem that has been identified on Eurone/Matsonic motherboards and is usually the result of an incompatible motherboard clock generator. Some clock generators support the Cyrix 120, 133, and 166-MHz models but exempt the 200-MHz model. Other clock generators support the 120, 150, 166, and 200-MHz models but exempt the 133 MHz model. So if you're using a 133-MHz or 200-MHz Cyrix CPU, you may be using the wrong clock generator. You will have to replace the CPU with a speed suitable to the particular clock generator or change the motherboard to one that will accommodate the particular CPU speed.

Symptom 5.45. When four eight-MB SIMMs are installed in the system (32 MB), the system only counts up to 24 MB. This is a known problem with Gigabyte motherboards (typically the GA-586ATE, ATM, and AP ver 1.x). The motherboard does not support double-sided SIMMs (2 MB, 8 MB, 32 MB, or 128 MB) in the center bank. Install the SIMMs in bank 0 and bank 2, leaving bank 1 empty. You may also choose to use single-sided memory modules.

> **NOTE**:   Some motherboards require the banks to be filled in sequential order or enable you to change the bank order with motherboard jumpers.

Symptom 5.46. Gold-plated SIMMs/DIMMs do not work properly in tin-plated sockets.   As a general rule, you should avoid mixing metal types when choosing memory modules. The metal in the SIMM/DIMM socket must be the same as the metal on the SIMM/DIMM itself. Otherwise, tin debris will transfer to the gold surface and oxidize. This will eventually result in memory errors that would suggest faulty SIMMs/DIMMs but can be corrected by removing, cleaning, and reinstalling the memory module(s).

Symptom 5.47. Even though all peripherals in the system are SCSI, Windows 95/98 will continue to detect the PCI IDE controller.   You notice that this occurs even though the controller was disabled in CMOS. This is a known problem with the Iwill P54TS motherboard, but you may encounter this with other motherboards also. Normally, Windows 95/98 will try to recognize and enable I/O devices, but it should not enable devices that are deliberately disabled in CMOS. This is typically a BIOS problem (the onboard IDE controllers were not properly disabled), so try upgrading your BIOS to the latest version. If the problem persists, you may need to upgrade the motherboard.

Symptom 5.48. You get an EISA CMOS configuration error when the system starts up. For EISA systems (which are *not* plug-and-play-compliant), you must run the *EISA Configuration Utility* (ECU) in order to properly set up the system. Without this step, the system will not be able to detect any possible resource conflicts. This type of problem is most common when installing a new EISA motherboard, when CMOS contents are lost, or when devices (such as memory) are added or removed.

Symptom 5.49. The Switching Module Processor (SMP) or dual processor mode refuses to run in Windows NT. The most common problem is an incompatibility with the SMP HAL shipped with Windows NT (versions prior to 3.51) and the motherboard's chipset. If you're upgrading from an older version of NT (prior to 3.51), first install NT as a standard PC (a single-processor kernel) and then install NT with the default multi-processor kernel it provides (NT will not recognize your dual CPUs if you upgrade straight to a multi-processor configuration).

Symptom 5.50. When attempting to upgrade your flash BIOS, you encounter an insufficient memory error. In most cases, you simply don't have enough conventional memory available to execute the flash program. Most flash programs require about 560 KB or conventional RAM. Try booting clean with a DOS diskette, and then run the flash upgrade utility directly from the diskette.

Symptom 5.51. You see a prolonged system message saying "Updating ESCD . . ." each time the system boots. The *Extended System Configuration Data* (ESCD) area is part of a plug-and-play system. One or more plug-and-play devices are attempting to update your BIOS settings. To stop this from occurring, set the BIOS to Program mode. If you cannot get the message to stop, you may need to check for hardware configuration problems between two or more devices in the system.

Symptom 5.52. You notice a yellow exclamation point over your USB port in the Device Manager. Windows 95/98 indicates that it has detected an unknown PCI device. In virtually all cases, the proper driver for the USB on your system has not been installed, and Windows 95/98 cannot recognize the USB hardware. You can usually correct this problem by updating your system BIOS to a newer version that supports the USB hardware better under Windows 95/98. If you're running an older version of Windows (Windows 95 OSR2), you may also consider upgrading to Windows 98/SE.

Symptom 5.53. The system hangs up after installing a Cyrix 6x86 CPU. There is probably a problem with the utilization of the system cache, which is causing the system to hang up. Try systematically disabling the internal (L1) and external (L2) cache through the CMOS Setup. A BIOS upgrade may correct cache utilization on some motherboards, so check with the motherboard manufacturer for possible patches or BIOS updates.

Symptom 5.54. When attempting to upgrade the BIOS version, you cannot use a key sequence such as Ctrl+Home to reboot the PC in order to start the flash process. The current BIOS version does not support such key sequences. To flash the BIOS, start the flash program manually from the DOS prompt. For example, try a command line such as the following:

```
A:\ZZZZZZ> AMIFL PAIV17.ROM <Enter>
```

Symptom 5.55. You find that a particular SVGA board refuses to work on a particular motherboard. However, the video board proves to be fine on other systems. In most cases, this is a compatibility problem between the video chipset and the motherboard's architecture. There may be a BIOS upgrade for the motherboard or video board that can overcome the problem, or you may simply have to use a different video board.

Symptom 5.56. When the on-board printer port is set to 3BCh (and EPP/SPP mode) and another parallel port add-on card is set to 378h or 278h, the BIOS only recognizes the add-on card. Port 3BCh seems to disappear. This may be a configuration problem with the Winbond chipset that specifies that LPT1 on the motherboard should be set at 378h (EPP or SPP), while add-on parallel ports should be set at 278h or 3BCh. The Winbond chip was designed this way for Windows 95. Check with the motherboard manufacturer for any available BIOS upgrades that may correct this issue.

Symptom 5.57. You cannot get parallel port devices to work on your motherboard. In most cases, you must set the proper parallel port mode (SPP/ECP/EPP) for the particular device you plan to use. Often, setting the port to Compatibility mode or Bidirectional will work for many common peripherals. Parallel port modes are selected through the CMOS Setup, usually under Integrated Peripherals or some similar heading.

Symptom 5.58. You notice that some configurations of memory provide less performance than others. This type of problem is most noted on motherboards with 440FX chipsets and is usually the result of a BIOS problem. Try updating your BIOS to the latest available version.

Symptom 5.59. You see no performance improvement when enabling PCI/IDE bus mastering. The problem is probably that you are using an older (or buggy) bus mastering driver. Make sure that you have installed the most recent bus mastering driver (Triton I, Triton II, and Natoma chipsets may use the same driver) for your particular motherboard chipset. Try to avoid generic bus mastering drivers in favor of motherboard-specific drivers.

Symptom 5.60. The BIOS banner displayed on power-on is showing the wrong motherboard model. In virtually all cases, this is a problem with the BIOS version where it cannot identify the correct hardware platform. Get the latest update for your motherboard BIOS.

Symptom 5.61. The Pentium P55CM BIOS shows a 150-MHz CPU even though the CPU is a 166-MHz model. Such incorrect speed identification is almost always due to a BIOS fault. You should upgrade to the very latest BIOS version for your particular motherboard. If you cannot flash the BIOS, replace the BIOS chip outright.

Symptom 5.62. You see the Static Device Resource Conflict error message after the system memory count. This is usually a problem with the PCI bus system on older motherboards, usually because of inadequate plug-and-play resource assignments. Press and hold the Insert key before turning on the computer. Release the Insert key when the video comes up. This forces the system to reassign PCI resources. If the error message still appears, remove all PCI cards (except for the video card) and try again. Reinsert one PCI card at a time until the problem returns. *That* is where the problem is.

CPU Issues

The CPU is the single most complex and expensive chip on the motherboard. It is responsible for processing every instruction and virtually all the data in memory at one time or another. Although CPU failures are somewhat rare, you should be familiar with the symptoms. When you suspect a CPU problem, make the following checks before proceeding:

- *Check the socket or slot.* Make sure that the CPU is inserted completely into its socket or slot. For a ZIF socket, see that the lever is closed completely and latched. For a Slot 1/Slot A receptacle, see that the processor cartridge is fully inserted and verify that the retention mechanism is secure.

- *Check the motherboard jumpers.* When upgrading a CPU, see that the motherboard is configured properly for the specific CPU type and clock setting. If you're using a jumperless motherboard, verify that the CPU voltage, clock, and multiplier settings are entered correctly in the CMOS Setup (usually in the Frequency/Voltage submenu).

- *Check for heat.* Make sure that the CPU's heat sink (or heat sink/fan assembly) is attached securely to the CPU. If there is a fan on the heat sink, see that the fan is running. You may need to reattach the heat sink using thermal grease.

CPU Symptoms

CPUs can experience a wide array of problems and this section provides possible solutions for many of them.

Symptom 5.63. The system is completely dead. You will usually see normal power indicators, and the hard drives may even spin up. The frustration with this kind of symptom is that the PC typically does not run long enough to execute its POST diagnostics, nor does the system boot to run any third-party DOS diagnostics. As a result, such dead systems require a bit of blind faith on the part of a technician, so be sure to start with the basics:

- *Check the power supply.* Use a voltmeter and check each output from the power supply. See that the motherboard power connectors are attached securely.

If any power level appears low or absent (especially the +5 volt supply), replace the power supply.

- *Check for hardware conflicts or a defective peripheral.* Strip the system of its peripherals and expansion boards, and then try the system again. If operation returns, one of the expansion devices is interrupting system operation. Reinstall one device at a time and check the system. The last expansion device to be installed when the PC fails is the culprit. Reconfigure or replace the offending device.

- *Replace the CPU.* Try a reliable CPU in the motherboard. When removing the original CPU, be *extremely* careful to avoid bending any of the pins (you may want to reinstall the CPU later) or damaging the processor cartridge connections. Use care when installing the new CPU as well. Bent pins or cartridge damage will ruin the chip. If a new CPU fails to correct the problem, replace the motherboard outright.

Symptom 5.64. You receive a beep code or I/O POST code indicating a possible CPU fault. In most cases, the CPU itself has failed, so one of the following steps must be made:

- *Check the power supply.* Use a voltmeter and check each output from the power supply. See that the motherboard power connectors are attached securely. If any power level appears low or absent (especially the +5 volt supply), replace the power supply.

- *Replace the CPU.* Try a reliable CPU in the motherboard. When removing the original CPU, be *extremely* careful to avoid bending any of the pins (you may want to reinstall the CPU later) or damaging the processor cartridge connections. Use care when installing the new CPU as well. Bent pins or cartridge damage will ruin the chip. If a new CPU

fails to correct the problem, replace the motherboard outright.

Symptom 5.65. The system boots with no problem, but it crashes or freezes when certain applications are run. It may seem as if the application may be corrupt. Thus, make the following checks:

- *Test the CPU.*   Try a diagnostic such as AMIDIAG from AMI or the Troubleshooter by AllMicro. Run repetitive tests on the CPU. Although the CPU may work in real mode, diagnostics can detect errors running protected-mode instructions and perform thorough register checking.

- *Check or update the application.*   Verify that the application has been tested with your particular type of hardware platform. In a few cases, you may need to patch or update the application itself in order to stabilize the system.

- *Replace the CPU.*   When an error code is returned suggesting a CPU fault, try a reliable CPU.

- *Expand the diagnostic.*   If a CPU fault is not detected, expand the diagnostic to test other portions of the motherboard. If the entire system checks properly, you may indeed have a corrupt file in your application.

Symptom 5.66. The system boots with no problem, but it crashes or freezes after several minutes of operation (regardless of the application being run). You may be dealing with excessive CPU heat. If you shut the system off and wait several minutes, the system will probably boot fine and run for several more minutes before stopping again. This behavior is typical of thermal failure, and the following checks will help you spot the problem:

- *Check for faulty connections.*   Make sure that the CPU is installed completely in its socket/slot. Also see that all cables, connectors, wiring, and expansion boards are secure.

■ *Check the CPU for heat.* See if the CPU is excessively hot. Use extreme caution when checking for heat since you can be easily burned. If the CPU is running very hot, be sure to add a heat sink/fan assembly.

■ *Check the heat sink/fan.* If the CPU is hot, see if the heat sink is equally hot. If not, the heat sink may not be attached properly to the CPU (it's not taking away any heat). Secure the CPU and try some thermal grease between the CPU and heat sink. If you are using a heat sink only, consider installing a heat sink/fan. If the fan is not running, replace the heat sink/fan unit.

Symptom 5.67. Some software locks up on systems running 5x86 processors. This is a frequent problem with high-end software such as AutoDesk's 3D Studio. Often, programs like 3D Studio use software timing loops in the code. The 5x86 processor executes these loop instructions faster than previous x86 CPUs and this interferes with timing dependent code inside the program. In most cases, the software manufacturer will offer a patch for the offending program. For 3D Studio, download the FSTCPUFX.EXE file from Kinetix *(ftp://ftp.fh-merseburg.de/pub/hardware/mainboard/asus/fstcpufx.exe)*. Run the excutable patch file and follow the instructions. The patch alters the 3D Studio executable file.

Symptom 5.68. The Windows 95 Device Manager identifies the CPU incorrectly. In many cases, the CPU is misidentified as a 486 or other, older CPU. This is due to an issue with Windows 95. The algorithm used in Windows 95 to detect the CPU was likely completed before the particular CPU was released, and therefore the CPU responds to the algorithm just as a 486 does. Use a diagnostic that will identify your particular

CPU correctly, or check with the CPU maker for a Windows 95 patch that will support proper identification. This problem happens often with Cyrix 6x86 CPUs and can be corrected by downloading a patch such as 6XOPT074.ZIP (see the Performance enhancement software bullet under the following "Cyrix 6x86 issues" section). In most cases, upgrading Windows should also correct this type of trouble.

Symptom 5.69. The heat sink/fan will not secure properly. The fan is not tight against the surface of the CPU. This can be a serious problem for the system because a loose heat sink/fan will not cool the processor correctly. Three classical solutions exist for this issue. First, make sure that you have the heat sink/fan model that is recommended for your particular CPU (a common error when building a new PC). For socket-mounted processors, make sure that the heat sink attaches to either the CPU chip itself or the ZIF socket that the CPU mounts in. Third, verify that the CPU has not been altered or faked. Faked or remarked CPUs are often ground down to remove their original markings and then new markings are placed on the CPU. The grinding process reduces the package thickness and can prevent the heat sink/fan from being secure (faked CPUs are a common occurrence in Europe).

Symptom 5.70. The Cyrix 6x86 system is crashing or freezing after some period of operation. This is almost always a heat-related problem caused by inadequate cooling of the 6x86. Thus, one of the following steps will bring a solution to the problem:

- *Check the cooling unit.* If you're not using a heat sink/fan, install one before continuing (be sure to use a thin layer of thermal grease to improve the heat transfer between the CPU and the heat sink). Make sure that you are using a good-quality heat sink/fan with plenty of capacity, and see that it is securely attached to the CPU. Also check that the CPU itself is secure in its socket.

- *Try a different CPU model.* You might also consider installing a different 6x86 model. The Type C028 version uses 3.52 volts, and the Type C016 uses 3.3 volts, so just changing models can reduce power demands. You might also try installing a version 2.7 or later 6x86, which is better able to deal with heat. Best yet, install a 6x86L CPU (and regulator).

- *Upgrade the BIOS.* A third possible cause of intermittent system operation is a poorly compatible BIOS. Check with the motherboard maker or system manufacturer and see if there is a BIOS upgrade to better support Cyrix CPUs.

Symptom 5.71. The Cyrix 6x86 system crashes and refuses to restart. This is another classic heat-related problem and may often indicate that the CPU or its associated voltage regulator has failed. Check the voltage regulator. Regulators are more susceptible to failure with Cyrix 6x86 CPUs because of the higher current demands. If the voltage regulator checks out, replace the CPU itself (perhaps with a lower power model, as mentioned in Symptom 5.91).

Symptom 5.72. You notice poor Cyrix 6x86 performance under Windows NT 4.0. In virtually all cases, NT has detected the 6x86 and has elected to shut down the system's write-back L1 cache completely. This results in the performance hit. Fortunately, this problem can be addressed in several ways. First, you can download a patch from the Cyrix Web site (*www.cyrix.com*) that re-enables the L1 cache under NT 4.0. This brings performance back up, but it also can cause instability for NT. A more practical resolution is to replace the CPU with a 6x86 version 2.7 or higher, or a 6x86L (and a suitable voltage regulator), as mentioned in Symptom 5.91.

Overclocking Symptoms

Various overclocking problems are discussed with solutions in this section.

Symptom 5.73. The system does not boot up at all after reconfiguring the system for overclocking. This is a common problem, which almost always means that you cannot overclock the CPU at the level you have chosen. Scale back the clock speed or the multiplier until the system starts up, or return the clock and multiplier to their original values.

Symptom 5.74. The system starts after overclocking but locks up or crashes after some short period of time. Overclocking causes substantial heat dissipation from the CPU, and cooling must be improved to compensate for this additional heat. Otherwise, the overheated CPU can lock up and crash the system. Check the heat sink/fan and see that it is attached correctly with a thin layer of thermal grease between the CPU and the heat sink. It may be necessary to upsize the heat sink/fan or use a Peltier cooler.

Symptom 5.75. You see memory errors after increasing the bus speed for overclocking. Memory performance is tightly coupled to bus speed (or clock speed). Most 60-nanosecond RAM types will work fine up to 66 MHz, but you may need high-end 50 nanosecond *Extended Data Output* (EDO) RAM or 10–12 nanosecond *Synchronous DRAM* (SDRAM) when pushing the bus speed to 75 or 83 MHz. Try some faster memory in the PC or do not attempt to overclock the system.

Symptom 5.76. After reconfiguring for overclocking, the system works, but you see a rash of CPU failures. Chances are that the CPU is running far too hot and is resulting in premature CPU failures. Check the cooling unit and see that it is securely attached using a thin layer of thermal grease between the CPU and the heat sink. It may be necessary to upsize the heat sink/fan or use a Peltier cooler.

Symptom 5.77. After reconfiguring for overclocking, you find that some expansion board or other hardware is no longer recognized or working. Since PCI and ISA clocks are typically tied to the system clock speed, increasing the clock speed may also increase the PCI and ISA clocks (on systems where these buses are ties to the front-side bus speed). This can upset the operation of some sensitive adapter boards. You may be able to replace the suspect hardware with a more tolerant adapter, but it is often safer to return the clock speed and multiplier settings to their original values.

Symptom 5.78. After reconfiguring for overclocking, you notice that a number of recent files are corrupt, inaccessible, or missing. In effect, the system is not stable. Check for excessive heat first and correct any overheating issues. Otherwise, you should not overclock this particular system. Try scaling back the overclocking configuration or return the clock speed and multiplier settings to their original values.

Memory Issues

The CPU relies heavily on the performance of memory in order to provide necessary data and instructions as needed. It then stores the processing results accurately. As a consequence, errors or faults in memory can easily crash the entire system. When you suspect a problem with your system memory, make the following checks before proceeding:

- *Check the memory module installation.* Make sure that each of your SIMMs, DIMMs, or RIMMs are installed correctly and completely in their sockets, and see that each module is clipped into place securely. If any clips are bent or snapped, you may need to secure the module with an elastic band or other means.

- *Check the CMOS Setup entries.* Open the CMOS Setup and see that the correct amount of RAM has been entered. Also check that the system is set for the proper number of wait states.

- *Check the motherboard jumpers.* When adding more memory, make sure that any motherboard jumpers are set properly to define bank 0, the number of active banks, or other memory attributes.

- *Check the memory speed.* See that the RAM in your system is fast enough to support your CPU. Do not mix memory speeds within the same bank. Also do not mix memory types (EDO and FPM). Never mix parity and non-parity RAM without turning the motherboard's parity checking off.

Contemporary Memory Symptoms

Typical contemporary memory problems and the solutions for them are discussed here.

Symptom 5.79. New memory is installed, but the system refuses to recognize it. New memory installation has always presented some unique problems since different generations of PCs deal with new memory differently. Make the following verifications:

- *Verify RAM identification.* The oldest PCs require you to set jumpers or DIP switches in order to recognize new blocks of memory. The vintage i286 and i386 systems (a PS/2) use a setup diskette to tell CMOS about the PC's configuration (including new memory). More recent systems incorporate an Installed Memory setting into a CMOS Setup utility in BIOS that must be updated after the memory is installed or removed. Late-model Pentium II/III systems actually auto-detect installed memory each time the system is booted (so it need not be entered in the CMOS setup, though Setup may need to auto-detect the new RAM amount on first boot).

- *Verify bank assignments.* Also check that a correct bank has been filled properly. The PC may not recognize any additional memory unless an entire bank has been filled, and the bank is next in line (Bank 0, then Bank 1, and so on). You may want to check the PC's user manual for any unique rules or limitations in the particular motherboard.

> **NOTE**: Many late-model Pentium II/III motherboards do not need banks filled in order, although that's usually the safest policy to follow when upgrading or troubleshooting any PC.

Symptom 5.80. New memory has been installed or replaced, and the system refuses to boot. Memory installations often proceed flawlessly, but when boot problems occur, you can usually narrow the problem down to several key areas:

- *Check the power.* Always start by checking AC power, the system power switch, and the power connection(s) to the motherboard. Check that none of the system cabling was dislodged during the memory installation.

- *Check the expansion devices.* See that all expansion boards are inserted evenly and completely in their expansion slots. Flexing the motherboard during memory installation may have pried one or more boards just slightly out of their slots.

- *Recheck the memory installation.* Your memory modules may not be inserted correctly. Take the modules out and seat them again, making sure the locking arm is holding the module securely in place.

- *Check the module type.* If the problem continues, you probably do not have the right memory module for that particular computer. Make sure that the memory module (SIMM or DIMM) is the correct part that is fully compatible with your motherboard.

- *Check the installation order.* Finally, check for any particular device order that may be required by the motherboard. Certain systems require that memory be installed in pairs or in descending order by size. Refer to the system or motherboard manual for specific details on your exact system.

Symptom 5.81. You see an "XXXX Optional ROM Bad, Checksum = YYYY" error message. Part of the POST sequence checks for the presence of any other ROMs in the system. When another ROM is located, a checksum test is performed to check its integrity. This error message indicates that an external BIOS ROM (such as a SCSI adapter BIOS or video card BIOS) has beem checked as bad or its address conflicts with another device in the system. In either case, system initialization cannot continue and the following checks must be made:

- *Check the ROM address setting.* If you have just installed a new peripheral device when this error occurs (a SCSI controller board), try changing the new device's ROM address jumpers to resolve the conflict.

- *Check the new device.* Remove the peripheral board and the fault should disappear. Try the board on another PC. If the problem continues on another PC, the adapter (or its ROM) may be defective. If this error has occurred spontaneously, remove one peripheral board at a time and retest the system until you isolate the faulty board, then replace the faulty board (or just replace its ROM if possible).

Symptom 5.82. You see a general RAM error with fault addresses listed. In actual practice, the error message may appear as any of the following examples, depending on the specific fault, where the fault was detected, and the BIOS version reporting the error:

- ```
  Memory address line failure at <XXXX>,
  read <YYYY>, expecting <ZZZZ>
  ```
  ```

- Memory data line failure at <XXXX>, read <YYYY>, expecting <ZZZZ>

- Memory high address failure at <XXXX>, read <YYYY>, expecting <ZZZZ>

- Memory logic failure at <XXXX>, read <YYYY>, expecting <ZZZZ>

- Memory odd/even logic failure at <XXXX>, read <YYYY>, expecting <ZZZZ>

- Memory parity failure at <XXXX>, read <YYYY>, expecting <ZZZZ>

- Memory read/write failure at <XXXX>, read <YYYY>, expecting <ZZZZ>

These errors indicate that at least one SIMM, DIMM, or RIMM has failed. A trial and error approach is usually the least expensive route in finding the problem. First, reseat each memory module and retest the system to be sure that each module is inserted and secured properly. Rotate a reliable SIMM/DIMM/RIMM through each occupied socket in sequence. If the error disappears when the module is in a slot, the old device that had been displaced is probably the faulty one.

Run a thorough system diagnostic if possible, and check for failures in other areas of the motherboard that affect memory (such as the interrupt controller, the cache controller, the DMA controller, or the memory management chips). If the problem prohibits a software diagnostic, use a POST board and try identifying any hexadecimal error code. If a support chip is identified, you can replace the defective chip or replace the motherboard outright.

Symptom 5.83. You see a "Cache Memory Failure—Disabling Cache" error. The cache system has failed. The tag RAM, cache logic (motherboard chipset), or cache memory on your motherboard is defective. Your best course is to replace the cache RAM IC(s) or *Cache-on-a-Stick* (COAST)) module. If the problem persists, try replacing the cache logic or tag RAM (or replace the entire motherboard). You will probably need a schematic diagram or a detailed block diagram of your system in order to locate the cache memory chip(s), so refer to the system or motherboard manual for detailed information.

Symptom 5.84. You see a "Decreasing Available Memory" error message.   This is basically a confirmation message that indicates a failure has been detected in extended or expanded memory, and that all the memory *after* the failure has been disabled to enable the system to continue operating (although at a substantially reduced level). Your first step should be to reseat each memory module and ensure that they are properly inserted and secured. Next, take a reliable SIMM, DIMM, or RIMM and step through each occupied module slot until the problem disappears. The device that was removed is probably the faulty one. Keep in mind that you may have to alter the system's CMOS Setup parameters as you move memory around the machine (an incorrect setup can cause problems during system initialization).

Symptom 5.85. You are encountering a memory error with HIMEM.SYS under DOS.   In many cases, this is a compatibility problem with system memory. For example, the Intel Advanced/AS motherboard is incompatible with two specific Texas Instruments EDO SIMMs (part numbers TM124FBK32S-60 and TM248GBK32S-60). Other EDO SIMMs from TI and other vendors will not cause this error. Try a SIMM from a different manufacturer. Also make sure that you're using the latest version of HIMEM.SYS.

Windows-Related Memory Errors

The following section will cover memory errors in Windows systems and provide solutions to these problems.

Symptom 5.86. Windows 95/98 "Protection" errors occur after adding SIMMs/DIMMs. Windows 95/98 stalls with Windows Protection errors during boot or randomly crashes with Fatal Exception errors when opening applications. This is a known problem with the Intel Thor motherboard using the 1.00.01.CNOT BIOS after installing 32 MB of RAM. This issue is usually due to certain third-party SIMMs/DIMMs operating at speeds other than 60 nanoseconds. The motherboard probably has tight memory specifications, and SIMMs/DIMMs that operate at correct speeds are required (not faster or slower, even though the modules are marked properly). For example, some SIMM manufacturers mark the SIMMs at 60 nanoseconds, but the SIMMs actually run at 45 nanoseconds. Try some memory modules from a different manufacturer. It is also possible that a BIOS upgrade may loosen timing enough to make the SIMMs/DIMMs usable.

Symptom 5.87. Windows returns a fault in the MS-DOS extender. This kind or error can occur in Windows 3.1, 3.11, 95, or 98 and usually happens in either of two formats: `Bad fault in MS-DOS extender` or `Fault outside of MS-DOS extender`. You may also see a *stack dump* with a format such as

```
Raw fault frame:

EC=0344  CS=031F  IP=85E2  AX=001D  BX=0005  CX=1800
DX=155F

SI=0178  DI=0178  BP=016E  DS=027F  ES=027F  SS=027F
SP=0166
```

An error such as `Bad fault in MS-DOS extender` generally occurs when the fault handler in DOSX. EXE (the DOS extender) generates another cascaded fault while trying to handle a protected-mode exception. This error is usually caused by one of the following factors:

- HIMEM.SYS is unable to control the A20 line (which may indicate a motherboard problem).

- DOS=HIGH is not functioning properly (perhaps HIMEM.SYS is not loaded or corrupt).

- Your RAM may be defective. You might try a RAM diagnostic to isolate any memory problems.

- You are not running MS-DOS (your system is running DR DOS).

- The third-party memory manager (386MAX) is not configured correctly.

- An `EMM386.EXE NOEMS x=A000-EFFF` command line is missing from the CONFIG.SYS file.

- You have an old, out-of-date BIOS ROM that isn't supporting the DOS extender properly.

- Your memory-related CMOS Setup configuration is incorrect.

- Your Windows files are old or corrupted. Run ScanDisk to test for file problems and then reinstall Windows if necessary.

- Your system is infected with a computer virus (Form, Forms, Noint, or Yankee Doodle are known to cause this type of problem). Check the system with a current anti-virus utility.

If you see an error such as `Standard mode fault outside MS-DOS extender`, the Windows kernel may be generating a processor exception during initialization (before it has installed its own exception handlers) or when the kernel determines that it cannot handle an exception. The underlying causes are almost always the same as outlined previously. The portion of the error display labeled `Raw fault frame` contains information generated by the 80286 or 80386 processor in response to the original fault.

Symptom 5.88. You see a memory error such as "Unable to control A20 line." This error is almost always related to the HIMEM.SYS driver. The A20 line controls access to the first 64 KB of extended memory known as the *high memory area* (HMA). The HIMEM.SYS device driver must control the A20 line in order to manage extended memory. The error message is reported by HIMEM. SYS if it incorrectly identifies the extended memory-handling mechanism of the computer or if the handling method in your PC's BIOS is unknown. This problem has two workarounds:

- *Set the machine switch.* Add the /M:x (the machine type) switch to the HIMEM.SYS command line in your CONFIG.SYS file (where x is the machine number between one through 14 or 16). Shut down and then restart your computer. For example,

  ```
  DEVICE=C:\DOS\HIMEM.SYS /M:1
  ```

  NOTE: An incorrect A20 machine handler may hang the system at boot up. You should have an MS-DOS version 5.0 (or Windows 95/98) bootable floppy disk available to boot from before you experiment with different machine switches.

- *Check the BIOS version.* It may be necessary to upgrade your machine's BIOS or contact your system vendor for assistance in modifying your CMOS settings. You may need to disable a FastGate (or similar) option.

Symptom 5.89. You see a memory error such as Cannot set up EMS buffer or Unable to set page frame base address. This is a known problem with many Dell Inspiron 7000 computers under Windows 98 and appears when starting a DOS-based program that requires *Expanded Memory* (EMS) page frames. EMS page frames normally require 64 KB of upper memory, but Dell Inspiron 7000-series computers can only provide 54

KB of upper memory. This is an issue with the Dell system design and generally cannot be corrected unless you turn off the program's use of EMS page frames (or run the program on another system).

Symptom 5.90. Memory contents are corrupted (or the PC halts) when entering a CPU power-down state under Windows 98. If your system's power management settings are configured to enable the processor to enter a C3 power state on a computer supporting the *Advanced Configuration and Power Interface* (ACPI) standard, you may encounter symptoms such as corrupted memory after several minutes of inactivity, or the computer may stop responding after several minutes of inactivity. This problem is due to an issue with the Intel 440BX chipset under Windows 98 (caused by Windows 98) that may enable memory contents to be corrupted when a CPU enters or leaves its power-down state. If that motherboard uses the Intel PIIX4-E IDE controller chip set, the computer might hang (which is known to occur if a bus mastering operation occurs while in the power-down state). Until a patch is available for Windows 98, you can work around this issue by preventing the CPU from entering the C3 power state. To accomplish this, exit Windows and reboot the computer. Enter your CMOS Setup and set the `lvl3_latency` entry to a value greater than 0x3E8h (1000 decimal). If `lvl3_latency` is greater than 0x3E8h, the Windows 98 ACPI driver does not enter the C3 state. You'll need to save your changes and reboot the PC for those changes to take effect.

Symptom 5.91. Windows 98 appears unstable after disabling virtual memory (the swap file). Not enough RAM is in the system. This can occur if you disable virtual memory with only 16 MB of RAM. Windows 98 has higher memory requirements than Windows 95, so although 16 MB may be a theoretical minimum for Windows 98, 32 MB of RAM or more would result in better system performance and stability. To resolve this problem, install more RAM in your computer, enable virtual memory (or both).

Symptom 5.120. You encounter a Windows 98 protection error involving NTKERN. This problem occurs when installing Windows 98 and restarting for the first time. You may see an error message such as

```
While initializing device NTKERN: Windows
Protection Error. You need to restart your
computer.
```

or you may receive an error message after the Windows 98 Setup is completed such as

```
Invalid VxD Dynamic Link Call to Device 3 Service B
```

or

```
While Initialing Device <filename> Windows
Protection Error. You need to restart your
computer.
```

If you try to start in the Safe Mode, you may receive a message like

```
HIMEM.SYS Has Detected Unreliable XMS Memory at
<address>.
```

In virtually every case, there is defective memory (RAM) in your computer. You'll need to systematically remove or replace the SIMMs, DIMMs, or RIMMs in your computer to eliminate any bad memory.

Symptom 5.93. After installing Windows 98, the Device Manager may show a yellow exclamation mark next to the PC Card (PCMCIA) network adapter. You may also see a status message such as Error Code 10 in the adapter's Properties. This is known to occur on laptops such as the DEC HiNote Ultra II when the PC Card network adapter uses memory that the computer's BIOS has reserved. Windows 98 determines a free range of memory and then assigns that range to the network adapter for use, but the network adapter driver may not be able to use the assigned range if it is reserved by the BIOS. To get around this problem, try excluding the memory range that is being reserved by the BIOS so that Windows 98 will not use it:

1. Click Start, highlight Settings, and click Control Panel.

2. Double-click the System icon.

3. Double-click Computer on the Device Manager tab.

4. Click the Reserve Resources tab and then click Memory.

5. Click Add, type CA000 in the Start Value box, and then type CB000 in the End Value box.

6. Click OK and click OK again.

7. Click the PC Card network adapter to highlight it and then click Remove.

8. Click OK and then click Close.

9. Restart your computer. The network adapter will be redetected and reinstalled by Windows 98.

Symptom 5.94. You encounter random "fatal exception" errors under Windows 95/98. You may also notice that more fatal exception errors take place under Windows 95/98 than under Windows 3.1x. The most common cause for these error messages is faulty physical memory (RAM) on the computer, so make the following checks:

- *Check for drivers.* Try starting the system in Safe Mode. If the fatal exception errors disappear, the problem may be with one or more buggy or corrupted drivers loading in the normal mode. You may then need to systematically disable background software and drivers in order to isolate the offending software.

▪ *Check the CMOS Setup.* In some circumstances, it may be possible to adjust the CMOS settings (such as changing memory wait states or disabling the motherboard's L2 cache) to stabilize Windows 95/98 successfully.

▪ *Check/replace the RAM.* To resolve fatal exception errors, it is often necessary to isolate and replace the defective memory module(s). In rare cases, the problem may be on the motherboard.

Symptom 5.95. You find that you cannot use 256-MB DIMMs that contain 64-Mbit RAM components. You should double-check the manufacturer's recommendations for your motherboard and verify the type of DIMM sizes and technologies best suited to the particular motherboard. Some motherboard models (such as Intel's JN440BX motherboard) cannot use such sophisticated RAM components on a DIMM of that capacity. This can cause the motherboard to produce invalid timing signals and cause unpredictable system behavior. Try smaller DIMMs or use DIMMs with less dense memory components on board.

Beep Codes

When a fault is detected before the video system is initialized, errors are indicated with a series of beeps (or beep codes). Since each BIOS is a bit different, the accuracy, precision, and quality of error detection and reporting varies from BIOS to BIOS. Although most POST routines today follow a remarkably similar pattern, the reporting style can vary greatly. Some routines (such as AMI) generate a continuous string of beeps, while other routines (such as Phoenix) create short beep sequences. This part of the chapter is

intended to help you understand and interpret the
beep codes produced by major BIOS makers:

- AMI (American Megatrends): Table 5.6
- AST: Table 5.7
- Dell (PowerEdge): Table 5.8
- Compaq (AlphaServer): Table 5.9
- IBM Desktop (classic): Table 5.16
- IBM Desktop (Aptiva): Table 5.11
- IBM ThinkPad: Table 5.12
- Mylex: Table 5.13
- Mylex 386: Table 5.14
- Phoenix Technologies: Table 5.15
- Quadtel: Table 5.16

> **NOTE**: All other beep code sequences indicate a motherboard fault, so try replacing the motherboard.

TABLE 5.6   AMI Beep Codes

Beeps	Error Message
1s	*System RAM Refresh Failure.* The *programmable Interrupt timer* (PIT) or *programmable interrupt controller* (PIC) has probably failed. Replace the motherboard.
2s	*Memory Parity Error.* A parity error has been detected in the first 64 KB of RAM. The RAM IC is probably defective. Replace the memory or motherboard.
3s	*Base 64KB Memory Failure.* A memory failure has been detected in the first 64 KB of RAM. The RAM IC is probably defective. Replace the memory or motherboard.
4s	*System Timer Failure.* The system clock/timer IC has failed.
5s	*CPU Failure.* The system CPU has failed. Try replacing the CPU or motherboard.

TABLE 5.6   **AMI Beep Codes**

Beeps	Error Message
6s	*Gate A20 Failure.* The keyboard controller IC has failed, so Gate A20 is no longer available to switch the CPU into protected mode. Replace the keyboard controller or motherboard.
7s	*Exception Error.* The CPU has generated an exception error due to a fault in the CPU or some combination of motherboard conditions. Try replacing the motherboard.
8s	*Video Memory Read/Write Error.* The system video adapter is missing or defective. Try replacing the video adapter.
9s	*ROM Checksum Error.* The contents of the system BIOS ROM do not match the expected checksum value. The BIOS ROM is probably defective and should be replaced.
10s	*CMOS Shutdown Register Read/Write Error.* The shutdown register for the CMOS memory has failed. Try replacing the RTC/CMOS IC.
11s	*Cache Error/L2 Cache Bad.* The L2 cache is faulty. Replace the L2 cache or integrated L2 cache hardware device.
1l-3s	*Memory Test Failure.* A fault has been detected in memory over 64 KB. Replace the memory or the motherboard.
1l-8s	*Display Test Failure.* The display adapter is missing or defective. Replace the video adapter board. If the video adapter is on the motherboard, try replacing the motherboard.

Legend: *l* = long *s* = short

TABLE 5.7   **AST Beep Codes**

Beeps	Error Message
1s	*CPU Register Test Failure.* The CPU has failed. Try replacing the CPU or replace the motherboard.
2s	*Keyboard Controller Buffer Failure.* The keyboard controller IC has failed.
3s	*Keyboard Controller Reset Failure.* The keyboard controller IC or its associated circuitry has failed.

(continues)

TABLE 5.7 AST Beep Codes

Beeps	Error Message
4s	*Keyboard Communication Failure*. The keyboard controller IC or its associated circuitry has failed. Try replacing the keyboard assembly. Try replacing the motherboard.
5s	*Keyboard Input Port Failure*. The keyboard controller IC has failed.
6s	*System Board Chipset Initialization Failure*. The chipset(s) used on the motherboard cannot be initialized. Either an element of the chipset(s) or the motherboard has failed.
9s	*BIOS ROM Checksum Error*. The BIOS ROM has failed. Try replacing the BIOS ROM or replace the motherboard.
10s	*System Timer Test Failure*. The master system clock IC has failed.
11s	*ASIC Register Test Failure*. Motherboard circuitry has failed. Replace the motherboard.
12s	*CMOS RAM Shutdown Register Failure*. The RTC/CMOS IC has failed. Try replacing the RTC/CMOS IC or replace the motherboard.
1l	*DMA Controller 0 Failure*. The DMA controller IC for channel 0 has failed.
1l-1s	*DMA Controller 1 Failure*. The DMA controller IC for channel 1 has failed.
1l-2s	*Video Vertical Retrace Failure*. The video adapter has failed. Replace the video adapter board.
1l-3s	*Video Memory Test Failure*. A fault has occured in video memory. Replace the video adapter.
1l-4s	*Video Adapter Test Failure*. The video adapter has failed. Replace the video adapter board.
1l-5s	*64-KB Base Memory Failure*. A failure has occurred in the low 64 KB of system RAM. Replace memory or replace the motherboard.
1l-6s	*Unable to Load Interrupt Vectors*. BIOS was unable to load interrupt vectors into low memory. Replace the motherboard.
1l-7s	*Unable to Initialize Video System*. There is a defect in the video system. Replace the video adapter board. Replace the motherboard.
1l-8s	*Video Memory Failure*. There is a defect in video memory. Replace the video adapter or replace the motherboard.

TABLE 5.8 **Dell (PowerEdge 6350) Beep Codes**

Beeps	Error Message
1-1-3	*NVRAM write/read failure.* The CMOS RAM has probably failed. Replace the main board.
1-1-4	*BIOS checksum failure.* The BIOS chip has probably failed. Replace the main board.
1-2-1	*Programmable interval-timer failure.* Replace the main board.
1-2-2	*DMA initialization failure.* Replace the main board.
1-2-3	*DMA page register write/read failure.* Replace the main board.
1-3-1	*Main-memory refresh verification failure.* Remove and reseat the DIMMs. If the problem persists, replace the memory module(s).
1-3-2	*No memory installed.* Remove and reseat the DIMMs and reboot the system. If the problem persists, replace the memory module(s).
1-3-3	*Chip or data line failure in the first 64 KB of main memory.* Remove and reseat the DIMMs and reboot the system. If the problem persists, replace the memory module(s).
1-3-4	*Odd/even logic failure in the first 64 KB of main memory.* Remove and reseat the DIMMs and reboot the system. If the problem persists, replace the memory module(s).
1-4-1	*Address line failure in the first 64 KB of main memory.* Remove and reseat the DIMMs and reboot the system. If the problem persists, replace the memory module(s).
1-4-2	*Parity failure in the first 64 KB of main memory.* Remove and reseat the DIMMs and reboot the system. If the problem persists, replace the memory module(s).
2-1-1 to 2-4-4	*Bit failure in the first 64 KB of main memory.* Remove and reseat the DIMMs and reboot the system. If the problem persists, replace the memory module(s).
3-1-1	*Slave DMA-register failure.* Replace the main board.
3-1-2	*Master DMA-register failure.* Replace the main board.
3-1-3	*Master interrupt-mask register failure.* Replace the main board.
3-1-4	*Slave interrupt-mask register failure.* Replace the main board.
3-2-4	*Keyboard-controller test failure.* Check the keyboard cable and connector for proper connection. If the problem persists, replace the main board.
3-3-1	*CMOS RAM failure.* Replace CMOS/RTC chip or the main board.
3-3-2	*System configuration check failure.* Replace the main board.

(continues)

TABLE 5.8   Continued.

Beeps	Error Message
3-3-3	*Keyboard controller not detected.*
3-3-4	*Screen initialization failure.* Verify that the monitor cable is correctly connected. If the problem persists, replace the main board.
3-4-1	*Screen-retrace test failure.* Ensure that the monitor cable is correctly connected. If the problem persists, replace the main board.
3-4-2	*Video ROM detection failure.* Replace the main board or install another video card.
4-2-1	*No timer tick.* Replace the main board.
4-2-2	*Shutdown failure.* Replace the main board.
4-2-3	*Gate A20 failure.* Replace the main board.
4-2-4	*Unexpected interrupt in protected mode.* Verify that all expansion cards are properly seated and then reboot the system.
4-3-1	*Improperly seated or faulty DIMM, DIMMs not installed in sets of four, or a faulty or improperly seated memory module.* Be sure that the DIMMs are installed in sets of four and in the proper sockets for each memory bank in use. If this does not resolve the problem, remove and reseat the DIMMs. If the problem persists, replace the DIMMs or the memory module(s).
4-3-3	*Defective system board.* Replace the main board.
4-3-4	*Time-of-day clock stopped.* Replace the battery. If the problem persists, replace the main board.
4-4-1	*Faulty I/O chip or Super I/O controller failure.* The system board is defective, so replace the system board.
4-4-2	*Parallel-port test failure.* The system board is defective, so replace the system board.
4-4-3	*Math coprocessor failure.* This means a defective microprocessor, so replace the microprocessor.
4-4-4	*Cache test failure.* This means a defective microprocessor, so replace the microprocessor.

TABLE 5.9   Compaq (AlphaServer) Beep Codes

Beeps	Error Message
1	No error
1-3	VGA monitor not plugged in. Graphics option card different from the one shipped with the system
1-1-2	A ROM data path error was detected while loading SRM/AlphaBIOS console code.

TABLE 5.9   Continued.

Beeps	Error Message
1-1-4	The SROM code is unable to load the console code or a FROM header area or checksum error is detected.
1-1-7	No boot block on floppy device
1-2-1	TOY NVRAM failure
1-2-4	B-cache error
1-3-3	No usable memory detected
3-3-1	Generic system failure
3-3-3	Failure of onboard SCSI controller

TABLE 5.10   IBM Desktop Beep Codes (Classic)

Beeps	Error Message
1s	Start of test
2s	Initialization error
1l-1s	System board error
1l-2s	Video adapter error
1l-3s	EGA/VGA adapter error
3l	Keyboard adapter error
999s	Power supply error

TABLE 5.11   IBM Desktop Beep Codes (Aptiva 2173)

Beeps	Error Message
1-1-3	*CMOS read/write error.* The system may be configured improperly. Run the system setup routine.
1-1-4	*ROM BIOS checksum error.* Replace the main board.
1-2-X	*DMA controller error.* Replace the main board.
1-3-X	*Memory module error.* Check, reinstall, or replace the memory module(s) or replace the main board.
1-4-4	*Keyboard error.* Check the keyboard and its installation. Replace the keyboard or the main board.
1-4-X	*Error detected in first 64 KB of RAM.* One or more memory modules may have failed. Try reseating the memory module(s), replace the memory module(s) and then replace the main board.
2-1-1	*System board fault.* Run the system setup routine or replace the main board.
2-1-2	*System board fault.* Run the system setup routine or replace the main board.

(continues)

TABLE 5.11   Continued.

Beeps	Error Message
2-1-X	*Error detected in first 64 KB of RAM.* One or more memory modules may have failed. Try reseating the memory module(s), replace the memory module(s), and then replace the main board.
2-2-2	*Video adapter fault.* The onboard video system has failed. Install a stand-alone video card or replace the main board.
2-2-X	*Error detected in first 64 KB of RAM.* One or more memory modules may have failed. Try reseating the memory module(s), replace the memory module(s), and then replace the main board.
2-3-X	*Memory module error.* Check, reinstall, or replace the memory module(s) or replace the main board.
2-4-X	*Memory module error.* Check, reinstall, or replace the memory module(s) or replace the main board.
3-1-X	*DMA register failed.* Replace the main board.
3-2-4	*Keyboard controller chip failed.* Replace the main board.
3-3-4	*Screen initialization failed.* The video system has failed. Replace the video adapter or replace the main board if the video system is integrated into the main board.
3-4-1	*Screen retrace test error.* The video system has failed. Replace the video adapter or replace the main board if the video system is integrated into the main board.
3-4-2	*Cannot locate video ROM.* The video system has failed. Replace the video adapter or replace the main board if the video system is integrated into the main board.
4	*Video adapter fault.* The onboard video system has failed. Install a stand-alone video card or replace the main board.
1l-1s	*Base 640-KB memory error or shadow RAM error.* Replace the defective memory module(s) or replace the motherboard.
1l-2s	*Video adapter fault.* The onboard video system has failed. Install a stand-alone video card or replace the main board.
1l-3s	*Video adapter fault.* The onboard video system has failed. Install a stand-alone video card or replace the main board.
3s	*Memory failure.* Check, reinstall, or replace the memory module(s) or replace the main board.
	Continuous beep: System board failure. Replace the motherboard.
	Repeating beeps: Stuck key on the keyboard, keyboard cable detached or damaged, or main board failure. Clean or replace the keyboard, or replace the motherboard.

TABLE 5.12   IBM ThinkPad Beep Codes

Beeps/Error	Error Message
Continuous beeps	System board failure
One beep and a blank, unreadable, or flashing LCD	LCD connector problem LCD backlight inverter problem Video adapter problem LCD assembly failure System board failure Power supply (DC/DC) failure
One beep and an `Unable to access boot source` message	Boot device (drive) failure System board failure
One long and two short beeps, and a blank or unreadable LCD	System board failure Video adapter problem LCD assembly failure
One long beep followed by four short beeps each time the power switch is operated	Low battery voltage. Connect the AC adapter or install a fully charged laptop battery
One beep every second. (System is shutting down due to low battery voltage.)	Low battery voltage. Connect the AC adapter or install a fully charged battery. (Allow the system to completely shut down before changing the battery.)
Two short beeps with error codes Two short beeps with blank screen.	POST error (refer to Table 19.1 for error code explanations) System board failure

TABLE 5.13   Mylex Beep Codes

Beeps	Error Message
1	Start of test
2	Video adapter error
3	Keyboard controller error
4	Keyboard error
5	PIC 0 error

(continues)

TABLE 5.13 Continued.

Beeps	Error Message
6	PIC 1 error
7	DMA page register error
8	RAM refresh error
9	RAM data error
10	RAM parity error
11	DMA controller 0 error
12	CMOS RAM error
13	DMA controller 1 error
14	CMOS RAM battery error
15	CMOS RAM checksum error
16	BIOS ROM checksum error

TABLE 5.14 Mylex 386 Beep Codes

Beeps	Error Message
1l	Start of test
2l	Video adapter fault (or adapter missing)
1l-1s-1l	Keyboard controller error
1l-2s-1l	Keyboard error
1l-3s-1l	PIC 0 error
1l-4s-1l	PIC 1 error
1l-5s-1l	DMA page register error
1l-6s-1l	RAM refresh error
1l-7s-1l	RAM data test error
1l-8s-1l	RAM parity error
1l-9s-1l	DMA controller 1 error
1l-10s-1l	CMOS RAM failure
1l-11s-1l	DMA controller 2 error
1l-12s-1l	CMOS RAM battery failure
1l-13s-1l	CMOS checksum failure
1l-14s-1l	BIOS ROM checksum failure
>1l	Multiple faults detected

TABLE 5.15 Phoenix Beep Codes for ISA/MCA/EISA POST

Beeps	Error Message
1-1-2	*CPU Register Test Failure*. The CPU has likely failed. Replace the CPU.
Low 1-1-2	*System Board Select Failure*. The motherboard is suffering from an undetermined fault. Try replacing the motherboard.

TABLE 5.15 **Continued.**

Beeps	Error Message
1-1-3	*CMOS Read/Write Failure.* The RTC/CMOS IC has probably failed. Try replacing the RTC/CMOS IC.
Low 1-1-3	*Extended CMOS RAM Failure.* The extended portion of the RTC/CMOS IC has failed. Try replacing the RTC/CMOS IC.
1-1-4	*BIOS ROM Checksum Error.* The BIOS ROM has probably failed.
1-2-1	*Programmable Interval Timer (PIT) Failure.* The PIT has probably failed.
1-2-2	*DMA Initialization Failure.* The DMA controller has probably failed.
1-2-3	*DMA Page Register Read/Write Failure.* The DMA controller has probably failed.
1-3-1	*RAM Refresh Failure.* The refresh controller has failed.
1-3-2	*64KB RAM Test Disabled.* The test of the first 64 KB of system RAM could not begin. Try replacing the motherboard.
1-3-3	*First 64KB RAM IC or Data Line Failure.* The first RAM IC has failed.
1-3-	*First 64KB Odd/Even Logic Failure.* The first RAM control logic has failed.
1-4-1	*Address Line Failure 64KB of RAM*
1-4-2	*Parity Failure First 64KB of RAM.* The first RAM IC has failed.
1-4-3	*EISA Failsafe Timer Test Fault.* Replace the motherboard.
1-4-4	*EISA NMI Port 462 Test Failure.* Replace the motherboard.
2-1-1	*Bit 0 First 64KB RAM Failure.* This data bit in the first RAM IC has failed.
2-1-2	*Bit 1 First 64KB RAM Failure*
2-1-3	*Bit 2 First 64KB RAM Failure*
2-1-4	*Bit 3 First 64KB RAM Failure*
2-2-1	*Bit 4 First 64KB RAM Failure*
2-2-2	*Bit 5 First 64KB RAM Failure*
2-2-3	*Bit 6 First 64KB RAM Failure*
2-2-4	*Bit 7 First 64KB RAM Failure*
2-3-1	*Bit 8 First 64KB RAM Failure*
2-3-2	*Bit 9 First 64KB RAM Failure*
2-3-3	*Bit 10 First 64KB RAM Failure*
2-3-4	*Bit 11 First 64KB RAM Failure*
2-4-1	*Bit 12 First 64KB RAM Failure*

(continues)

TABLE 5.15   Continued.

Beeps	Error Message
2-4-2	*Bit 13 First 64KB RAM Failure*
2-4-3	*Bit 14 First 64KB RAM Failure*
2-4-4	*Bit 15 First 64KB RAM Failure*
3-1-1	*Slave DMA Register Failure.* The DMA controller has probably failed.
3-1-2	*Master DMA Register Failure.* The DMA controller has probably failed.
3-1-3	*Master Interrupt Mask Register Failure.* The interrupt controller has probably failed.
3-1-4	*Slave Interrupt Mask Register Failure.* The interrupt controller has probably failed.
3-2-2	*Interrupt Vector Loading Error.* BIOS is unable to load the interrupt vectors into low RAM. Replace the motherboard.
3-2-3	. . . reserved . . .
3-2-4	*Keyboard Controller Test Failure.* The keyboard controller has failed.
3-3-1	*CMOS RAM Power Bad.* Try replacing the CMOS backup battery or RTC/CMOS IC. Also replace the motherboard.
3-3-2	*CMOS Configuration Error.* The CMOS configuration has failed. Restore the configuration. Replace the CMOS backup battery, the RTC/CMOS IC, and the motherboard.
3-3-3	. . . reserved . . .
3-3-4	*Video Memory Test Failed.* There is a problem with the video memory. Replace video memory or the video adapter board.
3-4-1	*Video Initialization Test Failure.* There is a problem with the video system. Replace the video adapter.
4-2-1	*Timer Tick Failure.* The system timer IC has failed.
4-2-2	*Shutdown Test Failure.* The CMOS IC has failed.
4-2-3	*Gate A20 Failure.* The keyboard controller has probably failed.
4-2-4	*Unexpected Interrupt in Protected Mode.* There is a problem with the CPU.
4-3-1	*RAM Test Address Failure.* System RAM addressing circuitry has failed.
4-3-3	*Interval Timer Channel 2 Failure.* The system timer IC has probably failed.
4-3-4	*Time of Day Clock Failure.* The RTC/CMOS IC has failed.

TABLE 5.15   Continued.

Beeps	Error Message
4-4-1	*Serial Port Test Failure.* A fault has developed in the serial port circuit.
4-4-2	*Parallel Port Test Failure.* A fault has developed in the parallel port circuit.
4-4-3	*Math Co-processor Failure.* Try replacing the math coprocessor.

TABLE 5.16   Quadtel Beep Codes

Beeps	Error Message
1s	Start of test
2s	CMOS IC error
1l-2s	Video controller error
1l>2s	Peripheral controller error

Video and Sound Troubleshooting

Video and sound are certainly two of the most exciting aspects of the PC. New video systems promise outstanding 2D and 3D performance at resolutions and color depths that simply were not practical just a few years ago. Enhanced video systems even provide support for features like video conferencing and MPEG video playback. Todays sound cards offer symphonic sound and MIDI wave table synthesis. Taken together, video and sound supply the backbone of a computer's multimedia capabilities. Still, the advances in video and sound have not come without a price, namely compatibility issues and the demand for computing power. This section looks at some background information and troubleshooting procedures for video and sound devices.

Video Display Hardware

The early days of PC development left users with a simple choice between monochrome or color graphics (all video adapters support text modes). In the years that followed, however, the proliferation of video adapters have brought an array of video modes and standards that you should be familiar with before upgrading a PC or attempting to troubleshoot a video system. This part of the chapter explains each of the video standards that have been developed in the last 20 years and shows you the video modes that each standard offers. Table 6.1 provides a comprehensive listing of the standard hardware and software-supported video modes for a 3Dfx Voodoo3 video accelerator.

TABLE 6.1 Index of Video Modes

Resolution	Number of Colors	Vertical Frequency (Hz)
320 × 200	256, 65K	70, 85
320 × 240	256, 65K	60, 70, 75, 85
400 × 300	256, 65K	60, 70, 75, 85
512 × 384	256, 65K	60, 70, 75, 85
640 × 200	16	70
640 × 350	16	70
640 × 400	256, 65K, 16.7M	70, 85
640 × 480	256, 65K, 16.7M	60, 72, 75, 85, 100, 120, 140, 160
720 × 480	256, 65K, 16.7M	60, 72, 85
720 × 576	256, 65K, 16.7M	72, 100
800 × 600	256, 65K, 16.7M	60, 72, 75, 85, 100, 120, 140, 160
920 × 760	256, 65K	60, 75, 85
1024 × 768	256, 65K, 16.7M	60, 70, 75, 85, 100, 120
1152 × 864	256, 65K, 16.7M	60, 70, 75, 85, 100, 120
1280 × 960	256, 65K	60, 75, 85
1280 × 1024	256, 65K, 16.7M	60, 70, 75, 85, 100
1600 × 024	256, 65K, 16.7M	60, 76, 85
1600 × 1200	256, 65K, 16.7M	60, 65, 70, 75, 80, 85, 100
1792 × 1344	256, 65K, 16.7M	60, 75
1856 × 1392	256, 65K, 16.7M	60, 75
1920 × 1080	256, 65K, 16.7M	60, 72, 75, 85
1920 × 1200	256, 65K, 16.7M	60, 76, 85
1920 × 1440	256, 65K, 16.7M	60, 75, 85
2046 × 1536	256, 65K, 16.7M	60, 75

NOTE: All of the display modes shown are not necessarily supported by all monitors or software. Check the capabilities of your monitor and the requirements of your software before choosing a given display mode or refresh rate.

Monochrome Display Adapter (MDA), 1981

The *Monochrome Display Adapter* (MDA) is the oldest conventional video adapter available for the PC. Text is available in an 80-column by 25-row format using 9 × 14-pixel characters. Being a text-only system, MDA offered no graphics capabilities, but it achieved popularity because of its relatively low cost, good text display quality, and an integrated printer (LPT) port. The nine-pin monitor connection uses four active *Time-to-Live* (TTL) signals: intensity, video, horizontal, and vertical. The video and intensity signals provide the on/off and high/low-intensity information for each pixel. The horizontal and vertical signals control the monitor's synchronization. MDA boards have long been obsolete and the probability of encountering one is remote at best.

Color Graphics Adapter (CGA), 1981

The *Color Graphics Adapter* (CGA) was the first to offer color text and graphics modes for the PC. A 160 × 200 low-resolution mode offered 16 colors, but such low resolution received very little attention. A 320 × 200 medium-resolution graphics mode allowed finer graphic detail, but with only four colors. The highest resolution mode provides 640 × 200 at two colors (usually black and one other color). The relationship between resolution and colors is important since a CGA *frame* requires 16 KB of video RAM. 640 × 200 resolution results in 128,000 pixels. With eight bits capable of representing eight pixels, (128,000/8) 16,000 bytes are adequate. 320 × 200 resolution results in 64,000 pixels, but with two bits needed to represent one pixel (four pixels/byte), (64,000/4) 16,000 bytes are still enough. You can see that video RAM is directly related to video capacity. Since typically much more video RAM is available than is needed for an image, video boards support multiple video pages. As with the earlier MDA design, CGA video signals reserve pins 1 and 2 as ground lines, while the horizontal sync signal is produced on pin 8 and the vertical sync signal is produced on pin 9. CGA is strictly a digital display system with TTL signals used on the Red (3), Green (4), Blue (5), and Intensity (6) lines.

Enhanced Graphics Adapter (EGA), 1984

It was not long before the limitations of CGA became painfully apparent. The demand for higher resolutions and color depths drove designers to introduce the next generation of video adapters known as the *Enhanced Graphics Adapter* (EGA). One of the unique appeals of EGA was its backward compatibility; an EGA board would emulate CGA and MDA modes on the proper monitor as well as its native resolutions and color depths when using an EGA monitor. EGA is known for its $320 \times 200 \times 16$, $640 \times 200 \times 16$, and $640 \times 350 \times 16$ video modes. More memory is needed for EGA and 128 KB is common for EGA boards (although many boards could be expanded to 256 KB).

TTL signals are used to provide Primary Red (3), Primary Green (4), and Primary Blue (5) color signals. By adding a set of secondary color signals (or color intensity signals) such as Red Intensity (2), Green Intensity (6), and Blue Intensity (7), the total of six color control signals enables the EGA to produce up to 64 possible colors. Although 64 colors are possible, only 16 of those colors are available in the palette at any one time. Pin 8 carries the horizontal sync signal, pin 9 carries the vertical sync signal, and pin 1 remains ground.

Professional Graphics Adapter (PGA), 1984

The *Professional Graphics Adapter* (PGA) was also introduced in 1984. This system offered a then-revolutionary display capability of $640 \times 480 \times 256$. Three-dimensional rotation and graphic clipping was included as a hardware function, and the adapter could update the display at 60 frames per second. The PGA was incredibly expensive and beyond the reach of all but the most serious business user. In actual operation, a PGA system required two or three expansion boards, so it also represented a serious commitment of limited system space. Ultimately, the PGA failed to capture any significant market acceptance. It is unlikely that you will ever encounter a PGA board. Most that ever saw service in PCs have long since been upgraded.

Multi-Color Graphics Array (MCGA), 1987

The *Multi-Color Graphics Array* (MCGA) was originally integrated into the motherboard of IBM's PS/2-25 and PS/2-30. MCGA supported all the CGA video modes and also offered several new video modes including a $320 \times 200 \times 256$ mode that was a preferred mode for game software of the day. MCGA was one of the first graphic systems to use analog color signals rather than TTL signals. Analog signals were necessary to enable MCGA to produce its 256 colors using only three primary color lines (red, green, and blue, or RGB).

IBM also took the opportunity to employ a new, high-density 15-pin sub-miniature "D-type" connector, as shown in Figure 6.1. One of the striking differences

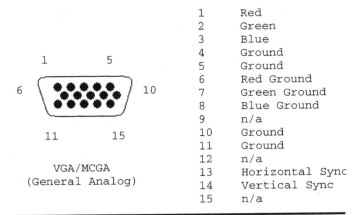

1	Red
2	Green
3	Blue
4	Ground
5	Ground
6	Red Ground
7	Green Ground
8	Blue Ground
9	n/a
10	Ground
11	Ground
12	n/a
13	Horizontal Sync
14	Vertical Sync
15	n/a

VGA/MCGA
(General Analog)

Figure 2.1 The index of video modes

between the analog connector and older TTL connectors is the use of individual ground lines for each color. Careful grounding is vital since any signal noise on the analog lines will result in color anomalies. If you inspect a video cable closely, you will find that one or both ends are terminated with a square metal box that actually contains a noise filter. It is important to realize that although the MCGA could *emulate* CGA modes, older TTL monitors were no longer compatible with analog RGB signal levels.

Although a number of notable technical improvements went into the PS/2 design, none of them could assure broad acceptance of the PS/2 series. However, the MCGA ushered in a new age of analog display technology, and virtually all subsequent video adapters now use the 15-pin analog format shown in Figure 6.1. Although MCGA adapters are also (technically) obsolete, the standard lives on in MCGA's cousins, VGA and SVGA.

Video Graphics Array (VGA), 1987

The *Video Graphics Array* (VGA) was introduced along with MCGA and implemented in other members of IBM's PS/2 series. The line between MCGA and VGA has always been a bit fuzzy since both were introduced simultaneously (both using the same 15-pin video connector), and VGA can handle every mode that MCGA could. For all practical purposes, we can say that MCGA is a subset of VGA.

It is VGA that provides the familiar $640 \times 480 \times 16$ display mode, which has become the baseline for Microsoft Windows 95/98 SafeMode displays. The use of analog color signals enables VGA systems to produce a palette of 16 colors from 262,144 possible colors. VGA also provides backward compatibility for all older screen modes. Although the PS/2 line has been discontinued, the flexibility and backward compatibility of VGA proved so successful that VGA adapters were soon developed for the PC. For a time, VGA support was considered to be standard equipment for all new PCs sold then, but SVGA boards have rapidly replaced VGA systems, and most SVGA adapters offer full VGA support.

8514, 1987

The 8514/A video adapter is a high-resolution system also developed for the PS/2. In addition to full support for MDA, CGA, EGA, and VGA modes, the 8514/A can display 256 colors at 640 × 480 and 1024 × 768 (interlaced) resolutions. Unfortunately, the 8514/A was a standard ahead of its time. The lack of available software and the demise of the PS/2 line doomed the 8514/A to extinction before it could become an accepted standard. The XGA standard rapidly became the PC standard for high-resolution/high-color display systems on MicroChannel PC platforms.

Super Video Graphics Array (SVGA)

Ever since VGA became the de facto standard for PC graphics, a strong demand from PC users has arisen to move beyond the 640 × 480 × 16 limit imposed by conventional VGA to provide higher resolutions and color depths. As a result, new generations of extended or *Super VGA* (SVGA) adapters have moved relentlessly into the PC market. Unlike VGA, which adhered to strict hardware configurations, no generally accepted standard exists on which to develop an SVGA board. Each manufacturer makes an SVGA board that supports a variety of different, and not necessarily compatible, video modes. For example, one manufacturer may produce an SVGA board capable of 1024 × 768 × 65K, while another manufacturer may produce a board that only reaches 640 × 480 × 16M (more than 16 million colors).

This mixing and matching of resolutions and color depths has resulted in a very competitive (but very fractured) market. No two SVGA boards are necessarily capable of the same things. This proliferation of video hardware also makes it impossible for application software to take advantage of *super* video modes without supplemental software called video drivers. Video drivers are device drivers (loaded before an application program is started) that enable the particular program to work with the SVGA board hardware. Video drivers are typically developed by the board manufacturer and are shipped on a floppy disk with the board. Windows 95/98 takes particular advantage of video drivers since the Windows interface enables all Windows applications to use the same graphics system, rather than having to write a driver for every application as DOS drivers must do. Using an incorrect, obsolete, or corrupted video driver can be a serious source of performance and stability problems for SVGA installations. The one common attribute of SVGA boards is that most offer full support for conventional VGA (which requires no video drivers), so Windows can always be started safely in the conventional 640 × 480 × 16 VGA mode. Only a handful of SVGA board manufacturers abandon conventional VGA support.

XGA, 1990

The XGA and XGA/2 are 32-bit, high-performance video adapters developed by IBM to support MicroChannel-based PCs. The XGA design with MicroChannel architecture enables the adapter to take control of the system for rapid data transfers. MDA, CGA, EGA, and VGA modes are all supported for backward compatibility. In addition, several color depths are available at 1024 × 768 resolution, and a photorealistic 65,536 colors are available at 640 × 480 resolution. To improve performance even further, fast video RAM and a graphics coprocessor are added to the XGA design. XGA is generally limited to high-performance applications in

MicroChannel systems. The migration to ISA-based PCs has been slow because the ISA bus is limited to 16 bits and does not support bus mastering as Micro-Channel buses do. For PCs, SVGA adapters using the high-performance PCI (and now the AGP) bus will likely provide extended screen modes as they continue to grow in sophistication as graphics accelerators.

Graphics Accelerators

Video designers seek to overcome the limitations of conventional video adapters by incorporating process-ing power onto the video board itself rather than rely-ing on the system *Central Processing Unit* (CPU) for graphic processing. By off-loading work from the sys-tem CPU and assigning the graphics processing to local processing components, graphics performance can be improved by a factor of three or more. Several means of acceleration exist depending on the sophisti-cation of the board. Fixed-function acceleration relieves the system CPU's load by providing adapter support for a limited number of specific functions such as BitBlt or line draws. Fixed-function accelerators are an improvement over frame buffers but do not offer the performance of more sophisticated accelerators. A graphics accelerator uses an application-specific chip or an *application-specific integrated circuit* (ASIC) that intercepts graphics tasks and processes them without the intervention of the system CPU. Graphics accelera-tors are perhaps the most cost-effective type of acceler-ator. Graphics coprocessors are the most sophisticated type of accelerator. The coprocessor acts as a CPU that is dedicated to handling image data. Older graphics coprocessors such as the TMS34010 and TMS34020 represent the *Texas Instruments Graphical Architecture* (TIGA), which is broadly used for high-end accelera-tors. Unfortunately, not all graphics coprocessors pro-vide increased performance to warrant the higher cost.

The core of a graphics accelerator is the graphics chip (or video chipset). The graphics chip connects directly with the PC expansion bus. Graphics commands and data are translated into pixel data that is stored in video RAM. High-performance video memory offers a second data bus that is routed directly to the video board's *Random Access Memory Video-to-Analog Converter* (RAMDAC). The graphics chip directs RAMDAC operations and ensures that *video RAM* (VRAM) data is available. The RAMDAC then translates video data into red, green, and blue analog signals along with horizontal and vertical synchronization signals. Output signals generated by the RAMDAC drive the monitor. This architecture may appear simple, but that is due to the extremely high level of integration provided by the chipsets being used.

Video Speed Factors

No one element defines the performance of a graphics accelerator board. Overall performance is actually a combination of five major factors: the video accelerator chips (the chipset), the video RAM, the video BIOS/drivers, the RAMDAC, and the expansion bus architecture. By understanding how each of these factors relate to performance, you can make the best recommendations for system upgrades or replacement boards.

Video Accelerator.   Of course, the video accelerator chip itself (usually the graphics chipset being used) is at the core of an accelerator board. The type of chip (fixed-function, graphics accelerator, or graphics coprocessor) loosely defines the board's capabilities. All other factors being equal, a board with a graphics accelerator will certainly perform better than a fixed-function accelerator. Companies like 3dfx, ATI, Advance Logic, Chips & Technologies, Matrox, Nvidia, S3, and Oak have developed many of the video accelerator chips in use today. Many of the chips provide a 32-bit data bus (though even newer designs are providing a 64-bit or 128-bit data bus), and they sustain very high data rates, but a data bottleneck across a 16-bit (ISA) expansion bus can seriously degrade the chip's effectiveness. This means you should match the recommended board to the particular system. A state-of-the-art graphics accelerator will not necessarily make your old i286 shine.

Video RAM.   Video adapters rely on RAM to hold image data, and video accelerator boards are no exception. Although the current amount of video RAM typically varies from 16 MB to 32 MB (some late-mode video adapters offer as much as 64 MB), the amount of RAM is not so important to a video accelerator as the RAM's speed. Faster memory can read and write image data faster, so adapter performance is improved. The introduction of specialized VRAM, memory devices with two separate data busses which can be read from and written to simultaneously, is reputed to be superior to conventional *dynamic RAM* (DRAM) or EDO RAM, such as the kind used for ordinary PC memory. Recent advances in DRAM speed have narrowed that gap while still remaining very economical.

At this point, adapters with *Extended Data Output* (EDO) RAM or *Synchronous DRAM* (SDRAM) are just about as fast as adapters with specialized video RAM for video modes up to $1024 \times 768 \times 256$. For higher modes and color depths found on high-end accelerators, specialized video RAM is still the way to go for optimum performance. *Double Data Rate SDRAM* (DDR-SDRAM) memory looks promising for both system and graphics memory. It effectively doubles its speed by using both edges of each clock cycle. Keep in mind that graphics board manufacturers are using the doubled rate in their specifications and advertising. AGP video boards are also being produced in different versions and prices depending on the type and speed of the memory provided on each adapter, and AGP video adapters can also access system RAM for certain video data storage.

Video BIOS and Drivers. Software is often considered as an afterthought in adapter design, yet it plays a surprisingly important role in accelerator performance. Even the finest accelerator board hardware can bog down when run under careless, loosely written code. You must be concerned with two classes of software: video BIOS and video drivers. The video BIOS is firmware (software that is permanently recorded on a memory device such as a ROM). Video BIOS holds the programming that enables the accelerator to interact with DOS applications software. Current adapters have flash upgradeable BIOS ROMs that enable the video adapter's firmware to be updated without removing the video adapter from the PC. VESA BIOS extensions are now being used almost universally as part of the video BIOS for many accelerators as well as conventional frame-buffer adapters. By adding VESA BIOS extensions to video BIOS, it eliminates the need to load another device driver under DOS.

However, video drivers have compelling advantages. Windows 95/98 works quite well with drivers (and generally ignores video BIOS entirely). Unlike BIOS ROMs that can be troublesome to upgrade, a video driver can change very quickly as bugs are corrected, enhancements are made, and performance is streamlined. The driver can be downloaded from a manufacturer's Web site on the Internet (or from another online information service such as AOL) and installed on your system in a matter of minutes without ever having to disassemble the PC. It is also possible for you to use third-party video drivers. Hardware manufacturers are not always adept at writing efficient software, and a third-party driver developed by an organization that specializes in software may actually let your accelerator perform better than the original driver shipped from the manufacturer.

NOTE: Reference drivers are often available from the video chipset maker's Web site. Video board manufacturers typically customize these drivers for their specific product. Customized reference drivers often include performance improvements but can be unstable because they have not been tested on or written for specific video cards.

The RAMDAC. Just about every analog video system in service today is modeled after the 15-pin VGA scheme that uses three separate analog signals to represent the three primary colors. The color for each pixel must be broken down into component red, green, and blue levels, and those levels must be converted into analog equivalents. The conversion from digital values to analog levels is handled by a *digital-to-analog converter* (DAC). Each conversion also requires a certain amount of time. Faster DACs are needed to support faster horizontal refresh rates. Current video boards incorporate RAMDAC rated at up to 350 MHz, which can support very high resolutions at reasonably high refresh rates. Remember that each video adapter uses a palette that is a subset of the colors that can possibly be produced. Even though a monitor may be able to produce "unlimited" colors, a VGA board can only produce 256 of these colors in any 256-color mode. Older video boards store the palette entries in registers, but the large-palette video modes now available (64K colors through 16 million colors) require the use of RAM. Boards that incorporate a RAMDAC are preferred since memory integrated with DACs tends to be much faster than accessing discrete RAM elsewhere on the board. Keep in mind that the RAM on a RAMDAC is used for holding palette information, not for the actual image.

The Expansion Bus Architectures. Finally, graphic data must be transferred between the PC motherboard and the adapter, as you saw early in this section. Such a transfer takes place across the PC's expansion bus. If data can be transferred between the PC and the adapter at a faster rate, video performance should improve. Consequently, the choice of bus architecture has a significant impact on video performance. Video accelerators are available to support three popular bus architectures: the *Industry Standard Architecture* (ISA), the *Peripheral Component Interconnect* (PCI), and the *Accelerated Graphics Port* (AGP).

ISA. The venerable ISA has remained virtually unchanged since its introduction with the PC/AT in the early 1980s. The ISA continues to be a mature interface standard for most IBM-compatible expansion devices. The sheer volume of ISA systems currently in service guarantees to keep the ISA on desktops for at least another 10 years. However, ISA's 16-bit data bus width, its lack of advanced features such as interrupt sharing or bus mastering, and its relatively slow 8.33-MHz operating speed form a serious bottleneck to the incredible volume of video data demanded by Windows 95/98 and most graphics-intensive DOS applications. ISA works, but it is no longer the interface of choice to achieve optimum video performance. When recommending an accelerator product, look to the newer buses for best results.

PCI. Intel's PCI bus was one of the newest and most exciting bus architectures to reach the PC. The PCI bus runs at a fixed frequency of 30 or 33 MHz and offers a full 64-bit data bus that can take advantage of new 64-bit CPUs such as Intel's Pentium (though most implementations of the PCI bus are designed for a 32-bit implementation). The PCI bus overcomes the speed and functional limitations of ISA, and the PCI architecture is intended to support all types of PC peripherals (not just video boards). Current PCI video boards now clearly outperform ISA- and VL bus-type video adapters.

AGP. Intel developed and introduced an advanced local bus architecture called AGP, a close cousin of PCI intended to meet the increasing demands for speed and bandwidth needed to support real-time 3D graphics. AGP is a dedicated high-speed bus that directly connects the chipset and the graphics controller. This creates a data channel specifically for graphics (unlike the PCI bus that must share bandwidth and system resources among the various PCI peripherals that are installed in any given system). The introduction of AGP removes data-hungry 3D and video data transfers from the PCI bus. PCI device performance can also benefit since video data transfers are no longer required. The system BIOS, chipset, and operating system (OS) must all support AGP to take advantage of AGP's performance capabilities. The only OSs that fully support AGP at this time are Windows 98 and Windows 2000. Windows 95 OSR 2.1 has limited AGP support, but any AGP performance benefit will be limited. DirectDraw (part of DirectX) is constantly being updated because it is responsible for controlling AGP's use of main system memory.

Although PCI specifications limit data transfer rates to a bandwidth of 132 MB/sec, the 32-bit 66-MHz AGP bus has a base bandwidth of 264 MB/sec. The AGP 2X specification supports a bandwidth of 533 MB/sec by transferring data on both the rising and falling edges of the 66-MHz clock (double-clocking) and also implements more efficient data transfer modes. The timing of data transfers is controlled by strobe signals rather than the standard method of clock cycles. Strobe signals are generated by the device sending the data (either the PC or the AGP board). Generating both the data and the strobe signals enables the sending device to precisely control the timing. Separating the data transfer timing from the bus clock also enables Intel to create an AGP 4X specification. By increasing the number of strobe signals from three to six, Intel defined a virtual clock speed of 264 MHz (4 X 66), and this improvement again doubles the potential bandwidth of the AGP connection to 1.06 GB/sec.

A significant AGP feature is its capability to access system memory directly during rendering. In this situation, system memory is referred to as *Non-Local Memory* (NLM). The OS can reserve portions of the system's main memory for use by the graphics controller. Two methods exist for using NLM supported by Intel's AGP specifications, and both require sup-port from the OS through an API (such as DirectDraw) to utilize NLM for texture map storage and some z-buffering. Z-buffering is the process of sorting 3D verticees to determine which are seen and which are hidden in any given space. The first method is through *Direct Memory Access* (DMA). The DMA mode only utilizes NLM for mass storage of information like texture data. This enables the graphic controller to keep fewer texture maps in local memory (on the video board) and is mainly a specification intended to reduce system cost. NLM can be used for texture maps, thus allowing applications (such as games) to use larger maps. This improves game realism and image quality without sacrificing performance or requiring more expensive local memory. *Direct Memory Execute* (DiME) is the second mode used by AGP adapters to utilize NLM. In this mode, often referred to as Execute mode, 3D functions are actually performed in NLM and the end result is then transferred to the graphics adapter for display. DiME can actually impair performance if the graphics adapter's resources are superior to the host system's components.

AGP has 32 multiplexed address and data lines. Eight additional lines are used for sideband addressing. These extra sideband address lines enable the graphics controller to issue new address and command data for read/write requests simultaneously while data continues to move from previous requests on the main 32 data/address lines. An additional AGP feature is known as Fast Write. The Fast Write feature enables the CPU to write directly to the graphics card's frame buffer without going through system memory. Fast Write is reported to be up to 30 percent faster than standard AGP 4X, and 2D as well as 3D applications are supposed to benefit from AGP 4X Fast Write. Fast Write also requires chipset support, which currently means an Intel i820 chipset or newer, but ALi and VIA should soon introduce chipsets with Fast Write support.

> **NOTE**:   Intel designed the AGP specifications for its Pentium Pro and newer CPUs, so they do not produce any chipsets to support both AGP and Socket 7 processors such as the AMD or Cyrix CPUs. If you want to take advantage of AGP performance using a Socket 7 processor, you will need to use a Super 7 motherboard with an AGP-compliant chipset from ALi or VIA.

3D Graphics Accelerators

Technically speaking, a 3D graphic is the graphical representation of a scene or object along three axes of reference (height, width, and depth) to make the scene look more realistic. This technique tricks the PC user into seeing a 3D image on a flat (2D) screen. There has been an astonishing rise in the demand for 3D video from all parts of the PC industry. 3D rendering has proven to be the technique of choice for many types of high-end games, business presentations, computer-aided designs, and multimedia applications. However, the use of 3D demands more of a PC than simply passing huge volumes of data across an expansion bus. 3D rendering requires complex mathematical calculations, determinations of coloring, the inclusion of special effects, and conversion of the rendered scene to a 2D plane (the display). In many cases, all this must be accomplished in real-time (15+ frames per second). Today most video systems are upgraded for the express purpose of supporting 3D animation (usually in 3D computer games such as Quake III).

Key 3D Speed Issues

Higher frame rates create realism and true-to-life atmospheres in 3D games. Speed is the main factor in providing faster frame rates. If the frame rate of a game is too slow, the game becomes unplayable because the time needed to react to an action in the game will be far too long. Consider playing a flight simulator if the display was only updated once or twice per second. Frame rate is largely dependent on the speed of a graphics accelerator. The speed of a 3D graphics engine is typically rated in terms of millions of texels (textured pixels) per second or Mtexels/sec. It is also frequently rated in polygons (or triangles) per second. Current 3D graphics accelerators can provide several million texels per second. For example, the 3Dfx Voodoo3 AGP card can render seven million triangles per second.

The speed of a 3D application is dependent on many tasks, but the most daunting tasks are 3D geometry and rendering. Geometry is the suite of calculations used to determine an object's position and color on the screen. Rendering (as you saw previously) is the actual drawing of the object onscreen. A typical graphics accelerator takes the load off of the CPU so that the CPU can devote more processing power to other functions. More advanced CPUs (such as the Pentium MMX, Pentium II, or Pentium III with SME technology) incorporate additional instructions that aid many of the calculation-intensive work needed in 3D environments. Three features that most often affect 3D speed are bus mastering, resolution, and color depth.

Bus Mastering. With a bus mastering graphics accelerator, a 3D graphics engine will never incur latency (or delays) during the rendering process. This happens because once the CPU has prepared all the triangles for rendering, the bus master will come and fetch the list of triangles asynchronously without requiring the CPU to wait. Bus mastering has two different implementations: the basic bus master and the scatter gather bus master. A basic bus master is capable of operating independently from the host CPU for short periods of time before it interrupts the host to ask for direction. During data-intensive operations like 3D, this minimizes the advantages of bus mastering. By contrast, a scatter-gather bus master can operate almost independently from the host CPU, achieving serious performance benefits. Bus mastering is eliminated if graphics are implemented through AGP since AGP is essentially a point-to-point connection between the graphics adapter and core logic, and the graphics adapter is always considered to be the master device.

Resolution. Because of limitations in OSs and graphics accelerators, most games and multimedia applications have been developed for low resolutions (such as 320 × 200) to achieve high performance. Increasing the resolution means displaying more pixels on the screen with every frame, which places more demand on the monitor and graphics board. Some applications developed in 320 × 200 can be played at 640 × 400, but the extra pixels are simply a replication of existing ones, making the image appear blocky. With today's standards in software and fast hardware accelerators, developers can include more unique pixel information in each frame, effectively increasing graphics detail at resolutions as high as 800 × 600 or 1024 × 768. This means gamers can play in high resolutions without any performance loss.

Color Depth. Using extra colors in 3D games makes the scenes much richer and more life-like. The more colors used in a scene, the more detailed and realistic it looks, but the more calculations are needed to determine the color of each rendered pixel. With the new generation of 3D graphics accelerators, higher color depths are supported without dramatic performance loss, and developers can now use more colors in each scene. For example, developers can now use 16-bit (65K) or 24-bit (16.7M) color instead of the traditional 8-bit (256) color.

Understanding DirectX

When Windows first emerged as a major OS, its focus was primarily on file management and utilities. High-performance graphics and other forms of multimedia were barely even dreamed of. This made it very difficult for Windows to support graphics-intensive applications such as games, DVD, PC-TV, or MPEG video (and is largely the reason why DOS lingered for so long on many PC platforms). Developers realized that in order for Windows to finally become independent of DOS, a means of supporting high-performance multimedia functions would be required, and DirectX technology was born. With Windows 95, DirectX has emerged as a key element in graphics, sound, and interaction for multimedia platforms. This part of the chapter offers a basic overview of DirectX and its components.

Contrary to popular belief, DirectX is not one single piece of software. Instead, DirectX is actually a comprehensive collection of Windows 95/98 *Application Programming Interfaces* (APIs) that provide a standardized set of features for graphics, sound, input devices, multi-player interaction, and application setup. DirectX software is categorized into three layers: a foundation layer, a media layer, and a components layer.

Determining the Installed Version of DirectX

Since DirectX is a collection of APIs, each application that uses DirectX is written to use a particular version of DirectX; the application needs the correct version of DirectX components installed under Windows 95/98. Otherwise, the application will not work. In most cases, DirectX is backward-compatible, so an application written for DirectX 3.x should work on a system with DirectX 5.x installed, but an application written for DirectX 5.x won't work on a system with DirectX 3.x. As a technician, you'll need to spot DirectX version issues. You can use the following procedure to check the current version of DirectX installed on a given system:

1. Using Windows Explorer or My Computer, locate the DDRAW.DLL file in the Windows\System folder.

2. Use the right mouse button to click the file DDRAW.DLL, and then click Properties on the menu that appears.

3. Click the Version tab.

4. Compare the version number on the File Version line with the following list:

   - 4.02.0095, DirectX 1
   - 4.03.00.1096, DirectX 2
   - 4.04.00.0068, DirectX 3 or 3a
   - 4.05.00.0155, DirectX 5
   - 4.05.01.1721, DirectX 5.1
   - 4.05.01.1998, DirectX 5.2 (Windows 98 and later)
   - 4.06.02.0436, DirectX 6.1
   - 4.06.03.0518, DirectX 6.1a
   - 4.07.00.0700, DirectX 7 and 7a

NOTE: DirectX versions 3 and 3a use the same version of the DDRAW.DLL file. To determine whether you are using version 3 or 3a of DirectX, use the previous procedure to check the version of the D3DRGBXF.DLL file:

   - 4.04.00.0068, DirectX 3
   - 4.04.00.0070, DirectX 3a

If the DDRAW.DLL file does not exist in the Windows\System folder, DirectX is probably not installed on your computer.

DirectX 6.1 and above include a useful utility named the DirectX Diagnostic Tool. In Windows 98, you can launch this utility from the System Information program in the System Tools menu folder under Accessories. You can also launch DirectX Diagnostic by clicking Start, selecting Run, and typing dxdiag in the text box. This tool reports detailed information about the DirectX components and drivers installed on your system. It lets you test functionality, diagnose problems, and make changes to your system configuration so that it works to its best potential.

AGP Overclocking

The AGP bus was designed as a 66-MHz bus architecture, and this 66-MHz signal is almost always derived from the motherboard's *Front Side Bus* (FSB) clock. When motherboards only offered a 66-MHz clock, this was not a problem for AGP since the FSB clock and AGP clock were basically the same thing. However, when motherboards went to 100 MHz and 133 MHz (and faster), the AGP bus needed to be "derived" from the FSB. In many cases, the AGP clock is set from a motherboard jumper or through an entry in the *Complementary Metal Oxide Semiconductor* (CMOS) Setup. You'll generally find these settings denoted as the AGP Ratio, and you can usually select 1:1, 2:3, and 1:2, depending on the FSB speeds available. You can see the following example of how this setting is used:

- If the FSB is 66 MHz, set the AGP Ratio to 1:1, and the AGP clock will be 66 MHz.

- If the FSB is 100 MHz, set the AGP Ratio to 2:3, and the AGP clock will be 66 MHz.

- If the FSB is 133 MHz, set the AGP Ratio to 1:2, and the AGP clock will be 66 MHz.

You can also see the potential for overclocking:

- If the FSB is 100 MHz, setting the AGP Ratio to 1:1 will cause the AGP clock to be 100 MHz.

- If the FSB is 133 MHz, setting the AGP Ratio to 2:3 will cause the AGP clock to be 88.7 MHz.

As a rule, it is unsafe to overclock the AGP bus, especially if you're using AGP in the 2X or 4X data modes. In most cases, an overclocked AGP bus will result in unstable video and system operation. In extreme cases, the overclocked AGP card will be damaged.

AGP and BIOS Settings

The number of video BIOS settings has been increasing steadily even before the introduction of AGP. Every video card should include a list of recommended BIOS settings with its documentation (or be available from the manufacturer's Web site), and you should see that your CMOS Setup is configured properly for your particular AGP video card. Table 6.2 lists the recommended settings for a Viper II Z200 card, and you get some idea of how important BIOS settings have become.

> **NOTE**:   Not all listed options will be available on all motherboards. Should particular setting combinations fail, try loading BIOS Defaults in the CMOS Setup.

TABLE 6.2   Typical BIOS Settings for an AGP Card

[BIOS Settings: PCI/AGP general]	
IRQ assignment	[toggle]
Boot with Plug and Plag OS	[enable]
Pallet snooping	[disable]
PCI bursting	[disable]
PCI latency timer	[128]
Peer concurrency	[disable]
Video ROM BIOS Shadow	[disable]
Video BIOS shadowing	[disable]
Video BIOS cacheable	[disable]

(continues)

TABLE 6.2   Continued.

[BIOS Settings: PCI/AGP general]	
Video RAM cacheable	[disable]
Video BIOS cacheable	[disable]
Video RAM cacheable	[disable]
Byte-merge	[disable]
Decouple Refresh	[disable]
Hidden Refresh	[disable]
USWC options	[Uncache Speculative Write Combining]
Video Memory Cache Mode	[UC]
Snoop Ahead	[disable]

[BIOS Settings: AGP specific]	
USB	[enabled]
PCI 2.1 compliance	[enable—also may assign IRQ to VGA]
Passive release/refresh	[enabled]
Delayed transactions	[enabled/disabled—toggle, may also enable PCI 2.1 compliance]
VGA BIOS sequence	[AGP-PCI, PCI-AGP, PCI]
AGP/graphics aperture size	[Target 1/2 installed RAM]
Write cache pipeline	[disable]
Read around write	[disable]
Primary frame buffer	[disable]
VGA frame buffer	[disable]
Frame buffer posted write	[disable]
RAS-CAS delay	[3T]
Cache read	[disable] (via motherboards)
CPU wait pipeline	[disable] (via motherboards)
AGP Master 1 WS write	[enable/disable]*
AGP Master 1 WS read	[enable/disable]*
AGP ratio	[set to 2/3 instead of 1/1]
AGP multi-trans timer	[disable]
AGP low-priority timer	[disable]
AGP 2x	[disable]
AGP turbo mode	[disable]
AGP bus turbo mode	[disable]
AGP transfer mode	[1x]

*Must both be set the same: enable/disable

Troubleshooting Video Adapters

A PC video system consists of four parts: the host PC itself, the video adapter/accelerator, the monitor, and the software (video BIOS and drivers). To deal with a failure in the video system, you must be able to isolate the problem to one of these four areas. When isolating the problem, your best tool is a working (or testbed) PC. With another PC, you can systematically exchange hardware to verify each element of the video system.

Isolating the Problem Area

The first step is to verify the monitor by testing it on a reliable working PC. Keep in mind that the monitor must be compatible with the video adapter on which it is being tested. If the monitor works on another PC, the fault lies in one of the three remaining areas. If the monitor fails on another machine, try the reliable monitor on the questionable machine. If the monitor then works on your questionable machine, you can be certain that the fault lies in your monitor, and you can refer to the appropriate chapter here for detailed troubleshooting if you want. If the monitor checks out, suspect the video adapter. Follow the same process to check the video adapter. Try the suspect video adapter on a reliable PC. If the problem follows the video adapter, you can replace the video adapter. If the suspect video adapter works in a good system, the adapter is probably good. Replace the adapter in the suspect machine, but try another expansion slot and make sure that the monitor cable is attached securely.

If both the monitor and the video adapter work in a capable PC but the video problem persists in the original machine, suspect a problem with the PC motherboard. Try the working video adapter in another expansion slot. Either the expansion slot is faulty or a fault has occurred on the motherboard. Run some PC diagnostics if you have some available. Diagnostics may help to pinpoint motherboard problems. You can then troubleshoot the motherboard further or replace the motherboard outright at your discretion.

When the video system appears to work properly during system initialization but fails with a particular application (or in Windows 95/98), strongly suspect a problem with the selected video driver. Since almost all video adapters support VGA at the hardware level, set your application (or change the Windows setup) to run in standard VGA mode (for Windows 95/98, you can start the PC in the Safe mode). If the display functions properly at that point, you can be confident that the problem is driver-related. Check with the manufacturer to see that you have the latest video driver available. Reload the driver from its original disk (or a new disk) or select a new driver. If the problem persists in VGA mode, the trouble may be in the video adapter. Problem isolation can be summarized with the following points:

- *Check the driver(s).* Video drivers are critically important in Windows 3.1x/95/98. Older drivers may contain bugs or be incompatible with certain applications. This accounts for the majority of all video problems. Obtain the latest video driver release and make sure it is properly installed on the system. If the driver is most current, try a generic video driver (usually available from the video chipset manufacturer).

- *Check the physical installation.* See that the video board is installed properly in its expansion slot, and make sure that any video card jumpers are set properly for the particular host system.

- *Check for memory conflicts.* The memory space used by video adapters is hotly contested territory in the upper memory area. Printer drivers, sound cards, tape backups, SCSI adapters, and scanners are just some of the devices that can step over the memory space needed by a video board. Many of today's video boards require you to exclude a range of upper memory through your memory manager (often A000h through C7FFh, though your particular video board may be different). Make sure that any necessary memory exclusions are made in CONFIG.SYS at the memory manager's command line. You may also have to add an `EMMExclude= A000-C7FF` line to the [386enh] section of your file SYSTEM.INI.

- *Suspect your memory manager.* Advanced real-mode memory managers such as QEMM or Netroom use very aggressive techniques to find memory. Often, this interferes with video operation. Try disabling any stealth or cloaking mode, or try disabling your real-mode memory manager outright.

- *Check your system's CMOS setup.* Today's motherboards sport all manner of advanced features. Try systematically disabling such attributes as video cache, video RAM Shadow, byte-merge, palette snoop, or decouple/hidden refresh. If PCI bus bursting is used on the video bus, try disabling that also. If the video system requires the use of an interrupt, make sure that the IRQ is not being used by another device. If the user manual for your video card lists any special settings for your CMOS Setup, verify that you've made the appropriate changes.

- *Compatibility.* Check the video adapter maker's (and motherboard maker's) Web site for any known compatibility issues. Current video adapters may have minimum power requirements or use some features not supported by the motherboard's chipset. This type of checking should be done before purchasing a video adapter for an upgrade.

Multiple Display Support Guide

Traditionally, only one video adapter is allowed on the system, but Windows 98 seeks to extend the desktop by supporting the use of more than one video adapter.

This enables more open windows and thus provides more information to the user at any given time. However, multiple display (or multi-monitor) support is far from perfect and must be used with the right combination of system BIOS, video adapter chipsets, and Windows 98/SE. This part of the chapter highlights some of the key hardware requirements and issues common to multi-monitor operation.

Video Adapters.   All the video adapters used in a computer with multi-monitor support must be PCI or AGP devices using the multi-monitor compliant display drivers that are included with Windows 98. *Industry Standard Architecture / Extended Industry Standard Architecture* (ISA/EISA) display adapters are specifically not supported. Keep in mind that the video adapters installed in your computer do not have to be identical. Each video adapter and monitor combination is separately enumerated by Windows 98 and can be configured to use different screen resolutions and color depths. For example, the primary display can be set to $1024 \times 768 \times 256$, and the secondary display can be set to $800 \times 600 \times 32K$.

Video Chipsets/Drivers.   Any combination of the following supported PCI-based video adapters can be used for multi-monitor operations. The following list will serve as primary and secondary adapters, but only this list can be used for secondary video adapters. The drivers in Table 6.3 are supported by Microsoft and are included on the Windows 98 CD.

> **NOTE**:   The basic Permedia chipsets cannot be used on multi-monitor platforms, but the Permedia NT and Permedia 2 can.

TABLE 6.3   Video Chipsets/Drivers Suitable for Multi-Monitor Operation

ATI Mach 64 GX (GX, GXD, VT)	ATIM64.DRV
ATI Graphics Pro Turbo PCI	
ATI Graphics Xpression	
ATI WinTurbo	
ATI Rage I, II, II+	ATI_M64.DRV
ATI All-In-Wonder	
ATI 3D Xpression+	
ATI 3D Xpression	
ATI 3D Xpression+	
ATI Rage Pro (AGP and PCI)	ATIR3.DRV
ATI Xpert@Work, four and eight MB	
ATI Xpert@Play, four and eight MB	
ATI All-In-Wonder Pro	
S3 765 (Trio64V+)	S3MM.DRV
S3 Trio64V2 (DX/GX)	S3MM.DRV
Diamond Stealth 64 Video 2001	
STB PowerGraph 64V+	
STB MVP 64	
Miro TwinHead 22SD	
Hercules Terminator 64/Video	
Number Nine 9FX Reality 332 (S3 Virge)	
Number Nine 9FX Reality 334 (S3 Virge GX/2)	
Number Nine 9FX Reality 772 (S3 Virge VX)	
California Graphics V2/DX	
Videologic GraphicsStar 410	
Cirrus 5436	CIRRUSMM.DRV
Cirrus Alpine	
Cirrus 5446	CIRRUSMM.DRV
STB Nitro 64V	
S3 ViRGE	S3V.DRV
ViRGE (325), ViRGE VX (988), ViRGE DX (385), and ViRGE GX (385)	
Diamond Stealth 3D 2000	
Diamond Stealth 3D 3000	
Diamond Stealth 3D 2000 Pro	
Number Nine 9FX Reality 332	
STB Nitro 3D	
STB PowerGraph 3D	
STB Velocity 3D	
STB MVP/64	

TABLE 6.3   Continued

STB MVP/64 3D	
STB WorkStation (2 and 4 output)	
Miro Crystal VR4000	
ET6000	ET6000.DRV
Hercules Dynamite 128/Video	
STB Lightspeed 128	
Compaq Armada	S3MM.DRV
Trident 9685/9680/9682	TRID_PCI.DRV
Jaton Video, 57P	

Enabling Multi-Monitor Support.   As you saw previously, the primary requirement for multi-monitor support is that the video adapters must be PCI or AGP devices. You can enable multi-monitor support with the following steps:

1. While the computer is turned off, add any additional video adapters and monitors.

2. Start Windows 98. Install the video adapter and monitor drivers (as necessary) and then restart your computer if you're prompted to do so.

3. Click Start, highlight Settings, and then click Control Panel.

4. Double-click the Display icon and then click the Settings tab.

5. In the Display box, click the adapter you want to use and then click the Extend my Windows desktop onto this monitor check box to select it.

6. Click OK.

Multi-Monitor Issues.   Multi-monitor display technology is fairly well-established under Windows 98/SE, but problems will arise. The easiest way to test your multi-monitor setup is to start Paint or WordPad under Windows 98. When Paint or WordPad is not running in full-screen mode, drag the program from one monitor to the other. If you can drag the program from one monitor to the other, you'll know that multi-monitor support is working correctly. If this presents problems, try the following tips to help isolate the trouble:

- Disable the secondary display adapter to confirm that your program works properly on the primary display adapter:

  1. Click Start, highlight Settings, click Control Panel, and then double-click the Display icon.
  2. On the Settings tab, click the secondary monitor icon.
  3. Click the `Extend my Windows desktop onto this monitor` check box to clear it and then click OK.

- Avoid programs that do not fully comply with multi-monitor support:

  - Programs or drivers that modify the GDI.EXE file or the display driver
  - Programs that use Adobe Type Manager
  - Remote control programs such as pcANY-WHERE

- Verify that the correct display driver is installed for the secondary display device:

  1. Click Start, highlight Settings, click Control Panel, and then double-click the Display icon.
  2. On the Settings tab, click Advanced and then click the Adapter tab.
  3. Verify that the installed video driver is the correct driver for the video adapter in your computer. If not, you should use the Update Driver wizard to install the correct driver(s).

- Verify that the secondary monitor displays the following message when you start your computer:

```
If you can read this message, Windows has
successfully initialized this display adapter.
To use this adapter as part of your Windows
desktop, open the Display option in the Control
Panel and adjust the settings on the Settings
tab.
```

If this message is not displayed, confirm that the secondary display adapter is installed:

1. Click Start, highlight Settings, click Control Panel, and then double-click the System icon.

2. On the Device Manager tab, double-click Display Adapters to confirm that all your video adapters have been correctly installed. If not, you should recheck the installation of any missing devices.

- Verify that the secondary display adapter has a supported chip set, as listed in Table 6.3.

- If you notice that the Extend my Windows desktop onto this monitor box is unavailable, you can select the secondary monitor and try extending the desktop again:

1. Click Start, highlight Settings, click Control Panel, and then double-click the Display icon.

2. On the Settings tab, click the secondary monitor icon. After you click the secondary monitor icon, the Extend my Windows desktop onto this monitor check box should become available.

Video Symptoms

This section will cover a variety of common video problems and provide solutions for them.

Symptom 6.1. The computer is on, but there is no display. The PC seems to initialize properly. Numerous problems can account for these symptoms:

- *Check for beeps.* If you hear a series of beeps during system initialization, refer to Section 5 to determine the error.

- *Check the monitor.* Make sure that the monitor is turned on and plugged into the video adapter properly. Also check that the monitor's brightness and contrast controls are turned up enough (it sounds silly, but it really does happen). Try the monitor on a reliable PC.

- *Check the video adapter.* If the monitor works properly, suspect the video adapter. Power down the PC and make sure the video adapter is seated properly in its expansion slot. If any of the board contacts are dirty or corroded, clean the contacts by rubbing them with an eraser. You can also use any electronics-grade contact cleaner. You may want to try the video board in another expansion slot.

- *Check the hardware configuration.* Chances are that the video adapter has at least one hardware jumper or *Dual Inline Package* (DIP) switch setting. Contact the manufacturer or refer to the owner's manual for the board and check that any jumpers or DIP switch settings on the board are configured properly. If this is a new installation, check the adapter board settings against the configuration of other expansion boards in the system. When the hardware settings of one board overlap the settings of another, a hardware conflict can result. When you suspect a conflict, adjust the settings of the video adapter (or another newly installed device) to eliminate the conflict.

- *Consider a memory conflict.* Some video adapters make unusual demands of upper system memory (the area between 640 KB and one MB). It is possible that an EXCLUDE switch must be added to the EMM386.EXE entry in a CONFIG.SYS file. Check with the adapter's instruction manual to see if any memory configuration changes or optimizations are required.

Symptom 6.2. There is no display, and you hear a series of beeps when the PC initializes.   The video adapter failed to initialize during the system's POST. Since the video adapter is not responding, it is impossible to display information. That is why a series of beeps are used. Bear in mind that the actual beep sequence may vary from system to system depending on the type of BIOS being used. You can probably find the beep code for your BIOS in Section 5. In actual practice, there may be several reasons why the video adapter fails and the following checks will help you discover what they are:

- *Check the video adapter.*   Power down the PC and check that the video adapter is installed properly and securely in an expansion slot. Make sure that the video adapter is not touching any exposed wiring or any other expansion board. Isolate the video adapter by trying another adapter in the system.

- *Check the hardware configuration.*   If the display works properly with another adapter installed, check the original adapter to see that all settings and jumpers are correct. If the problem persists, the original adapter is probably defective and should be replaced. If a new adapter fails to resolve the problem, there may be a fault elsewhere on the motherboard.

- *Check the POST codes.*   Install a POST board in the PC and enable the system to initialize. Each step of the initialization procedure corresponds to a two-digit hexadecimal code shown on the POST card indicators. The last code to be displayed is the point at which the failure occurred. POST cards are handy for checking the motherboard when a low-level fault has occurred. If a motherboard fault is detected, you may troubleshoot the motherboard or replace it outright at your discretion.

Symptom 6.3. You see large blank bands at the top and bottom of the display in some screen modes but not in others. Multi-frequency and multi-mode monitors sometimes behave this way. This is not necessarily a defect, but it can cause some confusion unless you understand what is going on. When screen resolution changes, the overall number of pixels being displayed also changes. Ideally, a multi-frequency monitor should detect the mode change and adjust the vertical screen size to compensate (a feature called auto-sizing). However, not all multi-frequency monitors have this feature. When video modes change, you are left to adjust the vertical size manually. Of course, if there is information missing from the display, there may be a serious problem with VRAM or the adapter's graphics controller chip. In this event, try another video adapter board.

Symptom 6.4. The display image rolls. Vertical synchronization is not keeping the image steady (horizontal sync may also be affected). This problem is typical of a monitor that cannot display a particular screen mode. Mode incompatibility is most common with fixed-frequency monitors but can also appear in multi-frequency monitors that are being pushed beyond their specifications. The best course of action here is to simply reconfigure your software to use a compatible video mode (or reduce the vertical refresh rate). If this is an unsatisfactory solution, you will have to upgrade to a monitor that will support the desired video mode.

If the monitor and video board are compatible, a synchronization problem is occurring. Try the monitor on a reliable PC. If the monitor also fails on a good PC, try the monitor on an original PC. If the monitor works on the suspect PC, the sync circuits in your original monitor have almost certainly failed. If the suspect monitor works on a reliable PC, the trouble is likely in the original video adapter. Try replacing the video adapter.

Symptom 6.5. An error message appears on system startup indicating an invalid system configuration. The system CMOS backup battery has probably failed, and the video type may have defaulted to EGA or MCA instead of VGA, resulting in the error. This is typically a symptom that occurs in older systems and the following checks can narrow down what is causing it:

- *Check your CMOS Setup.* If you enter your system setup (either through a BIOS routine or through a disk-based setup utility) and examine each entry, you will probably find that all entries have returned to a default setting, including the video system setting. Your best course is to replace the CMOS backup battery and enter each configuration setting again (hopefully you have recorded each setting on paper already or saved the CMOS contents to floppy disk using a CMOS backup utility). Once new settings are entered and saved, the system should operate properly.

- *Check the CMOS RAM.* If the CMOS still will not retain system configuration information, the CMOS RAM itself is probably defective. Use a software diagnostic to check the RTC/CMOS IC (and the rest of the motherboard) thoroughly. If a motherboard fault is detected, you can troubleshoot the motherboard or replace it outright at your discretion.

Symptom 6.6. Garbage appears on the screen or the system hangs up. The display may be distorted for a variety of reasons and the following checks are recommended:

- *Consider a monitor mismatch.* Check the video adapter jumpers and DIP switch settings and be sure that the video board will support the type of monitor you are using. It is possible that the video mode being used is not supported by your monitor. Try reconfiguring your application software to use a compatible video mode. The problem should disappear. If that is an unsatisfactory solution, you will have to upgrade to a monitor that will support the desired video mode.

■ *Check the monitor.* Some older multi-frequency monitors are unable to switch video modes without being turned off and then turned on again. When such monitors experience a change in video mode, they will respond by displaying a distorted image until the monitor is reset. If you have an older monitor, try turning it off, wait several minutes, and then turn it on again.

■ *Check for* Terminate and Stay Residents *(TSRs).* Conflicts between device drivers and TSR programs will upset the display and are particularly effective at crashing the computer. The most effective way to check for conflicts is to create a backup copy of your system startup files CONFIG.SYS and AUTOEXEC.BAT. From the root directory (or directory that contains your startup files), type

```
copy autoexec.bat autoexec.xyz
copy config.sys config.xyz
```

The extensions xyz suggest that you use any three letters, but avoid using "bak" since many ASCII text editors create backup file with this extension.

Now that you have backup files, go ahead and use an ASCII text editor (such as the text editor included with DOS) to REM out each driver or TSR command line. Then reboot the computer. If the problem disappears, use the ASCII text editor to re-enable one REMed-out command at a time. Reboot and check the system after each command line is re-enabled.

When the problem occurs again, the last command you re-enabled is the cause of the conflict. Check that command line carefully. You may be able to add command-line switches to the startup file that will load the driver or TSR without causing a conflict. Otherwise, you would be wise to leave the offending command line REMed out. If you encounter serious trouble in editing the startup files, you can simply recopy the backup files to the working file names and start again.

- *Check the video drivers.*   Video drivers also play a big part in Windows. If your display problems are occurring in Windows, make sure that you have loaded the proper video driver and that the driver is compatible with the video board being used. If problems persist in Windows, load the standard generic VGA driver. The generic VGA driver should function properly with virtually every video board and VGA (or SVGA) monitor available. If the problem disappears when using the generic driver setup, the original driver is incorrect, corrupt, or obsolete. Contact the driver manufacturer to obtain a copy of the latest driver version. If the problem persists, the video adapter board may be defective or incompatible with Windows. Try another video adapter.

Symptom 6.7. Your Viper II Z200 video card doesn't work on a VIA- or ETEQ-based system.   This is the same on both Super 7- and Slot 1-based systems. The Viper II Z200 card does not interact properly with the MVP3 or ETEQ chipsets. Check to see that the AGP driver and IRQ routing drivers have been installed properly before attempting to install the display adapter. All the necessary motherboard updates can be found in a file from *www.viatech.com/drivers/4IN1409.exe*. This patch is supposed to work for both the MVP3 and ETEQ chipset (Super 7) as well as the VIA Apollo Pro chipset (for Pentium II systems).

Symptom 6.8. Your Viper V770 video card doesn't work on an ALI-based system. This is the same on both Super 7- and Slot 1-based systems. This is probably because the ALI-based chipset requires an AGP driver in order to support AGP cards such as the V770. Ensure that the latest AGP driver from ALI has been installed from *www.acerlabs.com / acerlabs / drivers.htm*. This patch is supposed to work for both the Aladdin V chipset (Super 7) as well as the Aladdin Pro II chipset (for Pentium II systems and is also referred to as the BXPro).

Symptom 6.9. Your Viper II Z200 video card doesn't work on an AMD Athlon-based system. This is almost always because the Athlon motherboard requires an AGP miniport driver. Ensure that the latest AGP miniport driver has been installed from AMD by going to *www.1.amd.com / athlon / config*.

Symptom 6.10. Selecting a screen resolution over 640 × 480 causes an HP Pavilion system to reboot in the Safe mode. This is an HP BIOS problem. HP has a main board BIOS upgrade for the Pavilion that should fix this. The release notes for this new BIOS indicate that it fixes a problem with allocating IRQs to add-in AGP adapters (such as Nvidia-based display adapters). Check out the HP site at *www.hp.com*.

Symptom 6.11. When booting to Windows, you find a black screen or Windows indicates that the display adapter is not configured properly. You may also find a yellow exclamation mark on the video card in your Device Manager. In virtually all cases, this occurs because the video card does not have an adequate IRQ assigned to it. Boot into your system the CMOS Setup and look for an option such as `Assign IRQ for PCI VGA`. See that it's set to `enabled` or `auto`. If the video card is not assigned to a suitable IRQ, and the system BIOS does not have an option to assign an IRQ, you'll need to contact your motherboard manufacturer and check for a BIOS update.

Symptom 6.12. After installing 3D accelerator drivers, you find an error such as "Invalid VxD dynamic link call from h3vddd(01)+0000 4974."   In virtually every case, you're trying to use an AGP accelerator card under Windows 95 OSR2 without having a proper USB support update installed. The file USBSUPP.EXE can be found on your Windows 95 CD (if the CD is labeled With USB Support). In addition to proper USB support, this file also installs a new *Virtual Memory Manager* (VMM) that may be required for the AGP version of your accelerator card (the Monster Fusion) in Windows 95. If you do not have that file on your CD, it can be downloaded from *ftp://ftp.opti.com/pub/chipsets/system/861/ usbsupp.exe*. Upgrading the OS to Windows 98/SE should also correct this issue.

Symptom 6.13. After upgrading from an older video card, you can access higher colors but cannot use resolutions over 640 × 480.   This type of issue is seen frequently when upgrading an older Stealth 64 card. True color modes are accessible, but resolutions above 640 × 480 are not. This is almost always due to residual entries left in the Registry. Start your Registry editor and check the following key:

```
HKEY_LOCAL_MACHINE/Config/0001/Display/Settings
```

Right next to the Resolution setting is an entry called ScreenArea. This entry was left over from a former virtual desktop and was probably set to 640 × 480. Remove this key, save your changes, and reboot the system.

Symptom 6.14. Windows 95 reports a memory conflict with a PCI-to-PCI bridge and the AGP graphics adapter.   This PCI-to-PCI bridge is sometimes called the Intel 82443LX or 82443BX bridge. This is not a real error.

The memory conflict that appears between the PCI bridge and the AGP graphics adapter is a known conflict. This error is caused by the way Windows 95 reports memory usage and is not known to cause problems. Windows 98 does not report this problem, so you may ignore the issue or upgrade if you want.

Symptom 6.15. Problems occur with IE 5 after installing 3D accelerator drivers. For example, you may experience problems if you install Diamond Multimedia Monster Fusion video drivers on a computer running Internet Explorer 5. In one case, you may receive the following error after installing the Monster Fusion drivers on a system with IE 5 and restarting the PC:

```
EXPLORER caused an Invalid page fault in module
EXPLORER.EXE at 015f:00401f31
```

In another case, Windows 95/98 may not start if you download and install Diamond video drivers from the Diamond Web site and then restart your computer. This trouble can occur because some Diamond video drivers replace the COMCTL32.DLL file with a version that is not totally compatible with IE 5. Update the drivers to the latest versions. For example, Diamond Multimedia now has updated drivers that address this issue at *www.diamondmm.com*. As an alternative, you may extract a new copy of the file COMCTL32.DLL:

1. Start Windows in the native DOS mode (the Safe Mode Command Prompt).

2. Rename the COMCTL32.DLL file in the \Windows\ System folder to COMCTL32.OLD by typing

```
ren c:\windows\system\comctl32.dll comctl32.old
```

at the command prompt and then press Enter. Now type

```
extract c:\window~1\setupw95.cab comctl32.dll
/l c:\windows\system
```

and then press Enter.

3. Restart the computer normally.

Symptom 6.16. You notice a horizontal line scrolling down one side of the screen with multiple monitors under Windows 98/SE. This problem is almost always caused when your monitors are too close to a fluorescent light source (or you're using an unshielded monitor and you place it too close to another monitor). Most early monitors are unshielded, so they do not confine the magnetic field they emit. Later monitors are shielded so that most of the magnetic fields they emit are confined within the monitor. If you place an unshielded monitor too close to another monitor, the magnetic field emitted by the unshielded monitor may interfere with the other monitor. Move the unshielded monitor away from any monitors or fluorescent light sources it interferes with or place a shield (such as an ordinary cookie sheet) between the unshielded monitor and any monitors it interferes with. You may also choose to replace the unshielded monitor with a shielded model.

Symptom 6.17. You cannot drag a window from one monitor to another under Windows 98/SE. This problem can occur if the window you're trying to drag is maximized or your monitors are not positioned correctly. To work around this issue, restore the window to its previous size before you drag it to a different monitor. To do this, simply click the Restore button (the middle button in the upper-right corner of a window). You should also verify your monitor's position. Click Start, Help, and Index tab, then type `multiple display support`, and then double-click the Arranging Monitors topic for detailed information.

NOTE: A basic Permedia video adapter cannot currently be used as your primary video adapter (this excludes the Permedia NT and Permedia-2).

Symptom 6.18. You notice a black screen when you run a program requiring DirectX under Windows 95/98. When you run a DirectX-based program, your monitor may display a black screen (or may display only wavy lines on a black background). This fault can occur if the DirectX-based program changes the default refresh rate that your display adapter uses with the monitor. Change the refresh rate to an acceptable level for your monitor and selected resolution (such as 60 Hz or 72 Hz):

1. Click Start, highlight Settings, and then click Control Panel.

2. Double-click the Display icon, click the Settings tab, and then click Advanced.

3. Click the Adapter tab and then click Adapter Default in the Refresh Rate box.

4. Click OK when you're prompted to test the setting.

5. If the setting is displayed correctly, click Yes to keep the setting.

If this doesn't work, try reducing the hardware acceleration for the video adapter:

1. Click Start, highlight Settings, and then click Control Panel.

2. Double-click the System icon, click the Performance tab, and then click Graphics.

3. Move the Hardware Acceleration slider to one notch from the left (the Basic setting), click OK, click Close, and then click Yes when you're prompted to restart your computer.

Symptom 6.19. You encounter a blank screen after installing a secondary video adapter for Windows 98. This trouble can occur if your computer has a built-in video adapter and either your computer's BIOS does not provide support for multiple video adapters or the secondary video adapter is not supported for multiple display use. To resolve this behavior, update your computer's BIOS and/or obtain a different video adapter that's properly supported for Windows 98 multi-monitor service.

Symptom 6.20. You find that Riva 128 video adapters do not support multi-monitor operations. When you add a secondary video adapter to a system that uses a Riva 128 video adapter as the primary video adapter, the computer may hang up. This problem is almost always caused by an incompatible driver that is used by the Riva 128 video adapter. Consequently, Riva 128 video adapters are not supported for use with the multiple display feature. If you want to use multiple monitors, you should only use video adapters that are known to work in a multiple-monitor environment. Replace the incompatible video adapter with a model that is compatible with multi-monitor operation.

Symptom 6.21. You have trouble using the ATI Rage II PCI video card as a second video adapter. When you try the ATI Rage II PCI video adapter as a secondary display adapter under Windows 98, the secondary display adapter may not work properly (if at all). When you view the ATI Rage II PCI Properties dialog box in Device Manager, you may see an error message such as:

```
Multiple Display Support cannot start this device.
The area of memory normally used by video is in use
by another program or device. To enable Multiple
Display Support, remove EMM386 or other memory
managers from CONFIG.SYS and restart your computer.
```

Try adding an EMMExclude entry to the SYSTEM. INI file:

1. Open the SYSTEM.INI file using any text editor (such as Notepad).

2. Add the following line to the [386enh] section of the SYSTEM.INI file:

   ```
   emmexclude=c000-cfff
   ```

3. Save and then close the SYSTEM.INI file.

4. Restart your computer.

As an alternative, try adding the exclusion to the EMM386 command line of your CONFIG.SYS file:

1. Open the CONFIG.SYS file using any text editor (such as Notepad).

2. Add the following lines:

   ```
   device=<windows>\himem.sys

   device=<windows>\emm386.exe x=c000-cfff
   ```

   where <windows> is the path to the folder where Windows is installed.

3. Save and then close the CONFIG.SYS file.

4. Restart your computer.

Symptom 6.22. The screen image becomes distorted when changing resolutions.   This is known to occur with certain monitors under Windows 98 (such as the NEC 4FG). Some video adapters (such as the Diamond Stealth 64, Video 2001, and S3 Trio 64V+) default to a refresh rate of 60 Hz. NEC 4FG monitors can only support refresh rates of less than 60 Hz at a resolution of 1280 × 1024 or higher. For example, if you're using an NEC 4FG monitor and you change the display resolution to 1280 × 1024 or higher, your screen may become distorted. This trouble can occur if you're using a video adapter that defaults to a refresh rate of 60 Hz at such high resolutions. To correct this fault, optimize the refresh rate of your video adapter before you attempt change the display resolution:

1. Click Start, highlight Settings, and then click Control Panel.

2. Double-click the Display icon.

3. Select the Settings tab and then click Advanced.

4. Click the Adapter tab and then click Optimal in the Refresh Rate box.

5. Click OK and then click OK when you receive the following message:

   ```
   Windows will now adjust the refresh rate of
   your display. The screen may flicker for a few
   moments while the settings are being changed.
   If the display becomes garbled or unusable,
   simply wait and Windows will restore your
   original settings.
   ```

6. Click Yes when you're prompted to keep this setting and then click OK.

Symptom 6.23. You see wavy lines in the monitor's display. This is known to occur under Windows 98 with monitors such as the MAG DX-1795. This problem can occur if your video adapter is configured for 1600 × 1200 screen resolution and the Automatically detect Plug & Play monitors check box is selected on the Monitor tab in Display Properties. To correct this problem, manually install your monitor in Display Properties:

1. Click Start, highlight Settings, and then click Control Panel.

2. Double-click the Display icon.

3. Click the Settings tab and then click Advanced.

4. On the Monitor tab, click the Automatically detect Plug & Play monitors check box to clear it. Then click Change.

5. Click Next, click Display a list of all the drivers in a specific location, so you can select the driver you want, and then click Next.

6. Click Show All Hardware.

7. In the Manufacturers box, click `MAG Technology Co., Ltd.` and then click `MAG DX-1795` in the Models box.

8. Click Next and then follow the instructions on your screen to finish installing the monitor.

Symptom 6.24. When returning to Windows from a DOS application, the Windows screen splits from top to bottom. This is a DOS problem that is found under Windows and indicates an obsolete or corrupted video driver (for example, using a Windows 3.0 video driver under Windows 3.1). Chances are that the video adapter is running just fine. Make sure that the proper DOS "grabber" file is installed and specified in the file SYSTEM.INI. Check with the video board manufacturer to obtain the latest assortment of drivers and grabber files. Try reinstalling the drivers from their master disk. If you do not have the current drivers available, try switching to the generic VGA driver.

Symptom 6.25. The system hangs up during initialization, some characters may be missing from the display, or the screen colors may be incorrect. These are classic symptoms of a hardware conflict between the video adapter and one or more cards in the system or an area of memory. Some video boards use an area of upper memory that is larger than the classical video area. For example, the Impact SVGA board imposes itself on the entire address range between A0000h and DFFFFh. In this kind of situation, any other device using an address in this range will conflict with the video board. A conflict may occur when the video board is first installed or the board may work fine until another device is added or modified.

Resolving a hardware conflict basically means that something has to give. One of the conflicting elements (IRQ lines, DMA channels, or I/O addresses) must be adjusted to use unique system resources. As a technician, it rarely matters which of the conflicting devices you change, but remember that system startup files, device drivers, and application settings may also have to change to reflect newly selected resources. You may also be able to resolve some memory conflicts by adding the EXCLUDE switch to EMM386.EXE. The video adapter manual will indicate when an EXCLUDE switch is necessary.

Symptom 6.26. Your system is generating DMA errors with a VGA board in the system and video BIOS shadowing is disabled. This is a fairly rare symptom that develops only on some older i486 systems and is usually due to an eight-bit VGA board in a system equipped with a slower version of the i486 CPU (in the 25-MHz range). Eight-bit access takes so long that some DMA requests are ignored; thus, an error is generated. If you find such a problem, try enabling video ROM shadowing through the CMOS setup to enable faster access to video instructions. Also, you may try a newer revision of the i486 CPU.

Symptom 6.27. The system hangs up using a 16-bit VGA board and one or more 8-bit controllers. This is typically a problem that arises when 8-bit and 16-bit ISA boards are used in the same system. Due to the way that an ISA bus separates the 8-bit and 16-bit segments, accessing an 8-bit board when 16-bit boards are used in the system may cause the CPU to (falsely) determine that it is accessing a 16-bit board. When this occurs, the system will almost invariably crash. Try removing any 8-bit boards from the system. If the crashes cease, you have probably nailed down the error. Unfortunately, the only real correction is to either remove the 8-bit board(s) or reconfigure the board(s) to use a higher area of memory.

Symptom 6.28. You have trouble sizing or positioning the display, or you see error messages such as "Mode Not Supported" or "Insufficient Memory." These kinds of errors may occur in newer or high-end video boards if the board is not set up properly for the monitor it is being used with. Most new video boards include an installation routine that records the monitor's maximum specifications such as resolution (and refresh frequencies), horizontal-scanning frequencies, and vertical-scanning frequencies. If such data is entered incorrectly (or the monitor is changed) certain screen modes may no longer work properly. Check the video adapter's installation parameters and correct its setup if necessary.

Symptom 6.29. You frequently encounter General Protection Faults (GPFs) when using QuickTime for Windows 1.1. This is a notable problem with ATI Mach64 cards but has been known to occur with other advanced video boards. Often, the problem can be corrected by making a change in the Windows file SYSTEM.INI. For the ATI Mach64, you must turn DeviceBitmaps off under the [macx] section. As an alternative, start the ATI FlexDesk, type OPT (this starts a hidden window), and then uncheck the DeviceBitmap entry.

Symptom 6.30. The video board will not boot up when used in a particular motherboard. Generally speaking, noted cases of hardware incompatibility between certain video boards and motherboards have occurred. This usually causes a great deal of confusion because the video board may work just fine when tested in a different motherboard, and other video boards may work well in the original motherboard. The technician simply winds up chasing ghosts. A noted example of this problem is the Boca Research VGAXL1/2 refusing to work in a Micronics 486DX2/66 motherboard. The solution to this problem demands that U13 on the video board be a Texas Instruments TI-74F04. If U13 is a Motorola chip, you'll need to send the board back for rework, strange but true. For general troubleshooting purposes, if a certain video board and motherboard refuse to work together, don't waste your time chasing ghosts. Contact both the video board maker and PC (or motherboard) maker, and see if there are any reports of incompatibilities.

Symptom 6.31. Diagnostics refuse to show all of the available video modes for a particular board even though all video RAM was properly detected, or the board refuses to operate in some video modes.   When a video board does not respond to certain video modes (usually the higher video modes), it is usually because of a conflict in the upper memory area, and a memory range needs to be excluded. If a memory manager is at work (QEMM, 386MAX, or EMM386), try disabling the memory manager in CONFIG.SYS or boot the system from a clean floppy. Try your diagnostic(s) again; chances are that the problem has disappeared. To fix this problem on a more permanent basis, reenable the memory manager using an exclude command. Try x=B100h-B1FFh as the first parameter on the memory manager's command line. If that does not work, try x=A000h-BFFFh. Finally, try x=A000h-C7FFh.

Symptom 6.32. The characters shown in the display appear fuzzy.   This is often the result of a speed problem where the system is running too fast for the VL bus video board. In virtually all cases, you will find the VL bus to be running over 33 MHz. Try slowing down the VL bus speed. This will sacrifice video performance but should stabilize the system. Chances are also very good that the system has been locking up frequently. Slowing down the video board should also correct such lock-ups.

Symptom 6.33. Pixels appear "dropped" behind the mouse cursor, and graphic images appear to break up under Windows. Two major causes for this older type of problem exist: bad video RAM or the system ISA bus speed is too fast. Check the CMOS Setup for an entry in Advanced Setup such as AT Bus Clock, ISA Bus Speed, or AT Bus Speed. The corresponding entry should be set to 8.33 MHz. Otherwise, excessive speed may be resulting in lost video data. If the bus speed is set properly, run a diagnostic to check the integrity of video RAM (you may have to replace the video RAM or replace the video board entirely).

Symptom 6.34. You encounter video-related conflicts in Packard Bell systems. The system refuses to boot or starts with "garbage" and erratic screen displays. This symptom is encountered most frequently with Boca video boards on Packard Bell systems with video circuits already on the motherboard. Even when the onboard video has been disabled, reports indicate that the video circuitry remains active and then conflicts with the add-on video board. Packard Bell indicates that their Vxxx.16 BIOS will correct this problem, so contact Packard Bell for an appropriate BIOS upgrade.

Symptom 6.35. Text appears in an odd color. For example, text that should be green appears black. This is almost always the result of a problem with the palette-decoding registers on the particular video board and will typically appear when using higher color modes (64k or 16M colors). Make sure that the video drivers are correct, complete, and up to date. If the problem persists, you may need to replace the video board outright.

> **NOTE**: Remember that you can select a myriad of color and text schemes under Windows 95/98. Before you conclude that color problems are caused by a faulty video card, be sure to try the Windows Default desktop scheme.

Symptom 6.36. When an application is started (under Windows), the opening display appears scrambled. Although this might appear to be a video memory problem at first glance, it is actually more likely to be related to a buggy video driver. Upgrade the video driver to the latest version or try a generic video driver (a reference driver) that is compatible with your video chipset.

Symptom 6.37. The display colors change when exiting from a DOS shell under Windows. This problem has been noted with older video boards such as the Diamond SpeedStar Pro and is almost always the result of a video board defect (usually a palette problem). For the Diamond board, the product must be replaced with revision A2. For other video boards, such problems can usually be corrected by replacing the video board outright.

Symptom 6.38. The computer locks up or crashes when starting an .AVI file. This problem is encountered frequently as computer users first begin to try multimedia applications. Rather than being a problem with the video board specifically, the trouble is often from using an outdated version of Video for Windows. Make sure to use Video for Windows 1.1E or later. It can be downloaded from the Diamond Multimedia FTP site at *ftp://ftp.diamondmm.com/pub/misc/vfw11e.exe*. You may also need to edit the [DrawDib] section of the WIN.INI file and add an entry that says DVA=0. If no [DrawDib] section is present, you can add it. Remember to restart Windows after making any changes. You may also be able to correct this type of problem by upgrading to Windows 98/SE, which should contain many of the very latest drivers and support components.

Symptom 6.39. The computer is running very slowly (poor performance), and the hard drive light is continuously lit. This problem is particularly apparent with Diamond Edge 3D video boards on systems with more than 16 MB of RAM. The Diamond Edge 3D board comes with

both 1-MB and 6-MB MIDI bank files. Diamond rec-
ommends that you use only the 6-MB bank file on sys-
tems with over 16 MB of RAM. To change the size of
the MIDI bank file being used, right-click on My
Computer and choose Properties. Open the System
Control Panel and click on the Device Manager tab.
Click on the (+) symbol beside the Sound, Video, and
Game Controller line, then highlight the Diamond
EDGE 3D PCI Multimedia Device, and click on
Properties. Then click on Settings. You will see the 1-
MB and 6-MB MIDI bank selection. Select the 6-MB
option and choose OK. Restart your computer when
prompted.

**Symptom 6.40. You notice that .AVI files have distorted col-
ors or grainy playback.**   This usually occurs when playing eight-bit .AVI files that are not supported by DCI
and can usually be corrected by disabling the accelerated video playback features of the video board. For
example, the older Diamond ViperPro Video board is
noted for this problem, and you would need to edit the
COPRO.INI file located in the \Windows directory. In
the [VCP] area, change the VCPEnable=line to OFF.
Save the .INI file and restart Windows.

**Symptom 6.41. The PCI video board will not work under
Windows unless the system's PCI SCSI devices are disconnected.**   This type of problem occurs only on certain combinations of PCI system hardware. For
example, this type of symptom has been documented
using Phoenix BIOS 4.04 and a UMC8810P-AIO motherboard on systems with an NCR SCSI controller and
SCSI devices. You can often correct such problems by
correcting the Advanced System Setup in CMOS. Start
the CMOS Setup, go to the Advanced System Setup,
and select PCI Devices. Set up the PCI slot for the
SCSI controller as IRQ9 and LEVEL edge select. The
slot for the video board should have the IRQ set to
NONE and LEVEL edge select. Change the Base
Memory Address from 0080000000 to 0081000000.

Symptom 6.42. Boot problems occur when a new video board is installed. Typical problems include no video or eight beeps when the system is turned on. This is usually the result of an outdated system BIOS that is not capable of detecting the particular video chipset in use. The BIOS interprets this as meaning that no video board is in the system, and an error is generated accordingly. Contact the motherboard manufacturer (or PC maker) for an updated system BIOS. Most BIOS versions dated after the fall of 1994 should be able to detect most modern video chipsets.

Symptom 6.43. Boot problems occur when a PCI video board is installed. Two common problems account for this. First, the system BIOS did not complete the configuration of the video board correctly, and the board has not been enabled onto the PCI bus. The video board manufacturer may have a utility available that can remap the video card to a new address outside of physical memory. For the Matrox Millennium, use the PCIMAP.EXE utility. Other Matrox boards use the MGABASE.EXE utility. Other PCI video board manufacturers probably offer their own utilities. The second problem is that the system BIOS has assigned a base memory address to the video board that is used by another device or is reserved for use by the motherboard chipset. Although the utilities mentioned earlier may often help to correct this problem, a more permanent fix is usually to update the system BIOS. Investigate a BIOS upgrade from the motherboard (or PC) manufacturer.

Symptom 6.44. The monitor overscans when entering a DOS shell from Windows. This creates a highly distorted image and can (if left for prolonged periods) damage the monitor circuitry. The cause of this problem is usually a bug in the video driver. For example, this type of problem is known to happen when using the older Diamond SpeedStar Pro with drivers prior to version 1.06. Obtain the latest video driver from the video board maker, or try a generic video driver written by the video chipset maker.

Symptom 6.45. You encounter an intermittent Divide by Zero error. Although this type of error has several possible causes, they are all related to flaws in software. In this case, problems exist with the video driver or video toolkit that is installed with the particular video board. For example, `Divide by Zero` errors can be corrected with the Diamond Stealth 64 Video 2001 series by opening the InControl Tools package and changing a `Center to Viewport` selection to `Center to Desktop`. Similarly, the `Maximize to Viewport` selection should be changed to `Maximize to Desktop`. Often, upgrading the video driver or video support tools will eliminate this problem.

Symptom 6.46. During MPEG playback, the display flickers, shows low refresh rates, or appears to be in an interlaced mode. This is not necessarily an error. With some video boards (such as the Diamond MVP1100), MPEG files cannot play correctly at high refresh rates, typically over 72 Hz. When an MPEG file is played, the driver will automatically switch to a 72-Hz vertical refresh rate. This may result in an unexpected change to display quality during playback. After exiting from the MPEG player, the original (higher) refresh rate will be restored. If a vertical refresh rate lower than 72 Hz was originally selected, then the vertical refresh rate will not change during MPEG playback, so you should see no difference in the display.

Symptom 6.47. You receive an error such as "There is an undetectable problem in loading the specified device driver" when starting an MPEG player or other video tool. In almost all cases, the related driver is missing, installed improperly, or corrupt. Reinstall the MPEG playback driver(s) for your particular video board, and make sure to use the latest version. If problems persist, check for the driver under the files WIN.INI or SYSTEM.INI and see that there is only one load reference to the particular driver(s). Repeated references can cause conflicts or other loading problems. Similar drivers (other MPEG drivers) can also cause conflicts, so verify that the only drivers being loaded are the ones used by your current video adapter and/or playback software.

Symptom 6.48. On video boards with TV tuners, the TV window is blurry or fuzzy at 1024 × 768 or higher resolutions. This symptom is particularly noted with the Diamond DVV1100. Unfortunately, this type of symptom is usually the result of the particular video board's limited bandwidth, specifically of the video chipset. The only real option is to reduce the resolution to 800 × 600 or 640 × 480 when running the TV, and lower the refresh rate to 60 Hz. Contact your video board's manufacturer. An RMA or other replacement/upgrade program might be available to correct the issue.

Symptom 6.49. On video boards with TV tuners, the reception does not appear as good as that of an ordinary TV. This problem has been noted in conjunction with Matrox Media-TV boards and is usually due to the local cable company using the HRC carrier frequency instead of the standard carrier frequency. For Matrox boards, you can correct the problem by modifying the DVMCIMIL.INI file found in the \WINDOWS directory. Under the [Carrier] section, change the `CarrierType=0` entry to `CarrierType=1`. Other video/TV boards may utilize different .INI entries or enable carrier selection through the use of an onboard jumper, but poor reception is almost always the result of an unusual cable carrier.

Symptom 6.50. You encounter errors such as "Insufficient video memory." Not enough video memory on the board can handle screen images at the resolution and color depth you have selected. In most cases, the system may crash outright. Your immediate solution should be to select a lower resolution or a smaller color palette. If you are encountering such problems when attempting to play .AVI or MPEG files, you should be able to select smaller video windows and lower the color depth without altering your Windows setup. As a more long-term solution, you should consider adding more video memory, or replacing the video board with one that contains more video memory.

Symptom 6.51. The PCI video board is not working properly and there is a BIOS conflict with PCI interrupt 1Ah. The lower 32 KB of the ROM BIOS has been redirected for high memory use. Disable this memory with your memory manager by adding an exclude command such as x=f000-f7ff.

Symptom 6.52. You encounter video corruption or sporadic system rebooting when using an SLC-type motherboard. This particular symptom has been most noted when using Number Nine video boards with Alaris SLC2 motherboards. The SLC2 microprocessor uses a 32-bit internal data bus, but the external data bus (noticed by the motherboard) is 16-bit. Most of the registers on contemporary VL and PCI video boards are mapped as 32-bits and cannot be accessed as two 16-bit registers. As a result, the video board simply cannot be used together with the particular motherboard. You will have to upgrade the motherboard or use a different video board.

Symptom 6.53. Video playback experiences long pauses while the hard drive thrashes excessively. This is a problem that appears under Windows 95/98 and is almost always the result of disk caching problems. Start Windows Explorer and highlight the drivers responsible for video playback (for a Motion Pixels video board, highlight MPXPLAY.EXE and MPXPLAY.PIF). Click the right mouse button and select Properties. In the

Memory page, make sure that the Protected option has been set. Restart the video clip or restart Windows 95/98 if necessary. Also check your CONFIG.SYS and AUTOEXEC.BAT files and verify that no caching utilities are being loaded.

Symptom 6.54. You cannot use the loop-through feature of your video board. Typical examples include the Number Nine 9FX Motion 771 VGA loop-through connector with a Reel Magic board and a Number Nine driver. Unfortunately, this is often the result of a limitation with the video board's graphics processor chip (refusing to support loop-through functionality). To use loop-through, try the standard VGA driver.

Symptom 6.55. Windows appears with a black box cursor and/or icons that fail to appear on the screen. In most cases, the problem is caused by an incompatibility with the motherboard's non-compliant PCI BIOS (the motherboard's BIOS doesn't comply with the PCI backward-compatibility requirement). To overcome this problem, set the video board's memory aperture manually by editing the SYSTEM.INI file located in the \WINDOWS directory. For example, when working with a Number Nine 9GXE, find the [#9GXE] section of SYSTEM.INI and then add a command line such as APERTURE-BASE=0x8800 or APERTURE-BASE=31. Save the file and restart Windows. The actual section for your particular video board may be different.

Symptom 6.56. Video problems occur or the system locks up while using an anti-virus program. This error occurs frequently when using memory-resident virus checking. Some video boards allow you to compensate for this by editing the SYSTEM.INI file. For the Number Nine 9GXE board, find the [#9GXE] area in the file SYSTEM.INI and then set the FastMMIO= entry to OFF. Remember to save the .INI file and restart

Windows. The actual section for your particular video board may be different. As an alternative, you could also disable or remove the anti-virus program, or check with the anti-virus maker to see if there's a patch or update that might improve the program's compatibility.

Symptom 6.57. An error indicates that not enough memory exists for playback or resizing the playback window.   This program type is directly caused by a lack of system (not video) memory in the PC. If your system uses SMARTDRV (Windows 3.1x), try reducing the memory used for caching. Try unloading various unneeded programs from memory, and consider disabling any RAM drives that may be active. Finally, consider adding more system RAM to the PC.

Symptom 6.58. The video board refuses to accept a particular video mode.   Mode problems are most frequent when attempting to use unusual palette sizes such as 32K or 64K colors. Try setting the video board to 256 colors. If a higher color depth is needed, it may be possible to run the video board in a palletized or grayscale mode by adding command-line switches to the video driver. Refer to the instructions that accompany the particular video board for detailed information. You may also consider a video BIOS upgrade or try using an upgraded VESA driver (such as UNIVBE 5.3 from SciTech Software). Updated video drivers and/or firmware may also be available to correct the problem.

Symptom 6.59. The video system cannot lock memory using QEMM and linear video memory.   This is often a DOS problem with Motion Pixels video boards when using QEMM 7.04 and earlier versions. The DPMI has a bug when accessing physical memory above the DPMI's host memory. Upgrade the version of QEMM to 7.5 (or later) or play video under Windows instead.

Symptom 6.60. The video system cannot lock memory under Windows or the system hangs. This is also a problem noted most often with Motion Pixels video boards and is almost always related to the use of a WINDPMI.386 DPMI driver loaded through the file SYSTEM.INI. WINDPMI.386 reports the wrong amount of free lockable DPMI memory. If your Windows platform uses Borland's WINDPMI.386, manually reduce the cache size with the /c option, or remove (or disable) the driver from SYSTEM.INI entirely. You might also consider upgrading WINDPMI. 386 to a later version. Contact Borland technical support or the technical support department of the video board maker.

Symptom 6.61. Other devices don't work properly after the PCI video card is installed. For example, the sound card output is distorted or a fast modem loses data. This can happen often with newer video adapters. Some computers require that software wait for the hardware to be ready to receive new data. Newer video board drivers are not normally set to this because it slows them down slightly (and it's not necessary for most current computers). Under Windows 95/98, right-click on the Windows 95 desktop background. Click the Properties menu item and select the video board's Settings tab. Select the Advanced button and then click the Performance tab. Clear the Use automatic PCI bus retry check box. Finally, accept your changes and reboot the computer when instructed to do so. Under Windows 3.1x, edit the SYSTEM.INI file in your \Windows directory to add the line PciChipSet=1 to the particular video board's section (such as [mga.drv]).

Symptom 6.62. A Windows 95/98 game doesn't start or runs slower than normal. The program uses the Microsoft DirectX interface. DirectX may not be installed, or an older version of DirectX is installed. Most programs that use DirectX install it as part of their installation, but some do not. Also, some older programs may install an earlier version of DirectX (overwriting a later version). To see if DirectX is installed, perform the following steps:

1. Right-click on the Windows 95/98 desktop.

2. Click the Properties menu item and select the video adapter's Settings tab.

3. Click the Advanced button and click the Information tab.

4. Look at the Microsoft DirectX Version label. DirectX 5.x (or later) should be the current version.

If the current version of DirectX is installed, you're finished. Otherwise, you'll need to install DirectX.

NOTE: If the DirectX setup program asks if you want to replace the existing display drivers, click No.

Symptom 6.63. You replace an older 3D accelerator with a new one, but the new accelerator is not working properly. You often see this kind of trouble when replacing a 3Dfx Voodoo card or Monster I card with a new card such as a Monster Fusion. You'll need to remove the original Voodoo graphics card and clean out all of the old references to the card:

NOTE: 3Dfx provides an .INF file to remove these references. You can download it from *www.3dfx.com/view_io.asp?ID=96*.

Also, always make a complete backup of your Registry to a bootable floppy disk before making any changes to the system Registry.

1. Click Start, select Run, and then type regedit.

2. Locate the HKEY_LOCAL_MACHINE/Enum/PCI key and delete the VEN_121A&DEV folder.

3. Locate the HKEY_LOCAL_MACHINE/Software key and delete the 3Dfx Interactive folder.

4. Locate the HKEY_LOCAL_MACHINE/Software/ Diamond key and delete the Monster3D folder.

5. Locate the HKEY_LOCAL_MACHINE/Software/ Microsoft/Windows/CurrentVersion/ControlsFolder/ Display/shellex/Property Sheet Handlers key and delete any folders pertaining to the original Voodoo card.

6. Save your changes to the Registry and then use Windows Explorer to open the c:\windows\ inf\other folder.

7. Delete any *.INF file pertaining to the Monster3D, 3Dfx Interactive, the Monster Fusion, and so on.

8. Click Start, select Find, and then choose Files and Folders. Search for any references to glide, and delete any file references that you find.

9. Search for files such as DD3DFX.DRV, DD3DFX16. DLL, DD3DFX32.DLL, and MM3DFX*.*, and delete those files if you find them.

10. Search for the FXMEMMAP.VXD file and delete it as well.

11. Finally, search for SST1INIT*.* and delete it.

12. Restart the computer and reinstall the drivers for the new Monster Fusion device.

Sound Boards

Sound is an area of the PC that has been largely over-looked in early systems. Aside from a simple, oscillator-driven speaker, the early PCs were mute. Driven largely by the demand for better PC games, designers developed stand-alone sound boards that could read sound data recorded in separate files and then recon-struct those files into basic sounds, music, and speech. Since the beginning of the 1990s, those early sound boards have blossomed into an array of powerful, high-fidelity sound products capable of duplicating voice, orchestral soundtracks, and real-life sounds with uncanny realism. Not only have sound products helped the game industry to mature, but they have been instrumental in the development of multimedia technology (the integration of sound and picture) as well as Internet Web phones and other powerful communication tools. This part of the chapter explains the essential ideas and operations of a contemporary sound board and shows you how to isolate a defective sound board when problems arise.

Inside a Sound Board

Take a look at a simplified block diagram of a sound board (see Figure 6.2). It is important to note that your own particular sound board may differ somewhat, but all contemporary boards should contain these subsections. The core element of a sound board is the *digital signal processor* (DSP). A DSP is a variation of a microprocessor that is specially designed to manipulate large volumes of digital data. Like all processor components, the DSP requires memory. A ROM contains all the instructions needed to operate the DSP and direct the board's major operations. A small quality of RAM serves two purposes: it provides a scratch pad area for the DSP's calculations and serves as a buffer for data traveling to or from the PC bus.

Signals entering the sound board are passed through an amplifier stage and provided to an A/D converter. When recording takes place, the DSP runs the A/D converter and accepts the resulting conversions for processing and storage. Signals delivered by a microphone are typically quite faint, so they are amplified significantly. Signals delivered to the "line" input are often much stronger (such as the output from a CD player or stereo preamp), so it receives less amplification.

For signals leaving the sound board, the first (and often most important) stop is the mixer. It is the mixer that combines CD audio, DSP sound output, and synthesizer output into a single analog channel. Since most sound boards now operate in a stereo mode, there will usually be two mixer channels and amplifier stages.

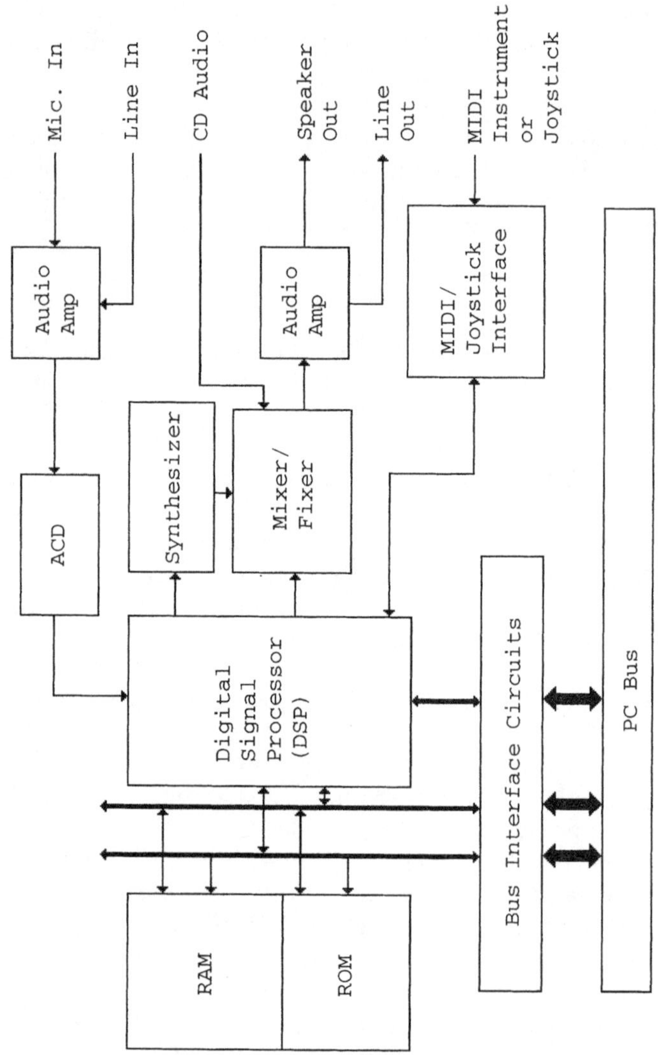

Figure 6.2 Video chipsets/drivers suitable for multi-monitor operation

The audio amplifier stages boost the analog signal for delivery to stereo speakers. If the sound will be driving a stereo system, a "line" output provides a separate output. Amplifier output can be adjusted by a single master volume control located on the rear of the board.

Finally, a MIDI controller is provided to accommodate the interface of a MIDI instrument to the sound board. In many cases, the interface can be jumpered to switch the controller to serve as a joystick port. That way, the sound board can support a single joystick if a MIDI instrument will not be used. MIDI information processed by the DSP will be output to the onboard synthesizer.

Decibels

No discussion of sound concepts is complete without an understanding of the *decibel* (dB). Decibels are used because they are logarithmic; you see, human hearing is not a linear response. If you increase the power of your stereo output from 4W to 16W, the sound is not four times louder. In fact, it is only twice as loud. If you increase the power from 4W to 64W, the sound is only three times as loud. In human terms, amplitude perception is measured logarithmically. As a result, very small decibel values actually relate to substantial amounts of power. The accepted formula for decibels is

$$\text{gain (in dB)} = 10 \log_{10} \frac{P_{out}}{P_{in}}$$

Don't worry if this formula looks intimidating. Chances are that you will not need to use it, but consider what happens when output power is greater than input power. Suppose a 1mW signal is applied to a circuit, and a 2mW signal leaves. The circuit provides a gain of +3dB. Suppose the situation is reversed where a 2mW signal is applied to the circuit, and a 1mW signal leaves it. The circuit would then have a gain of − 3dB. Negative gain is a loss, also called attenuation.

As you see, a small dB number represents a large change in signal levels.

Frequency Response

Expressed simply, the frequency response of a sound board is the range of frequencies that the board will handle uniformly. Ideally, a sound board should be able to produce the same amount of power (0dB) across the entire working frequency range (usually 20 Hz to 20 KHz). This would show up as a flat line across a graph. In actual sound cards, however, this is not practical, and there will invariably be a rolloff of signal strength at both ends of the operating range. A good-quality sound board will demonstrate sharp, steep rolloffs. As the rolloffs get longer and more shallow at high and low frequencies, the board has difficulty producing sound power at those frequencies. The result is that bass and treble ranges may sound weak, and this affects the sound's overall fidelity. By looking at a frequency response curve, you can anticipate the frequency ranges where a sound board may sound weak.

Signal-to-Noise Ratio

The *signal-to-noise ratio* (SNR) of a sound board is basically the ratio of maximum undistorted signal power to the accompanying electronic noise being generated by the board (primarily hum and hiss) expressed in decibels. Ideally, this will be a very large dB number that would indicate that the output signal is so much stronger than the noise signal that for all intents and purposes the noise is imperceptible. In actual practice, a good-quality sound board will enjoy an SNR of 85 dB or higher, but these are difficult to find. For most current sound boards with SNR levels below 75 dB, there may be an audible hum and hiss present during silent periods as well as a certain amount of sound grit underlying sound and music reproduction. Some very inexpensive sound boards are on the market with SNR levels as low as 41 dB (noise may be noticeable and actually annoying).

You may also find the SNR value expressed as an A-weighted decibel number. The reason for this is that human hearing is not equal at all frequencies, so we cannot hear all noise equally. The process of A-weighting emphasizes the noise levels at frequencies we are most sensitive to. Resulting SNR values are often several dB higher (better) than non-weighted SNR values. Be careful here; a sound board with a low SNR may use the A-weighted value in the specification sheet. If this is the case, subtract about three or four dB for the actual SNR figure.

Total Harmonic Distortion

Sound and music are rich in harmonics (overtones), which are basically integer multiples of an original frequency signal (although at much lower levels). As a consequence, harmonics are a valuable attribute of sound. The number and amplitude of harmonics provide the sound characteristics that allow you to distinguish between a guitar, flute, piano, or any other musical instrument played at the same note. Without harmonics, every instrument would just produce flat tones, and every instrument would sound exactly the same.

However, when sound is produced in an electronic circuit, other unwanted harmonics are generated that can alter the sound of the music being produced (thus the term harmonic distortion). The *total harmonic distortion* (THD) of a sound board is the *root-mean squared* (RMS) sum of all unwanted harmonic frequencies produced, expressed as a percentage of the total undistorted output signal level. In many cases, the RMS value of noise is added to THD (expressed as THD + N). The lower this percentage is, the better. THD + N values over 0.1 percent can often be heard and suggest a less than adequate sound board design.

Intermodulation Distortion

Intermodulation distortion is related to harmonics. When two or more tones are generated together, amplifiers create harmonics as well as tone combinations. For example, if a one-KHz and a 60-Hz tone are mixed together, intermodulation harmonics will be generated (940 Hz, 880 Hz, 1060 Hz, 1120 Hz, and so on). It is this intermodulation that gives sound a harsh overtone. Since intermodulation is not related to sound quality, it is a form of distortion that should be kept to a very low level. Like THD, *intermodulation distortion* (IMD) is the RMS sum of all unwanted harmonic frequencies expressed as a percentage of the total undistorted output signal level. IMD should be under 0.1 percent on a well-designed board.

Sensitivity and Gain

Although it does not directly affect the fidelity of sound reproduction, sensitivity can be an important specification. Sensitivity is basically the amplitude of an input signal (such as a microphone signal) that will produce the maximum undistorted signal at the output(s) with volume at maximum.

By itself, sensitivity is hard to apply to a sound board, but if you consider the board's output power versus its input signal power and express the ratio as a decibel, you would have the gain of the sound board. Many sound boards offer a potential gain of up to six dB. However, it is important to note that not all sound boards provide positive gain. Some boards actually attenuate the signal even with the volume at maximum. In practical terms, this usually forces you to keep the volume control at maximum.

3D Audio (A3D)

The A3D audio technology in your sound card (part of your Diamond Multimedia Sonic Impact A3D audio system) was developed by Aureal Semiconductor and is the result of many years of research into human hearing and digital audio reproduction. In the real world, anyone can close their eyes, listen to a sound, and pinpoint its direction, distance, and motion. Our ears allow us to hear 360 degrees in all directions, while our eyes cover only about 140 degrees in the direction we're facing. The eyes and ears work in close cooperation to provide us with a seamless perception of reality. When the ears hear a sound from behind, we decide to turn our head and look at an object.

A3D audio is based on the following premise: we can hear sounds in three dimensions by using only our ears, so it's possible to create sounds from two speakers (or a set of headphones) that have the same effect. Several listening "cues" enable us to hear sounds three-dimensionally. Split-second differences exist between what each ear hears when listening to a sound. Sound waves usually appear earlier and louder at the ear closest to the sound source. That same sound (originating from various locations around a listener) will sound different because of the changes in the way it gets reflected and filtered by the shoulders, face, and the outer ear before reaching the ear drum. These listening effects can be summarized in a set of audio filters called *Head-Related Transfer Functions* (HRTFs).

A3D technology uses advanced signal processing algorithms and HRTF measurement techniques. This digitally recreates these hearing cues along with the absorption, reflection, and doppler shift effects, which affect sound waves as they travel from a sound source, through an environment, to the listener's ears. The result is a life-like audio experience that "surrounds" the listener with sound that seems like it's in three dimensions using only a single pair of ordinary speakers or headphones.

> **NOTE**: DirectSound and DirectSound3D are DirectX wave audio playback APIs that enable you to simultaneously play multiple wave files and move sound sources within a simulated 3D space (DirectSound3D).

They take advantage of sound-accelerator hardware (found on many high-end sound cards such as the Sonic Impact A3D board) to improve performance and minimize CPU usage.

Microphone Issues

Three types of microphones exist: dynamic, condenser, and electret condenser. You will find all three microphone types available for sound boards:

- *Dynamic.* Dynamic microphones are typically hand-held or desktop units. They have a larger response range and typically sound better than condenser microphones. A dynamic microphone does not require phantom power because the diaphragm element in the microphone can create enough electric current for the sound board to use.

- *Condenser.* Condenser microphones are the small multimedia microphones that typically come with computers. When you open a new sound board and take the microphone out of the box, it is almost always a condenser microphone. They do not have as good a response range as dynamic microphones, and they also have a smaller diaphragm. This demands phantom power for the sound board.

- *Electret condenser.* Electret condenser microphones are basically condenser microphones with a built-in battery for power. They have the same response as a condenser microphone, but they do not require phantom power to operate. Some electret condenser microphones will enable you to remove this internal battery. With the battery not installed, phantom power would be required.

Phantom Power

So the next question is "what is phantom power?" Phantom power is simply a small, low-current power supply on the sound board that is used to power some microphones. Devices like dynamic microphones can produce enough current on their own to avoid the use of phantom power, but condenser microphones demand phantom power as a current source.

Here's the main problem with today's sound boards. Not all of them provide switchable phantom power. Ideally, sound boards (like the Ensoniq Soundscape) would provide phantom power and enables you to jumper the phantom power on or off depending on which microphone you plan to use. If you use a dynamic microphone, you'd switch phantom power off. If you use a condenser microphone, you'd switch phantom power on. When a sound board does not provide phantom power at all, you're stuck using a dynamic microphone or a powered electret condenser microphone. If a sound board provides full-time phantom power (and you cannot turn it off), you'll need to stay with a condenser microphone.

You can probably see the potential for trouble here. If you use a condenser microphone on an unpowered sound board, the microphone will not work at all (or generate little more than faint noise). On the other hand, plugging a dynamic or electret microphone into a powered sound board will usually result in severe clipping. Once again, you'll capture little more than noise.

Choosing a Microphone

Whether you're choosing a microphone for yourself or recommending one to someone else, some considerations should be kept in mind. Perhaps the most important issue is the application. If you just need a basic, inexpensive microphone to record a few simple voice notes, a condenser or electret microphone would work just fine, and your sound board will require a phantom power supply. If you want to record more professional vocals or prepare a presentation, a dynamic microphone will generally provide the best results, and no phantom power is needed.

Troubleshooting a Sound Board

Traditionally, sound boards use many of the same chipsets and basic components, but since each board is designed a bit differently, it is very difficult for commercial diagnostic products to identify failed IC functions. For the most part, commercial and shareware diagnostics can only identify whether a brand-compatible board is responding or not. As a result, this chapter will take the subassembly replacement approach. When a sound board is judged to be defective, it should be replaced outright. This part of the chapter reviews the problems and solutions for sound boards under both DOS and Windows 95/98. The following tips may help you nail down a sound problem most efficiently:

- Check to see that your speakers are connected, powered, and turned on.

- Check that the speaker volume and sound card master volume are turned up.

- Check to see that the mixer volume and master volume are set properly.

- Make sure that the music or sound file(s) are installed properly.

- Check that all sound card and multimedia drivers are installed.

- Make sure that the drivers are up to date.

- Check for resource conflicts between the sound card and other devices in the system.

- Make sure that the sound card is selected and configured properly (especially for DOS apps).

- The sound device should be enabled and configured under CMOS (for sound functions incorporated on the motherboard).

Drivers and Driver Order

Unlike most other expansion devices that are driven by system or supplemental BIOS, sound boards make use of small device drivers to set up their operations. These drivers are generally included in CONFIG.SYS and AUTOEXEC.BAT and are called when the system is first initialized. Most sound board drivers are only used to initialize and set up the board, so they do not remain resident. This is good since it reduces the load on conventional and upper memory. However, these initialization routines vary from board to board. For example, the files installed for a Creative Labs Sound Blaster will not support a Turtle Beach MultiSound board. When you elect to replace a sound board, you must also disable any current sound board drivers and include any new supporting driver files. The process is not difficult; just follow the installation instructions for the board, but the software consideration does add another wrinkle to the replacement process.

If problems occur when you are installing or upgrading a sound board, one of the first issues to suspect is the driver loading order. Sound boards are typically multi-function devices that require several drivers in CONFIG.SYS and AUTOEXEC.BAT. If the drivers are installed in the wrong order, the sound board (or other features of the board) may not function. As a rule, the drivers should be loaded in the following order after your memory managers.

Here is the order for the sound board's device driver:

- DEVICE=C:\SB16\DRV\SB16.SYS /A:220: The CD-ROM port setup driver (if the sound board is so equipped)

- DEVICE=C:\SB16\DRV\CDSETUP.SYS /P:340: The CD-ROM driver (if the sound board is so equipped)

- DEVICE=C:\SB16\DRV\MTMCDAE.SYS /D:MSCD001 /P:340 /A:0 /T:5 /I:11

Full-Duplex Drivers

Many current sound board designs are compatible
with multimedia communication technologies such as
Internet Phone, Web phone, and communication tools.
These tools require full-duplex operations; that is,
sound is digitized with the microphone and received
sound is played through the speakers simultaneously.
This demands full-duplex drivers. If you plan to use
communication tools, you'll need to install full-duplex
sound card drivers that are appropriate for your particular sound board and OS. For example, the Creative
Labs SB32, AWE32, and AWE64 require the Windows
95/98 full-duplex driver file (SBW95UP.EXE) available
from the Creative Labs Web site (*www.creaf.com*). To
use those same devices for full-duplex under Windows
NT 4.0, you'd need the AWENT40.EXE driver file. As a
rule, always check with the sound board maker for current full-duplex drivers.

> **NOTE**:   You may find that full-duplex drivers are not
> available for older sound boards or sound boards run-
> ning under OS/2 and Windows NT. In that case, you
> cannot support full-duplex applications.

.WAV Playback Problems Under Windows 95/98

Of all the sound board problems reported, perhaps the
most common is the failure to play wave files (ordinary
sound files with the .WAV extension) under Windows
95/98. This problem usually manifests itself during the
Windows startup or shutdown when the accompanying
sounds are not played. A variety of issues can prevent
.WAV files from playing.

Program-Specific Problems. If you cannot play .WAV
files from a specific program that you use in Windows
95/98, check to see if the same problem occurs when
you play the file from another program. If the problem
occurs only with one particular program, the files

associated with that program may be damaged or that program may not be configured correctly under Windows 95/98. If you cannot get .WAV files to play under any application, chances are that another issue is responsible.

The Sound Device Is Not Configured Properly. If you cannot play any .WAV files in Windows 95/98 (or if .WAV files are not played at the proper volume), you may not have a sound device selected, or the sound device that you have selected may not be configured properly. To select and configure a sound device in Windows 95/98:

1. Open the Control Panel and double-click the Multimedia icon.

2. In the Playback area under the Audio tab, click the playback device that you want to use in the Preferred Device list, and then move the Volume slider to the value you want (usually 50 to 75 percent volume is adequate).

3. In the Recording area under the Audio tab, click the playback device that you want to use in the Preferred Device list and then move the Volume slider to the value you want.

4. Make sure that the speakers are properly connected to the sound card, and that the speakers are turned on.

The Mixer Settings Are Not Configured Properly. If you cannot play any .WAV files under Windows 95/98 (or if .WAV files are not played at the proper volume), the mixer control settings may not be configured properly. You can use the mixer control program included with Windows 95/98 to adjust the volume for playback, recording, and voice commands. To configure mixer control settings for Windows 95, perform the following steps:

1. Click the Start button, point to Programs, point to Accessories, point to Multimedia, and then click Volume Control.

2. Make sure that the Mute All check box below the Volume Control slider and the Mute check box below the Wave slider are not selected, and that the Balance sliders for Volume Control and Wave are in the center of the scale.

3. Move the Volume Control and Wave sliders at least halfway to the top of the scale. You may need to adjust the current Volume Control or Wave settings to play .WAV files at the volume level you want.

   NOTE: If the Volume Control and Wave sliders do not appear, click Properties on the Options menu and then click the Volume Control and Wave check boxes in the `Show the following volume controls` box to select them.

The Sound Hardware Is Not Configured Properly.   It is possible that your sound card may not be compatible with the type of .WAV file you are attempting to play, or a resource conflict may be taking place between your sound card and another device installed in your computer. Check the Device Manager to see if any resource conflicts exist because of sound board problems. To determine whether your sound card supports the .WAV file format you are attempting to play, contact the sound card's manufacturer.

The Sound Files Are Damaged.   If you cannot play certain .WAV files in Windows 95/98 (or if the .WAV files are not played properly), the .WAV files themselves may be damaged. To check if a .WAV file is damaged, use the right mouse button to click the .WAV file in Windows Explorer, click Properties on the menu, and then click the Details tab. The Audio Format line should contain information about the type of compression used to compress the file, the sound quality of the file, and whether or not the file is in stereo. If this information is missing, the .WAV file is probably damaged and should be reinstalled or recopied to the drive.

> **NOTE**:   If you can play other .WAV files of a similar format, chances are good that the suspect file is indeed damaged. If you can play .WAV files of different formats, but NOT .WAV files of a particular format, it may be that your sound board does not support the particular format.

Compression-Related Problems.   Windows 95/98 includes 32-bit versions of several common *compressor/decompressors* (CODECS) including *Adaptive Delta Pulse Code Modulation* (ADPCM), *Interactive Multimedia Association* (IMA) ADPCM, *Group Special Mobile* (GSM) 6.10, *Consultative Committee for International Telephone and Telegraph* (CCITT) G.711 A-Law and u-Law, and Truespeech from DSP. These 32-bit CODECS are installed by default during the Windows 95/98 Setup and are used by multimedia programs even if a 16-bit version of the same CODEC is available. Make sure that .WAV file format is supported by an available CODEC. Otherwise, you may need to install an appropriate CODEC.

Sound Symptoms

The following section will outline various sound problems and provide solutions for them.

Symptom 6.64. A noticeable buzz or hum is being produced in one or both speakers.   Low-cost speakers use unshielded cables. Unfortunately, strong signals from AC cords and other signal-carrying conductors can easily induce interference in the speaker wires. Try rerouting speaker cables clear of other cables in the system. If problems persist, try using higher quality speakers with shielded cables and enclosures. In most cases, that should resolve everyday noise problems. If the noise continues regardless of what you do, a fault may exist in the sound board amplifier. Try moving the sound board to another bus slot away from other boards or the power supply. If that does not resolve the problem, try a new sound board.

Symptom 6.65. No sound comes from the speaker(s). The lack of sound from a sound board can be due to any one of a wide range of potential problems, and the following checks can help spot the problem:

- *Check the application(s).* If the sound board works with some applications but not with others, it is likely that the problem is due to an improperly installed or configured application. See that the offending application is set up properly (and make sure it is even capable of using the sound card).

- *Check the drivers.* See that the proper sound driver files (if any) are loaded into CONFIG.SYS and AUTOEXEC.BAT as required. In many cases, one or two sound-related environment variables are set in AUTOEXEC.BAT. Make sure that your startup files are configured properly.

- *Check your speakers.* See that they are turned on and set to a normal volume level. The speakers should be receiving adequate power and should be plugged properly into the correct output jack .If speakers have been plugged into the wrong jack, no sound will be produced. If the cable is broken or questionable, try a new set of speakers. Also see that the master volume control on the sound board is turned up most (or all) of the way.

- *Check the hardware configuration.* If problems continue, a resource conflict may exist between the sound board and another device in the system. Examine the IRQ, DMA, and I/O settings of each device in the system. Make sure that no two devices are using the same resources. If problems persist, and no conflict is present, try another sound board.

Symptom 6.66. CD audio will not play through the sound card. This problem can occur under both DOS and Windows 95/98. First, make sure that the sound board is actually capable of playing CD audio (older boards may not be compatible). If the sound card is playing sound files but is not playing CD audio, several things must be checked. First, open the PC and make sure that the CD audio cable (a thin, four-wire cable) is attached from the CD-ROM drive to the sound board. If this cable is broken, disconnected, or absent, CD audio will not be passed to the sound board. If the cable is intact, make sure that the CD audio player is configured properly for the sound board you are using, and check the startup files to see that any drivers and environment variable needed by CONFIG.SYS and AUTOEXEC.BAT are available. If the CD audio fails to play under Windows 95/98, make sure that an *multimedia control interface* (MCI) CD audio driver is included in the Drivers dialog box under your Windows Control Panel.

Symptom 6.67. You see an error such as "No interrupt vector available." The DOS interrupt vectors used by the sound board's setup drivers (usually INT 80h to BFh) are being used by one or more other drivers in the system. As a consequence, there is a software conflict. Try disabling other drivers in the system one at a time until you see the conflict disappear. Once you have isolated the offending driver(s), you can leave them disabled, or (if possible) alter their command-line settings so that they no longer conflict with the sound board's software.

Symptom 6.68. There is no MIDI output. Make sure that the file you are trying to play is a valid MIDI file (usually with a .MID extension). In most cases, you will find that the MIDI Mapper under Windows is not set up properly for the sound board. Load the Windows MIDI Mapper applet from the Control Panel and set it properly to accommodate your sound board.

Symptom 6.69. Sound play is jerky. Choppy or jerky sound playback is typically the result of a hard drive problem. More specifically, the drive cannot read the sound file to a buffer fast enough. In most cases, the reason for this slow drive performance is excessive disk fragmentation. Under DOS, the sound file(s) may be highly fragmented. Under Windows, the permanent or temporary swap files may be highly fragmented. In either case, use a reliable DOS defragmenter such as PC Tools or Norton Utilities (leave Windows before defragmenting the disk) and defragment the disk thoroughly.

Symptom 6.70. You see an error such as "Out of environment space." The system is out of environment space. You will need to increase the system's environment space by adding the following line to the file named CONFIG.SYS:

```
shell=c:\command.com /E:512 /P
```

This command line sets the environment space to 512 bytes. If you still encounter the error message, change the E entry to 1,024.

Symptom 6.71. Regular clicks, stutters, or hiccups occur during the playback of speech. This may also be heard as a garbled sound in speech or sound effects. In virtually all cases, the system CPU is simply not fast enough to permit buffering without dropping sound data. Systems with i286 and slower i386 CPUs typically suffer with this kind of problem. This is often compounded by insufficient memory (especially under Windows) that automatically resorts to virtual memory. Since virtual memory is delivered by the hard drive, and the hard drive is much slower than RAM anyway, the hard drive simply can't provide data fast enough. Unfortunately, little can be done in this kind of situation (aside from adding RAM, upgrading the CPU, or changing the motherboard). If it is possible to shut off various sound features (music, voice, effects, and so on), try shutting down any extra sound features that you can live without. Make sure that no TSRs or other applications are running in the background.

Symptom 6.72. The joystick is not working or not working properly on all systems. This problem only applies to sound boards with a multi-function MIDI/joystick port being used in joystick mode. Chances are that the joystick is conflicting with another joystick port in the system. Disable the original joystick port or the new joystick port. Only one joystick port (game adapter) can be active at any one time in the system. Since joystick performance is dependent on CPU speed, the CPU may actually be too fast for the joystick port. Disable the joystick port, or try slowing the CPU down.

Symptom 6.73. You install a sound board and everything works properly, but now the printer does not seem to work. An interrupt conflict is taking place between the sound board and an IRQ line used by the printer. Although parallel printers are often polled, they can also be driven by an IRQ line (IRQ5 or IRQ7). If the sound board is using either one of these interrupts, try changing to an alternative IRQ line. When changing an IRQ line, be sure to reflect the changes in any sound board files called by CONFIG.SYS or AUTOEXEC.BAT.

Symptom 6.74. You see the message "Error MMSYSTEM 337: The specified MIDI device is already in use." This problem often occurs with high-end sound boards such as the Creative Labs AWE64. This error is often caused by having the sound board's mixer display on with the wavetable synthesizer selected (the LED display in the Creative Mixer is turned on and Creative Wave Synthesizer is selected as the MIDI playback device). You can usually correct the problem by turning the mixer display off.

Symptom 6.75. You see the message "Error: Wave device already in use when trying to play wave files while a MIDI file is playing." This problem often occurs with high-end sound boards such as the Creative Labs AWE64 and is usually the result of a device configuration problem. If "full-duplex" is turned on and you try to play a .WAV file and a MIDI file at the same time with the wavetable synthesizer (the Creative Wave Synthesizer) selected as the MIDI play back device, an error will occur. To resolve this problem, you need to turn off the full-duplex mode:

1. Hold down the Alt key and double-click on My Computer.

2. Select the Device Manager tab. There should be a listing for Sound, Video, Game Controllers in the Device Manager. Double-click on the listing to expand it.

3. You should now see a listing for sound board (Creative AWE32 16-Bit Audio). Double-click on the listing and then select the Settings tab. Uncheck the box labeled `Allow full-duplex operation`. Click OK until you are back to the Control Panel.

4. Now try to play a .WAV and MIDI file at the same time.

Symptom 6.76. You hear pops and clicks when recording sound under Windows 95/98. An insufficient cache cannot adequately support the recording process (or the cache is improperly configured). Try the following procedure to alter the way cache is allocated:

1. Open Notepad and load SYSTEM.INI

2. Locate the area of SYSTEM.INI labeled [vcache].

3. Add the following line below [vcache]:

```
maxfilecache=2048
```

4. Save your changes to the SYSTEM.INI file.

5. From the desktop, right-click on My Computer and then select Properties.

6. Select the Performance page and then click on File System.

7. Find the slider marked Read-ahead optimization and then pull the slider to None.

8. Save your changes and restart Windows 95/98.

Symptom 6.77. You notice high frequency distortion in one or possibly in both channels. In many cases, the AT Bus Clock is set over eight MHz, and data is being randomly lost. This problem usually occurs in very fast systems using an ISA sound board. Enter the system's CMOS Setup and check the AT Bus Clock under the Advanced Chipset Setup area. See that the bus clock is set as close as possible to eight MHz. If the bus clock is derived as a divisor of the CPU clock, you may see an entry such as /4. Make sure that divisor results in a clock speed as close to eight MHz as possible. If problems still persist, try increasing the divisor to drop the bus speed below eight MHz (note that this may have an adverse effect on other ISA peripherals).

Symptom 6.78. You hear pops and clicks when playing back pre-recorded files under Windows 95/98. There is an excessive processing load on the system that is often caused by virtual memory and/or 32-bit access. Start by disabling virtual memory. Open the Control Panel and double-click on the System icon. Select the Performance page and click on Virtual Memory. Set the swap file to None and save your changes. Try the file playback again. If problems persist, try disabling 32-bit file access. If that still does not resolve the problem, try disabling 32-bit disk access.

Symptom 6.79. You hear pops and clicks on new recordings only; pre-existing files sound clean. This is often due to issues with software caching. If you are using

DOS or Windows 3.1, disable SmartDrive from both CONFIG.SYS and AUTOEXEC.BAT. Then restart the computer for your changes to take effect. If problems continue (or you are using Windows 95/98), there may be an excessive processing load on the system due to virtual memory or 32-bit access.

Symptom 6.80. You hear pops and clicks when playing back or recording any sound file.   In most cases, there is a wiring problem with the speaker system. Check all of your cabling between the sound board and speakers. If the speakers are powered by AC, make sure that the power jack is inserted properly. If the speakers are powered by battery, make sure that the batteries are fresh. Check for loose connections. If you cannot resolve the problem, try some new speakers. If the problem persists, replace the sound board.

Symptom 6.81. The sound board will playback fine, but it will not record.   The board probably records fine in DOS, but not in Windows. If the sound board is using 16-bit DMA transfer (typical under Windows), two DMA channels are in use. Chances are that one of those two DMA channels is conflicting with another device in the system. Determine the DMA channels being used under Windows and then check other devices for DMA conflicts. If you are using Windows 95/98, check the Device Manager and look for entries marked with a yellow icon.

Symptom 6.82. A DMA error is produced when using a sound board with an Adaptec 2842 controller in the system. This is a known problem with the Digital Audio Labs' DOC product and the Adaptec 2842. You will need to alter the controller's FIFO buffer. Go in the controller's setup by hitting Ctrl + A when prompted during system startup. Select the advanced configuration option and then select the FIFO threshold. Chances are that it will be set to 100 percent. Try setting the FIFO threshold to zero percent and see if this makes a difference.

Symptom 6.83. A DMA error is produced when using a sound board with an Adaptec 1542 controller in the system. This is a known problem with the Digital Audio Labs' DOC sound product and the Adaptec 1542. The problem can usually be resolved by rearranging the DMA channels. Place the Adaptec controller on DMA 7. Then place the sound board on DMA 5 for playback, and DMA 6 for recording.

Symptom 6.84. The sound card will not play or record. The system just locks up when either is attempted. The board will probably not play in either DOS or Windows, but it may run fine on other systems. This is a problem that has been identified with some sound boards and ATI video boards. ATI video boards use unusual address ranges that sometimes overlap the I/O address used by the sound board. Change the sound board to another I/O address.

Symptom 6.85. The sound card will record but will not playback. Assuming that the sound board and its drivers are installed and configured properly, chances are that a playback oscillator on the sound board has failed. Try replacing the sound board outright.

Symptom 6.86. The sound application or editor produces a significant number of DMA errors. This type of problem is known to occur frequently when using the standard VGA driver that accompanies Windows. The driver is poorly written and cannot keep up with screen draws. Try updating your video driver to a later, more efficient version. If the driver is known to contain bugs, try using a generic video driver written for the video board's chipset.

Symptom 6.87. The sound board will not record in DOS.
Several possible problems can account for this behavior and the following checks will help you narrow the problem down:

- *Check for hardware conflicts.*   Suspect a hardware conflict between the sound board and other devices in the system. Make sure that the IRQs, DMA channels, and I/O port addresses used by the sound board are not used by other devices.

- *Check the drivers.*   If the hardware setup appears correct, suspect a problem between DOS drivers. Try a clean boot of the system (with no CONFIG.SYS or AUTOEXEC.BAT). If sound can be run properly now, there is a driver conflict. Examine your entries in CONFIG.SYS or AUTOEXEC.BAT for possible conflicts or for older drivers that may still be loading to support hardware that is no longer in the system.

- *Check the drive controller.*   Try setting up a RAM drive with RAMDRIVE.SYS. You can install a RAMdrive on your system by adding the line:

  ```
  device=c:\dos\ramdrive.sys /e 8000
  ```

  The 8000 is for eight MB worth of RAM. Make sure enough RAM is in the PC. Once the RAMdrive is setup, try recording and playing from the RAMdrive (you may have to specify a new path in the sound recorder program). If that works, the hard drive controller may simply be too slow to support the sound board, and you may need to consider upgrading the drive system.

Symptom 6.88. When recording sound, the system locks up if a key other than the recorder's hot keys are pushed.
This is a frequent problem under Windows 3.1x. The system sounds (generated under Windows) may be interfering with the sound recorder. Try turning off

system sounds. Go to the Main icon, choose the Control Panel, and then select Sounds. A box in the lower-left corner is marked `Enable system sounds`. Click on this box to remove the check mark and then click OK.

Symptom 6.89. After the sound board driver is loaded, Windows locks up when starting or exiting.   In virtually all cases, you have a hardware conflict between the sound board and another device in the system. Make sure that the IRQs, DMA channels, and I/O port addressed used by the sound board are not used by other devices.

Symptom 6.90. When using Windows sound editing software, the sound board refuses to enter the digital mode and always switches back to the analog mode.   Generally speaking, this is a software configuration issue. Make sure that your editing (or other sound) software is set for the correct type of sound board (an AWE32 instead of a Sound Blaster 16/Pro). If problems persist, the issue is with your sound drivers. Check the [drivers] section of the Windows SYSTEM.INI file for your sound board driver entries. If there is more than one entry, you may need to disable the competing driver. This is a known problem with the Digital Audio Labs CardDplus and is caused by incorrect driver listings. For example, the proper CardDplus driver must be entered as

```
Wave=cardp.drv
```

and the companion driver must be listed as

```
Wave1=tahiti.drv
```

You will need to make sure that the proper driver(s) for your sound board are entered in SYSTEM.INI. You may also need to restart the system after making any changes.

Symptom 6.91. The microphone records at very low levels (or not at all). Suspect your microphone itself. Most sound boards demand the use of a good-quality dynamic microphone. Also, Creative Labs and Labtec microphones are not always compatible with sound boards from other manufacturers. Try a generic dynamic microphone. If problems persist, chances are that your recording software is not configured properly for microphone input. Try the following procedure to set up the recording application properly under Windows 95:

1. Open your Control Panel and double-click on the Multimedia icon.

2. The Multimedia Properties dialog will open. Select the Audio page.

3. In the Recording area, make sure to set the Volume slider all the way up.

4. Also see that the Preferred device and Preferred quality settings are correct.

5. Save your changes and try the microphone again.

Symptom 6.92. The sound card isn't working in full-duplex mode. Virtually all current sound boards are capable of full-duplex operations for such applications as Internet phones. Check the specifications for your sound board and see that the board is in fact capable of full-duplex operations. If it is, and full-duplex isn't working, your audio properties may be set up incorrectly. Thus, perform the following steps:

1. Open your Control Panel and double-click on the Multimedia icon.

2. The Multimedia Properties dialog will open. Select the Audio page.

3. If the Playback device and the Record device are set to the same I/O address, this is only half-duplex.

4. Change the Playback device I/O address so it is different from the Record device.

5. Hit the Apply button and then hit the OK button.

6. You should now be in Full-Duplex mode.

> **NOTE**:   Some of the latest sound boards (such as the Ensoniq SoundscapeVIVO 90) will carry full-duplex operations with the same playback and record device selected.

Symptom 6.93. You encounter DMA errors using an older sound board and an Adaptec 1542.   In many cases, you can clear DMA issues by slowing down the 1542 using the /n switch. Add the /n switch to the ASPI4DOS command line in CONFIG.SYS:

```
device=c:\aspi4dos.sys /n2
```

If slowing the 1542 down with an /n2 switch doesn't fix the problem, then you should strongly consider upgrading the sound board. This is a known problem with the older Digital Audio Labs CardD sound board.

Symptom 6.94. The microphone records only at very low levels or not at all.   Check your phantom power settings first. In many cases, the microphone's gain is set too low in the sound board's mixer applet. Start the sound board's mixer, make sure that the microphone input is turned on, and then raise the microphone's level control. Remember to save the mixer settings before exiting the mixer. You should not have to restart the system.

Symptom 6.95. Your dynamic microphone clips terribly, and recordings are noisy and faint.   This is probably due to phantom power being switched on in your sound board. Try turning the phantom power off. If you cannot turn phantom power off, try plugging the dynamic microphone into the sound board's line input jack. Remember to start the sound board's mixer applet and set the line input level properly.

Symptom 6.96. You have trouble using Creative Labs or Labtec microphones with your (non-Creative Labs) sound board. This is a common complaint among Ensoniq sound board users. It turns out that Ensoniq sound boards are not compatible with Creative Labs or Labtec microphones. Try a generic microphone instead.

Symptom 6.97. You hear static at the remote end when talking through a voice application such as Web Phone. Noise is occurring at the line input or microphone input that is being transmitted to the remote listener. Check the line input signal. You might try reducing or turning off the line input mixer level. If the problem persists, check your phantom power setting and your microphone. Try reducing the microphone level in the sound board's mixer or try a different microphone.

Symptom 6.98. You encounter pops and cracks during recording or playback. This is a known problem with SoundBlaster Live and Windows 98 on a VIA motherboard using either an Apollo VP3 (VT82C597) or an Apollo MVP3 (VT82C598) system controller chipset and a VIA IDE bus master driver version 2.1.33 update. Follow these steps to remove the popping/cracking sound:

1. Run SETUP.EXE of the VIA IDE Bus master driver version 2.1.33 again.

2. Select the Enable/Disable (Ultra) DMA option instead and then press the Next button.

3. Unselect/uncheck the available devices and then press the Next button.

4. Reboot the system.

Please check the VIA web site at *www.viatech.com* for updates on your motherboard.

Symptom 6.99. You encounter short bursts of sound when playing a .WAV file. This problem happens when you're using a SoundBlaster Live card on a VIA motherboard with the Apollo VP3 (VT82C597) or Apollo MVP3 (VT82C598) system controller chipset. This combination causes repeated buffering during a .WAV playback on Windows 98 (Version 4.10.1998). To resolve this problem, download and install the VIA PCI IRQ Miniport driver version 1.3a Setup program. This program can be obtained from the VIA Web site at *www.via.com.tw*. Reboot the system after installing the update.

Symptom 6.100. The sound card's SB16 emulation is causing IRQ conflicts on the PC. You'll need to disable this device:

1. Click Start, highlight Settings, and click Control Panel.

2. Double-click the System icon and then click the Device Manager tab.

3. Click the plus sign (+) next to Creative Miscellaneous Devices.

4. Click the sound card's SB16 Emulation to highlight it and then click Properties.

5. Put a check mark in the Disable This Device In This Hardware Profile box.

6. Click OK, click OK again, and then click Close.

NOTE: This will disable your sound device in DOS mode.

Symptom 6.101. You stop hearing sounds after the system resumes from suspend mode under Windows 98/SE. If your computer enters the suspend mode while a program using DirectSound is running, you may no longer hear sounds from the program after you resume the computer. This problem can occur if the DirectSound components of your platform do not resume properly due to using an older version of DirectX. To correct the issue permanently, download and install the latest version of DirectX from Microsoft at *http://windows update.microsoft.com*. You can work around the problem and restore sound to the program by rebooting the system.

Symptom 6.102. No .WAV sounds are played with Ensoniq PCI sound cards under Windows 98/SE. When you're using an Ensoniq PCI sound card, .WAV files may not be played properly (or at all), even though MIDI files can be heard normally. This problem occurs if the preferred audio playback device is set to "Use any device." To hear .WAV file playback, set the Ensoniq card as the preferred device:

1. Click Start, highlight Settings, and then click Control Panel.

2. Double-click the Multimedia icon.

3. Click the Audio tab.

4. In the Playback section, click Ensoniq in the Preferred Device box.

5. Click OK and reboot the PC if necessary.

Symptom 6.103. Your USB speakers don't work after upgrading to Windows 98/SE. This trouble will occur if another sound card is detected as the preferred audio playback device during the installation of Windows 98/SE. To correct this problem, select the USB audio device as the preferred playback device:

1. Click Start, highlight Settings, and then click Control Panel.

2. Double-click the Multimedia icon.

3. Click the Audio tab.

4. In the Playback section, click your USB audio device in the Preferred Device box.

5. Click OK and reboot the PC if necessary.

Symptom 6.104. You get no volume from Yamaha USB speakers. This is a known problem for the Yamaha YSTMS55D USB speakers under Windows 98/SE. After you install the Yamaha USB speakers, the speakers may produce little (or no) volume when you use the volume control knob on the speakers. This problem is almost always caused by an incompatible Yamaha driver. You'll need to reinstall or update the device drivers and applications software for your speakers. For the Yamaha speakers, reinstall the Windows 95/98 driver for the Yamaha USB device, the Yamaha Human Interface Device, and the Yamaha Sound Recorder from the original installation media:

1. Click Start, highlight Settings, click Control Panel, and then double-click the System icon.

2. On the Device Manager tab, double-click the Sound, video and game controllers branch, and then double-click the Yamaha USB device.

3. On the Driver tab, click the Update Driver button, click Next, click Display a list of all the drivers in a specific location, so you can select the driver you want, and then click Next.

4. Click the appropriate Yamaha driver, click Next, click Next, click Finish, and then click Yes to restart your computer.

5. After you change the drivers, open the Volume Control tool and move the volume settings to the highest level. You can then use the volume knob on the speakers to control the sound level.

Symptom 6.105. An Aztech 2316 sound card is mistakenly identified as a SoundBlaster Pro. When you use the Add New Hardware wizard under Windows 98/SE to detect your Aztech 2316 sound card, it may be incorrectly identified as a SoundBlaster Pro sound card. To fix this error, use the Device Manager to install your Aztech 2316 sound card manually:

1. Click Start, highlight Settings, click Control Panel, and then double-click the System icon.

2. Click the Device Manager tab, double-click the `Sound, video and game controllers` entry, and then double-click Sound Blaster Pro.

3. Click the Driver tab, click Update Driver, and then click Next.

4. Click `Display a list of all the drivers in a specific location` and then click Next.

5. Click Show all hardware, click Aztech Labs, and click `Aztech 2316 Compatible Legacy Audio (WDM)`.

6. Click Next and then click Finish.

7. Restart your computer.

Symptom 6.106. Your sound card delivers a DSP timeout. This often happens on 440GX motherboards under Windows 98, and you'll find this happens even though you switch card slots and reinstall/update the sound card's drivers. The problem is with the motherboard's 440GX chipset. You must download the .INF update utility for the GX chipset from your system or motherboard manufacturer. This motherboard is newer than Windows 98 and must have this patch installed for PCI and AGP devices to function correctly.

Symptom 6.107. You replace a legacy ISA sound card with a PCI sound card and now you get a virtual device driver (VxD) error at boot time.   The problem is almost always caused by the old sound card drivers (not the new sound card drivers). Chances are that you did not remove or uninstall the old sound card's drivers and application software, and it's still trying to load when the system boots. Since the old card is no longer installed, the drivers show an error and refuse to load.

You'll need to remove the old sound card's drivers and uninstall the old application software.

Symptom 6.108. You find that your speakers "sleep" or the bass is too low. This is a known problem with Cambridge 4 Point surround speakers and is almost always caused by a driver problem. Aureal has released a set of drivers (2030_22rc or later) that should address this issue. Go to *www.a3d.com/html/download/drivers* and download the complete drivers for the Vortex 2 chipset. These drivers will enable the bass to function normally in both stereo and quad modes.

Symptom 6.109. You cannot install a sound card's software before installing the sound card. This is a known problem with Phoenix BIOS and LiveWare 2.0 when you're installing a SoundBlaster Live card. To install the sound software, you should install the sound card and its drivers first. Install the sound card and reboot your PC. After the PC has restarted, Windows 95/98 will attempt to detect your audio card and install drivers for it. Insert the original installation disc that comes with your sound card into the CD-ROM drive. When prompted to install the drivers, do the following:

1. Choose to install the drivers provided by your hardware manufacturer (found in the installation disc).

2. Specify the location and path where the driver software is located.

3. Now run the software setup program.

Symptom 6.110. You encounter an error such as "Setup cannot detect the sound card on your system." The sound application's setup program cannot detect the sound card hardware, so you'll need to make a few quick checks to isolate the problem:

1. Check that the sound card is listed and enabled under your Device Manager.

2. Use another mouse device or disconnect it entirely.

3. Restart the system to your CMOS Setup and see that your PNP OS INSTALLED option is set to Yes.

4. Try moving the card to another PCI slot.

7

Controller
Troubleshooting

Controllers basically perform two sets of functions. They manage system drives, such as hard drives, floppy drives, and *CD-rewritable disk* (CD-RW) drives, and they provide I/O capabilities (serial ports, parallel ports, game ports, and so on). Today most controller circuitry can easily be integrated onto the motherboard. However, it is impossible to add new controller features to the motherboard without replacing the entire motherboard, so stand-alone "controller boards" remain a popular and cost-effective way to introduce new features to an existing system. This chapter covers symptoms and solutions for three types of controllers: drive controllers, I/O controllers, and *Small Computer Systems Interface* (SCSI) controllers.

Drive Controllers

The term *drive controller* refers to the device that handles your *Ultra Direct Memory Access* (UDMA)/ *Enhanced Integrated Development Environment* (EIDE)/ IDE hard drives and floppy drives. Floppy drives use a 34-pin interface, and UDMA-type hard drives use a

40-pin interface. In today's PC, the drive controller circuits are typically located on the motherboard. Really only three circumstances occur in which you will see a stand-alone drive controller:

- *Older PCs.* You are working on an older system that requires a drive controller board because the motherboard does not incorporate an adequate controller.

- *System upgrade.* The motherboard's drive controller will not support such things as 2.88-MB floppy drives or Ultra-DMA/66 hard drives, and an advanced drive controller must be installed (the motherboard drive controller(s) must be disabled to upgrade the system.

- *Controller repairs.* The motherboard drive controller has failed. Rather than replace the entire motherboard, a stand-alone drive controller board may be installed to restore drive access.

Drive Controller Symptoms

Here we'll discuss several typical drive controller problems and offer solutions for remedying them.

Symptom 7.1. You cannot get the drive adapter software to install properly. When installing or upgrading drive controller software, it is not uncommon to encounter problems, usually due to the many advanced features of the drive controller itself. If you cannot get new software installed, try the following steps to overcome the problem.

- *Check the Complementary Metal Oxide Semiconductor (CMOS) Setup.* You should start the CMOS Setup and disable the high-performance features usually related to drive controllers: IDE Block Mode, Multi-Sector Transfer, and 32-bit Disk Access. If other options exist for the secondary drive controller channel, try disabling them as well.

- *Check for resource conflicts.* Try moving the controller BIOS address range (change the address range from C800h to CF00h).

- *Check for overlay software.* If you still cannot get the controller software installed, there may also be trouble with overlay software (such as Ontrack's Disk Manager or EZ-Drive software) used to partition and format a drive. You may need to uninstall the overlay software and update the CMOS Setup by enabling *Logical Block Addressing* (LBA) support for the drive. If you can't uninstall the overlay software, you can run FDISK /MBR to overwrite the overlay software. Once the overlay software is removed, repartition and reformat the drive. If you cannot wipe the drive clean, check with the drive manufacturer for such a utility. You should now be able to install the new drive software.

    NOTE: This step is destructive to any data on the drive. Be sure to make a complete system backup (and have a bootable diskette on hand) before removing the overlay software.

Symptom 7.2. The controller will not support a drive with more than 1,024 cylinders. This often happens when building a new system or piecing together a system from used parts. In order to support a drive with more than 1,024 cylinders, the controller must support LBA, and the feature must be enabled. The following checks can help discover the problem:

- *Check the controller.* The controller's onboard BIOS should support LBA, but you may need to install a driver for the controller in order to support LBA (for example, a Promise Technology controller needs the DOSEIDE.SYS driver to support LBA). If the controller is integrated onto the motherboard, the motherboard BIOS must support LBA. If not, you'll need to upgrade the motherboard BIOS or install a drive adapter with an LBA-aware BIOS.

- *Check the drive.*   The hard drive itself must support LBA. Make sure the drive is an EIDE hard drive. Finally, check the CMOS Setup and verify that the drive is using the LBA mode rather than the older CHS mode. You may need to repartition and reformat the hard drive.

Symptom 7.3. Loading a disk driver causes the system to hang or generate a bad or missing COMMAND.COM error. This is a known problem with some versions of the DTC DTC22XX.SYS or DOSEIDE.SYS drivers, but it frequently occurs with other controller makers that use disk drivers. The controller is probably transferring data too fast to the drive. The following checks are recommended:

- *Check/update the driver.*   When the disk driver loads, it obtains information from the drive, including drive speed. Sometimes the drive reports that it can support PIO mode 4 or PIO mode 3 when it actually cannot. In many cases, the original drivers are outdated, and the immediate solution is to slow down the data transfer rate manually. Download and install the newest drivers. Until then, you may be able to add a command line switch to the disk driver. For example, DTC recommends adding a switch to their DOSEIDE.SYS driver such as

```
DOSEIDE.SYS /v /dx:m0 /dx:p0
```

where x is the drive designation.

- *Check the driver loading characteristics.*   If your problems started after loading the disk drivers high (into the upper memory area), adjust CONFIG.SYS to load the drivers into conventional memory.

- *Check the CMOS Setup.*   Some drive adapters have reported better success with driver software when the Hidden Refresh feature is enabled in CMOS Setup (in the Advanced CMOS Setup area). This alters the way in which the system timing refreshes

RAM and may better support the disk drivers. Also try disabling advanced controller options such as IDE Block Mode, Multi-Sector Transfer, and 32-bit Disk Access.

■ *Check the overlay software.* If you're using overlay software (such as Disk Manager), the disk driver may not work with the overlay software. You'll then need to remove the overlay software and repartition and reformat the drive before the disk driver will work.

Symptom 7.4. Drive performance is poor; data transfer rates are slow. This often happens when installing a replacement drive controller and the following checks will correct the problem:

■ *Check for software conflicts.* Make sure that you're not running any anti-virus software. Anti-virus utilities that load at boot time can degrade drive performance.

■ *Check the controller's configuration.* If the controller uses a speed jumper, make sure you have properly configured the jumper settings on card to match the speed of the IDE drive and processor (this is a known issue with DTC's 2278VL and 2270 controllers).

■ *Check the CMOS Setup.* Make sure that the highest possible data transfer rate is selected in the CMOS Setup (PIO Mode 4 for older setups, or UDMA/33 or UDMA/66 for newer systems).

■ *Check/update the device driver(s).* If the drive adapter uses a disk driver for optimum performance, make sure that the correct disk driver software is loaded and see that any necessary command-line switches are entered.

■ *Check the overlay software.* Remove any third-party software (such as Disk Manager or EZ-Drive) that may have shipped with the drive itself.

Symptom 7.5. The PC refuses to boot after a drive adapter is installed. Many possible reasons exist for this kind of problem. See that the drive adapter is installed properly and completely into its bus slot. Then verify that the drive signal cables are oriented and attached properly. If the drive adapter uses jumpers to match the drive and processor speeds (such as the DTC 2278VL or 2270), make sure that the adapter is configured correctly. Verify that the drive itself is properly jumpered as a master or slave. Finally, check the CMOS Setup and confirm that the proper drive parameters are being used. Try disabling advanced features like IDE Block Mode and 32-bit Disk Access. If the problem still persists, try repartitioning and reformatting the drive.

Symptom 7.6. Windows generates a "Validation Failed 03,3F" error. This type of problem most frequently occurs after loading the Windows disk driver and is almost always due to a 1,024-cylinder limit in the drive system. Make sure that the drive and drive controller are able to support more than 1,024 cylinders (both UDMA or EIDE). Check the CMOS Setup and verify that the LBA mode is selected. Once the proper hardware is configured correctly, try reinstalling the disk driver.

Symptom 7.7. Windows hangs or fails to load files after loading the controller's driver. In most cases, Windows hangs, or every file after the offending driver is unable to load. In some cases, you may see an error message such as `Cannot find KRN.386`. Load SYSTEM.INI into a text editor and move the controller's driver (WINEIDE.386) to the last line in the [386enh] section. Also make sure that the classic WDCTRL driver is commented out, such as

```
;device=*WDCTRL
```

If problems persist, the controller's driver may be old or buggy. Download and install the newest disk driver version from the controller maker. If all else fails, disable the block mode and mode speed using the driver's internal switches or setup routine. For example, the WINEIDE.386 driver provides the switch WINEIDESWITCH that you can use, such as the following:

```
device=wineide.386

wineideswitch= /dx:m0 /dx:p0
```

Symptom 7.8. After replacing a drive adapter with a different model, the hard drive is no longer recognized. This can happen frequently with all types of IDE drives and controllers. You will find that the new controller is probably not using the same translation geometry used when the drive was originally partitioned. Verify that the drive geometry and LBA settings are as close as possible to the settings used on the older controller. You may need to use user-defined settings rather than auto-detect to ensure that the geometry settings are identical. If you cannot recreate the identical translation geometry for the drive, you'll have to repartition and reformat the drive with FDISK and FORMAT. Reinstall the original controller and perform a complete system backup before continuing.

Symptom 7.9. System problems occur after installing a VL drive adapter. This is a symptom usually found in older VL-based motherboards. It is quite common for a combination of components on VL-bus systems to exceed the tolerance limits for that specific motherboard. VL-bus noise generated by the motherboard chipset can easily contribute to floppy, floppy tape, and other drive failures. This may cause the system to hang on boot up and render it unable to access the hard drive. VESA video and controller cards also contribute to the load on the VL bus. If the load on the VL bus for a given motherboards is too high, then you will see compatibility problems with VESA video cards, intermittent system crashes, and *hard disk drive* (HDD) controller failures. System problems can manifest themselves in a wide variety of ways:

- Incompatibility with some VESA video cards (devices with S3 chipsets)

- Incompatibility with Colorado Floppy Tape

- Floppy disk failures

- System hangs on boot or when trying to access IDE hard drive

- Drive won't hold a partition

- Performance not improved with new drive adapter

- Intermittent system crash in Windows or other graphics program

- Modem status failures

In some cases, upgrading the disk controller to a later revision VL board that causes less loading and signal issues may provide a proper solution. For an immediate solution, try rearranging the VL devices or slowing the VL-bus speed to stabilize VL-bus operation. If you cannot correct the problem, consider upgrading the motherboard to a current model.

Symptom 7.10. You cannot enable 32-bit Disk Access under Windows. In most cases, you're using the wrong protected-mode driver, or the driver should be upgraded with a newer version. Download and install the latest disk drivers for your drive adapter. Before installing the new driver(s), be sure to disable advanced data transfer features such as IDE Block Mode and 32-bit Disk Access (if enabled). Load SYSTEM.INI into a text editor. Make sure that the protected-mode disk driver is installed under the [386enh] section, and verify that the WDCTRL driver is remarked out. Note that many Windows drivers will not support an IBMSLC2 processor or Ontrack's Disk Manager and will not work with 32-bit disk access.

Symptom 7.11. The IDE-type drive adapter's secondary port refuses to work. If the drive adapter has a secondary drive channel, that secondary channel is not working. In many cases, this type of problem occurs when the drive adapter relies on a disk driver for proper operation. Often, the secondary channel must be enabled specifically through the disk driver's command line in CONFIG.SYS, such as

```
DEVICE=DOSEIDE.SYS /V /2
```

Make sure that the drive attached to the secondary channel is jumpered as the master drive, and verify that the signal cable between the drive and controller is oriented properly. Also remember that a secondary drive channel requires a unique interrupt (usually IRQ 15). Make sure there is no hardware conflict between the secondary port's IRQ and other devices in the system. Try disabling advanced data transfer features in the CMOS Setup like IDE Block Mode and 32-bit Disk Access. If your hard drive is an older IDE drive, it may not support Multi-Sector Transfer. Try disabling Multi-Sector Transfer in the CMOS Setup, or by adding the necessary command-line switch to the disk driver command line in CONFIG.SYS, such as

```
DEVICE=DOSEIDE.SYS /V /2 /D0:M0
```

Symptom 7.12. The drive adapter's BIOS doesn't load. First, make sure that the BIOS is enabled (usually through a jumper on the drive adapter) and see that the BIOS chip is seated correctly and completely in its socket on the drive adapter. If problems persist, try changing the BIOS address. It's probably conflicting with another BIOS in the system. Also check the IRQ and I/O port assignments for the drive adapter for possible conflicts. If all else fails, try another drive controller.

Symptom 7.13. The drive adapter BIOS loads, but the system hangs up. First, make sure that the drive parameters are set properly in the CMOS Setup. Inexperienced users frequently mistake the parameters for a second drive in CMOS with a drive on the secondary channel. When there is no drive in the primary slave position, the second drive should be "none" or "not installed." If you have an onboard drive controller, make sure to disable it. Otherwise, you'll have a hardware conflict between the two drive controllers. Check the individual drives attached to the controller and verify that each drive is jumpered as a unique master or slave device (try reversing the drive order or working with only one drive). Finally, try disabling some of the advanced drive performance parameters in CMOS such as IDE Block Mode.

Symptom 7.14. The ATAPI CD-ROM is not recognized as the slave device versus an IDE master. First, verify that the CD-ROM is in fact ATAPI-compatible and suitable for use on an IDE-type interface. Second, make sure that the proper *low-level* (LL) ATAPI driver for the CD-ROM drive is in use. If the driver is old, try downloading and installing the newest version of the driver. If problems persist, the trouble is probably due to a fast IDE-type device coexisting with a slower IDE ATAPI device. Reconfigure the CD-ROM as the master device on the secondary drive controller channel. You may need to update the ATAPI driver command line in CONFIG.SYS.

Symptom 7.15. Hard drives are not recognized on the secondary drive controller channel. Make sure that all the hard drives are jumpered correctly. If only one drive is on the secondary channel, it should be configured as the single or master drive. If two drives exist on the secondary channel, verify that the drives are jumpered as master and slave. If the drive adapter uses a disk driver to support UDMA/EIDE or secondary-channel operations, make sure that the command line in CONFIG.SYS uses the correct switch(es) to enable the secondary drive channel. For example, the Promise Technologies 2300 would add an /S switch to the command line such as

```
device=c:\eide2300\eide2300.sys /S
```

Check that your system's power management features are not enabled on IRQ 15 (and confirm that no other devices are conflicting with IRQ 15). If the drive is set to auto-configure in the CMOS Setup, try entering the drive's parameters specifically (the drive may be too old to understand the *Identify Drive Command* [IDC] needed for auto-configuration). Finally, try booting the system clean (with just disk driver software if necessary) to see if any other driver or *Terminate and Stay Resident* (TSR) conflicts arise.

Symptom 7.16. The drive adapter can only support 528 MB per disk. First, make sure that the LBA mode is enabled. This is often accomplished through the CMOS Setup, but it may also be necessary to enable an LBA support jumper on some older EIDE drive adapters. If problems persist, the drive adapter's BIOS is probably too old and should be upgraded to a new version. If you cannot upgrade the drive adapter BIOS, install a new drive adapter outright.

Symptom 7.17. You get a code 10 error relative to the drive adapter. You notice that Windows 95/98 is running in DOS Compatibility mode, and the system only boots in Safe mode. You'll probably find one or more devices (including the drive adapter) marked with a yellow exclamation. Disk overlay software (such as Disk Manager, EZ-drive, or MaxBlast) will often cause problems when used in conjunction with drive adapters that use their own disk driver software. The disk overlay must be removed before installing the adapter's disk drivers. Remove the overlay software or simply repartition and reformat the drive (remember to do a complete backup before repartitioning). Next, remove or disable any 32-bit disk drivers previously installed under Windows. With Promise Technology drive adapters, you'll probably see the following under SYSTEM.INI:

```
[386enh]

device=*int13

;device=*wdctrl

;device=c:\windows\system\eide2300.386          (for
eide2300plus)

;device=ontrackw.386

;device=c:\windows\system\pti13.386 (for the 4030)

;device=c:\windows\system\ptictrl.386   (for   the
4030)

;device=wdcdrv.386

;device=c:\windows\system\maxi13.386    (for   the
eidemax)

;device=c:\windows\system\maxctrl.386   (for   the
eidemax)

32bitdiskaccess=off
```

When first installing the disk driver (such as the Promise Windows 95/98 driver), follow these next steps below (note that some UDMA drive adapters, especially new ones, do not require special drivers):

1. Open the Control Panel and double-click the System icon.

2. Choose Device Manager and double click on Hard Disk Controller.

3. Click once on the driver (standard IDE/ESDI driver) and click on Remove.

4. Reboot the computer.

5. Reopen the Control Panel and start the Add/New Hardware wizard.

6. Answer No when prompted for Windows 95/98 to auto-detect the device(s).

7. Select Hard Disk Controller and click on Have Disk.

8. Either insert the floppy diskette or choose Browse and move to the subdirectory where the disk drivers are located.

9. Follow the prompts and choose Finish, but do not reboot the computer yet.

10. Open the Control Panel and double-click the System icon.

11. Choose Device Manager and double-click on Hard Disk Controller. Click once on the installed driver and choose Properties. Select the Resource tab. If you see Basic Configuration of 1, IRQ 15, change this to Basic Configuration of 0, IRQ 14.

12. Now reboot the computer so that your changes can take effect.

There may also be a *Direct Memory Access* (DMA) conflict. Some drive adapters take advantage of DMA when the parallel port is in the ECP mode (the conflict occurs most often with the sound board). In order to find out which devices use DMA, open the Control Panel, double-click on the System icon, select Device Manager, and double-click on Computer. Choose Direct Memory Access. You can then either switch the controller's use of DMA or disable it altogether. You may need to alter the DMA setting on the drive controller itself and then switch the parallel port's mode to *Enhanced Parallel Port* (EPP).

Symptom 7.18. You encounter mouse problems after changing the drive adapter. This is a known problem with Logitech pointing devices or standard pointing devices using Logitech drivers. In most cases, you can correct the problem by downloading and installing version 7.0 or later Logitech drivers, or by switching to the Windows 95/98 serial mouse driver:

1. Open the Control Panel and double-click on the System icon.

2. Select Device Manager and double-click on Mouse.

3. Click once on Logitech and choose Remove.

4. Start the Add/New Hardware wizard in the Control Panel.

5. Choose No when Windows prompts to auto-detect the device.

6. Select Mouse. Click on Standard Serial Mouse. Click on Finish.

7. Reboot the computer.

Another solution may also be to disable the COM port's FIFO buffer. Open the Control Panel and choose the System icon. Click on Device Manager and double-click on Ports [COM & LPT]. Choose the Communications Port that the mouse uses (COM 1) by clicking on it once and then click on Properties. Select Port Settings and choose Advanced. Uncheck the box next to Use FIFO buffers and then click OK.

Symptom 7.19. You cannot run Norton Anti-Virus (NAV) 95 with Promise drive adapters. This appears to be an issue with the *Norton Anti-Virus* (NAV) software itself. According to Symantec (*www.symantec.com*), a patch has been released that corrects this problem.

Symptom 7.20. The system hangs after counting through system memory. You may also receive error messages such as Get Configuration Failed! or HDD Controller Failure. First, make sure that you have at least one hard drive attached to the controller and see that the signal cable is oriented properly at both ends. It is also possible that you may have a problem when more than one drive is connected. See that the drives are jumpered in the desired master and slave relationship. Try working with only one drive or reverse the drive jumper relationship (make the master drive the slave, and vice versa). In all cases, verify that the CMOS Setup entries accurately reflect the drives that are connected. If your drive adapter uses onboard RAM, the RAM may be bad. Try replacing the controller's onboard RAM or replace the drive controller outright.

Symptom 7.21. After replacing/upgrading a VL drive adapter, the system hangs intermittently during use.   This is a somewhat common complaint with older VL motherboards and drive adapters and is often due to bad memory on the drive controller or a bad VL-bus slot. Try replacing the RAM on the drive adapter. If the problem persists, try putting the drive controller in a different VL-bus slot. If you have a VESA VL video card also, try swapping in a 16-bit (ISA) video card. Some motherboards may become unstable with two VL cards in the system, especially when the VL bus is being run over 33 MHz (there is a great likelihood of this happening at 50 MHz). If you cannot correct the problem, upgrade the motherboard to a current model.

Symptom 7.22. Errors occur reading or writing to floppies after replacing/upgrading a drive adapter.   This is almost always due to a hardware conflict between the floppy adapter on the new controller, and another floppy adapter elsewhere in the system. Here you disable the floppy adapter port on the new drive controller card. If you're using the new floppy port, disable the floppy port already in the system.

> **NOTE**:   If you cannot successfully disable a current or pre-existing floppy controller, you'll need to remove the new drive controller and install a controller without a floppy port (or one that can be disabled properly).

Symptom 7.23. Your drive controller won't function with a 75-MHz bus speed. This occurs because the odd bus speed results in a PCI bus clock of about 37.5 MHz (which is higher than the 33 MHz that the PCI bus is designed for). This effectively overclocks the PCI bus and can often result in unstable or erratic operations for sensitive PCI devices such as the drive controller. The best solution here is to drop the motherboard's 75-MHz bus speed to 66 MHz where the clock can be divided down to 33 MHz for the PCI bus.

Symptom 7.24. You cannot use APM with hard drives oper-ated from a new drive controller. This is a known issue with high-end UDMA/66 controllers such as the Promise FastTrack66. In most cases, this is because the system sees the new controller card as a SCSI con-troller. Using IDE commands for APM will not work since the card is seen as a SCSI card. SCSI commands for APM will not work because the drives are IDE-type devices.

Symptom 7.25. You can't boot from a new IDE controller if you've got a SCSI card in the system already. Chances are that you'll need to tweak the setup of your new IDE controller (a Promise Ultra66 card) and existing SCSI card. If you have an actual SCSI controller in the sys-tem, the computer will attempt to boot from whichever controller is seen first. To get one controller to be shown before another, you must get its BIOS to load first. Manipulating the BIOS address that the card is set to use normally takes care of this.

However, virtually all IDE-type controllers are fully *plug-and-play* (PnP). This means that only the PnP BIOS on the motherboard can control which resources the card uses. Generally, the PCI slot with the highest priority will be assigned the lowest BIOS address. On most motherboards, the PCI slot with the highest pri-ority is PCI slot 1. If you cannot assign a specific memory address or loading order to your PCI devices through the CMOS Setup, try inserting the IDE drive controller so that it's in PCI slot 1.

Symptom 7.26. EMM386 fails to load after installing a new IDE controller. This is a known issue with some Promise IDE controllers (such as the FastTrack66 card) and is caused by the way motherboard memory handles memory. No workaround exists for this problem at the moment, but check for an updated controller BIOS from the manufacturer. If no update is available, you'll need to disable the use of EMM386.

Symptom 7.27. You cannot get QuickBooks 5.0 to start with an IDE controller in the system. This is a known issue with some Promise controllers, such as the Ultra33, and is caused by the controller's driver. We have found that if you use the Ultra33 driver version 1.33 and set it to Business mode with the UltraTune utility, QuickBooks will start. You can download this driver version from *ftp://ftp.promise.com/Controllers/ ftp://ftp.promise.com/Controllers/ IDE/U33_133.zip.*

Symptom 7.28. You find that your IDE controller is conflicting with the USB controller. This is a BIOS problem with the IDE controller itself. Check to see if a new BIOS version is available for your controller. For a Promise Ultra66, a new BIOS has been released to fix the conflict. You can download the BIOS from *ftp://ftp.promise.com/Controllers/IDE/Ultra66/U66_0628.zip.*

I/O Controllers

The PC also depends on a series on important ports to communicate with peripheral devices. Serial (COM) ports drive serial printers and modems. Parallel (LPT) ports operate parallel printers and other types of parallel port devices (parallel port tape drives and so on). Other ports also consist of game ports, light pens, and so on. Motherboards typically provide at least one COM port and one LPT port, but occasionally you may use a stand-alone I/O controller for the following reasons:

■ *Older PCs*.   Older PCs are usually fitted with UARTS that are now obsolete. Newer external modems demand a 16550A or later UART. It may be necessary to disable the motherboard's COM ports and use more efficient ports from an I/O controller. Remember to disable the motherboard's COM ports.

■ *System upgrade*.   You may need to add a second LPT port or COM port to the system. In this case, you do not need to disable the motherboard's ports, but you must make sure to set the new ports to different IRQs and address ranges to avoid hardware conflicts.

■ *Controller repairs*.   The I/O port on the motherboard has failed. Rather than replace the entire motherboard, a stand-alone I/O controller can be used to replace the failed port. Note that you still have to disable the corresponding port on the motherboard.

I/O Controller Symptoms

Here we'll discuss typical I/O controller problems and offer solutions to them.

Symptom 7.29. When an I/O board is installed, the parallel port does not print to its assigned port.   This is a known problem with several IBM PS/2 systems with built-in parallel ports. Check the motherboard BIOS. In IBM PS/2 systems, a BIOS bug causes this problem. LPT1 operates as LPT3, LPT 2 operates as LPT1, and LPT3 operates as LPT2. Try upgrading the system BIOS. For non-PS/2 systems, check for BIOS bugs also.

Symptom 7.30. You cannot configure a parallel port to LPT3. This may be a limitation of the particular I/O controller, so these checks are recommended:

- *Check the jumpers.* LPT3 resides at port 3BCh. If you can set the parallel port to that address, you can use the port as LPT3. Otherwise, you will have to use 378h (LPT1) or 278h (LPT2). Note that some I/O boards simply do not offer support for LPT3.

- *Check for hardware conflicts.* Make sure that no other devices in the system are using the 3BCh address area.

Symptom 7.31. The PC does not see COM3 or COM4 after adding an I/O controller. This is usually a limitation of the particular system BIOS rather than the I/O controller. Thus, make the following checks:

- *Check the ports.* Make sure that COM3 and COM4 are enabled on the I/O controller. Also make sure no other devices in the system are using the address ranges assigned to COM3 and COM4.

- *Upgrade the system BIOS.* Consider a BIOS upgrade to a version that will initialize COM3 and COM4 properly.

- *Try an initialization utility.* Some DOS utilities (such as DOSPORTS.EXE from the Boca Research Web site) can help to initialize COM3 and COM4 if the system BIOS cannot. Such utilities are generally placed in the AUTOEXEC.BAT file.

Symptom 7.32. The system fails to detect a mouse after an I/O controller is installed. In virtually all cases, one of the new COM ports is conflicting with the mouse's existing COM port. Check for hardware conflicts, and disable any unused COM ports. If you intend to keep the mouse on its existing COM port, disable the corresponding port on the new I/O card. If you intend to use the new COM port(s), disable the original COM port(s) and move the mouse to the new port.

Symptom 7.33. The new I/O controller's EPP will not drive the printer properly.   In most cases, the cable itself is at fault. The following checks will help you pin down the problem:

- *Check the I/O board.*   Make sure that you have configured the parallel port as EPP. This is often accomplished through a jumper on the board. Also be sure to disable any corresponding parallel port on the motherboard.

- *Check the printer.*   Make sure that the printer is compatible with EPP operation. If not, you may need to set the port back to Compatibility mode.

- *Check the cable.*   Make sure that the printer cable conforms to IEEE1284 specifications and is the correct length. Otherwise, you may need to set the port back to Compatibility mode.

SCSI Controllers

SCSI has been an icon of advanced computing since the late 1980s. SCSI enables you to chain devices together on the same bus without having to add controllers or deal with the configuration issues that are present with more traditional devices. Unlike other controllers, SCSI controllers (also called *host adapters*) are rarely integrated onto the motherboard. As a result, almost all SCSI-equipped PCs use stand-alone SCSI controllers. Although SCSI simplifies the addition of some devices, you must be aware of some special needs:

- *Termination.*   Both ends of the SCSI device chain must be electrically terminated with a set of terminating resistors. If the SCSI chain is terminated improperly, you will receive device and data errors.

- *Drivers.* SCSI driver software is required to operate the SCSI controller as well as SCSI devices such as CD-ROM drives, tape drives, and scanners. SCSI drivers consume memory and suffer from bugs and incompatibilities just like other drivers.

- *Device IDs.* The SCSI controller and every SCSI device on the chain requires its own unique device ID (that is, ID0 to ID7). Hardware conflicts can result if two or more devices use the same SCSI ID.

- *Device dependence.* SCSI devices are very dependent on the particular controller. For example, hard drives formatted with one SCSI controller may not work properly with another SCSI controller. If you replace the SCSI controller, you may need an entirely new set of drivers.

SCSI Termination

Although more conventional drive systems like floppy drives and UDMA drives integrate termination into each drive, SCSI configurations can be very diverse, and terminating every device would impair signal timing, so you must be able to specifically terminate the SCSI chain properly. Terminating a SCSI chain may sound easy, but it can sometimes be confusing in actual practice. Since termination problems cause a majority of SCSI problems, the following rules may help you avoid common mistakes:

- The SCSI bus needs exactly two terminators, never more, never less.

- The device located at each end of the SCSI bus must be terminated and all other devices must be unterminated.

- Devices on the SCSI bus should form a single chain that can be traced from a device at one end to a device at the other. No cable Ts are allowed and the cable length should be kept as short as possible.

- All unused connectors on the SCSI cable must be placed between the two terminated devices.

- The host adapter (controller) is a SCSI device.

- Host adapters may have both an internal and an external connector. These are tied together internally and should be thought of as an "in" and an "out." If you have only internal or external devices, the host adapter is terminated; otherwise, it is not.

- SCSI IDs are only logical assignments. They have nothing to do with where they should go on the SCSI bus or if they should be terminated.

- Just because an incorrectly terminated system happens to work now, don't count on it continuing to do so. Fix any termination issues wherever you encounter them.

SCSI Symptoms

This section covers SCSI malfunctions and offers solutions for correcting them.

Symptom 7.34. After initial SCSI installation, the system will not boot from the floppy drive. You may or may not see an error code corresponding to this problem. Thus, perform the following checks:

- *Check the SCSI host adapter.* There may be an internal fault with the adapter that is interfering with system operation. Check that all of the adapter's settings are correct and that all jumpers are intact. If the adapter is equipped with any diagnostic *light-emitting diodes* (LEDs), check for any problem indications. When adapter problems are indicated, replace the adapter board.

- *Check the drive cable.* If a SCSI hard drive has been installed and the drive light is always on, the SCSI signal cable has probably been reversed between the drive and adapter. Be sure to install the drive cable properly.

- *Check the SCSI BIOS.* Look for the SCSI adapter BIOS message generated when the system starts. If the message does not appear, check for the presence of a ROM address conflict between the SCSI adapter and ROMs on other expansion boards. Try a new address setting for the SCSI adapter. If a BIOS wait state jumper is located on the adapter, try changing its setting. If you see an error message indicating that the SCSI host adapter is not found at a particular address, check the I/O setting for the adapter.

- *Check for hardware conflicts.* Some more recent SCSI host adapters incorporate a floppy controller. This can cause a conflict with an existing floppy controller. If you choose to continue using the existing floppy controller, be sure to disable the host adapter's floppy controller. If you'd prefer to use the host adapter's floppy controller, remember to disable the pre-existing floppy controller port.

Symptom 7.35. The system will not boot from the SCSI hard drive. Start by checking the system's CMOS setup. When SCSI drives are installed in a PC, the corresponding hard drive reference in the CMOS setup must be changed to none or not installed (this assumes that you will not be using UDMA/EIDE hard drives in the system). If previous hard drive references have not been mapped out, do so now, save the CMOS Setup, and reboot the PC. If the problem persists, check that the SCSI boot drive is set to ID 0. You will need to refer to the user manual for your particular drive to find how the ID is set.

Next, check the SCSI parity to be sure that it is selected consistently among all SCSI devices. Remember that all SCSI devices must have SCSI parity enabled or disabled. If even one device in the SCSI chain does not support parity, it must be disabled on all devices.

Check the SCSI cabling to be sure that all cables are installed and terminated properly. Finally, be sure that the hard drive has been partitioned and formatted properly. If not, boot from a floppy disk and prepare the hard drive as required using FDISK and FORMAT.

Symptom 7.36. The SCSI drive fails to respond with an alternate HDD as the boot drive.   Technically, you should be able to use a SCSI drive as a non-boot drive (drive D:) while using a UDMA/EIDE drive as the boot device. If the SCSI drive fails to respond in this kind of arrangement, check the CMOS setting to be sure that drive 1 (the SCSI drive) is mapped out (or set to none or not installed). Save the CMOS Setup and reboot the PC. If the problem persists, check that the SCSI drive is set to SCSI ID 1 (the non-boot ID). Next, make sure that the SCSI parity is enabled or disabled consistently throughout the SCSI installation. If the SCSI parity is enabled for some devices and disabled for others, the SCSI system may function erratically. Finally, check that the SCSI cabling is installed and terminated properly. Faulty cables or termination can easily interrupt a SCSI system. If the problem persists, try another hard drive.

> **NOTE**:   Later SCSI host adapters use BIOS, which enables SCSI drives to boot even WITH IDE/EIDE drives in the system. In such a configuration, the Boot Order entry in CMOS Setup determines whether A:, C:, or SCSI will be the boot device.

Symptom 7.37. The SCSI drive fails to respond with another SCSI drive as the boot drive.   This typically occurs in a dual-drive system using two SCSI drives, so make the following checks:

- *Check the CMOS Setup.*   Make sure that both drive entries in the setup are set to none or not installed. Save the CMOS Setup.

- *Check the SCSI IDs.* The boot drive should be set to SCSI ID 0, while the supplemental drive should be set to SCSI ID 1 (you will probably have to refer to the manual for the drives to determine how to select a SCSI ID).

- *Check the drive preparation.* The hard drives should have a DOS partition and format. If not, create the partitions (FDISK) and format the drives (FORMAT) as required.

- *Check the SCSI parity.* See that the SCSI parity is enabled or disabled consistently throughout the SCSI system. If some devices use parity and other devices do not, the SCSI system may not function properly.

- *Check the cabling and termination.* Make sure that all SCSI cables are installed and terminated properly. If the problem persists, try systematically exchanging each hard drive.

Symptom 7.38. The system works erratically. The PC hangs or the SCSI adapter cannot find the drive(s). Such intermittent operation can be the result of several different SCSI factors. Making the following checks will help spot the problem:

- *Check the applications software.* Before taking any action, be sure that the application software you were running when the fault occurred did not cause the problem. Unstable or buggy software can seriously interfere with system operation. Try different applications and see if the system still hangs up (you might also try any DOS diagnostic utilities that accompanied the host adapter).

- *Check the SCSI parity.* Check each SCSI device and make sure that parity is enabled or disabled consistently throughout the SCSI system. If parity is enabled in some devices and disabled in others, erratic operation can result.

- *Check the SCSI setup.*   Make sure that no two SCSI devices are using the same ID. Cabling problems are another common source of erratic behavior. Make sure that all SCSI cables are attached correctly and completely. Also check that the cabling is properly terminated.

- *Check for resource conflicts.*   A resource conflict may exist between the SCSI host adapter and another board in the system. Check each expansion board in the system to be sure that nothing is using the same IRQ, DMA, or I/O address as the host adapter (or check the Device Manager under Windows 95/98). If you find a conflict, you should alter the most recently installed adapter board. If problems persist, try a new drive adapter board.

Symptom 7.39. You see an 096xxxx error code.   This is a diagnostic error code that indicates a problem in a 32-bit SCSI host adapter board. Check the board to be sure that it is installed correctly and completely. The board should not be shorted against any other board or cable. Try disabling one SCSI device at a time. If normal operation returns, the last device to be removed is responsible for the problem (you may need to disable drivers and reconfigure termination when isolating problems in this fashion). If the problem persists, remove and reinstall all SCSI devices from scratch or try a new SCSI adapter board.

Symptom 7.40. You see a 112xxxx error code.   This diagnostic error code indicates a problem in a 16-bit SCSI adapter board. Check the board to be sure that it is installed correctly and completely. The board should not be shorted against any other board or cable. Try disabling one SCSI device at a time. If normal operation returns, the last device to be removed is responsible for the problem (you may need to disable drivers and reconfigure termination when isolating problems in this fashion). Try a new SCSI host adapter board.

Symptom 7.41. You see a 113xxxx error code. This is a diagnostic code that indicates a problem in a system (motherboard) SCSI adapter configuration. If a SCSI BIOS ROM is installed on the motherboard, be sure that it is up to date and installed correctly and completely. If problems persist, try replacing the motherboard's SCSI controller IC or replace the system board. It may be possible to circumvent a damaged motherboard SCSI controller by disabling the motherboard's controller and then installing a SCSI host adapter card.

Symptom 7.42. You see a 210xxxx error code. There is a fault in a SCSI hard disk. Check that the power and signal cables to the disk are connected properly. Make sure the SCSI cable is correctly terminated. Try repartitioning and reformatting the SCSI hard disk. Finally, try a new SCSI hard disk.

Symptom 7.43. A SCSI device refuses to function with the SCSI adapter even though both the adapter and device check properly. This is often a classic case of basic incompatibility between the device and host adapter. Even though SCSI-2 and later standards help to streamline compatibility between devices and controllers, situations will occur when the two just don't work together. Check the literature included with the finicky device and see if there are any notices of compatibility problems with the controller (perhaps the particular controller brand) you are using. If there are warnings, there may also be alternative jumper or *Dual Inline Package* (DIP) switch settings to compensate for the problem and enable you to use the device after all. A call to technical support at the device's manufacturer may help shed light on any recently discovered bugs or fixes (an updated SCSI BIOS, SCSI device driver, or host adapter driver). If problems remain, try using a similar device from a different manufacturer (try a Connor tape drive instead of a Mountain tape drive).

Symptom 7.44. You see a "No SCSI Controller Present" error message. Immediately suspect that the controller is defective or installed improperly. Check the host adapter installation (including IRQ, DMA, and I/O settings) to see if the proper suite of device drivers has been installed correctly. If the system still refuses to recognize the controller, try installing it in a different PC. If the controller also fails in a different PC, the controller is probably bad and should be replaced. However, if the controller works in a different PC, your original PC may not support all the functions under the interrupt 15h call required to configure SCSI adapters (such as an AMI SCSI host adapter). Consider upgrading the PC BIOS ROM to a new version, especially if the PC BIOS is older. There may also be an upgraded SCSI BIOS or host adapter driver to compensate for this problem.

Symptom 7.45. The PCI SCSI host adapter is not recognized, and the SCSI BIOS banner is not displayed. This often occurs when installing new PCI SCSI host adapters. The following checks are recommended:

- *Check the PCI bus revision.* The host computer must be PCI REV. 2.0 compliant (or later). The motherboard BIOS must also support *PCI-to-PCI Bridges* (PPB) and bus mastering. This is typically a problem (or limitation) with some older PCI motherboard chipsets, and you'll probably find that the PCI SCSI adapter board works just fine on newer systems. If the system doesn't support PPB, it may not be possible to use the PCI SCSI adapter. You can try an ISA SCSI adapter instead or upgrade the motherboard to one with a more recent chipset.

- *Upgrade the BIOS.* If the system hardware does offer PPB support and the problem persists, the motherboard BIOS may still not support PPB features as required by the PCI 2.0 standard. In this case, try a motherboard BIOS upgrade if one is available.

■ *Check the slot configuration.*   If the problem continues, either the board is not in a bus mastering slot or the PCI slot is not enabled for bus mastering. Configure the PCI slot for bus mastering through the CMOS Setup or through a jumper on the motherboard (check your system's documentation to see exactly how).

Symptom 7.46. During boot-up, you see a "Host Adapter Configuration" error message.   In virtually all cases, there is a problem with the PCI slot configuration for the SCSI host adapter. Try enabling a IRQ for the SCSI adapter's PCI slot (usually accomplished through the CMOS Setup). Make sure that any IRQ being assigned to the SCSI adapter PCI slot is not conflicting with other devices in the system.

Symptom 7.47. You see an error message such as "No SCSI Functions in Use."   Even when a SCSI adapter and devices are installed and configured properly, this kind of an error has several possible causes and the following checks will help determine where the problem lies:

■ *Check the drivers.*   Make sure that no hard disk drivers are installed when no physical SCSI hard disks exist in the system. Also make sure that no hard disk drivers are installed (in CONFIG.SYS) when the SCSI host adapter BIOS is enabled. HDD drivers aren't needed then, but you could leave the drivers in place and disable the SCSI BIOS.

■ *Check the drive format.*   This error can occur if the HDD was formatted on another SCSI controller that does not support ASPI or uses a specialized format. For example, Western Digital controllers only work with Western Digital HDDs. In this case, you should try a more generic controller.

Symptom 7.48. You see an error message such as "No Boot Record Found." This is generally a simple problem that can be traced to several possible issues. First, chances are that the drive has never been partitioned (FDISK) or formatted as a bootable drive (FORMAT). Repartition and reformat the hard drive. If you partitioned and formatted the drive with a third-party utility (TFORMAT), be sure to answer yes if asked to make the disk bootable. A third possibility can occur if the disk was formatted on another manufacturer's controller. If this is the case, there may be little alternative but to repartition and reformat the drive again on your current controller.

Symptom 7.49. You see an error such as "Device fails to respond—No devices in use. Driver load aborted." In most cases, the problem is something simple such as the SCSI device not being turned on or cabled correctly. Verify that the SCSI devices are on and connected correctly. In other cases, the SCSI device is on but fails the *inquiry* command. This happens when the SCSI device is defective or not supported by the host adapter. The device may need default jumper settings changed (the drive should Spin up and Come Ready on its own). You may find that the SCSI device is sharing the same SCSI ID with another device. Check all SCSI devices to verify that each device has a separate SCSI ID. You may have the wrong device driver loaded for your particular device type. Check CONFIG.SYS to make sure the correct driver is loaded for the drive type (TSCSI.SYS for a hard disk, not a CD-ROM).

Symptom 7.50. You see an error such as "Unknown SCSI Device or Waiting for SCSI Device." The SCSI hard disk has failed to boot as the primary drive. Check that the primary hard disk is set at SCSI ID 0. Make sure that the drive is partitioned and formatted as the primary drive. If necessary, boot from a floppy with just the

ASPI manager loaded in CONFIG.SYS and no other drivers. Then format the drive. It may also be that the SCSI cable termination is not correct (or TERMPWR is not provided by the hard disk for the host adapter). Verify the cable terminations and TERMPWR signal.

Symptom 7.51. You see an error such as "CMD Failure XX." This typically occurs during the format process. The XX is a vendor-specific code (and you'll need to contact the vendor to determine what the error means). The most common problem is trying to partition a drive that is not LL formatted. If this is the case, run the LL format utility that accompanied the SCSI drive and then try partitioning again. If you're suffering a different error, you may need to take other action depending on the nature of the error.

Symptom 7.52. After the SCSI adapter BIOS header appears, you see a message like "Checking for SCSI target 0 LUN 0." The system pauses about 30 seconds and then reports BIOS not installed, no INT 13h device found. The system then boots normally. In most cases, the BIOS is trying to find a hard drive at SCSI ID 0 or 1, but no hard drive is available. If you do not have a SCSI hard drive attached to the host adapter, then it is recommended that the SCSI BIOS be disabled.

Symptom 7.53. The system hangs up when the SCSI BIOS header appears. This is usually caused by a terminator problem. Make sure that the SCSI devices at the end of the SCSI chain (either internally or externally) are terminated. Check all device IDs to make sure that they are unique and also check for system resource conflicts (BIOS address, I/O address, and interrupts). You may also need to disable the Shadow RAM feature in the CMOS Setup.

Symptom 7.54. The SCSI BIOS header is displayed during system startup. Then you get the message, "Host Adapter Diagnostic Error."   The card either has a port address conflict with another card or the card has been changed to port address 140h and the BIOS is enabled. Some SCSI host adapters can use the BIOS under port address 140h, so check for I/O conflicts. You may need to reconfigure the SCSI host adapter.

Symptom 7.55. When a VL bus SCSI adapter is installed, the system hangs at startup.   Chances are that the VL SCSI adapter is a bus mastering device and requires that the VL slot support full 32-bit bus mastering. Most VL bus systems have either slave slots and/or master slots. The SCSI adapter must be inserted into a master slot. If you are not sure if the system supports bus mastering or if you have a master slot, contact the system manufacturer. Also, the slot that the SCSI VL card is inserted into must be a 5Vdc slot that operates at 33 MHz or less. The VL bus speed is typically set through a jumper on the motherboard. It should be set in the greater than 33-MHz position. The motherboard may also need to be set for write-through caching. This may be set in the motherboard's CMOS Setup utility or it may be configured via a jumper on the motherboard (if there is both a CMOS setting and a jumper, be sure they are both set the same way).

Symptom 7.56. When upgrading a VL bus system CPU to a faster model, the system locks up with a SCSI VL card installed or won't boot from the SCSI HDD.   Most likely there is a DMA or other timing discrepancy between the SCSI adapter and the VL local bus. The SCSI adapter probably works fine on VL bus systems running up to 33 MHz. Faster CPUs can increase the VL bus speed beyond 33 MHz. Above this 33-MHz speed, variations in motherboard, chipset, or CPU design may cause the SCSI adapter to function intermittently or to fail. In some cases, this problem can be resolved in a variety of ways:

- The motherboard may have jumpers that govern the VL bus speed. Be sure that the VL bus speed jumper is set in the greater than 33 MHz position. This may also be set in the motherboard's CMOS setup.

- In the CMOS setup, you can disable the CPU external cache or change the caching method to write-through instead of write-back.

- The internal cache on some CPUs may cause the VL SCSI adapter to hang as well. Try disabling the CPU's internal cache.

- Reducing the CPU speed may be necessary to enable the SCSI adapter to function reliably.

- Try disabling the system's turbo setting during the boot-up sequence. Then re-enable the turbo setting after the system has booted.

Symptom 7.57. The VL SCSI adapter won't work with an SLC-type CPU. This is a problem that typically occurs with older VL-based motherboards. VL SCSI adapters often refuse to run with SLC-type CPUs because the SLC uses 16-bit architecture, rather than 32-bit at the VL bus. Some VL SCSI adapters will run in this configuration, but it is rare. Use an ISA SCSI adapter instead of an VL adapter in this circumstance.

Symptom 7.58. When running the Qualitas 386MAX memory manager software on ISA or VL systems with an SCSI host adapter, the system crashes when booting. 386MAX is known to cause problems with SCSI systems, and you'll need to adjust the 386MAX command line. Do not allow 386MAX to load during boot up and then include the key NOIOWRAP on the 386MAX command line. This will allow you to boot with 386MAX loaded.

Symptom 7.59. When installing an EISA SCSI adapter and running the EISA configuration utility, you see an "EISA configuration slot mismatch" or "board not found in slot x" error. This error is caused by the fact that your board is not completely seated in the EISA slot. You can verify this by booting to a floppy diskette and running the DOS debug command. After typing Debug, you will receive the debug prompt (a dash). Then type i (space) Xc80 in which X is the EISA slot where your board is physically installed. If a 04 is returned, the board is correctly seated and the problem lies elsewhere. If FF is returned, the board needs to be pushed down further. Power down your system before reseating your board.

Symptom 7.60. You cannot configure an EISA SCSI adapter in Enhanced mode. You get the error Unable to initialize host adapter or the system hangs after the SCSI BIOS scans the SCSI devices. These errors are usually limited to motherboards that do not support LEVEL INT triggering. These chipsets (such as the Hint and SIS) require a few modifications be made to the host adapter's EISA configuration (.CFG) file. Make the following changes to the !ADP000X.CFG file:

```
CHOICE = "Enhanced Mode"

FREE

INT=IOPORT(1) LOC (7 6 2 1 0) 10000B

LINK

IRQ=11|12|10|15|14|9

SHARE = "AHA-1740"              (Change to: SHARE = NO)

TRIGGER = LEVEL                        (Change       to:
TRIGGER = EDGE)

INIT=IOPORT(3) LOC(4 3 2 1 0) 10010B | 10011B |
10001B | 1010B | 10101B | 10000B

(Change first zero in each binary number to a one;
Example: 10010B = 11010B)
```

Another option is to download the latest .CFG file for your SCSI adapter card (ASWC174.EXE). Reconfigure the card with a new .CFG file and select `edge-triggered IRQ`.

Symptom 7.61. Adaptec EasySCSI software causes an invalid page fault error under Windows 95/98. When you reinstall the Adaptec EZ-SCSI version 4.0x software, you may receive the following error message:

```
ADPST32 caused an invalid page fault in module
MSCUISTF.dll at 015f:007d1bf7.
```

After you receive this error message, the computer may hang up. This problem can be caused when an Adaptec 3940UW Dual Channel SCSI adapter is installed on your computer, when you previously set the Write and Read Cache settings to Enable in SCSI Explorer (included with EZ-SCSI 4.0x), or when you uninstalled the EZ-SCSI software and then restarted the computer before attempting to reinstall the EZ-SCSI software. You should restore the firmware defaults for the SCSI BIOS:

1. Reboot the computer. When you see the SCSI BIOS banner, press Ctrl + A to start the SCSI BIOS Setup program.

2. In the SCSI BIOS Setup program, press F6 (or another appropriate key) to restore the factory default settings. You must do this for both channels if you're using a dual-channel SCSI host adapter.

3. Turn your computer off and back on.

4. Uninstall and then reinstall the EZ-SCSI software.

Symptom 7.62. You encounter problems with a BusLogic PCI SCSI controller. If your computer includes a PCI BusLogic SCSI controller, the Windows 95/98 Device Manager displays an exclamation point in a yellow circle next to the PCI BusLogic SCSI controller or the system performance is not a good as you expect with the controller. This fault can occur if the BusLogic card is not configured as a true PCI device. To configure the BusLogic card as a true PCI device, remove the jumpers in the bottom-right corner of the card. If you remove the jumpers, the card can be enumerated. If you leave the jumpers on the card, the card is detected as a legacy device and is not enumerated by the PnP system. Also, if you leave the jumpers on, the I/O range is set to a standard address (such as 330h, 334h, 130h, or 134h) instead of a high PCI address. As a rule, if the version number in the top-right corner of the BusLogic card is -01-4.23K or later, the card is supported in true PCI mode and you should remove the jumpers. If the version is earlier than -01-4.23K, leave the jumpers on the card.

Symptom 7.63. You encounter problems with an Adaptec SCSI controller and CD-RW drive. Your computer may hang up when you start your Windows 98 computer, or your computer may run slowly when you try to access drives in your computer. This problem can occur if you're using an Adaptec AHA-2940U2W SCSI host adapter with a SCSI CD-RW drive. The AIC78U2.MPD driver file included with the Adaptec AHA-2940U2W SCSI adapter is not completely compatible with Windows 98. To correct this problem, download the 7800W9X.EXE file from Adaptec's Web site. This self-extracting file contains updated drivers for the Adaptec AHA-2940U2W SCSI adapter.

Symptom 7.64. Windows 98 cannot locate the SCSI CD-ROM after upgrading. When Windows 98 Setup restarts your computer for the first time, Setup may be unable to access your SCSI CD-ROM drive, and you may receive error messages stating that files cannot be found (the file names vary depending on your computer's hardware). Once Setup is completed and you attempt to start Windows 98, your computer may hang up, and only a blinking cursor may be displayed on a black screen. In virtually every case, this problem will occur if the HIDE120.COM file (a file related to an LS120 drive) is being loaded from the AUTOEXEC. BAT file. Open your AUTOEXEC.BAT file and disable (REM-out) the HIDE120 command line, such as

```
d:\lsl120\hide120.com
```

Command Reference

There is no doubt that Windows 95/98 and *plug-and-play* (PnP) technology have gone a long way toward "automating" the configuration of a PC. The automatic detection of hardware, installation of protected-mode drivers, and reduced dependence on startup batch files (CONFIG.SYS and AUTOEXEC.BAT) have simplified many of the difficult and time-consuming configuration issues of years past. However, when working on PCs *without* Windows 95/98 (or when Windows fails to start), you will need to fall back to DOS commands and utilities in order to restore system operation. This chapter provides you with a DOS command reference that also covers utilities and batch file-specific functions.

DOS Shortcut Keys

The DOS shortcut keys are as follows:

- **F1** brings the last command back one letter at a time. You will have to press F1 repeatedly until the entire command string comes back.

- **F2** brings back the last command to the specified letter. For example, if the original command is

```
dir windows /p
```

the command F2 and N will bring the command back to

```
dir wi
```

- **F3** brings back the entire previous command.
- **F4** deletes everything in the command after the letter you specify (opposite of F2).
- **F5** copies the current command line to a template.
- **F6** produces a Ctrl-Z character that is typically used in command lines.

DOS Commands and Functions

This section will list the DOS commands, discuss their functions, and break down their code lines.

APPEND

This enables programs to open data files in specified directories as if they were in the current directory. Its syntax is as follows:

```
APPEND [[drive&]path[;...]][/X[&ON |
:OFF]][/PATH:ON | /PATH:OFF][/E]&]
```

- `[drive&]path` specifies a drive and directory to append.
- `/X:ON` applies appended directories to file searches and application execution.
- `/X:OFF` applies appended directories only to requests to open files.
- `/PATH:ON` applies appended directories to file requests that already specify a path.
- `/PATH:OFF` turns off the effect of `/PATH:ON`.
- `/E` stores a copy of the appended directory list in an environment variable named APPEND. `/E` can be

used only the first time you use APPEND after starting your system.

Type APPEND ; to clear the appended directory list. Type APPEND without parameters to display the appended directory list.

ASSIGN

This command redirects requests for disk operations on one drive to a different drive. Here is its syntax:

```
ASSIGN [x[&]=y][...]]&]
ASSIGN /STATUS
```

- X specifies the drive letter to reassign.
- Y specifies the drive that x: will be assigned to.
- /STATUS displays current drive assignments.

Type ASSIGN without parameters to reset all the drive letters to the original assignments.

ATTRIB

This command displays or changes file attributes. Its syntax is as follows:

```
ATTRIB [+R | -R][+A | -A][+S | -S][+H | -
H][[drive&][path]filename][/S]
```

- [+] sets an attribute.
- [-] clears an attribute.
- R is a read-only file attribute.
- A is an archive file attribute.
- S is a system file attribute.
- H is a hidden file attribute.
- /S processes files in all directories in the specified path.

BACKUP

This command backs up one or more files from one disk to another. Here is its syntax:

```
BACKUP source destination:
[/S][/M][/A][/F[&size]][/D:date[/T:time]]
[/L[drive&][path]logfile]]
```

- `source` specifies the file(s), drive, or directory to back up.
- `destination` specifies the drive to save backup copies onto.
- `/S` backs up the content of subdirectories.
- `/M` backs up only files that have changed since the last backup.
- `/A` adds backup files to an existing backup disk.
- `/F:[size]` specifies the size of the disk to be formatted.
- `/D:date` backs up only files changed on or after the specified date.
- `/T:time` backs up only files changed at or after the specified time.
- `/L[&[drive&][path]logfile]` creates a log file and entry to record the backup operation.

BREAK

This command sets or clears extended Ctrl+C checking. Its syntax is as follows:

```
BREAK [ON | OFF]
```

Type BREAK without a parameter to display the current BREAK setting.

BUFFERS

This command sets the number of buffers allocated from memory. Here is its syntax:

```
BUFFERS=x
```

x is the number of buffers required.

CALL

This command calls one batch program from another. Its syntax is as follows:

```
CALL [drive&][path]filename [batch-parameters]
```

batch-parameters specifies any command-line information required by the batch program.

CD or CHDIR

This command displays the name of the current directory or changes it. Here is its syntax:

```
CHDIR [drive&][path]
CHDIR[..]
CD [drive&][path]
CD[..]
```

Type CD drive: to display the current directory in the specified drive. Type CD without parameters to display the current drive and directory.

CHCP

This command displays or sets the active code page number. Its syntax is as follows:

```
CHCP [nnn]
```

nnn specifies a code page number. Type CHCP without a parameter to display the active code page number.

CHKDSK

This command checks a disk and displays a status report. Here is its syntax:

```
CHKDSK [drive&][[path]filename][/F][/V]
```

- [drive&][path] specifies the drive and directory to check.
- filename specifies the file(s) to check for fragmentation.
- /F fixes errors on the disk.
- /V displays the full path and name of every file on the disk.

Type CHKDSK without parameters to check the current disk.

CHOICE

This command enables input for multiple choices. Its syntax is as follows:

```
CHOICE /C:xxx.. [text]
```

- /C:xxx.. lists the numbers used in the selection (1234 and so on).
- [text] is the label that appears for the choices.

CLS

This command clears the screen. Here is its syntax:

```
CLS
```

COMMAND

This command starts a new instance of the MS-DOS command interpreter. Its syntax is as follows:

```
COMMAND  [[drive&]path][device][/E:nnnnn][/P][/C
string][/MSG]
```

- [drive&]path specifies the directory containing the COMMAND.COM file.
- device specifies the device to use for command input and output.

- /E:nnnnn sets the initial environment size to nnnnn bytes.

- /P makes the new command interpreter permanent (it can't exit).

- /C string carries out the command specified by the string and then stops.

- /MSG specifies that all error messages be stored in memory. You need to specify /P with this switch.

COMP

This command compares the contents of two files or sets of files. Here is its syntax:

```
COMP [data1][data2][/D][/A][/L][/N=number][/C]
```

- data1 specifies the location and name(s) of the first file(s) to compare.

- data2 specifies the location and name(s) of the second files to compare.

- /D displays differences in decimal format. The default is hexadecimal.

- /A displays differences in ASCII characters.

- /L displays line numbers for differences.

- /N=number compares only the first specified number of lines in each file.

- /C disregards the case of ASCII letters when comparing files.

To compare sets of files, use wildcards in data1 and data2 parameters.

COPY

This command copies one or more files to another location. Its syntax is as follows:

```
COPY [/A | /B] source [/A | /B][+ source [/A |
/B][+ ...]][destination [/A | /B]][/V]
```

- `source` specifies the file or files to be copied.
- `/A` indicates an ASCII text file.
- `/B` indicates a binary file.
- `destination` specifies the directory and/or file-name for the new file(s).
- `/V` verifies that new files are written correctly.

To append files, specify a single file for the destination, but specify multiple files for the source (using wildcards or `file1 1 file2 1 file3` format).

CTTY

This command changes the terminal device used to control your system. Here is its syntax:

```
CTTY device
```

`device` is the terminal device you want to use (such as COM1).

DATE

This command displays or sets the date. Its syntax is as follows:

```
DATE [date]
```

Type `DATE` without parameters to display the current date setting and a prompt for a new one. Press Enter to keep the same date.

DEBUG

This command runs Debug, a program testing and editing tool. Here is its syntax:

```
DEBUG [[drive&][path]filename [testfile-parameters]]
```

- [drive&][path]filename specifies the file you want to test.

- testfile-parameters specifies command-line information required by the file you want to test.

After Debug starts, type ? to display a list of debugging commands.

DEFRAG

This command reorganizes file clusters into contiguous disk areas. Its syntax is as follows:

```
DEFRAG [/switches] [sorting]
```

- /F defragments files and consolidates all empty space at the end of the disk.

- /U defragments files but leaves empty space alone.

- /V verifies that all files have been rewritten correctly.

- /B restarts the computer after DEFRAG has run.

- /S is the sorting options:

  - Alphabetically by name
  - Reverse alphabetically
  - Alphabetically by extension
  - Reverse alphabetically by extension
  - Date and time, earliest first
  - Date and time, latest first
  - Smallest to largest
  - Largest to smallest

DEL or ERASE

These commands delete one or more files. Here is its syntax:

```
DEL [drive&][path]filename [/P]

ERASE [drive&][path]filename [/P]
```

- `[drive&][path]filename` specifies the file(s) to delete. Specify multiple files by using wildcards.

- `/P` prompts for confirmation before deleting each file.

DELTREE

This command deletes an entire directory. Its syntax is as follows:

```
DELTREE [path]
```

DEVICE

This command loads a device driver in CONFIG.SYS. Here is its syntax:

```
DEVICE=[path and filename] [/switches]

DEVICEHIGH=[path and filename] [/switches]
```

- `path and filename` is the complete path to the device driver file.

- `/switches` is any command-line switches used for the driver.

DIR

This command displays a list of files and subdirectories in a directory. Its syntax is as follows:

```
DIR [drive&][path][filename][/P][/W][/A[[&]
attributes]][/O[]sort order]][/S][/B][/L]&]
```

- `[drive&][path][filename]` specifies the drive, directory, and/or files to list.

- `/P` pauses after each screenful of information.

- /W uses wide list format.
- /A displays files with specified attributes: Directories (D), Read-only files (R), Hidden files (H), Archive files (A), and System files (S).
- /O lists files in sorted order.
- sort order is N (by alphabetic name), S (by size, with the smallest first), E (by alphabetic extension), D (by date and time), or G (group directories first).
- /S displays files in a specified directory and all sub-directories.
- /B uses bare format (no heading information or summary).
- /L uses lowercase.

Switches may be preset in the DIRCMD environment variable.

DISKCOMP

This command compares the contents of two floppy disks. Here is its syntax:

```
DISKCOMP [drive1: [drive2&]][/1][/8]
```

- /1 compares the first side of the disks.
- /8 compares only the first eight sectors of each track.

DISKCOPY

This command copies the contents of one floppy disk to another. Its syntax is as follows:

```
DISKCOPY [drive1: [drive2&]][/1][/V]
```

- /1 copies only the first side of the disk.
- /V verifies that the information is copied correctly.

The two floppy disks must be the same type. You can specify the same drive for drive1 and drive2.

DOSKEY

This command edits command lines, recalls MS-DOS commands, and creates macros. Here is its syntax:

```
DOSKEY        [/REINSTALL][/BUFSIZE=size][/MACROS]
[/HISTORY][/INSERT | /OVERSTRIKE][macroname=[text]]
```

- `/REINSTALL` installs a new copy of DOSKEY.

- `/BUFSIZE=size` sets the size of the command history buffer.

- `/MACROS` displays all DOSKEY macros.

- `/HISTORY` displays all commands stored in memory.

- `/INSERT` specifies that any new text you type is inserted in old text.

- `/OVERSTRIKE` specifies that new text overwrites old text.

- `macroname` specifies a name for a macro you create.

- `text` specifies commands you want to record.

The following are special function keys under DOSKEY:

- UP and DOWN ARROWS recall commands.

- ESC clears the command line.

- F7 displays the command history.

- ALT+F7 clears the command history.

- F8 searches the command history.

- F9 selects a command by number.

- ALT+F10 clears the macro definitions.

The following are some special codes in DOSKEY macro definitions:

- $T is the command separator and it enables multiple commands in a macro.

- $1-$9 are the batch parameters and are the equivalent of %1-%9 in batch programs.

- $* is the symbol replaced by everything following the macro name on the command line.

DOSSHELL

This command starts MS-DOS Shell. Its syntax is as follows:

```
DOSSHELL [/T[&res[n]]][/B]&]
DOSSHELL [/G[&res[n]]][/B]&]
```

- /T starts MS-DOS Shell in text mode.

- :res[n] is a letter (L, M, H) and a number indicating screen resolution.

- /B starts MS-DOS Shell using a black-and-white color scheme.

- /G starts MS-DOS Shell in graphics mode.

ECHO

This command displays messages or turns command echoing on or off. The following is its syntax:

```
ECHO [ON | OFF]
ECHO [message]
```

Type ECHO without parameters to display the current echo setting.

EDIT

This command starts MS-DOS Editor, which creates and changes ASCII files. Here is its syntax:

```
EDIT [[drive&][path]filename][/B][/G][/H][/NOHI]
```

- `[drive&] [path] filename` specifies the ASCII file to edit.

- `/B` enables the use of a monochrome monitor with a color graphics card.

- `/G` provides the fastest update of a CGA screen.

- `/H` displays the maximum number of lines possible for your hardware.

- `/NOHI` enables the use of a monitor without high-intensity support.

EDLIN

This command starts Edlin, a line-oriented text editor. Its syntax is as follows:

```
EDLIN [drive&][path]filename [/B]
```

`/B` ignores end-of-file (Ctrl+Z) characters.

EMM386

This command turns on or off EMM386 expanded memory support. The following is its syntax:

```
EMM386 [ON | OFF | AUTO][W=ON | W=OFF]
```

- `ON | OFF | AUTO` activates or suspends the EMM386. EXE device driver or places it in auto mode.

- `W=ON | OFF` turns on or off Weitek coprocessor support.

EXE2BIN

This command converts .EXE (executable) files to binary format. Here is its syntax:

```
EXE2BIN   [drive1&][path1]input-file   [[drive2&]
[path2]output-file]
```

- `input-file` specifies the .EXE file to be converted.
- `output-file` specifies the binary file to be created.

EXIT

This command quits the COMMAND.COM program (command interpreter). Its syntax is as follows:

```
EXIT
```

EXPAND

This command expands one or more compressed files. The following is its syntax:

```
EXPAND [-r] Source [Destination]
```

- -r automatically renames expanded files but is only valid for files compressed with the -r switch.
- Source is a source file specification and may consist of multiple file specifications. Wildcards may be used.
- Destination is the destination file/path specification and may be a directory. If Source is multiple files and -r is not specified, Destination must be a directory. Wildcards may not be used.

FASTOPEN

This command decreases the amount of time needed to open frequently used files and directories. Here is its syntax:

```
FASTOPEN drive:[[=]n][drive:[[=]n][ ...]][/X]
```

- drive: specifies the hard disk drive you want Fastopen to work with.
- n specifies the maximum number of file locations Fastopen retains in its filename cache.
- /X creates the filename cache in expanded memory.

FC

This command compares two files or sets of files and displays the differences between them. Its syntax is as follows:

```
FC[/A][/C][/L][/LBn][/N][/T][/W][/nnnn][drive1&]
[path1]filename1 [drive2&][path2]filename2
```

or

```
[&@CP1X:FC /B [drive1&][path1]filename1 [drive2&]
[path2]filename2
```

- /A displays only the first and last lines for each set of differences.

- /B performs a binary comparison.

- /C disregards the case of letters.

- /L compares files as ASCII text.

- /LBn sets the maximum consecutive mismatches to the specified number of lines.

- /N displays the line numbers on an ASCII comparison.

- /T does not expand tabs to spaces.

- /W compresses white space (tabs and spaces) for comparison.

- /nnnn specifies the number of consecutive lines that must match after a mismatch.

FDISK

This command configures a hard disk for use with MS-DOS. The following is its syntax:

```
FDISK
```

FIND

This command searches for a text string in a file or files. Here is its syntax:

```
FIND    [/V][/C][/N][/I]    "string"    [[drive&]
[path]filename[ ...]]
```

- /V displays all the lines not containing the specified string.

- /C displays only the count of lines containing the string.

- /N displays line numbers with the displayed lines.

- /I ignores the case of characters when searching for the string.

- "string" specifies the text string to find.

- [|bul|drive&][path]filename specifies a file or files to search.

If a path name is not specified, FIND searches the text typed at the prompt, or piped from another command.

FOR

This command runs a specified command for each file in a set of files. Its syntax is as follows:

```
FOR %variable IN (set) DO command [command-
parameters]
```

- %variable specifies a replaceable parameter.

- (set) specifies a set of one or more files. Wildcards may be used.

- command specifies the command to carry out for each file.

- command-parameters specifies parameters or switches for the specified command.

To use the FOR command in a batch program, specify %%variable instead of %variable.

FORMAT

This command formats a disk for use with MS-DOS. The following is its syntax:

```
FORMAT  drive:  [/V[&label]][/Q][/U][/F:size][/B  |
/S]&]

FORMAT    drive:    [/V[&label]][/Q][/U][/T:tracks
/N:sectors][/B  |  /S]&]

FORMAT  drive:  [/V[&label]][/Q][/U][/1][/3][/4][/B
|  /S]&]

FORMAT  drive:  [/Q][/U][/1][/3][/4][/8][/B  |  /S]
```

- /V[&label] specifies the volume label.
- /Q performs a quick format.
- /U performs an unconditional format.
- /F:size specifies the size of the floppy disk to format (such as 160, 180, 320, 360, 720, 1.2, 1.44, or 2.88).
- /B allocates space on the formatted disk for system files.
- /S copies system files to the formatted disk.
- /T:tracks specifies the number of tracks per disk side.
- /N:sectors specifies the number of sectors per track.
- /1 formats a single side of a floppy disk.
- /3 formats a 3.5-inch, 720K floppy disk in a high-density drive.
- /4 formats a 5.25-inch, 360K floppy disk in a high-density drive.
- /8 formats eight sectors per track.

GOTO

This command directs MS-DOS to a labeled line in a batch program. Here is its syntax:

```
GOTO label
```

label specifies a text string used in the batch program as a label. You type a label on a line by itself, beginning with a colon.

GRAFTABL

This command enables MS-DOS to display an extended character set in graphics mode. Its syntax is as follows:

```
GRAFTABL [xxx]
GRAFTABL /STATUS
```

- xxx specifies a code page number.
- /STATUS displays the current code page selected for use with GRAFTABL.

GRAPHICS

This command loads a program that can print graphics. The following is its syntax:

```
GRAPHICS    [type][[drive&][path]filename][/R][/B]
[/LCD][/PRINTBOX:STD | /PRINTBOX:LCD]
```

- type specifies a printer type (see User's Guide and Reference).
- [drive&][path]filename specifies the file containing information on supported printers.
- /R prints white on black as shown on the screen.
- /B prints the background in color for COLOR4 and COLOR8 printers.
- /LCD prints using a *Liquid Crystal Display* (LCD) aspect ratio.
- /PRINTBOX:STD | /PRINTBO:LCD specifies the print-box size, either STD or LCD.

IF

This command performs conditional processing in batch programs. Here is its syntax:

```
IF Note ERRORLEVEL number command

IF Note string1==string2 command

IF Note EXIST filename command
```

- NOTE specifies that MS-DOS should carry out the command only if the condition is false.
- ERRORLEVEL number specifies a true condition if the last program run returned an exit code equal to or greater than the number specified.

- `command` specifies the command to carry out if the condition is met.

- `string1==string2` specifies a true condition if the specified text strings match.

- `EXIST filename` specifies a true condition if the specified filename exists.

JOIN

This command joins a disk drive to a directory on another drive. Its syntax is as follows:

```
JOIN [drive1: [drive2&]path]
JOIN drive1: /D
```

- `drive1:` specifies the disk drive that will appear as a directory on `drive2`.

- `drive2:` specifies the drive that you want to join `drive1` to.

- `Path` specifies the directory that you want to join `drive1` to. It must be empty and cannot be the root directory.

- `/D` cancels any previous `JOIN` commands for the specified drive.

Type `JOIN` without parameters to list currently joined drives.

KEYB

This command configures a keyboard for a specific language. The following is its syntax:

```
KEYB    [xx[,[yyy][,[drive&][path]filename]]][/E]
[/ID:nnn]
```

- `xx` specifies a two-letter keyboard code.
- `yyy` specifies the code page for the character set.

- `[drive&] [path]filename` specifies the keyboard definition file.

- `/E` specifies that an enhanced keyboard is installed.

- `/ID:nnn` specifies the keyboard in use.

LABEL

This command creates, changes, or deletes the volume label of a disk. Here is its syntax:

```
LABEL [drive&][label]
```

LASTDRIVE

This command specifies the maximum number of drives in the system. Its syntax is as follows:

```
LASTDRIVE=x
```

`x` is the last drive letter in the system.

LH or LOADHIGH

These commands load a program into the upper memory area. The following is its syntax:

```
LOADHIGH [drive&][path]filename [parameters]

LH [drive&][path]filename [parameters]
```

`parameters` specifies any command-line information required by the program you want to load.

LOADFIX

This command loads a program above the first 64K of memory and runs the program. Here is its syntax:

```
LOADFIX [drive&][path]filename
```

Use `LOADFIX` to load a program if you have received the message `Packed file corrupt` when trying to load it in low memory.

MD or MKDIR

These commands create a directory. Its syntax is as
follows:

```
MKDIR [drive&]path
MD [drive&]path
```

MEM

This command displays the amount of used and free
memory in your system. The following is its syntax:

```
MEM [/PROGRAM | /DEBUG | /CLASSIFY]
```

- /PROGRAM or /P displays the status of programs
  currently loaded in memory.

- /DEBUG or /D displays the status of programs, internal drivers, and other information.

- /CLASSIFY or /C classifies programs by memory
  usage. It lists the size of the programs, provides a
  summary of the memory in use, and lists the largest
  memory block available.

MIRROR

This command records information about one or more
disks. Here is its syntax:

```
MIRROR [drive:[ ...]][/1][/Tdrive[-entries][ ...]]
MIRROR [/U]
MIRROR [/PARTN]
```

- drive: specifies the drive for which you want to
  save information.

- /1 saves only the latest disk information (it does not
  back up previous information).

- /Tdrive loads the deletion-tracking program for
  the specified drive.

- -entries specifies the maximum number of entries in the deletion-tracking file.

- /U unloads the deletion-tracking program.

- /PARTN saves hard disk partition information to a floppy diskette.

MODE

This command configures a system device. Its syntax is as follows:

```
Printer port: MODE LPTn[&] [COLS=c] [LINES=l]
[RETRY=r]&]

Serial port: MODE COMm[&] [BAUD=b] [PARITY=p]
[DATA=d] [STOP=s] [RETRY=r]&]

Device Status: MODE [device] [/STATUS]

Redirect printing: MODE LPTn[&]=COMm]&]

[&@T1:Prepare code page: MODE device CP
PREPARE=((yyy[...]) [drive&][path]filename)

Select code page: MODE device CP SELECT=yyy

Refresh code page: MODE device CP REFRESH

Code page status: MODE device CP [/STATUS]

Display mode: MODE [display-adapter][,n]

MODE CON[&][COLS=c][LINES=n]&]

Typematic rate: MODE CON[&] [RATE=r DELAY=d]&]
```

MORE

This command displays output one screen at a time. The following is its syntax:

```
MORE |less| [drive&][path]filename

command-name | MORE
```

- [drive&][path]filename specifies a file to display one screen at a time.

- command-name specifies a command whose output will be displayed.

MOVE

This command transfers files among directories. Here is its syntax:

```
MOVE [source path][destination path]
```

MSAV

This command scans the computer for viruses. Its syntax is as follows:

```
MSAV [drive][switches]
```

- `drive` is the drive letter to be scanned.
- `/S` activates the Detect button.
- `/C` activates the Detect and Clean button.
- `/R` creates a report file (MSAV.RPT) in the scanned drive's root directory.
- `/A` scans all drives but floppy drives.
- `/L` scans all diskette and floppy drives.
- `/P` disables the program's graphic interface for general scanning.
- `/N` disables the program's graphic interface for batch file scanning.
- `/F` prevents naming all scanned files (used with `/P` and `/N`).
- `/VIDEO` displays video and mouse options.

MSCDEX

This command is the DOS CD-ROM drive extension. The following is its syntax:

```
MSCDEX [/D:device] [switches] [/L:letter]
```

- `/D:device` is the label used by the *low-level* (LL) device driver when it loads. A typical label is MSCD000.

- /M:x is the number of two-KB buffers allocated to the CD-ROM drives.

- /L:letter is the optional drive letter for the CD-ROM.

- /N forces MSCDEX to show memory usage statistics on the display each time the system boots.

- /S is the switch used with CD-ROM installations in network systems.

- /K instructs MSCDEX to use Kanji (Japanese) file types on the CD if present.

- /E enables MSCDEX to use expanded memory for buffers.

NLSFUNC

This command loads country-specific information. Here is its syntax:

```
NLSFUNC [path]
```

PATH

This command displays or sets a search path for executable files. Its syntax is as follows:

```
PATH [[drive&]path[;...]]
PATH ;
```

Type PATH ; to clear all search-path settings and direct MS-DOS to search only in the current directory. Type PATH without parameters to display the current path.

PAUSE

This command suspends the processing of a batch file and displays a message. The following is its syntax:

```
PAUSE
```

PRINT

This prints a text file while you are using other MS-DOS commands. Here is its syntax:

```
PRINT [/D:device] [/B:size] [/U:ticks1]
[/M:ticks2] [/S:ticks3] [/Q:qsize] [/T]
[[drive&][path]filename[  . . . ]] [/C] [/P]
```

- /D:device specifies a print device.

- /B:size sets the internal buffer size in bytes.

- /U:ticks1 waits the specified maximum number of clock ticks for the printer to be available.

- /M:ticks2 specifies the maximum number of clock ticks it takes to print a character.

- /S:ticks3 allocates the scheduler the specified number of clock ticks for background printing.

- /Q:qsize specifies the maximum number of files allowed in the print queue.

- /T removes all files from the print queue.

- /C cancels printing of the preceding filename and subsequent filenames.

- /P adds the preceding filename and subsequent filenames to the print queue.

Type PRINT without parameters to display the contents of the print queue.

PROMPT

This command changes the MS-DOS command prompt. Its syntax is as follows:

```
PROMPT [text]
```

text specifies a new command prompt. PROMPT can be made up of normal characters and the following special codes:

- $Q: = (equal sign)
- $$: $ (dollar sign)
- $T: Current time
- $D: Current date
- $P: Current drive and path
- $V: MS-DOS version number
- $N: Current drive
- $G: > (greater-than sign)
- $L: < (less-than sign)
- $B: | (pipe)
- $H: Backspace (erases previous character)
- $E: Escape code (ASCII code 27)
- $_: Carriage return and linefeed

Type PROMPT without parameters to reset the prompt to the default setting.

QBASIC

This command starts the MS-DOS QBasic programming environment. The following is its syntax:

```
QBASIC   [/B][/EDITOR][/G][/H][/MBF][/NOHI][[/RUN]
[drive&][path]filename]
```

- /B enables the use of a monochrome monitor with a color graphics card.
- /EDITOR starts the MS-DOS Editor.
- /G provides the fastest update of a CGA screen.
- /H displays the maximum number of lines possible for your hardware.
- /MBF converts the built-in functions MKS$, MKD$, CVS, and CVD to MKSMBF$, MKDMBF$, CVSMBF, and CVDMBF, respectively.

- /NOHI enables the use of a monitor without high-intensity support.

- /RUN runs the specified Basic program before displaying it.

- [[drive&][path]filename] specifies the program file to load or run.

RD or RMDIR

These commands remove a directory. Here is its syntax:

```
RMDIR [drive&]path
RD [drive&]path
```

RECOVER

This command recovers readable information from a bad or defective disk. Its syntax is as follows:

```
RECOVER [drive&][path]filename
RECOVER drive:
```

REM

This command records comments (or remarks) in batch files or CONFIG.SYS. The following is its syntax:

```
REM [comment]
```

It is useful for commenting out lines in a batch file without having to remove the line entirely.

REN or REMANE

These commands rename a file or files. Here is its syntax:

```
RENAME [drive&][path]filename1 filename2
REN [drive&][path]filename1 filename2
```

Note that you cannot specify a new drive or path for your destination file.

REPLACE

This command is used to replace files. Its syntax is as follows:

```
REPLACE  [drive1&][path1]filename  [drive2&][path2]
[/A][/P][/R][/W]

REPLACE   [drive1&][path1]filename[drive2&][path2]
[/P][/R][/S][/W][/U]
```

- `[drive1&][path1]filename` specifies the source file or files.

- `[drive2&][path2]` specifies the directory where files are to be replaced.

- `/A` adds new files to the destination directory. It cannot be used with `/S` or `/U` switches.

- `/P` prompts for confirmation before replacing a file or adding a source file.

- `/R` replaces read-only files as well as unprotected files.

- `/S` replaces files in all subdirectories of the destination directory. It cannot be used with the `/A` switch.

- `/W` waits for you to insert a disk before beginning.

- `/U` replaces (updates) only files that are older than source files. It cannot be used with the `/A` switch.

RESTORE

This command restores files that were backed up using the BACKUP command. The following is its syntax:

```
RESTORE drive1:drive2:[path[filename]][/S][/P]
[/B:date][/A:date][/E:time] [/L:time][/M][/N][/D]
```

- `drive1:` specifies the drive where the backup files are stored.

- `drive2:[path[filename]]` specifies the file(s) to restore.

- `/S` restores files in all subdirectories in the path.

- /P prompts before restoring read-only files or files changed since the last backup (if appropriate attributes are set).

- /B restores only files last changed on or before the specified date.

- /A restores only files changed on or after the specified date.

- /E restores only files last changed at or earlier than the specified time.

- /L restores only files changed at or later than the specified time.

- /M restores only files changed since the last backup.

- /N restores only files that no longer exist on the destination disk.

- /D displays files on the backup disk that match specifications.

SCANDISK

This command is the DOS disk drive analysis tool. Here is its syntax:

```
SCANDISK drive: [/all] [/switches]
SCANDISK /undo [undo-drive&]
SCANDISK /fragment [path]
```

- /all checks and repairs all local drives at once.

- /autofix fixes errors without asking first.

- /checkonly checks for errors but will not repair them.

- /custom runs ScanDisk using settings in the [CUSTOM] section of SCANDISK.INI.

- /fragment checks files for fragmentation.

- /mono uses a monochrome display instead of color.

- /nosave deletes all lost clusters found by ScanDisk.

- /nosummary prohibits a full-screen summary after each drive.

- /surface performs a surface analysis without asking first.

- /undo uses an undo diskette to undo any repairs that have been made.

SET

This command displays, sets, or removes MS-DOS environment variables. Its syntax is as follows:

```
SET [variable=[string]]
```

- variable specifies the environment-variable name.

- string specifies a series of characters to assign to the variable.

Type SET without parameters to display the current environment variables.

SETVER

This command sets the version number that MS-DOS reports to a program. The following is its syntax:

```
Display current version table: SETVER
[drive:path]
```

Add entry: SETVER [drive:path] filename n.nn

```
Delete entry: SETVER [drive:path] filename /DELETE
[/QUIET]
```

- [drive:path] specifies the location of the SETVER.EXE file.

- filename specifies the filename of the program.

- n.nn specifies the MS-DOS version to be reported to the program.

- /DELETE or /D deletes the version-table entry for the specified program.

- /QUIET hides the message typically displayed during deletion of the version-table entry.

SHARE

This command installs file-sharing and locking capabilities on your hard disk. Here is the syntax:

```
SHARE [/F:space] [/L:locks]
```

- /F:space allocates file space (in bytes) for file-sharing information.

- /L:locks sets the number of files that can be locked at one time.

SHIFT

This command shifts the position of replaceable parameters in batch files. Its syntax is as follows:

```
SHIFT
```

SORT

This command sorts input. The following is its syntax:

```
SORT [/R] [/+n] |less| [drive1&][path1]filename1 [>
[drive2&][path2]filename2] [command |] SORT [/R]
[/+n] [> [drive2&][path2]filename2]
```

- /R reverses the sort order; that is, it sorts Z to A, then 9 to 0.

- /+n sorts the file according to the characters in column n.

- [drive1&][path1]filename1 specifies a file to be sorted.

- `[drive2&][path2]filename2` specifies a file where the sorted input is to be stored.

- `command` specifies a command whose output is to be sorted.

SUBST

This command associates a path with a drive letter. Here is its syntax:

```
SUBST [drive1: [drive2&]path]
SUBST drive1: /D
```

- `drive1:` specifies a virtual drive that you want to assign a path to.

- `[drive:2]path` specifies a physical drive and path you want to assign a virtual drive to.

- `/D` deletes a substituted (virtual) drive.

Type SUBST with no parameters to display a list of current virtual drives.

SYS

This command copies MS-DOS system files and command interpreter to a disk you specify. Its syntax is as follows:

```
SYS [drive1&][path] drive2:
```

- `[drive1&][path]` specifies the location of the system files.

- `drive2:` specifies the drive the files are to be copied to.

TIME

This command displays or sets the system time. The following is its syntax:

```
TIME [time]
```

Type TIME with no parameters to display the current time setting and a prompt for a new one. Press Enter to keep the same time.

TREE

This command graphically displays the directory structure of a drive or path. Here is its syntax:

```
TREE [drive&][path][/F][/A]
```

- /F displays the names of the files in each directory.

- /A uses ASCII instead of extended characters.

TYPE

This command displays the contents of a text file. Its syntax is as follows:

```
TYPE [drive&][path]filename
```

UNDELETE

This command recovers files that have been deleted. The following is its syntax:

```
UNDELETE [[drive&][path]][filename] [/LIST | /ALL]
[/DT | /DOS]
```

- /LIST lists the deleted files available to be recovered.

- /ALL undeletes all specified files without prompting.

- /DT uses only the deletion-tracking file.

- /DOS uses only the MS-DOS directory.

UNFORMAT

This command restores a disk erased by the FORMAT command or restructured by the RECOVER command. Here is its syntax:

```
UNFORMAT drive: [/J]
UNFORMAT drive: [/U][/L][/TEST][/P]
UNFORMAT /PARTN [/L]
```

- `drive:` specifies the drive to unformat.
- `/J` verifies that the mirror files agree with the system information on the disk.
- `/U` unformats without using MIRROR files.
- `/L` lists all file and directory names found or, when used with the `/PARTN` switch, displays current partition tables.
- `/TEST` displays information but does not write changes to disk.
- `/P` sends output messages to the printer connected to LPT1.
- `/PARTN` restores disk partition tables.

VER

This command displays the MS-DOS version. Its syntax is as follows:

```
VER
```

VERIFY

This command tells MS-DOS whether to verify that your files are written correctly to a disk. The following is its syntax:

```
VERIFY [ON | OFF]
```

Type `VERIFY` without a parameter to display the current `VERIFY` setting.

VOL

This command displays a disk volume label and a serial number. Here is its syntax:

```
VOL [drive&]
```

VSAFE

This command runs the DOS anti-virus checking utility. Its syntax is as follows:

```
VSAFE [/option] [/switches]
```

- 1 warns of formatting attempts that could erase the drive.
- 2 warns of a virus attempting to load into memory.
- 3 prevents programs from writing to the drive.
- 4 checks each program for viruses as they are executed.
- 5 checks all disks for boot sector viruses.
- 6 warns of attempts to write to the boot sector or partition of a hard drive.
- 7 warns of attempts to write to the boot sector of a diskette.
- 8 warns of attempts to modify program files.

The switches for VSAFE are as follows:

- /N enables network virus checking.
- /D turns off the checksum feature.
- /U removes VSAFE from memory.
- /NE prevents VASFE from loading into expanded memory.
- /NX prevents VSAFE from loading into extended memory.
- /AX sets a VSAFE screen hotkey as Alt-V.
- /CX sets a VSAFE screen hotkey as Ctrl-V.

XCOPY

This command copies files (except hidden and system files) and directory trees. The following is its syntax:

```
XCOPY source [destination][/A | /M][/D:date][/P][/S
[/E]][/V][/W]
```

- `source` specifies the file(s) to copy.

- `destination` specifies the location and/or name of new files.

- `/A` copies files with the archive attribute set yet doesn't change the attribute.

- `/M` copies files with the archive attribute set and turns off the archive attribute.

- `/D:date` copies files changed on or after the specified date.

- `/P` prompts you before creating each destination file.

- `/S` copies directories and subdirectories except empty ones.

- `/E` copies any subdirectories, even if empty.

- `/V` verifies each new file.

- `/W` prompts you to press a key before copying.

DOS Error Messages

DOS provides myriad error messages to indicate problems or issues that we should be aware of. Unfortunately, DOS error messages are cryptic at best, and there is precious little documentation to explain the causes of these errors (and even less help in correcting these errors). The following list provides a general index of DOS error messages, explains the potential causes of the error, and offers some practical solutions.

> **NOTE**: The exact wording of these errors may vary slightly between DOS versions, and not all errors may be reported in all DOS versions.

ABORT, RETRY, or FAIL

This message has several causes, but they all mean that there's a problem with the disk(ette) DOS/Windows is trying to access. The drive is not reading a disk in the drive that you've instructed DOS/Windows to check. First, see that you typed the correct drive letter in the command line and that the diskette is in the correct drive (if you have more than one diskette drive). Next, check that the diskette is fully inserted into the drive (label side up) and that the drive door is closed properly. Then press R to retry. This message also could mean the disk you're using is damaged. Try the diskette in a different drive or try a different diskette.

ACCESS DENIED

You just tried to change a file that is: (1) on a write-protected diskette, (2) locked, or (3) a read-only file. Write-protected diskettes can be read but not be written to (some commercial software is write-protected). A locked file is one that can't be altered in a common way (such as adding or deleting data, moving the file, or changing the name of the file). A read-only file is one that a programmer has added a command to so that users can only view the information or a file that resides in *read-only memory* (ROM). There's usually a good reason why you aren't being allowed to change the file. You may need to change the attributes of the file before you're allowed to modify it.

BAD COMMAND OR FILE NAME

DOS/Windows didn't recognize the command you just typed or can't find a file you referred to in the command line entry. The most likely problem is that you mis-spelled either the command or the file name. Another possibility is that you haven't established the right path to a file. Recheck the location of the file and be sure to enter the path correctly when you retype the command. Finally, it may be possible that the version of DOS/Windows you're running doesn't recognize this command. You'll need to see if your version has an equiv-alent command or update the DOS/Windows version.

BAD OR MISSING COMMAND INTERPRETER

This means DOS can't find COMMAND.COM, and your CONFIG.SYS file doesn't have a SHELL statement telling DOS where to look for COMMAND.COM. Your COMMAND.COM file may have been damaged or deleted, or your SHELL command was removed from the CONFIG.SYS file. It may also be that the wrong version of COMMAND.COM is copied to the disk. Your hard drive may also be damaged (or infected with a virus), preventing DOS from accessing the DOS directory. Boot from an emergency bootable diskette that contains the same version of COMMAND.COM that should be on the hard drive. Then copy the file COMMAND.COM to the root directory of your hard drive and reboot. You may want to add a SHELL statement to the CONFIG.SYS file indicating the exact location of the COMMAND.COM file. You may also want to reinstall DOS (or Windows 95/98) outright.

BAD OR MISSING FILE NAME

A command in your CONFIG.SYS file is entered incorrectly. You should get this message only if you recently changed something in this file. Go back and check to be sure you typed the recent addition or change correctly. If you have not made changes to the file, the file(s) being referred to in CONFIG.SYS may be corrupt or deleted. Verify that any files referred to in the CONFIG.SYS file are present.

> **NOTE**: Anytime you make a change to the files CONFIG.SYS or AUTOEXEC.BAT, make a backup copy of the original file(s) prior to making the changes.

CANNOT FIND A DEVICE FILE THAT MAY BE NEEDED TO RUN WINDOWS

The error also goes on to say, Make sure that the PATH line in your AUTOEXEC.BAT points to the directory that contains the file and that it exists on your hard disk. If the file does not exist, try running Setup to install it or remove any references in your SYSTEM.INI file. C:\directory\filename. Press a key to continue. Although this message does tell you what to do to fix the problem, it is still largely unclear. It means a given file that may or may not be necessary to run Windows isn't where DOS thinks it should be.

The offending file is listed in the second to last sentence of the error message, and the path given is the location where DOS expected to find the file. It may be a file that was installed with an application you've since removed (when you remove an application from your system, a reference to a file from that program often remains in your SYSTEM.INI file). You may be able to simply press a key to continue and experience no difficulty. To be sure you don't encounter a more serious problem, however, you'll want to either install the offending file in the location DOS specified, point DOS to the real location of the file, or remove mention of the file from the file SYSTEM.INI file so DOS won't try to look for it anymore.

CANNOT FIND SYSTEM FILES

This message appears when you try to make a bootable diskette, but DOS can't find the necessary system files. Make sure that you're in the directory containing these files (which is usually your C:\ root directory). Switch drives and/or directories if necessary, and then try making the system diskette again.

DIRECTORY ALREADY EXISTS

You've tried to create a directory with the same name as one that already exists. Just choose a different name for the new directory or use the existing directory if it's appropriate.

DISK FULL

This message appears during a copy operation when the destination diskette is full. Remove some unneeded files from the diskette to make room for the full copy to fit or use another diskette to receive the additional files.

DRIVE A: DOES NOT EXIST

This message can be caused by a dirty diskette drive (the diskette cannot be read). Get a diskette drive cleaner kit and follow its instructions to clean the drive. If this doesn't solve the problem, you may have a bad floppy disk drive or floppy disk controller.

DUPLICATE FILE NAME OR FILE(S) NOT FOUND

This message occurs when you try to use the REN command to rename a file. It means that either you're trying to rename the file using a name that is already in use, or the file you want to rename couldn't be found. Check your spelling and check whether the new name is already in use in the directory. Then try the REN command again, typing carefully and using a new name.

EXISTING FORMAT DIFFERS FROM THAT SPECIFIED

If you're reformatting a disk or diskette to a different capacity, you actually want to see this message. It means you're doing the right thing, but you'll need to tell DOS that it's OK to continue. The reason to reformat a diskette to a different capacity is to make it match the capacity of the drive. You can use a low-capacity diskette in a high-capacity drive, but not the other way around. It's best to match the capacity of the diskette to the maximum drive capacity.

FILE CANNOT BE COPIED ONTO ITSELF

This message probably means you forgot to give a destination location for a file you're trying to copy. Type the COPY command again (being sure to include the destination). If you're unsure how to use the COPY command correctly, type help copy and press Enter for more information.

FILE CREATION ERROR

This means one of two things: either you're trying to create a file with the same name as an existing file or the disk you're using is write-protected. Check the tab on the diskette to be sure it isn't in the write-protected position. If it isn't, try using a different file name. If neither of these solutions works, try using another diskette with the new file name.

FILE EXISTS

You're trying to name your new file with a file name already in use. Choose another name. If you're unsure of which names you've used before, use the DIR command to check out the files in the current directory.

FILE NOT FOUND

You've typed a file name in a command incorrectly, the file doesn't exist, or the file is in a location other than the one you specified. Check for accuracy and enter the command again.

FORMATTING WHILE COPYING

This is one of the DOS messages that's more informational. It's telling you the diskette you're using needs to be formatted in order to hold the information you're copying to it. You should be aware, however, that formatting a diskette takes longer while copying than if you're just formatting it.

HELP NOT AVAILABLE FOR THIS COMMAND

Either you've asked for help with a command or utility program that there is no help information for in the version of DOS you're running or you typed the command incorrectly.

INCORRECT DOS VERSION

The program you're trying to run has found a version of COMMAND.COM other than the one it expected. You probably upgraded DOS versions at some point and now have more than one version of some DOS files on your system (and the program found an older or newer one than it wanted). You may need to reinstall DOS or Windows 95/98 to fix this problem.

INSERT SYSTEM DISK

This just means you need to insert your bootable diskette into a diskette drive, usually when installing or repartitioning a hard drive.

INSUFFICIENT DISK SPACE

You don't have enough room on your hard disk or diskette to complete the command. Use another diskette or delete/compress some files to make more space available.

INSUFFICIENT MEMORY

This message means that you don't have enough memory (RAM) available to complete the command. Remove any unnecessary *Terminate and Stay Resident* (TSR) programs and try the command again. TSRs (also known as memory-resident programs) remain loaded in memory even when they're not running, so they can be quickly activated for specific tasks while you're running other applications. If you're relying on a swap file on your hard drive to emulate RAM, you may have a shortage of drive space or there may be some other problem with the swap file.

INVALID DATE/INVALID TIME

You've used an improper format for a date/time. To check the proper format, use the DATE/TIME command. Make note of the correct format and try again.

INVALID DIRECTORY

DOS/Windows can't find the directory you specified. Either you typed the directory's name incorrectly, or it doesn't exist (at least not on the drive you specified). Check your typing and the location of the directory. It may be that it's in a subdirectory.

INVALID DRIVE IN SEARCH PATH

This probably means that you have made a hardware change and haven't updated the PATH command in your AUTOEXEC.BAT file to reflect the drives that are now in your computer. Update the PATH command and try again.

INVALID DRIVE SPECIFICATION

DOS/Windows can't find the drive you tried to switch to. Either you made a typing error (asking your computer to find a drive that doesn't exist) or the drive you asked for is not working. If you get this message when trying to switch to your hard drive, the drive may be suffering from corrupted partition information or the drive may be defective.

INVALID FILENAME

DOS/Windows can't find the file you're looking for. Check the name and location of the file and try again (be sure to check your typing). Be sure to include any underscores, dashes, periods, or other valid filename characters.

INVALID MEDIA TYPE

The diskette you're trying to use is defective or not formatted properly for the particular floppy drive. Reformat the floppy disk or try a different one.

INVALID PARAMETER

You've entered a command parameter incorrectly. A *parameter* is something you add to the end of a command to tell it what to operate on (also called a *command-line switch*). For example, in the command dir a:, the a: tells DOS you want a list of the contents of the A: drive, regardless of which drive you're currently in. Check the format of the command and re-enter it. The other possibility is that you're using a parameter not used in the utility program you're trying to use.

NON-SYSTEM DISK OR DISK ERROR. REPLACE AND STRIKE ANY KEY.

Before computers had hard drives, the OS was stored on a diskette called the *system diskette*, *bootable diskette*, or *DOS disk*. That diskette was kept in the A: drive where the computer would look for it when it was started. Although OSs are now on the hard drive, most computers still look at the diskette drive before checking the hard drive. If they don't find anything in the A: drive, they check the hard drive, usually the C: drive. If they find a non-system diskette in the A: drive, you'll get this message. The most common reason for this message is that you forgot to remove a diskette from the A: drive when you last used it. Remove the diskette and strike any key to continue. Another possibility is that you have a computer (probably an old one) that boots from a system diskette. In that case, this message means you need to put a bootable diskette in the A: drive and continue.

The last scenario is a bit more serious. If neither of the previous situations applies to you, the first step is to get a DOS system diskette and try booting the computer from it. This should get you to an A:\> prompt. At the A:\> prompt, type C: and press Enter. If you get a C:\> prompt, the drive is running, but your OS is lost. Type `cd dos` at the prompt and press Enter. Then type `sys c:` and press Enter again. That should replace the OS. On the other hand, if you get a message saying `Invalid drive specification` when you try to switch to the C: drive, your hard drive is not working properly. The drive will have to be replaced.

OUT OF MEMORY

This means a program can't complete its task because you don't have enough free memory. Close some other running programs and try again. If no other programs are running, you may need to add memory to your computer. Before buying more memory, you may want to try EMM386 (a driver included with DOS 6.0 that provides expanded memory) or a memory manager such as Quarterdeck's QEMM. These tools can move some drivers and TSRs into the *Upper Memory Area* (UMA) and free some additional conventional memory.

PATH NOT FOUND

A path is the set of directions you give DOS/Windows to tell it how to find something. For example, the path C:\DOS\EDIT.HLP tells DOS to find the file EDIT.HLP in the DOS directory on your C: drive. If you get this message, DOS couldn't find the path you entered. Check your typing and reenter the path carefully. If that doesn't work, it means the path doesn't exist.

PROCEED WITH FORMAT (Y/N)?

This message means you will lose any information that is on the diskette when you format it. Press Y to continue with the format if you're sure you won't lose any important information, or N to stop the process if you want to check the contents of the diskette before formatting it.

READ ERROR

DOS has found a problem with a sector of your disk. There was either damage during the formatting process or a fault in one of the sectors. Run ScanDisk (version 6.2 or newer) to find the bad spot and rescue as much data as possible. If the error occurs on a floppy diskette, you should reformat or discard the diskette.

STACK OVERFLOW — SYSTEM HALTED

Reboot your system and edit your CONFIG.SYS file so the value of `stacks=` is increased to 10 or more and then try again.

SYNTAX ERROR

You've either made a typing error in a command or you've used terminology DOS doesn't recognize (or at least your version of DOS). Check your typing for accuracy and try again.

TERMINATE BATCH JOB (Y/N)?

Either you've interrupted a batch file in progress or the batch file is incomplete or incorrect. If you didn't mean to interrupt the batch job, type N to let DOS return to work. If the batch file is defective, type Y to return to the DOS prompt.

THIS DISK CANNOT BE UNFORMATTED

UNFORMAT is a command that can sometimes save data if you accidentally format a disk or diskette containing data you didn't mean to eliminate. Depending upon the type of format you performed and whether you've written new data to the location, UNFORMAT may not work. If it does not, try again. If you get the same message, your data is irretrievable.

TOO MANY OPEN FILES

You've tried to open too many files at one time. Open your CONFIG.SYS file and increase the number of files specified in the Files= command. Restart your system and try again. You should now be able to have more files open at a time.

WRITE-PROTECT ERROR

You've tried to format a diskette that is write-protected. Remove the write protection from the disk and try again.

A

The A+ Checklist

If you're planning to enter the field of PC troubleshooting and repair, you're going to want some industry-recognized certification behind you. This means you're going to want A+ certification before you sit down for that important interview. This appendix outlines the essential elements of the A+ certification and illustrates the major areas of knowledge that you'll need to master.

About A+ Certification

A+ is a testing program sponsored by the *Computer Industry Technology Association* (CompTIA) that certifies the basic competency of entry-level service technicians (those with about six months experience) in the computer industry. No other prerequisites exist for A+ certification, so the exam is open to anyone. Earning A+ certification tells prospective employers that you possess the knowledge, skills, and customer relations skills essential to start a career in computer service. These competencies have been defined by experts from companies across the industry. The computer industry has widely accepted the A+ exam as a fundamental measure of knowledge, and as of late 1999, there were over 150,000 A+ certified technicians. This number is growing daily.

The test itself (which is actually administered by Sylvan Prometric) was first available in July 1993, but the exam has been completely reworked in July 1998. The exam questions cover a broad range of hardware and software technologies, most of which are covered in this book, but the questions are not related to any vendor-specific products. To become certified, you must pass two parts: the Core module and the DOS/Windows module. When both the Core and the DOS/Windows portions are passed within 90 calendar days, you will receive the A+ designation. Once you're A+-certified, you do not need to retake the exam as it's updated.

Scheduling the Exam

Registering for the A+ exam is a relatively simple matter. You'll need to contact your local Sylvan Prometric location at 800-776-4276 and register. The exam code for the Core exam is 220-101, and the code for the DOS/Windows module is 220-102. The cost is $117 (United States) if you (or your employer) is a CompTIA member, or $167 if you're not. Have your credit card handy and plan on some lengthy hold times, but once you're registered, it's just a matter of studying until the exam day.

The Core Examination (Circa 1998)

The Core examination tests the essential competencies for a break/fix computer hardware service technician with roughly six months of on-the-job experience. You must demonstrate the knowledge needed to properly install, configure, upgrade, troubleshoot, and repair microcomputer hardware. This includes basic knowledge of desktop and portable systems, basic networking concepts, and printers. You must also demonstrate a knowledge of safety and common preventive maintenance procedures. The Core examination also includes questions that measure your knowledge of effective behaviors that contribute to customer satisfaction. Note that the customer satisfaction questions will be scored but will not impact the final pass/fail score on this examination.

Installation, Configuration, and Upgrading

Here you require the knowledge and skills to identify, install, configure, and upgrade microcomputer modules and peripherals while following established procedures for the system assembly and disassembly of field-replaceable modules. This includes the ability to identify and configure *interrupt request lines* (IRQs), *Direct Memory Access* (DMA), *input/output* (I/O) addresses, and set switches and jumpers. The tasks that you will have to perform are outlined as follows:

- Identify the basic terms, concepts, and functions of system modules, including how each module should work during normal operation. These concepts and modules include
  - *Basic Input/Output System* (BIOS)
  - Boot process
  - *Complementary Metal Oxide Semiconductor* (CMOS)
  - Firmware
  - Memory
  - Modem
  - Monitor
  - Power supply
  - Processor/*Central Processing Unit* (CPU)
  - Storage devices
  - System board

- Identify the basic procedures for adding and removing field-replaceable modules such as

- Input devices
- Memory
- Power supply
- Processors/CPUs
- Storage devices
- System boards

- Identify available IRQs, DMAs, and I/O addresses and understand the procedures for configuring them for device installation including

  - Floppy drives
  - Hard drives
  - Modems
  - Standard IRQ settings

- Identify common peripheral ports, associated cabling, and their connectors including

  - *British Naval Connector* (BNC)
  - Cable orientation
  - Cable types
  - DB-25
  - DB-9
  - Pin connections
  - PS2/MINI-DIN
  - RJ-11
  - RJ-45
  - Serial versus parallel

- Identify the proper procedures for installing and configuring *Integrated Development Environment* (IDE)/*Enhanced IDE* (EIDE) devices including

  - Devices per channel
  - Master/slave

- Identify the proper procedures for installing and configuring *Small Computer Systems Interface* (SCSI) devices such as
  - Address/termination conflicts
  - Cabling
  - Internal versus external
  - Switch and jumper settings
  - Types (regular, wide, ultra-wide)

- Identify the proper procedures for installing and configuring peripheral devices including
  - Modems
  - Monitor/video cards
  - Storage devices

- Identify the important concepts and procedures relating to BIOS such as
  - Methods for upgrading
  - When to upgrade

- Identify the hardware methods of system optimization and understand when to use them on
  - Memory
  - Hard drives
  - CPUs
  - Cache memory

Diagnosing and Troubleshooting

You must apply your knowledge relating to the diagnosis and troubleshooting of common module problems and system malfunctions. This includes a knowledge of the symptoms relating to common problems. The principle problem areas are covered:

- Identify the common symptoms and problems associated with each module and how to troubleshoot and isolate the problems for devices such as

  - BIOS
  - CMOS
  - Floppy drive failures
  - Hard drives
  - Modems
  - Monitor/video
  - Motherboards
  - Mouse
  - Parallel ports
  - Power-on self-test (POST) audible/visual error codes
  - Power supply
  - Processor/memory symptoms
  - Slot covers
  - Sound card/audio
  - Troubleshooting tools (multimeter)

- Identify the basic troubleshooting procedures and good practices for eliciting problem symptoms from customers (related to customer service) such as

  - Troubleshooting/isolation/problem determination procedures
  - Determining whether something is a hardware or software problem
  - Gathering information from the user regarding customer environment
  - Gathering information from the user regarding symptoms/error codes
  - Gathering information from the user regarding the situation when the problem occurred

Safety and Preventive Maintenance

Here you're required to have a working knowledge of safety and preventive maintenance. Safety includes recognizing the potential hazards to personnel and equipment when working with lasers, high-voltage equipment, *electrostatic discharge* (ESD), and items that require special disposal procedures that comply with environmental guidelines. Preventive maintenance includes a knowledge of preventive maintenance products, procedures, environmental hazards, and precautions when working on microcomputer systems. The tasks that you will have to perform are outlined as follows:

- Identify the purpose of various types of preventive maintenance products and procedures and when to use/perform them. This includes

  - Liquid cleaning compounds

  - Types of materials to clean contacts and connections

  - Vacuuming out systems, power supplies, and fans

- Identify the procedures and devices for protecting against environmental hazards, such as

  - Determining the signs of power issues

  - The proper methods of storage of components for future use

  - *Uninterruptible Power Supply* (UPS) and suppressers

- Identify the potential hazards and proper safety procedures relating to lasers and high-voltage equipment such as

  - *Cathode Ray Tubes* (CRTs)

  - High-voltage equipment

  - Lasers

  - Power supply

- Identify items that require special disposal procedures that comply with environmental guidelines including
  - Batteries
  - Chemical solvents and cans
  - CRTs
  - *Material Safety Data Sheets* (MSDSs)
  - Toner kits/cartridges

- Identify *electrostatic discharge* (ESD) precautions and procedures, including the use of ESD protection devices including:
  - What ESD can do and how it may be apparent or hidden
  - Common ESD protection devices
  - Situations that could present a danger or hazard

Motherboards, Processors, and Memory

You must understand the specific terminology, facts, and methods of dealing with classifications, categories, and principles of motherboards, processors, and memory in modern microcomputer systems. The tasks that you will have to perform are outlined as follows:

- Distinguish between the popular CPU chips in terms of their basic characteristics such as
  - The number of pins
  - If cache is onboard or not
  - Physical size
  - Sockets
  - Speeds
  - Voltage

- Identify the categories of *Random Access Memory* (RAM) terminology, its location, and physical characteristics such as

- *Dynamic Random Access Memory* (DRAM)
- *Dual Inline Memory Modules* (DIMMs)
- *Extended Data Output RAM* (EDO RAM)
- Memory bank
- Memory chips (8-bit, 16-bit, and 32-bit)
- Parity chips versus non-parity chips
- *Single Inline Memory Modules* (SIMMS)
- *Static RAM* (SRAM)
- *Video RAM* (VRAM)
- *Windows Accelerator Card RAM* (WRAM)

- Identify the most popular type of motherboard, its components, architecture (bus structures and power supplies), and its basic compatibility guidelines including
  - AT (Full and Baby)
  - ATX
  - Communication ports
  - *Extended Industry Standard Architecture* (EISA)
  - External cache memory (Level 2)
  - *Industry Standard Architecture* (ISA)
  - PC Card (PCMCIA)
  - Pulse Code Modulation (PCI)
  - Processor sockets
  - SIMM AND DIMM
  - *Universal Serial Bus* (USB)
  - *VESA local bus* (VL-Bus)

- Identify the purpose of CMOS, what it contains, and how to change its basic parameters including
  - Boot sequence
  - Date/time

- Disable COM/serial port

- Disable/enable uni-directional, bi-directional, *Extended Capabilities Port* (ECP), and *Enhanced Parallel Port* (EPP)

- Enable/disable floppy drive or boot, speed, and density

- Hard drive size and drive type

- Memory address and interrupt request

- Memory parity and non-parity

- Passwords

- Printer parallel port

Printers

Here you must have a knowledge of basic printer types, basic printer concepts, and printer components. You should know how a printer works, how it prints a page, the paper path, care and service techniques, and be familiar with common problems. The tasks that you will be required to do are outlined as follows:

- Identify basic concepts, printer operations, and printer components for

  - Dot matrix

  - Ink jet

  - Laser

- Identify care and service techniques and common problems with primary printer types including

  - Errors

  - Feed and output

  - Paper jams

  - Preventive maintenance

- Print quality
- Safety precautions

■ Identify the types of printer connections and configurations such as

- Network
- Parallel
- Serial

Portable Systems

This area of the Core exam requires a knowledge of portable computers and their unique components and problems. The tasks that you will be required to do are outlined as follows:

■ Identify the unique components of portable systems and their unique problems including

- AC adapter
- Battery
- Docking stations
- Hard Drive
- *Liquid Crystal Display* (LCD)
- Memory
- Network cards
- *T*ype I, II, and III cards

Basic Networking

This part of the exam requires a knowledge of basic network concepts and terminology, the ability to determine whether a computer is networked, a knowledge of procedures for swapping and configuring *network interface cards* (NICs), and a knowledge of the ramifications of repairs when a computer is networked. The tasks that you will be required to do are outlined as follows:

- Identify basic networking concepts including how a network works such as
  - Network access
  - Protocol
  - NICs
  - Full-duplex
  - Cabling such as Twisted Pair, Coaxial, Fiber Optic
  - The ways to network a PC

- Identify the procedures for swapping and configuring NICs
- Identify the ramifications of repairs on the network such as
  - Loss of data
  - A network slowdown
  - Reduced bandwidth

Customer Satisfaction

You must understand and be sensitive to the behaviors that contribute to satisfying customers, including the quality of technician/customer personal interactions, the way you conduct yourself professionally within the customer's business setting, and the credibility and confidence you project. This area is not a test of specific company policies or procedures. The tasks that you will be required to do are outlined as follows:

- Differentiate effective from ineffective behaviors as these contribute to the maintenance or achievement of customer satisfaction such as
  - Communicating and listening (face-to-face or over the phone)
  - Establishing personal rapport with the customer
  - Handling complaints and upset customers, conflict avoidance, and resolution

- Helping and guiding a customer with problem descriptions

- Interpreting verbal and nonverbal cues

- Professional conduct (punctuality and accountability)

- Responding appropriately to the customer's technical level

- Responding to and closing a service call

- Sharing the customer's sense of urgency

- Showing empathy and flexibility

The DOS/Windows exam (Circa 1998)

The DOS/Windows part of the A+ examination measures essential OS competencies for a break/fix microcomputer hardware service technician with six months of on-the-job experience. You must demonstrate a basic knowledge of DOS, Windows 3.x, and Windows 95 for installing, configuring, upgrading, troubleshooting, and repairing microcomputer systems.

Function, Structure Operation, and File Management

This part of the exam requires a knowledge of DOS, Windows 3.x, and Windows 95 in terms of function and structure, managing files and directories, and running programs. It also includes navigating through the OS from DOS command-line prompts and Windows procedures for accessing and retrieving information. The tasks that you will be required to do are outlined as follows:

- Identify the OS's functions, structure, and major system files including
  - Ansi.sys
  - Autoexec.bat
  - Command.com
  - Config.sys

- Contrasts between Windows 3.x and Windows 95
- Emm386.exe
- Functions of DOS, Windows 3.x, and Windows 95
- Gdi.exe
- HIMEM.SYS
- Io.sys
- Krnlxxx.exe
- The major components of DOS, Windows 3.x, and Windows 95
- Msdos.sys
- Progman.ini
- regedit.exe
- System.dat
- System.ini
- User.dat
- User.exe
- Win.com
- Win.ini

- Identify ways to navigate the OS and to access needed technical information such as
  - Procedures for navigating through DOS to perform such things as locating, accessing, and retrieving information
  - Procedures for navigating through the Windows 3.x/Windows 95 OS as well as accessing and retrieving information

- Identify the basic concepts and procedures for creating, viewing, and managing files and directories, including the procedures for changing file attributes and the ramifications of those changes such as
  - Command syntax
  - File attributes

- File-naming conventions
- Read-Only, Hidden, System, and Archive attributes

- Identify the procedures for basic disk management including
  - Backing up
  - Defragmenting
  - FAT32
  - *File allocation tables* (FAT)
  - Formatting
  - Partitioning
  - ScanDisk
  - Using disk management utilities
  - *Virtual file allocation tables* (VFAT)

Memory Management

This part of the DOS/Windows exam requires a knowledge of the types of memory used by DOS and Windows and the potential for memory address conflicts. The tasks that you will be required to do are outlined as follows:

- Differentiate between types of memory such as
  - Conventional
  - Extended/upper memory
  - High memory
  - Expanded memory
  - Virtual memory
- Identify typical memory conflict problems and how to optimize memory use such as
  - *General Protection Fault* (GPF)
  - HIMEM.SYS
  - How it happens

- Illegal operations occurrences
- MemMaker or other optimization utilities
- SmartDrive
- System monitor
- Expanded memory blocks (using EMM386.EXE)
- What a memory conflict is
- When to employ utilities

Installation, Configuration, and Upgrading

This part of the exam requires a knowledge of installing, configuring, and upgrading DOS, Windows 3.x, and Windows 95. This includes a knowledge of the system boot sequences. The tasks that you will be required to do are outlined as follows:

- Identify the procedures for installing DOS, Windows 3.x, and Windows 95, and for bringing the software to a basic operational level including
  - Formatting the drive
  - Loading the drivers
  - Creating the partition
  - Running the appropriate setup utility

- Identify steps to perform an OS upgrade including
  - Upgrading from DOS to Windows 95
  - Upgrading from Windows 3.x to Windows 95

- Identify the basic system boot sequences and some alternative ways to boot the system software, including the steps to create an emergency boot disk with utilities installed such as
  - Files required to boot
  - Creating an emergency boot disk
  - Startup disk

- Safe mode
- DOS mode

- Identify procedures for loading/adding device drivers and the necessary software for certain devices such as
  - Windows 3.x procedures
  - Windows 95 Plug and Play

- Identify the procedures for changing options, configuring, and using the Windows printing subsystem

- Identify the procedures for installing and launching typical Windows and non-Windows applications

Diagnosing and Troubleshooting

This part of the DOS/Windows exam requires you to diagnose and troubleshoot common problems relating to DOS, Windows 3.x, and Windows 95. This includes your understanding of normal operations and the symptoms of common problems. The tasks that you will be required to do are outlined as follows:

- Recognize and interpret the meaning of common error codes and startup messages from the boot sequence, and identify steps to correct the problems such as
  - A device referenced in SYSTEM.INI could not be found
  - Bad or missing COMMAND.COM
  - An error in CONFIG.SYS line XX
  - HIMEM.SYS not loaded
  - An incorrect DOS version
  - Missing or corrupt HIMEM.SYS
  - No operating system found
  - Safe mode
  - Swap file

- Recognize Windows-specific printing problems and identify the procedures for correcting them such as

  - The print spool is stalled.
  - An incorrect/incompatible driver is being used to print.

- Recognize common problems and determine how to resolve them such as

  - An application will not start or load.
  - ATTRIB.EXE
  - You cannot log on to the network.
  - DEFRAG.EXE
  - Device Manager
  - EDIT.COM
  - EXTRACT.EXE
  - FDISK.EXE
  - GPFs
  - Illegal operations
  - Invalid working directory
  - MEM.EXE
  - MSD.EXE
  - Option will not function
  - ScanDisk
  - SYSEDIT.EXE
  - System lock up

- Identify the concepts relating to viruses and virus types, their danger, their symptoms, the sources of viruses, how they infect, how to protect against them, and how to identify and remove them, including

  - What they are
  - Their sources
  - How to determine their presence

Networks

This final part of the DOS/Windows exam requires a knowledge of the network capabilities of DOS and Windows and how to connect to networks, including what the Internet is about, its capabilities, the basic concepts relating to Internet access, and generic procedures for system setup. The tasks that you will be required to do are outlined as follows:

- Identify the networking capabilities of DOS and Windows including the procedures for connecting to the network such as

  - The network type and network card

  - Sharing disk drives

  - Sharing print and file services

- Identify concepts and capabilities relating to the Internet and basic procedures for setting up a system for Internet access such as

  - Dial-up access

  - Domain names for Web sites

  - E-mail

  - FTP

  - HTML

  - HTTP

  - ISP

  - TCP/IP

Taking the A+ Exam

If you're planning to take the A+ exam, you should arrive at the testing center at least 15 minutes before the test is scheduled to begin. The testing center administrator will demonstrate how to use the computer-based testing system before the test begins. In most cases, two forms of identification are required. One must have a picture (such as a driver's license) and both must have a signature. The other can be a major credit card. Books, calculators, laptop computers, or other reference materials are not allowed during any test. Also, since the test is computer-based, pens, pencils, or paper will not be needed.

The Core portion of the exam includes 69 questions, and the DOS/Windows portion of the exam includes 70 questions. You have one hour to complete the Core module, and one hour and 15 minutes to complete the DOS/Windows module. The passing grade for the Core exam is 65 percent, and the passing grade for the DOS/Windows exam is 66 percent. As soon as the test is finished, a final score will be generated, and this score will immediately be shown on the computer screen. A hard copy of the score report is also provided at the testing center. The score report shows whether you passed the examination or not. It will also show, by section, your performance on the test (please hold on to your score report).

After you pass the examination(s) successfully, your certificate and ID card will be forwarded by Sylvan Prometric in two to three weeks. Should you need a replacement (or a correction) to your certificate or ID card, contact Sylvan Prometric at 1-800-776-4276 if you live in the United States, Canada, or Puerto Rico. If you live outside this area, call your regional Sylvan Prometric site. If you do not pass the examination, you can register at any time to take it again. You will be able to retest after payment has been made.

> **NOTE**: Remember that the A+ exam has two test components (the Core and DOS/Windows portions) and these must be taken within 90 calendar days of each other. If you fail to pass both examinations within 90 calendar days, you will not be granted the A+ certification. You would then have to retake the Core examination, even if you had passed it previously, *and* retake the other portion.

The Future of A+

The A+ exam is not a traditional exam where the questions and the format never change. Technology is changing every day, and you can expect the A+ exam to be updated every few years. By April of 2000 (before this book is published), you'll probably see the following changes to the A+ exam:

- Elimination of the Windows 3.1 objectives and items
- Elimination of the customer satisfaction objectives and items
- New test objectives and items in the following areas:
  - Windows 98
  - Windows 2000
  - Windows NT, version 4.0
  - Linux (baseline, elementary information only)

According to CompTIA, these new test items will be beta tested around May/June 2000. However, these items will not be scored and *will not* count toward an individual's pass/fail score. Depending on how this beta testing phase works out, you may see such new questions appear permanently by the end of 2000. You can stay abreast of the latest developments with the A+ exam by visiting the CompTIA Web site at *www.comptia.org*.

> **NOTE**:   Once you're A+-certified, you're certified for life. There is no need to recertify.

Index

E

X–Y

About the Author

Stephen J. Bigelow is the founder and president of Dynamic Learning Systems, a technical writing, research, and publishing company specializing in electronic and PC service topics. Bigelow is the author of 15 feature-length books for TAB/McGraw-Hill and over 100 major articles for mainstream electronics magazines such as *Popular Electronics*, *Electronics NOW*, *Circuit Cellar INK*, and *Electronic Service & Technology*. Bigelow is a contributing columnist for CNET (*www.cnet.com*) and is a regular online instructor for PC building, repair, and A+ courses at SmartPlanet (*www.smartplanet.com*) and ElementK (*www.elementk.com*). Bigelow is also the editor and publisher of *The PC Toolbox*, a premier PC service newsletter for computer enthusiasts and technicians. He is an electrical engineer with a BS EE. You may contact the author at the following address:

Dynamic Learning Systems
PO Box 402
Leicester, MA 01524-0402
www.dlspubs.com